.J.

.ls of n

Fundamentals of Microcomputer Programming

T. J. WAGNER

University of Texas at Austin

G. J. LIPOVSKI

University of Texas at Austin

FUNDAMENTALS OF MICROCOMPUTER PROGRAMMING

Macmillan Publishing Company

New York

Collier Macmillan Publishers

London

Dedicated to our wives
Nancy and Belle

Copyright © 1984, Macmillan Publishing Company, a division of Macmillan, Inc.

Printed in the United States of America

Macmillan Publishing Company
866 Third Avenue, New York, New York 10022

Collier Macmillan Canada, Inc.

Library of Congress Cataloging in Publication Data

Wagner, T. J. (Terry John)
  Fundamentals of microcomputer programming.

  Includes index.
  1. Microcomputers—Programming. 2. Motorola 6809
(Computer)—Programming. 3. Assembler language (Computer
program language) I. Lipovski, G. Jack. II. Title.
QA76.6.W3   1984   001.64′2   83-11249
ISBN 0-02-423710-8

Printing: 1 2 3 4 5 6 7 8   Year 4 5 6 7 8 9 0 1 2

ISBN   0-02-423710-8

PREFACE

Programming is an essential engineering skill. It is as important to an electrical engineer as circuit design, to a civil engineer as statics, and to a chemical engineer as heat transfer. The engineer has to learn to program in high-level languages to solve problems. He or she also has to learn assembly language programming because microcomputers are components in many systems designed, marketed, and maintained by engineers, and these components are usually programmed in assembly language. The first goal of this book then is to teach engineers the skill of assembly language programming on any computer. The second goal is to teach the engineer what can be done on a small computer from the programming point of view, in particular, how the microcomputer is interfaced to the outside world. Even the nonprogramming engineer should understand these issues. Although this book is written for engineers, it will serve equally well for anyone, even hobbyists, interested in these two goals.

The reader is taught the principles of assembly language programming by being shown how to program a particular microcomputer, the Motorola MC6809. The important thing about the MC6809 is that it has a very straightforward yet powerful instruction set and is perhaps the nicest computer of *any size* on which to learn assembly language principles. The best way to learn these principles is to write a lot of programs, debug them, and see them work on a real machine.

This hands-on experience can be obtained very inexpensively with the MC6809. For example, the TRS-80 color computer, which uses the MC6809, is available for under $300 in a version that does everything needed for this book. (This price includes the color computer, software, cassette recorder, and monitor.)

The following discussion outlines the book and explains several decisions that were made when we wrote the book. Each chapter is sketched and the main skills taught in it are summarized.

Chapters 1 to 3 discuss programming using hand-translated machine code. The assembler is not introduced until Chapter 4. This gives the engineering student a fine feeling for the machine and how it works, and helps him resolve problems encountered later with timing in input/output programming or with the use of addressing modes in managing data structures. Chapter 1 introduces computer organization to explain the way a microprocessor interacts with the memory and to explain the instruction cycle. The explanation focuses on a microcomputer and is simplified to provide just enough background for the remainder of the text. Simple instructions and elementary programs are introduced next. Pointing out that there is no best program to solve a problem, Chapter 1 concludes with a discussion of what makes a good program and encourages the reader to develop a good programming style.

The MC6809 has an extensive set of addressing modes that can be used with most instructions. Thus it is useful to introduce the addressing modes before discussing the complete instruction set of this machine. Chapter 2 covers the addressing modes and Chapter 3 covers the instruction set. In Chapter 2, the different addressing modes are introduced with a goal of explaining why these modes are useful as well as how they work. Examples at the end of the chapter illustrate the use of these modes with the simple instructions introduced in Chapter 1. In Chapter 3, the main concepts are the alternative forms of the same kind of instruction. Rather than listing the instructions alphabetically, as is desirable in a reference book, we group together instructions that perform the same type of function. Our groups are the classical ones, namely, the move, arithmetic, logical, edit, control and input/output groups. Although other groupings are also useful, this one seems to encourage the student to try alternative instructions as a way of looking for the best instruction for his or her purpose.

Chapters 4 and 5 show how a program can be more easily written and how a program can incorporate earlier program segments so they do not have to be rewritten. Chapter 4 introduces the assembler, explains assembler directives, symbolic addresses, and the limitations of forward referencing in a two-pass assembler. In a laboratory accompanying a course using this text, the student puts in a substantial effort learning the use of an assembler, text editor, and operating system at this time. Chapter 4 is designed to support this effo t. A general discussion of other programs related to the assembler, such as compilers and interpreters, is given along with a discussion of macros. Assembly language examples that build on the examples from previous chapters conclude Chapter 4. Chapter 5 introduces subroutines. The techniques used to pass arguments to a subroutine are discussed at an abstract level (such as call by name and its alternatives) and at an implementation level (such as passing arguments in registers or on the stack). The trade-offs between macros and subroutines as a means to insert the same program segment into different places in a program are discussed. The notion of a subroutine as a test module, the notion of a top-down design, and testing top-down or bottom-up are explored. Chapters 4 and 5 simplify the problem of writing in assembly language by showing how assemblers, subroutines, and macros are used.

Chapter 6 covers elementary data structures. The simplest, including the character string used in earlier chapters, and the more involved deque and linked list structures are related to the addressing modes available in the MC6809. The main theme of this chapter is that the correct storage of data can significantly improve the efficiency of a program.

Chapter 7 covers arithmetic routines. Conversion between different bases is discussed and examples are given illustrating conversion from ASCII decimal to binary and vice versa. The discussion of multiple-precision integer arithmetic is completed by examining the details of multiple-byte division and multiplication. Floating-point representations are introduced and the mechanics of common floating-point operations are discussed. Stack operation and Polish notation are shown to be useful in arithmetic routines of any complexity.

Chapter 8 introduces input/output programming. The discussion focuses on what a user (rather than a designer) of input/output hardware and software should know. Hardware and software basics are developed for simple input/output systems (as apart from the systems using the commercially available LSI input/output chips). Interrupts and direct memory access are discussed, and the basis is laid for further study of the use of microcomputers as components in larger systems. The discussion of the design of input/output hardware and software is available in other texts that are referenced at the end of the chapter.

Chapter 9 shows how the assembly language of a different microcomputer might be learned once that of the MC6809 has been learned. Although we would like to discuss other popular microcomputers, we believe that we could fill another book doing that. To illustrate the idea, we look at the near relatives of the MC6809, in particular, the MC6801, MC6800, and MC6805. We also discuss briefly the MC68000. The main theme is that once you understand the instruction set of one microcomputer, you can learn to program efficiently on other microcomputers in a short time.

This book systematically develops the concepts of programming a microcomputer in assembly language. It also covers the principles of good programming practice through top-down design and the use of data structures. It is suitable as a text for a core course in an engineering curriculum on assembly language programming or as the first course on microcomputers that demonstrates what a small computer can do. It may also be used by those who want to delve more deeply into assembly language principles and practices. You should find, as we have, that programming is a skill that magnifies the knowledge and control of the programmer, and you should find that programming, though very much an important engineering skill, is fun and challenging. This book is dedicated to show you that.

An instructors manual is available from the publisher. This includes solutions to all the text exercises, suggested assignments, and tests.

A number of people contributed to this book. The reviewers of an early draft provided many helpful suggestions. Our students gave us steady feedback on our changes, and were able to point out many elusive errors. One student, Paul Vaughn, was particularly helpful in this respect. One colleague from Liberal Arts, John Weinstock, even endured one of our classes and gave us a different perspective of how this material is received. We wish to thank them all.

T.J.W

G.J.L

CONTENTS

The **TRS-80 Color Computer** with an audio cassette recorder/player, a television set and the **EDTASM+** (editor, assembler, and debugger) **ROM** cartridge, all that is needed to run the programs in the text.

CHAPTER 1

Basic Computer Structure and the MC6809

Computers, and microcomputers in particular, are possibly the most useful tools that man has developed. They are not mysterious half-human forces that the news media seems to imply when they say "The computer will decide . . ." or "It was a computer error!". No, computers are actually like levers; as a lever amplifies what the human arm can do, so the computer amplifies what the human brain can do. Good actions by the programmer are amplified, and the computer is a great tool, but bad actions are likewise amplified. These bad actions can be a result of good plans incorrectly programmed into the computer. This tool has to be studied and exercised to make it useful: that is the purpose of this book. The computer also has to be used with insight and consideration for its effects on society, but that will not be studied in this book.

We are going to study the computer in the manner in which an engineer studies any tool—we begin by finding out just how it ticks. There is a trade-off in where we start, for if we start at too primitive a level or if we dwell too long on the introductory material, we will not have time to show how the tool is used. We use the well-designed Motorola MC6809 microcomputer to make our discussion concrete, but we are interested in this particular microcomputer only as a means of teaching the operations of microcomputers in general. In this chapter we introduce the basic structure of the microcomputer. We discuss what a memory is and how words in this memory are read to tell the microcomputer what to do, as well as how the words are written and read to save data that are used by the microcomputer. We describe a small but useful subset of the instructions of the MC6809, enough to show the mechanism used by all computers to read an instruction and carry it out. These few instructions are enough to introduce very simple programs and, using these programs, we will discuss the idea of programming.

After reading this chapter, you should be able to approach a typical instruction, to be introduced in the next two chapters, with an understanding about what the mnemonic, the machine code, and a sequence of memory reads (and writes) may mean for that instruction. This chapter then provides the background for the discussion of instructions that we will present in the next two chapters.

1—1

BASIC COMPUTER STRUCTURE

What is a microcomputer, and how does it execute the instructions that a programmer writes for it? This question is explored now at a level of abstraction that will be adequate for this text.

We do know that many readers will object to one aspect of the following discussion, and we want to answer that objection a priori, so that those readers will not miss the point. We will introduce a seemingly large number of terms. Don't miss the objective: we are really introducing concepts. The reader should think about the concepts rather than memorize definitions. Like your physics text, this text has to use terms in a fairly precise way to avoid ambiguity. Your physics text, you may recall, used the word "work" in a very precise way, as the product of force times distance, which is a bit different from the conversational use of the word "work" as used in the expression, "He's doing a lot of work." We will use terms such as "read" and "fetch" in a similar way. We define them and use them in later discussions to avoid confusion. We ask you to learn the term and its meaning even though you do not have to memorize the wording of the definition. But take heart, because although we do have a few concepts that have to be learned, and we have to learn the terms for those concepts, we do not have any formulas or equations to deal with. Accept our challenge and study these terms; then you will enjoy the latter discussions even more than if you muddle through this section without thinking about the terminology.

You probably know what microcomputers and computers are, to some degree, but let us discuss the term "computer" so that if you get into an argument about whether a hand calculator is a computer, you can respond knowledgeably. A microcomputer is a kind of computer or, more accurately, a kind of *von*

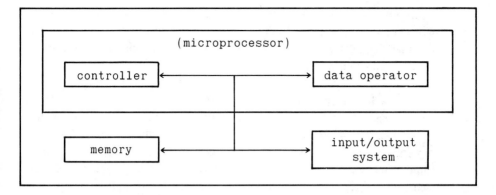

FIGURE 1-1. Simplified Computer Structure

Neumann computer, named after the scientific giant of our century who invented it. All (von Neumann) computers have four components: *memory*, *controller*, *data operator* (sometimes called an *arithmetic/logic unit*), and *input/output*. A simplified diagram of a computer is shown in Figure 1-1 where the various lines indicate that information may flow between the components. Some paths of information flow may be slightly different on specific computers. Briefly, the memory stores the data and the program, while the input/output provides the communication with the outside world. In a conventional large computer system this communication is done through peripherals such as terminals, card readers, line printers, keyboards, and so on. In typical microcomputer applications the input/output may be thought of as providing the necessary connections, or interfacing, to the device of which the microcomputer is a component, such as an automobile, kitchen appliance, toy, or laboratory instrument. The data operator performs arithmetic and logical operations, such as addition, logical AND, and so forth, on data. The controller controls the flow of information between the components, directing what computation is to be done, what data are to be stored and where. The input/output, controller, and data operator may themselves contain a small amount of memory held in devices called *registers*.

A microcomputer is a computer that is implemented using low cost integrated circuits, and is therefore cheap enough to be used in an incredible range of applications where a large computer would be infeasible. For the purposes of this book, if the data operator and the controller are together on a single integrated circuit, that integrated circuit is called a *microprocessor*, and the computer that uses a microprocessor is called a *microcomputer*. (Look again at Figure 1-1.)

Some aspects of microcomputers apply to all computers. We will often discuss an aspect of the computer and, of course, that aspect applies to microcomputers, on which we are concentrating. The term microprocessor is used so often that we will abbreviate it. Following common terminology, we abbreviate it (MPU) (microprocessor unit). The abbreviation CPU (central processor unit) is often used to denote the controller and data operator, but that term leads subtly to the idea that the CPU is central and most important. This idea is misleading and actually dangerous when the MPU is the cheapest part of the microcomputer and when a computer system has many MPUs, none of which is "central."

We now look more closely at the memory and the MPU. (The input/output unit is discussed in Chapter 8.) A diagram of a model memory is shown in Figure 1-2. The memory we choose here illustrates the principles that are of importance to us, but we point out that different computers may have somewhat different memories. We can think of the memory as a large number of cells, each able to store a 0 or a 1—that is, a binary digit or one *bit* of memory. The bits are grouped together in units called *bytes*, which consist of 8 bits. Within a particular byte the bits are labeled b_7, ..., b_0 as shown.

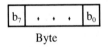
Byte

The right-hand bits are called lower-order or least significant, and the left-hand bits are called higher-order or most significant. There is nothing sacred about this labeling and, in fact, many computer manufacturers reverse it. A *word* in memory is the number of bits that are typically handled as a whole. In most microcomputers, a word is one byte so that the terms "word" and "byte" are often used interchangeably. This will be the case in this text. In the memory shown in Figure 1-2, each word or byte is given an *address*, an integer between

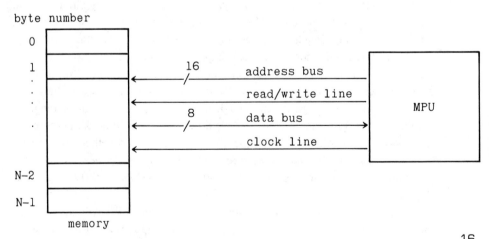

FIGURE 1-2. Model Memory and Its Connection to the MPU. The notation " /¹⁶ " indicates a bus with 16 lines.

0 and N - 1, where N is the total number of bytes in the memory. With the MC6809, N can be at most 2^{16}, so that each address can be described by its 16-bit binary representation (see Appendix 1).

The MPU controls the memory by means of a clock and a read/write line, and communicates to it by an address bus and a data bus (see Figure 1-2). A *line* is a wire that carries information by the level of voltage on it; a threshold level is established and any voltage above it is a *high signal*, and any voltage below it is a *low signal*. Each line can carry a high or a low signal, which is interpreted as a logical ''1'' or a logical ''0'' at each instance of time; a line can thus carry a bit of information. A *bus* is a collection of lines that can move a word or an address in parallel, so that one bit of a word or address is on one line of the bus. The *data bus* moves an 8-bit word to or from memory, from or to the MPU, and the *address bus* moves a 16-bit address from the MPU to the memory. A *clock* is a signal that is alternately a low signal and a high signal, staying with each signal level for the same time in a square wave, as shown below. The clock signal from a falling edge (a transition from high to low) to the next falling edge is called a *clock cycle* and the frequency at which high to low transitions occur is called the *clock rate*.

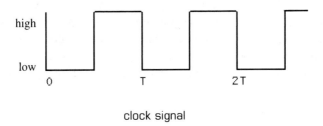

clock signal

In one clock cycle, the MPU can *read* a word from the memory by putting an address on the address bus and making the read/write line high for the cycle, and then picking up the word on the data bus at the end of the cycle. It can also *write* a word into the memory in one clock cycle by putting the address on the address bus and putting the word on the data bus, and making the read/ write line low for the cycle. A read or a write to memory is also called an *access* to memory.

We can enlarge our description of how the memory works. Assume that we want to get the contents of a particular word or byte from memory, that is, read a word from memory. The MPU first puts a high signal for read on the read/ write line and then puts the address of the desired word or byte on the address bus. This is done throughout the duration of a clock cycle. The memory is designed so that at the end of the clock cycle, the desired word is put on the data bus. The MPU then places a copy of the contents of the word or byte on the data bus into some register inside the MPU as required by the instruction that it is executing. This is done without changing the contents in memory of the word or byte addressed.

To put a word into memory, or write into memory, the address of the word is put on the address bus, the word is put on the data bus, and on the read/ write line, the low write signal is given for a full clock cycle. The memory is designed to store the word at that address at the end of the clock cycle. After the word is stored at the given address, the MPU may still retain a copy of the word that has just been written into memory in one of its registers.

In the model just discussed we assumed that we could read and write in every byte of memory in one clock cycle. Such a memory is usually called random access memory or *RAM* since each byte is equally accessible or can be selected at random without changing the time of the access. With microcomputer applications, it is not unusual to have part of the memory bytes in *ROM* (read only memory). A ROM is capable of a read operation but not a write operation; its words are written when it is made at the factory and are retained even when the power is turned off. If the data in a RAM are lost when power is turned off, the RAM is termed *volatile*; otherwise, it is termed *nonvolatile*. Most RAM memories are volatile. The term RAM is also used almost universally to imply memories that you can read and write in, even though ROM memories can be randomly accessed with a read operation. The part of memory that is in ROM is typically used to store a program for a microcomputer that only executes one program. For example, the microcomputer used for controlling various operating parameters in an automobile would be running the same program every time it is used, so that the part of the memory that is used for storing these instructions is in ROM.

1-2

THE INSTRUCTION

We now examine the notion of an *instruction*, one of operations performed by the MPU. It can be described statically as a collection of bits stored in memory or as a line of a program or, dynamically, as a sequence of actions by the controller. In this discussion we begin with a simplified dynamic view of the instruction and then develop a static view. Examples are offered to combine these views to explain the static aspects of the operation code, addressing mode, machine code, and mnemonics. We conclude with an expanded view of the dynamic aspects of the instruction cycle.

The controller will send commands to memory to read or write, and will send commands to all other parts of the computer to effectively carry out the intentions of the programmer. The specification of what the control unit is to do is contained in a *program*, a sequence of instructions stored, for the most part, in consecutive bytes of memory. To execute the program, the MPU controller repeatedly executes the *instruction cycle* (or *fetch/execute cycle*):

1. Read the next instruction from memory.
2. Execute the instruction.

As we shall see with the MC6809 MPU, reading an instruction from memory will require that one or more bytes be read from memory. To execute the instruction, some bytes will also be read or written. These two activities, read and execute, seem to be read or write operations with the memory, but are quite different to the MPU and we use different terms for them. To *fetch* means to read a word from memory to be used as an instruction in the controller. The first step in the cycle shown above is called the *fetch phase*. To *recall* means to read a word into the MPU that is not part of the instruction. The recall and write operations are done in the second step of the instruction, which is called the *execute phase*. Thus, when we talk about fetching a word, you can be sure that we are talking about reading the instruction, or part of the instruction. We will not use the word fetch to describe an operation of reading data to be input to the data operator.

Some of the registers and logic blocks of the MC6809 are shown in Figure 1-3, where the longer registers hold 16 bits and the shorter ones hold 8 bits. In particular, the 8-bit registers A and B are called *accumulators* because arithmetic operations can be done with their contents with the results placed back in the registers to "accumulate" the result. This accumulating aspect of registers A and B will be assumed to be understood so that we can refer to (register) "A" or "B" rather than "accumulator A" or "accumulator B." Another register, called the *program counter* (PC), is used to fetch the instruction. It is called a counter because it normally increments each time it is used, as we shall soon see.

At the beginning of the instruction cycle it is assumed that the program counter contains the address of the first byte of the instruction. As each byte of the instruction is fetched, the PC is incremented by 1 so that the PC always has the address of the next byte of the instruction, if any, to be read from memory. When the instruction cycle is completed, the PC then automatically contains the address of the first byte of the next instruction.

We now look at the instruction statically as one or more bytes in memory or as a line of a program. This discussion will introduce new concepts, but we have tried to keep the number down so that the examples can be discussed without your having too many terms to deal with. The examples will help to clarify the concepts that we introduce below.

Each instruction in a microcomputer carries out an operation. The types of operations provided by a von Neumann computer can be categorized as follows:

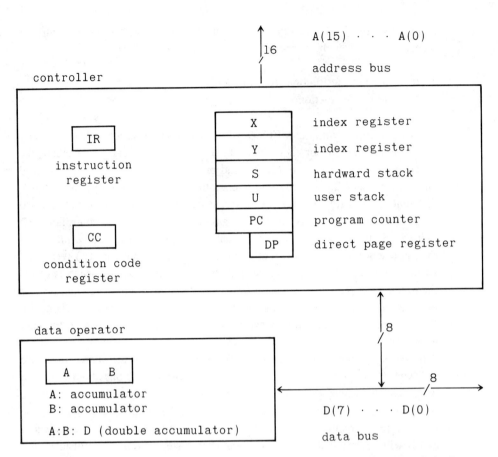

FIGURE 1-3.   The MC6809 MPU. The shorter registers hold 8 bits and the longer ones hold 16.

1. Move.
2. Arithmetic.
3. Logical.
4. Edit.
5. Control.
6. Input/output.

We will examine these in detail later. For now, we are interested in how instructions are stored in memory as part of a program and how they are executed by the MC6809.

After the instruction is fetched, the execute phase of the fetch/execute cycle will often use an address in memory for the input data of the operation or for the location of the result of the operation. This location is called the *effective address*. The Motorola MC6809, like most microcomputers, is a *one-address computer* because each instruction can specify at most one effective address in memory. For instance, if an instruction were to move a word from location 100 in memory into register A, then 100 is the effective address. This effective address is generally determined by some bits in the instruction. The *addressing mode* specifies how the effective address is to be determined, and there are binary numbers in the instruction that are used to determine the address. The effective address is calculated at the beginning of the execute phase, just after the instruction is fetched and before any of the operations actually take place to execute the instruction.

An instruction in the MC6809 is stored in memory as one or more bytes. The first, and possibly only, byte of the instruction is called the *operation code byte*. It contains the *operation code* (op code, for short), the specification of what operation is to be carried out, and the specification of the addressing mode. The remaining bytes of the instruction, if any, specify the effective address according to the given addressing mode. The bytes representing the instruction can be represented as a sequence of ones and zeros, that is, a binary number. The trouble with this is that it is hard to remember and to check an 8-bit or longer string of ones and zeros. To make it easier, we can represent the bit pattern as a *hexadecimal number*. A hexadecimal number will be prefixed by a dollar sign ($) to distinguish it from a decimal number. (For example, 193 = $C1. If you are unfamiliar with hexadecimal numbers, see Appendix 1.) When the op code, addressing modes, and constants used to determine the address are represented either as binary or hexadecimal numbers, we call this representation the *machine code* because it is the actual format used to store the instruction in the *machine* (microcomputer), and this format is used by the machine to determine what is to be done.

Machine code is quite useful for making small changes in a program that is being run and corrected or *debugged*. However, writing even a moderately long program in machine code is a punishment that should be reserved for the fifth level of Dante's Inferno. To make it easier to remember the instructions, a three- or four-character *mnemonic* is used to describe the operation. These mnemonics and the addressing mode are exact replacements for the hexadecimal operation code bytes and they can be converted into their hexadecimal equivalents using Appendix 2. Also, we may give the address in decimal, and it can be converted to hexadecimal so that it can be entered into the microcomputer memory and executed. You can do this yourself (by hand). In Chapter 4 we discuss how this conversion can be done for you by the computer. In the meantime, we want to avoid this easy way out of work because we want you to see clearly just how the computer ticks, and we have found that this is best done by using mnemonics and converting them to hexadecimal by hand.

We now look at one instruction in detail, to show these concepts about instructions in general. The load instruction belongs to the move class of instructions. It will move a byte from memory to an accumulator register, either

A or B. We will look at the simplest addressing mode that can be used with this instruction.

One can put a specific number, say $2F, in accumulator A with the *immediate addressing* mode. The instruction for this is written

```
LDA        #$2F
```

where the symbol "#" denotes immediate addressing and the symbol "$"is used to indicate that the number which follows is in hexadecimal. (When the instruction is written in this way, with an operation mnemonic and an address in some mode, we will refer to it also as a "mnemonic." Which mnemonic we mean will always be clear.) The addressing mode, immediate, is actually specified in the first byte of the instruction together with the operation. The immediate mode uses the value in the second byte of the instruction as the value to be loaded into the accumulator. The instruction is stored in memory as the two consecutive bytes

(Look in Appendix 2 for the operation code byte for LDA and find $86 in the "Immediate addressing" column. In the drawing above, and all like it that follow, the memory will be portrayed as in Figure 1-2, that is, lower-numbered addresses toward the top of the drawing. We will usually use hexadecimal numbers when displaying memory contents in this type of drawing.)

We will now review the dynamic operation of the fetch/execute cycle in more detail. The general pattern will be laid out first, and then the load instruction example will be extended to illustrate these more detailed steps. Looking again at an instruction, we have an operation (e.g., add, subtract, load, clear, etc.) with one or more inputs (or *operands*) and a result. With the MC6809, at most one address in memory is used for one of the operands or result (see Figure 1-4). This is the effective address. We can now enlarge the instruction cycle description as follows.

1. Fetch the first byte of the instruction from memory.
2. Increment the PC by one.
3. Decode the op code that was fetched in step 1.
4. Repeat steps 1 and 2 to fetch all bytes of the instruction.
5. Calculate the effective address to access memory, if needed.

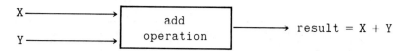

The add operation has two operands, with values X and Y.

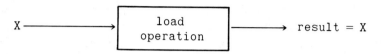

The load operation has one operand, whose value is X.

FIGURE 1-4. Instruction Operations

6. Recall the operand from memory, if needed.
7. Execute the instruction, which may include writing the result into memory.

As we shall see, memory reads may be required in step 5, and more than one memory read may be required in step 6. Also, we mention that some instructions for the MC6809 require two operation code bytes, or an operation code byte and a post byte. The instruction cycle takes a number of clock cycles to carry out, called MPU cycles in the instruction set summary of Appendix 2. Figure 1-5 depicts what goes on in each of the two clock cycles used for the instruction LDA #\$42 where the number \$42 is loaded into A.

PC	into	ADDRESS BUS	
PC + 1	into	PC	1
M(ADDRESS BUS)	into	DATA BUS	
DATA BUS	into	IR	
PC	into	ADDRESS BUS	
PC + 1	into	PC	2
M(ADDRESS BUS)	into	DATA BUS	
DATA BUS	into	REGISTER A	

FIGURE 1-5. Steps in the Execution of LDA #\$42. In this figure M(ADDRESS BUS) denotes the contents of the memory location given by the address on the address bus. The last step of the second clock cycle is actually done in the first part of the next clock cycle while the operation code byte of the next instruction is being fetched.

A FEW INSTRUCTIONS AND SOME SIMPLE PROGRAMS

Now that we have examined the notion of an instruction from several viewpoints, we will look at some simple programs. The machine code for these programs will be described explicitly so that you can try out these programs on a real MC6809 and see how they work, or at least so that you can clearly visualize this experience. The art of determining which instructions have to be put where is introduced together with a discussion of the bits in the condition code register. We will discuss what we consider to be a good program versus a bad program, and we will discuss what is going to be in Chapters 2 and 3. We will also introduce an alternative to the immediate addressing mode using the load instruction. Then we bring in the store, add, software interrupt, and add with carry instructions to make the programs more interesting as we explain the notions of programming in general.

We first consider some variations of the load instruction to illustrate different addressing modes and representations of instructions. We may want to put another number into register A. Had we wanted to put $3E into A rather than $2F, only the second byte of the instruction would be changed, with $3E replacing $2F. The same instruction as

```
LDA      #$3E
```

could also be written using a decimal number as the immediate operand; for example,

```
LDA      #62
```

It would be converted to machine code and stored in memory as follows:

$86
$3E

(With this instruction and all that follow, one obtains the operation code byte from the operation code bytes table in Appendix 2.) The foregoing instructions loaded accumulator A. We can load register B using a different op code byte. Had we wanted to put $2F into accumulator B, the first byte would be changed to $C6 and the instruction mnemonic would be written

```
LDB      #$2F
```

We now introduce the direct addressing mode. Although the immediate mode is useful for initializing registers when a program is started, the immediate mode would not be able to do much work by itself. We would like to load words that are at a known location but whose actual value is not known at the time the program is written. One could load accumulator B with the contents of memory location $3C2F. This is called *direct addressing* as opposed to immediate addressing. The addressing mode, direct, uses the sign ">" and a 2-byte address value as the effective address; it loads the byte at this address into the accumulator. The instruction mnemonic for this is

    LDB   >$3C2F

and the instruction appears in memory as the three consecutive bytes

$F6
$3C
$2F

Notice that the "#" has been replaced by ">" in this mnemonic since we are using direct addressing instead of immediate addressing. Also, the second two bytes of the instruction give the address of the operand, high byte first.

The store instruction is like the load instruction described earlier except that it works in the reverse manner (and a STA or STB with the immediate addressing mode is neither sensible nor available). It moves a word from a register in the MPU to a memory location specified by the effective address, and does not change the register contents. The mnemonic for store from A is STA and the instruction

    STA   >193

will store the byte in A into location 193 (decimal). Its machine code is

$87
$00
$C1

where we note that the number 193 is stored in hexadecimal as $00C1. With direct addressing, two bytes are always used to specify the address even though the first byte may be zero.

The ADD instruction is used to add a number from memory to the number in an accumulator, putting the result into the same accumulator. Its use is obvious. The ADD instruction that adds the number 37 to A has the form

```
ADDA        #37
```

and, since this is immediate addressing, the 2-byte instruction is stored in memory as

$88
$25

(Note that 37 in decimal equals $25.) Similarly, if we want to add the contents of memory location $47AC to accumulator B, the three-byte instruction with direct addressing becomes

$FB
$47
$AC

in memory and the instruction is written

```
ADDB        >$47AC
```

We need an instruction to end a program. Although the instruction SOFTWARE INTERRUPT (mnemonic SWI) is a more general instruction, it will serve as a halt instruction in the first few chapters. When you see SWI, think "halt the program execution."

These four instructions can be used for the simple sequence of instructions below, in which the two numbers in locations 40 and 41 are added together, with the result put into location 42.

Memory Location (hex)	Memory Contenst (hex)	Mnemonic	Comments
000D	B6	LDA >40	First number into A
000E	00		
000F	28		
0010	BB	ADDA >41	Add second number into A
0011	00		
0012	29		
0013	B7	STA >42	Store sum into 42
0014	00		
0015	2A		
0016	3F	SWI	Halt

The instruction sequence is stored in locations 13 through 22, or $000D through $0016 in hexadecimal.

We will now look at *condition code bits* in general and the carry bit in particular. The carry bit is really pretty obvious. When you add by hand, you may write the carry bits above the bits that you are adding so that you will remember to add it to the next bit. When the microcomputer has to add more than eight bits, it has to remember the carry bit from one byte to the next, just as you remembered the carry bits in adding by hand. For example, when adding the 2-byte numbers $349E and $2570, we can add $9E and $70 to get $0E, the low byte of the result, and then add $34, $25, and the carry bit to get $5A, the high byte of the result. The *carry bit* (or *carry* for short) in the *condition code register* is used in exactly this way.

The carry bit is also an error indicator after the addition of the most significant bytes is completed. As such, it may be tested by conditional branch instructions, to be introduced later. Other characteristics of the result are similarly saved in the controller's condition code register. These are, in addition to the carry bit C, N (*negative or sign bit*), Z (*zero bit*), V (*two's-complement overflow bit* or *signed overflow bit*), and H (*half-carry bit*) (see Figure 1-6). How each instruction of the MC6809 affects these bits is shown in Appendix 2.

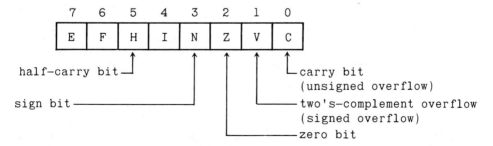

FIGURE 1-6.   Bits in the Condition Code Register

We can look at a simple example that uses the carry bit C. This example shows two equally good programs to make a point that there is no way of having exactly one correct answer to a programming problem. After the example, we consider some ways to know if one program is better than another. Suppose that we want to add the two 16-bit numbers in locations 10, 11 and 12, 13, putting the sum in locations 14, 15. For all numbers, the higher-order byte will be in the smaller-numbered location. One possibility for doing this is the following instruction sequence, where, for compactness, we give only the memory location of the first byte of the instruction.

ML (hex)	MC (hex)	Mnemonics	Comments
20	B6 00 0A	LDA >10	First number into A:B
23	F6 00 0B	LDB >11	
26	FB 00 0D	ADDB >13	Add second number into A:B
29	B9 00 0C	ADCA >12	
2C	B7 00 0E	STA >14	Put result in locations
2F	F7 00 0F	STB >15	14 and 15
32	3F	SWI	Halt

In the program segment above, the instruction ADCA >12 adds the contents of A with the contents of location 12 and C, putting the result in A. At that point in the sequence, this instruction adds the two higher-order bytes of the two numbers together with the carry generated from adding the two lower-order bytes previously. This is, of course, exactly what we would do by hand as seen in Figure 1-7. Note that we can put this sequence in any 19 consecutive bytes of memory as long as the 19 bytes do not overlap with data locations 10 through 15. Finally, the notation A:B is used for putting the accumulator A in tandem with B or concatenating A with B. This concatenation is just the double

$\downarrow C$

(10)	(11)

+

(12)	(13)

(14)	(15)

FIGURE 1-7. Addition of Two-Byte Numbers. In this figure, C is the carry bit obtained from adding the contents of locations 11 and 13; (m) is used to denote the contents of memory location m, where m may be 10, 11, 12 . . . etc.

accumulator D. We could also have used just one accumulator with the following instruction sequence.

ML (hex)	MC (hex)	Mnemonics	Comments
20	B6 00 0B	LDA >11	Low byte of #1 into A
23	BB 00 0D	ADDA >13	Add in low byte of #2
26	B7 00 0F	STA >15	Store low byte of result
29	B6 00 0A	LDA >10	High byte of #1 into A
2C	B9 00 0C	ADCA >12	Add in high byte of #2
2F	B7 00 0E	STA >14	Store high byte of result
32	3F	SWI	Halt

In this new sequence, the load and store instructions do not affect the carry bit. (See Appendix 2. We will understand why this is so as we look at more examples.) Thus, when the instruction ADCA >12 is performed, the carry bit has been determined by the ADDA >13 instruction as required.

The two programs above were equally acceptable. However, there are guidelines to writing good programs, and we want to discuss them early in the book so that you can be aware of them to know what we are expecting for answers to problems, and so that you can develop a good programming style. A good program is shorter, faster, and clearer than a bad program that solves the same problem. Unfortunately, the fastest program is almost never the shortest or the clearest. The measure of a program has to be made on one of the qualities, or on one of the qualities based on reasonable limits on the other qualities. The measure must be selected according to the application environment in which the program will work. Also, the quality of clarity is difficult to measure, but is often the most important quality of a good program. Nevertheless, we discuss the shortness, speed, and clarity of programs to help you develop good programming style.

The number of bytes in a program, or its length, and the execution time of a program are something we can measure. A short program is desired in applications where program size affects the cost of the end product. Consider two manufacturers of computer games. These products feature high sales volume and low cost, of which the microcomputer and its memory are a significant part. If one company uses the shorter program, its product may need fewer ROMs to store the program, may be substantially cheaper, and so may sell in larger volume. A good program in this environment is a short program. Among all programs doing a specific computation will be one that is the shortest. The *static efficiency* of one of these programs is the ratio of the number of bytes of the shortest program to the number of bytes in the particular program. Although we never compute the static efficiency of a program, we will say that one program is more statically efficient than another, to emphasize that it takes fewer bytes than the other program.

The speed or execution time of a program is prized in applications where the microcomputer has to keep up with a fast environment, such as in some communication switching systems, or where the income is related to how much computing can be done, and thus where a faster computer can do more computing and thus make more money. However, speed is often overemphasized: "My computer is faster than your computer." To show you that this may be irrelevant, we like to tell this little story about a computer manufacturer. This is a true story, but we will not use the manufacturer's real name for obvious reasons. How do you make a faster version of a computer that executes the same instruction? The proper answer is that you run a lot of programs, and find instructions that are used most often. Then you find ways to speed up the execution of those often used instructions. Our company did just that. It found one instruction that was used very, very often; it found a way to really speed up that instruction. The machine should have been quite a bit faster, but it wasn't! The most common instruction was used in a routine that waited for input/output devices to finish their work. The new machine just waited faster than the old machine that it was to replace. The moral of the story is that many computers spend a lot of time waiting for input/output work to be done. A faster computer will just wait more. Sometimes speed is not as much a measure of goodness as it is cracked up to be, but then in other environments, it is the most realistic measure of a program. As we shall see in later chapters, the speed of a particular program can depend on the input data to the program. Among all the programs doing the same computation with specific input data, there will be a program that takes the fewest number of clock cycles. The ratio of this number of clock cycles to the number of clock cycles in any other program doing the same computation with the same input data is called the *dynamic efficiency* of that program. Notice that dynamic efficiency does depend on the input data but not on the clock rate of the microprocessor. Although we never calculate dynamic efficiency explicitly we do say that one program is more dynamically efficient than another to indicate that first program performs the same computation more quickly than the other one over some range of input data.

The *clarity* of a program is hard to evaluate, but has the greatest significance in large programs that have to be written by many programmers and that have to be corrected and maintained for a long period. Clarity is improved if you use good documentation techniques, such as comments on each instruction that explain what you want them to do, and flowcharts and precise definitions of the inputs, outputs, and the state of each program, as explained in texts on software engineering. Some of these issues are discussed in Chapter 5. Clarity is also improved if you know the instruction set thoroughly and use the correct instruction. How this is done is developed in the next two chapters.

The normal way to introduce an instruction set is to discuss operations first and then addressing modes. The MC6809 is best described in the opposite way, however, because some instructions are better explained as addressing modes incorporated into other instructions. Thus we will devote Chapter 2 to the discussion of addressing modes, and Chapter 3 to the survey of instructions.

In summary, you should aim to write good programs. As we saw with the example above, there are equally good programs, and generally there are no best programs. Short, fast, clear programs are better than the opposite kind. Yet the shortest program is rarely the fastest or the clearest. The decision as to which quality to optimize is dependent on the application. Whichever quality you choose, you should have as a goal the writing of clear, efficient programs. You should fight the tendency to write sloppy programs that just barely work, or that work for one combination of inputs but fail for others. Therefore, we will arbitrarily pick one of these qualities to optimize in the problems at the end of the chapters. We want you to optimize static efficiency in your solutions, unless we state otherwise in the problem. Learning to work toward a goal should help you write better programs for any application when you train yourself to try to understand what goal you are working toward.

1–4

SUMMARY AND FURTHER READING

In this chapter we examined the computer and the instruction in some detail. You should be prepared to study each of the instructions in the MC6809 in the following two chapters with respect to the details that we introduced for the load instruction in this chapter. We will expand the ideas of programming, introduced at the end of this chapter, as we progress through the book. Many questions may remain unanswered, though, after reading this chapter. We want you to continue reading the following chapters as we discuss the way to use this marvelous tool.

If you would like additional or supplementary reading material, we can suggest several books. We introduced the fact that the MC6809 is a one-address computer when we discussed the idea of the effective address. Did you know that there are two- and three-address computers, and even zero-address computers? These ideas are discussed in books on computer architecture. One of the better books is *Computer Hardware and Organization* (M. E. Sloan, Science Research Associates, Inc., Chicago, 1976). You may also want supplemental reading on programming in general and on programming the MC6809 in particular. The former is discussed in several excellent books, including *Introduction to Computer Organization and Data Structures: PDP-11 Edition* (H. S. Stone and D. P. Siewiorek, McGraw-Hill Book Company, New York, 1975) and *Introduction to Microprocessors: Software, Hardware, Programming*

(L. A. Leventhal, Prentice-Hall Inc., Englewood Cliffs, N.J., 1978). The latter is covered in some of Motorola's applications notes and programming manuals, such as the *MC6809-MC6809E Microprocessor Programming Manual* (Motorola, Inc., Schaumburg, Ill., 1981.) Finally, if you are already an accomplished assembly language programmer on another computer or microcomputer, you may find this book too simple and spread out. We might offer Chapter 1 of the text *Microcomputer Interfacing* (G. J. Lipovski, Lexington Books, Lexington, Mass., 1980) by one of the authors of this book, as a condensed summary of much of the material in this text.

PROBLEMS

1. Is a Hewlett-Packard 21 (or any programmable calculator that you may select) a (von Neumann) computer, and why?
2. What do the following terms mean: memory, controller, data operator, input/output? What is a microcomputer and a microprocessor?
3. Describe the terms: clock, data bus, address bus and read/write line. Discuss the operation of reading a word from memory using these terms.
4. How many memory reads are needed for the following instructions? How many are fetch operations, and how many are recall operations?
   (a) LDA #18
   (b) LDB #18
   (c) ADDA >$3F62
   (d) ADDA >23
   (e) STA >199
5. While executing a particular program, (PC) = 182, (A) = 7, and (B) = 213 before the following sequence is executed:

   ```
   LDA #10
   ADDA >42
   STA >39
   ```

   If the contents of memory locations 39 through 43 are as shown below before the sequence is executed, what will be the contents of A, B and PC after the sequence is executed? (ML is the memory location, or address, and MC is the memory contents. All numbers given are in decimal.) What will the C bit be equal to after the sequence is executed?

ML	MC
39	8
40	7
41	16
42	251
43	19

6. Give a reasonable guess for the steps in the execution of the instruction ADDA >$29. Your answer should follow the format of Figure 1-5.

7. Write a program to add two 3-byte numbers in the same manner as the last program segment of this chapter.

8. Select goals for good programs in the following applications and give a reason for the goals. The goals should be: static or dynamic efficiency or clarity.
   (a) A 75,000-instruction program.
   (b) A program for guidance of a space satellite.
   (c) A controller for a drill press.
   (d) An automobile engine controller.
   (e) Programs for sale to a large number of users (like a Basic Interpreter).

9. The machine code for the instruction LDA >$396 is as follows:

Assuming that the program counter is loaded with the address of the first byte of this instruction, show the position of the program counter after each fetch in the instruction cycle. Use the notation

to indicate that the program counter contains the address L or "points" to location L.

10. What is the effective address in the following instructions?
   (a) LDA >122
   (b) LDA #122
   (c) ADDA >$3452
   (d) ADDA #125

11. How many clock cycles does it take to execute the following program? (See the operation code bytes table in Appendix 2.)

```
LDA     >$1473
ADDA    >$1474
STA     >$1475
SWI
```

12. Explain which of the registers A, B, CC, and PC would have to be changed if the designer of the MC6809 wanted to have more bytes in memory. What would happen to the address bus?

The **TRS-80 Color Computer** with the cover removed. The rightmost eight small chips above the keyboard are the **RAM** memory chips. The large chip in the upper righthand corner of the board is the **MC6809**.

CHAPTER 2

Addressing

We would like to share a simple idea with you that, judging from the way many programmers work, is a rather well kept secret. A program is more than just a sequence of instructions. It also has a *data structure,* the way data is stored in memory. If the data used by the program is kept in a structure that is easy to use in the program, the program is shorter, faster, and simpler. That is not too profound, but it is very important, and it is often missed.

Recall from Chapter 1 that an instruction consists of an operation with at most one address in memory for an operand and/or result. How that address is determined is called *addressing* and the different ways that the address is determined are called addressing *modes.* The data is *accessed* in a program, that is, read or written, by an instruction with the addressing modes available in the computer. These modes correspond to the data structures that can be easily managed in that computer. If you want to handle a particular structure, such as a string of characters, an addressing mode such as postincrement is very useful, as we discuss in more detail in Chapter 6. This chapter introduces the addressing modes of the MC6809, modes which provide the tools that make handling the most useful data structures so easy on this machine. Learning the rich set of addressing modes here will also make it easier later to learn about the common data structures.

This chapter introduces the following general aspects of addressing. The level of addressing indicates how many times an address must be read from memory to get the actual or effective address of the operand or result used with the instruction. This is first introduced to show several addressing modes, and to introduce the need for the indexing modes, which are discussed next. Relative modes are then discussed to show the important concept of position independence. We give examples that rework the addition program of Chapter 1 to illustrate data structure ideas and position independence using these addressing modes. Finally, we consider some architectural thoughts about addressing, such as multiple address instructions and the effective address computation in the fetch/execute cycle.

Upon completion of this chapter, you should be able to use the addressing modes described here with any instruction that is introduced in Chapter 3. You should be able to determine what has been done to compute the effective address, what that effective address will be, and what side effects are generated when some modes are used. This will prepare you to use good data structures in your programs, and thus to write shorter, faster, and clearer programs as you progress through this material.

2-1

LEVELS OF ADDRESSING

This section discusses levels of addressing, the number of times an address must be read from memory to get the effective address of the operand and/or result used with the instruction. We have already introduced this idea in an ad hoc manner in Chapter 1 when we discussed immediate and direct addressing. Now we approach it a bit more systematically in order to show the range of useful addressing modes that have to do with these levels. (See Table 2-1 as a guide to this systematic analysis of addressing modes.)

The two key ideas are the flexibility in changing the data being used, and keeping commonly accessed data where shorter, faster access to it is available. The first two modes, immediate and inherent, require no memory reads to get an address, so they are called zero-level address modes. The next two modes, direct (discussed in Chapter 1) and direct page, require that an address be read from memory, so they are one-level addressing modes. The final mode, indirect, requires two addresses to be read from memory, so it is a two-level addressing mode. The zero-level inherent mode and the one-level direct page mode are used for most commonly accessed data to improve static and dynamic efficiency. When we conclude this section, you should agree that immediate addressing is

TABLE 2-1

Mode	Example	Where Used
Inherent	DECA	Most commonly used variables
Immediate	LDA #160	Get constants
Direct	LDA >1000	Least commonly used variables
Direct page	LDA <100	Fairly commonly used variables
Indirect	LDA [1000]	Least commonly used variables whose address changes
Pointer	LDA ,X	Commonly used variables whose address changes
Postincrement	LDA ,X+	Variables in a data structure
Predecrement	LDA ,-X	Variables in a data structure
Index, 8-bit offset	LDA <1,X	Variables in a data structure
Index, 16-bit offset	LDA >1000,X	Variables in a data structure
Accumulator indexed	LDA B,X	Variables in a data structure
Indirect indexed	LDA [<2,S]	Arguments passed into a subroutine
Relative, 8-bit offset	LDA <L,PCR	Data close to program
Relative, 16-bit offset	LDA >L,PCR	Data more than one byte from the program

the most inflexible since it fixes the value of the data. The one-level mode permits the value to vary but fixes the location, and the two-level mode permits the location to vary as well as the value. The advantages of these modes will be made clear as we bring you to that conclusion.

Some instructions do not involve any address from memory for an operand or a result. One way to avoid going to memory is to use only registers for all the operands. The DEC instruction decrements (subtracts one from) the value in an accumulator so that DECA and DECB are really the same operation, with the registers A and B serving as the addresses for the operand *and* result. Motorola considers DECA and DECB to be different instructions, whereas other manufacturers would call them the same instruction with a register address that indicates which register is used. Either case has some merits but we will use Motorola's convention. There is also an instruction

```
DEC      >100
```

which recalls the word at location 100, decrements that word, and writes the result in location 100. That instruction uses direct addressing (as discussed in Chapter 1), whereas DECA does not use direct addressing. Because the instruction mnemonic for instructions such as DECA make it clear which registers are being used, at least for simple instructions, Motorola calls this type of addressing *inherent* or *implied*. It is a zero-level mode. The Motorola MC6809 has 37 instructions that use inherent addressing. For instance, CLRA clears accumulator A (puts its contents to zero) and uses inherent addressing, whereas

```
CLR        >1000
```

clears the word at location 1000 and uses direct addressing. Several other instructions, such as SWI, which we are using as a halt instruction, have been included in the inherent category since the operation code byte of the instruction contains all of the addressing information necessary for the execution of the instruction.

We have used the immediate addressing mode in Chapter 1, where the value of the operand is part of the instruction, as in

```
LDA        #67
```

which puts the number 67 into accumulator A (see Figure 2-1). The adjective immediate is used because when the instruction is being fetched from memory the program counter contains the address of the operand, and no further memory reads beyond those required for the instruction bytes are necessary to get its value. Thus this is a zero-level mode.

You should use inherent addressing wherever it will shorten the program storage or speed up its execution. For example, by keeping the most frequently used data in registers as long as possible, their use will involve only inherent addressing. Immediate addressing should be used to initialize registers with constants or provide constants for other instructions, such as ADDA.

One-level modes allow the data to be variable, as opposed to the fixed data in the zero-level immediate mode. There are two one-level modes, direct and direct page, in the MC6809 to allow for accessing any word in memory, yet allow for accessing the most common words more efficiently.

We introduced the direct mode in Chapter 1. It is really the only mode required for any program that one would write if we are not concerned about efficiency and if we permit the program to modify one of its own instructions. Indeed, that was the way the first computer was programmed. However, if one examines a program that changes its instructions, it will be very unclear. An example of this type of program, using what is called *self-modifying code,* is given in the problems at the end of this chapter. To avoid self-modifying code and to improve efficiency, other addressing modes will be introduced. In the direct mode, the address of the operand or result is supplied with the instruction. For example,

```
LDA        >103
```

puts the contents of location 103 into accumulator A. We could also have written this

```
LDA        >$67
```

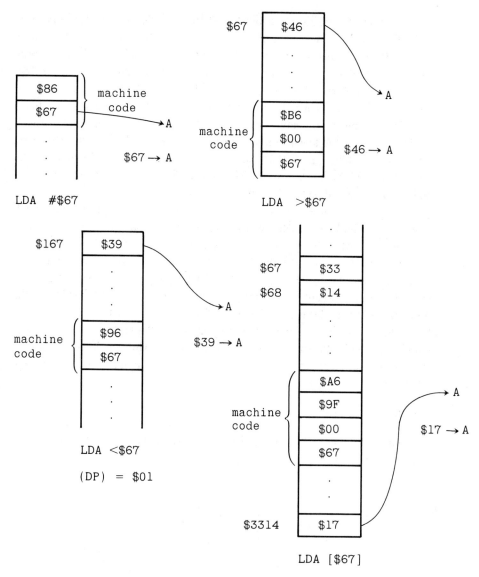

FIGURE 2-1. Addressing Mode Examples Using LDA

(see Figure 2-1). The operation code for this instruction is $B6 and the instruction is stored in memory as the sequence

$B6
$00
$67

(One can find the operation code bytes of the instructions in the table of operation code bytes in Appendix 2.) In the direct mode, a full 16 bits are always used to describe the address even though the first byte may consist of all zeros. With Motorola, the description of a 16-bit address is always higher-order byte first; that is, the higher-order byte has the lower-numbered memory location. Unfortunately, Motorola calls direct addressing "extended addressing." Almost all other computer companies use the traditional term "direct addressing." Because we intend to teach general principles, using the MC6809 as an example rather than teaching the MC6809 only, we will stick to the traditional term. But when you read Motorola's literature, remember to translate their "extended addressing" into "direct addressing."

Experience has shown that most of the accesses to data are to a rather small number of highly used data words. To improve both static and dynamic efficiency, the MC6809 has a compact and fast version of one-level addressing to be used with the most commonly accessed data words. It uses an 8-bit *direct page* register (refer to the register labeled DP in Figure 1-3.) This register is normally cleared when the computer is turned on, but can be loaded by the programmer, as we discuss in Chapter 3. The *direct page* mode is an addressing mode that forms the effective address by taking its higher-order byte, or *page* number, to be the contents of the direct page register while the lower-order byte is supplied by the 8 bits in the instruction. For example, if the direct page register contains $1,

```
LDA        < $67
```

will put the contents of location $0167 into accumulator A (see Figure 2-1). This instruction is stored in memory as

$96
$67

The symbol "<" is used in the instruction to remind us that direct page addressing is being used instead of direct addressing. In direct page addressing then, the direct page register supplies the page number of the address while the instruction supplies the byte number on that particular page.

The symbol "<" will be used in several addressing modes that we will learn. It will generally mean that a short 8-bit number in the instruction is used in the calculation of the effective address. The symbol ">," used above for direct addressing, will also be used in several addressing modes. It will generally denote that a 16-bit number in the instruction is used in the calculation of the effective address. In Chapter 4 we will find that these symbols can usually be dropped when the instruction mnemonics are automatically translated into machine code, because the computer that does the translation can figure out whether an 8-bit or a 16-bit value must be put in the instruction. Until then, to enhance your understanding of how the machine works and to simplify hand translation of mnemonics into machine code we will use the symbols "<" and ">" to designate 8-bit and 16-bit values, respectively.

In the MC6800, the predecessor of the MC6809, direct page addressing was used and given the name "direct addressing." This nonstandard use of the term confuses everyone who uses or studies a variety of machines. When you read Motorola's literature, you need to be aware that when Motorola uses the term "direct addressing," it is really "direct page addressing." Do not confuse it with our use of the term "direct addressing."

Clearly, direct page addressing uses fewer bits in an instruction, and thus the instruction can be fetched faster than with direct addressing. For the purposes of this book we will usually take zero to be in the DP register, the value it is initialized with when the microprocessor is powered-up. Page zero, which is the collection of words at addresses zero to 255, should then be used for the most commonly accessed data, and direct page addressing should be used to access these words. Nevertheless, direct page addressing can be used to access any word in memory, and you can resort to it whenever you need to.

Which mode should you use? In this book we will write many short programs that use only a few variables. All of these variables can fit on page zero, and direct page addressing will be preferred for improved static and dynamic efficiency. However, many programs that you write in your later work will be longer, and will have more variables, so that you will have to use direct addressing for the general case.

For example, if you want to add two numbers together and put the result in a third location, similar to the programs in Chapter 1, then the numbers and result should be stored on page zero and the program executed with direct page addressing. In the simplest case of 1-byte numbers stored at locations 10 and 11 with the result stored at location 12, the program becomes

```
LDA       < 10
ADDA      < 11
STA       < 12
SWI
```

This will be shorter, faster, and perhaps even clearer than the same sequence using direct addressing that you saw in Chapter 1.

A two-level addressing mode, which is doubly removed from the immediate mode, is *indirect* addressing. In this mode, the address giving the location of the operand is in the instruction. For example,

```
LDA       [$67]
```

loads accumulator A with the contents of the word at the address contained in locations $67 and $68. (We defer discussing the machine code representation of this mode of addressing because it is implemented in the MC6809 as a special case of index addressing that is discussed in Section 2-2.) The high byte of the effective address is stored in location $67 and the low byte in location $68; [ ] is used to denote indirect addressing. If location $67 contains $33 and location $68 contains $14, the instruction above loads the word from location $3314 into accumulator A (see Figure 2-1). Motorola calls this "extended indirect" because a full two bytes must be used to describe the address of the location of the operand. There is no analogous form of indirect addressing that uses an 8-bit number in the instruction together with the contents of the direct page register to get the address of the location of the operand. Thus the symbol > is not needed in the indirect mode.

Indirect addressing can be used where the address changes, as well as the data, although a variation of indirect addressing discussed in the next section is usually used for that purpose. Nevertheless, ignoring the next section, we can present the notion of indirect addressing in a pedagogically clean way as an extension of direct addressing. Suppose that an instruction is used many times (in a loop, as we discuss shortly), and that each time it is used it uses a different address. For instance, the first time it is used, it uses address $6712, the second time, $6713, the third time, $6714, and so on. The instruction LDA >$6712 would be stored as shown when the program is loaded into memory.

	$86
$1000	$67
$1001	$12

If the last two bytes of the instruction, $67 and $12, are at locations $1000 and $1001, then just after this instruction is executed, the program could read the two words at locations $1000 and $1001, increment the double word, and put it back into locations $1000 and $1001. When the instruction is executed again, the address would be $6713. Using direct addressing, we have to change the instruction bits themselves. This is an example of *self-modifying code* and, as discussed earlier, is almost universally regarded as unclear. Besides, the program may be in ROM, so that it is impossible to modify the instruction bits. Indirect addressing can be used instead. If locations $3F45 and $3F46 are in RAM and not in ROM, then after each use of the instruction LDA [$3F45], we could increment the contents of the double word at locations $3F45 and $3F46 to prepare for the next address.

Consider another simple example. Suppose that we wish to add the word at location $100 to that at location $101 and put the result in location $102, much like an example in Chapter 1. Then the program should use direct addressing because the variables are on page 1. The sequence would be

```
LDA        >$100
AAAD       >$101
STA        >$102
```

If we were to add any two words in memory, putting the result in a different word in memory, and we did not know which locations they would be at until the program was run, we could put the address of the first number in locations $201 and $202, the address of the second number in locations $203 and $204, the address of the result in locations $205 and $206 and execute

```
LDA        [$201]
ADDA       [$203]
STA        [$205]
```

All addresses above are stored higher-order byte first, as usual.

The next section will introduce a better way to handle variable addresses, although that way is really a simple extension of the technique introduced above. Moreover, the technique described above can always be resorted to if necessary.

This section introduced some of the simpler addressing modes: inherent, direct, direct page, and indirect. We saw that inherent addressing should be used when data is kept in registers, typically for the most frequently used data. Direct page addressing, where data is kept on page zero, should be used for the rest of the frequently used data. We saw that immediate, direct, and indirect modes are used where the data is constant, the address is constant, and the address is variable, respectively. This nice little series of concepts introduces the first group of addressing modes. We now turn to the next group, which is based on the use of other registers in the addressing mode.

2-2

INDEX ADDRESSING MODES

This section introduces a collection of addressing modes that use registers in the address calculation, rather like the direct page register used in direct page addressing. Computer designers realized that, as good as indirect addressing is, it is not particularly efficient because it takes a couple of recall cycles to get the address of the operand or result from memory. To improve efficiency, the controller could be provided with a few registers that could be indirectly addressed to get the data. These registers are called *pointer* or *index* registers.

Indirectly addressing through a pointer or index register would be faster since the number of bits needed to specify one of a few registers is much less than the number of bits needed to specify any word in memory that holds the address. Moreover, it has turned out to be the most efficient mode to handle many data structures, such as character strings, vectors, and many others, as we discuss later. With this potential, index registers have been used in a number of similar addressing modes, called collectively *index addressing* modes, and these are introduced below.

The controller in the MC6809 is supplied with four index/pointer registers, called X, Y, U, and S (see Figure 1-3 again). Although these are all pretty much equal in capabilities, the S register has to be treated with some respect, in the words of a popular comedian, as we will discuss later. Registers X and U are slightly better than Y, and S is used for quite different applications, but all the addressing modes described for X below also apply to the others. First, there are load instructions that can load these registers. For example, the instruction

```
LDX        #$6712
```

will load the 16-bit X register with $6712. It is machine coded very much like the LDA immediate instruction. (See Appendix 2.)

$8E
$67
$12

The other registers can be loaded with similar instructions (although some of the op codes are two bytes long), and other addressing modes can be used to get the two bytes to be put in the index register. In all cases, the effective address determined by the instruction is used to get the byte to be put into the high byte of the index register. The effective address plus one is used to get the byte to be put into the low byte of the index register. Other operations on these registers are discussed in Chapter 3.

Before we get into the modes of index addressing we have to discuss the idea of a *post byte*. As noted earlier, the MC6809 is the successor of the MC6800. The latter had only the modes inherent, immediate, direct page (with page zero), direct, and one form of index addressing discussed below. To keep the same customers that they had for the MC6800 happy with the newer machine, Motorola opted to make the MC6809 as similar as possible to the MC6800. But to introduce more addressing modes, they needed more room in the instruction. The MC6809 is as similar to the MC6800 as possible, using the same op codes in many cases. The extra addressing modes were provided by including an extra byte, right after the op code byte, for addressing information only and then only for variations of index addressing that are used on the MC6809. This byte is called the *post byte*.

The indirect addressing mode, which was not in the MC6800 but is in the MC6809, is handled this way too, as we implied above. That is, because the MC6800 did not have indirect addressing and the MC6809 does, this mode is implemented on the MC6809 as an index addressing option even though it is not conceptually an index addressing mode. The instruction LDA [$3F45] is coded in machine code as an index addressing "option" with a post byte of $9F:

$A6
$9F
$3F
$45

(See Appendix 2, and find $A6 in the row labeled "LDA" and the column labeled "Index." The post byte is shown for all index addressing modes or options in the table of post bytes for index addressing options. See $9F in the row "Indirect Mode." The last two bytes are the address that is specified in the instruction.) This type of post byte will also be used for all of the index addressing modes below.

The simplest type of index addressing is called *pointer* addressing. It is denoted by a comma and the name of the index register, as in the instruction

```
LDA        ,X
```

which loads the contents of the location contained in X into accumulator A. This form of addressing is typically used to improve efficiency when several accesses to the same location have to be made. Suppose, for example, that one wants to access the address contained in locations $1231 and $1232. The sequence

```
LDX        >$1231
LDA        ,X
```

performs the same load operation as

```
LDA        [$1231]
```

but is one byte longer and one clock cycle slower than its indirect counterpart. However, if several accesses are made to this address, and if this address can be kept in X for all of these accesses, then the sequence

```
LDX          >$1231
LDA          ,X              First access
  .
  .
  .
STA          ,X              Second access
  .
  .
  .
LDA          ,X              Third access
```

is more statically and dynamically efficient than

```
LDA          [$1231]         First access
  .
  .
  .
STA          [$1231]         Second access
  .
  .
  .
LDA          [$1231]         Third access
```

In short, addresses requiring several accesses are kept in index registers, if possible, and utilize the more efficient pointer addressing. Less frequently used addresses that change can be kept in memory, and indirect addressing can be used with them.

In the case of pointer addressing, one also has the option of either *postincrementing* or *predecrementing* the index register once or twice in the execution of the addressing mode itself. For example, if X had the value $6712,

```
LDA          ,X+
```

loads the contents from location $6712 into A and then increments the contents of X by 1. The machine code for these modes is left as an exercise at the end of the chapter. Notice that this is what was needed when we wanted to access locations $6712 through $6714 in the loop discussed earlier for indirect addressing.

Consider the simple addition problem again. If you want to add the word at location $100 with the word at location $101, putting the result at location $102, you could execute

```
LDX        #$100
LDA        ,X+
ADDA       ,X+
STA        ,X+
```

Other predecrement/postincrement modes can increment or decrement by a count of one or two. For example,

```
LDA        ,--X
```

first decrements the contents of X by 2 and then loads A from the location whose address is the contents of X. Note that these increment and decrement modes produce a side effect. They not only compute the effective address, they also change the value in the index register used to get the address. No other addressing mode has such a side effect. We will see how useful these options are when we look at some examples later in this chapter.

The next type of index addressing is also called *index* addressing. Here a number called the *offset* is added to the contents of an index register, say X, to get the effective address of the operand or result in memory. Once again, experience has shown that desired addresses are frequently within 100 locations of the location to which the index register points. Thus, for greater efficiency, a shorter 8-bit option is used for many accesses, but a full 16-bit index option is also available. (An even shorter mode with a 5-bit offset is available, and will be introduced in Chapter 4 when we discuss the Motorola assembler. We omit it from our discussion here because it does not add any new concepts and the Motorola assembler does not have a symbol that specifically designates this option. All the other symbols used in this chapter are syntactically correct for the Motorola assembler.) The 8-bit option is denoted by a < symbol, like the direct page mode, and a comma and index register after the address value, like the pointer mode. For example, if X contains the value 3000,

```
LDB        <17,X
```

loads the number contained in location $17 + 3000$ into accumulator B. Similarly, if index register Y contains the value 114,

```
LDB        <-14,Y
```

gets the contents for accumulator B from the location $-14 + 114$, or location 100 (see Figure 2-2). The 8-bit option allows access to words from -128 to 127 away from the value in the index register because the offset is treated as an 8-bit two's-complement number. This index option can be used to access the most commonly used words.

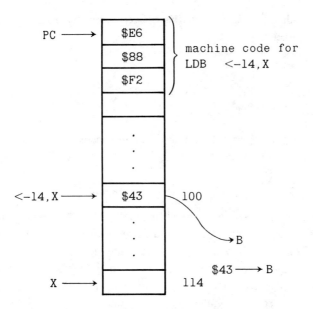

FIGURE 2-2. Index Addressing. This figure illustrates the instruction LDB < − 14,X assuming that the machine code for the instruction is above the locations accessed in memory.

The machine code for LDB < − 14,Y is given by

$E6
$A8
$F2

where $E6 is the op code byte for any index option with LDB, $A8 is the post byte, and $F2 is the 8-bit two's-complement representation of − 14. (To find $E6, look at the operation code bytes table in Appendix 2 and find $E6 in the row labeled "LDB" and the column labeled "Index." To find the post byte, use the table of post bytes for index addressing options and find $A8 in the row labeled "8-bit offset" and the column labeled "direct." Be sure to substitute 01 for Y in the two bits labeled "RR.")

Consider our addition example again. To add the word at $100 with the word at $101, putting the result in $102, use

```
LDX        #$100
LDA        ,X
ADDA       <1,X
STA        <2,X
```

In the preceding sequence, the contents of X are not changed as was the case with the previous example using postincrementing.

When a larger offset is needed, the full 16-bit offset option can be used. It is denoted with ">" replacing "<." For example, if the contents of X is 1, the instruction

```
LDA        >$3012,X
```

will load the byte at location $3013 into accumulator A. Once again, the value in the index register is not changed by this mode. The machine code for this instruction is

$A6
$89
$30
$12

where $A6 is the op code byte for any index option with LDA, $89 is the the post byte and $3012 is the 16-bit two's-complement offset. (To find $A6, use the operation code bytes table in Appendix 2 and find $A6 in the row labeled "LDA" and the column labeled "Index." To find the post byte, use the table of post bytes for index addressing options and find $89 in the row labeled "16-bit offset" and the column labeled "direct." Be sure to substitute 00 for X in the two bits labeled "RR.")

The examples given later in this chapter will make it clear just how convenient index addressing is, and problems at the end of this chapter will exercise your ability to derive the machine code for instructions that use these modes. The index addressing mode has several options for the choice of the size of the offset. The pointer addressing mode executes faster than the other possibilities when the offset is zero since there is no need to add zero to X to recalculate the address, saving one or more clock cycles over the other options. In general, one should pick the index option that describes the offset with the fewest number of bytes or, in the case of a zero offset, one should use the pointer mode because the instruction will be executed faster.

Sometimes, the effective address is the sum of two numbers, neither of which is a constant. The index register can be used to hold one of the variables, and an accumulator can hold the other variable used to compute the effective address. This is called *accumulator indexed* addressing. One may use the contents of A, B, or D as an offset as in

```
LDB        A,X
```

or

```
LDX        D,Y
```

The contents of the registers A and B are treated as 8-bit two's-complement numbers in these instructions while the contents of D may be treated as a 16-bit two's-complement number or an unsigned 16-bit number since the sum of the contents of D and the contents of any 16-bit index register, truncated to 16 bits, is the same unsigned 16-bit number in either case.

Finally, indirect addressing can be combined with almost all forms of index addressing discussed above. The instruction

```
LDA        [ ,X ]
```

will use the value in the index register X as an address, use the word at that address and the word at the next address as another address, and load accumulator A with the word at the latter address. For instance, if X contains the value $100, location $100 contains $02, and location $101 contains $00, LDA [,X] will load the word at $200 into accumulator A. This combined form of indexing and indirect addressing will be useful in such operations as passing arguments to and from subroutines, as we will see in Chapter 5.

The idea of using a register to form the effective address is very powerful. Several addressing modes were introduced that use this idea. The pointer mode uses the contents of the register without modification. It happens to be the shortest and fastest addressing mode in the MC6809 except for the zero level modes. It should be used, whenever possible, to hold an address that changes in a program. The most common change to an address is to increment or decrement it. Two special modes are provided to automatically increment the value in the index register after it is used, or decrement it before it is used, by one or by two. Index addressing modes allow you to add a constant to the address in an index register to form the effective address without modifying the contents of the index register. These should be used whenever one would otherwise be adding a constant to the index register before each access, if pointer addressing were used, because index addressing does that automatically. Moreover, if pointer addressing were used and the index register value were changed often, an error could be made if you forgot where you left it, while index addressing leaves the value of the index register alone. Thus index addressing is better than pointer addressing if you are going to access many words in the vicinity of a particular location. This will be quite common in some data structures that we meet later. A mode that adds the values of an accumulator to the value of an index register permits one to compute addresses that are derived from two variable values, rather than from a variable and a fixed value. Finally, these modes may be combined with indirect addressing for some special applications. With these modes of addressing, the MC6809 is a very powerful microprocessor. With this power, we can show you how to use data structures intelligently to make your programs shorter, faster, and clearer.

RELATIVE ADDRESSING AND POSITION INDEPENDENCE

The microcomputer is very much like any other computer; however, the use of ROMs in microcomputers raises an interesting problem that is met by the last mode of addressing that we discuss. The problem is that a program may be put in a ROM such that the program starts at location $1000 and ends at $2000. Suppose that someone buys this ROM, but his microcomputer has another program in a ROM that starts at location $1000 and ends at $2000. We would like to be able to use this new ROM so that the new program would start at location $4000 and end at location $5000, for instance, or wherever there is room in the address space of the microcomputer. However, since the program is in a ROM, it cannot be changed by the buyer. A program that works the same way whether it starts at $1000 or at $4000 is said to be *position independent.*

The programs that we have seen so far happen to be position independent when the location of the data is fixed and, in fact, most program segments that do not use jump or branch instructions, which are discussed shortly, are position independent. As we see below, jump or branch instructions will have to use a different mode of addressing if the program segment containing them is to be position independent. We will introduce this mode of addressing with the familiar LDA instruction and then discuss its use with jump and branch instructions.

Program counter relative addressing, or simply *relative* addressing, adds a two's-complement number, called a *relative offset,* to the value of the program counter to get the effective address of the operand. Relative addressing is implemented using an 8-bit signed relative offset or a 16-bit signed relative offset, denoted by the "<" before and "PCR" after for the 8-bit offset and by the ">" before and ",PCR" after for the 16-bit offset. (The machine code uses a post byte in this mode since it is implemented as an index option. See Appendix 2.) For example,

```
LDA        <L,PCR
```

can load any word into A that can be reached by adding an 8-bit signed number to the program counter. (Recall that the PC is pointing to the next instruction just below the LDA instruction when the effective address L is calculated.) The instruction

```
LDA        >L,PCR
```

can be used to access words that are farther away than -128 to $+127$ locations from the address of the next instruction; it adds a 16-bit offset to the current value of the program counter to get the effective address L. Although the machine coding of relative addressed instructions is the same as that of index addressed instructions, we do not want you to dwell on that similarity because the offset put in the machine code is determined differently, as explained in the following discussion of the branch instruction.

A *jump* or *branch* instruction is an instruction that may change the value of the program counter other than just to increment it, as has always been done until now. The use of program counter relative addressing in this type of instruction is so common that the branch instructions are defined to use this mode only, while the jump instruction can use any addressing mode to determine where to go. A branch instruction is implicitly program counter relative, so that we drop some of the notation needed to distinguish program counter relative from other modes in other instructions.

In order to discuss an important branching instruction below, we look briefly at the zero bit in the condition code register discussed at the end of Chapter 1. This bit, labeled Z, is put equal to 1 if the result in a load, store, or add instruction is zero. Otherwise, Z is put equal to 0. (There is a great temptation to reverse this description, so be careful.) Almost all other instructions also set the Z bit if the result of the operation is zero. The *conditional branch* instructions will branch depending on the value of one or more of the condition code bits, and the one that we discuss now depends only on the Z bit. The "branch if not equal to zero" instruction

BNE   L

causes the program counter to be loaded with the address L if $Z = 0$ in the condition code register. If $Z = 1$, the program counter is unchanged so that it points to the first byte after the BNE instruction. The amount added to or subtracted from the program counter to get to location L is the relative offset and, in the preceding instruction, is assumed to be described by an 8-bit two's-complement number. (See Figure 2-3 and note particularly that L is the effective address of the instruction.) Consider the following example. Suppose that a branch instruction was in a location so that the next instruction below it is at location $1000, and L is a label that is used for an instruction that is at location $1020. The relative offset is $20 and the machine code for this instruction would be

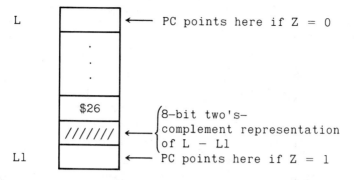

FIGURE 2-3. Relative Addressing. This figure illustrates the use of relative addressing with the instruction BNE L. As shown, the relative offset L − L1 is negative. The op code byte for BNE is $26.

If the relative offset is outside the 8-bit range, one uses a *long branch* equivalent,

    LBNE   L

which uses a 16-bit two's-complement relative offset. It does not need the ">" and ",PCR" symbols in the instruction because the long branch instruction only uses relative addressing with 16-bit relative offsets.

The relative addressing mode is used to implement position independence. If the program segment above was in a ROM and that ROM was installed so that the instruction following the BNE was at $4000, the BNE instruction would still have the relative offset $20. If Z is 0 when the instruction is executed, the program counter would be changed to $4020. That would be the address of the instruction that had the label L. The program would execute the same way whether it was stored at location $1000 or $4000. This makes the program position independent.

A program is not position independent if any instruction in it causes it to do something different when the program is moved, intact, to a different location. The only real test for a program's position independence is to show that it may be moved without changing its operation. One necessary condition, however, is that all changes to the program counter be position independent, and using branch instructions in place of jump instructions will generally make that possible. The relative addressing mode is generally used with data that moves with the program, such as constants that are on the same ROM as the program, and with instructions that compute the address to jump to in a manner to be introduced later. Used with other instructions, then, the relative mode allows programs to be position independent, and that may be very important in a microcomputer that uses a lot of ROMs.

EXAMPLES

We now tie together some of the ideas that were introduced above using some examples. The examples presented illustrate a basic loop that will be used repeatedly in the text and, at the same time, give you some experience with addressing modes and the more frequently used instructions.

Suppose that we want to add N 1-byte numbers which are stored consecutively beginning in location 40. The value of N is stored in location 39 and the result is to be placed in location 38 (see Figure 2-4). The sequence below does this for either unsigned or signed (two's-complement) numbers. If the numbers are unsigned, the result will be correct as long as there is no *unsigned overflow,* that is, the sum can be expressed with an 8-bit unsigned number. If the numbers are signed, the result will likewise be correct as long as there is no *signed overflow,* that is, the result can be expressed with an 8-bit two's-complement number. Note that accumulator B is initially loaded with the number of times that the loop is to be executed. This *loop counter* (accumulator B in this case) is decremented by DECB, and the next instruction branches back to the location L if the (B) is not zero after it is decremented. [The notation (R) is used to denote the contents of any register R.] The loop from location L to the BNE instruction is repeated N times, where N is the initial value in accumulator B.

ML	MC (hex)			Mnemonics		Comments
	8E	00	28	LDX	# 40	Point X to first number
	D6	27		LDB	<39	Initialize B with N
	4F			CLRA		Initialize sum
L	AB	80		ADDA	,X+	Add next number to A
	5A			DECB		Decrement counter
	26	FB		BNE	L	Branch to add next number
L1	97	26		STA	<38	Place result
	3F			SWI		Halt

In the program above, register A is used to accumulate the result, register B holds the number of remaining bytes to be added, and the index register X contains the address or *points* to the next byte to be added. Notice that this sequence can be put anywhere in memory that does not overlap with the data locations and, even though the value of L changes as the instruction sequence is moved in memory, the two bytes representing the instruction

    BNE   L

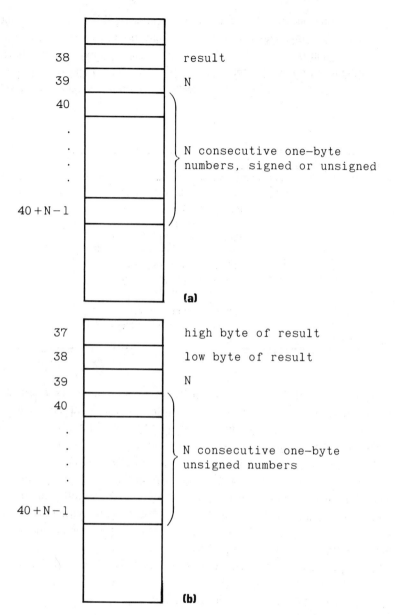

FIGURE 2-4. Data Structures for (a) First Example and (b) Second Example

do not change because the value of relative offset L − L1, which is the second byte of the machine code for the BNE instruction, stays equal to −5 (or $FB). Notice also that a symbol must be used for the effective address of the BNE instruction unless we fix where we are going to place the instruction sequence.

Assuming that the numbers are unsigned numbers, we can find the 2-byte representation of the sum by incrementing location 37 if C = 1 after the addition step. The following sequence does this, where the branching instruction BCC causes a branch if C = 0 or if "C is clear." The locations and machine code are omitted, but notice that the relative offsets for BCC J and BNE L are 2 and −9, respectively, regardless of where the instruction sequence is placed (see Figure 2-4).

ML	Mnemonics		Comments
	LDX	#40	Point X to the first number
	LDB	<39	Put N into B
	CLRA		Initialize the sum
	CLR	<37	Initialize the high byte of result
L	ADDA	,X+	Add next number to current sum
	BCC	J	Skip next instruction if C = 0
	INC	<37	Increment high byte of result
J	DECB		Decrement counter
	BNE	L	Add next number if any are left
	STA	<38	Otherwise, store low byte of result
	SWI		Halt

Suppose now that we want to add the two N-byte numbers where the first begins in location 20, the second begins in location 30, and the result is to be stored beginning in location 40. (For simplicity, we will not worry here about either signed or unsigned overflow.) The value of N is stored in location 19 and we will assume that each number has its N bytes stored consecutively with the lower-order bytes first. (Storing numbers in this way is an example of an elementary data structure called a *vector* or an *array*.) The following instruction sequence uses only one index register and has the basic loop used in the previous two examples. A new instruction ANDCC #$FE is used which puts C = 0 in the condition code register while leaving all other bits there unchanged. In the loop of this sequence, the instructions LDA, STA, DEC, and BNE do not affect the carry bit, so that when ADCA <−10,X is performed, the carry bit is determined by the addition of the previous two lower-order bytes (see Figure 2-5).

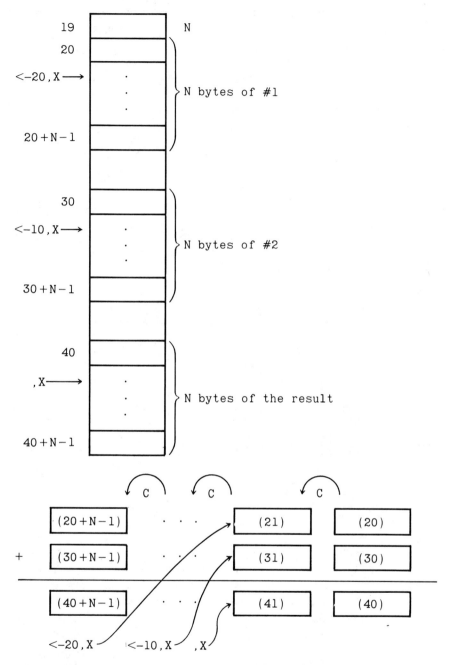

FIGURE 2-5. Data Structure for Adding Two N-Byte Numbers with One Index Register

ML	MC (hex)			Mnemonics		Comments
	8E 00 28			LDS	#40	Point X to result
	D6 13			LDB	<19	Put N into B
	1C FE			ANDCC	#$FE	Clear carry
L	A6 88 EC			LDA	<−20,X	Load next byte of #1
	A9 88 F6			ADCA	<−10,X	Add next byte of #2
	A7 80			STA	,X+	Store result; increment X
	5A			DECB		Decrement counter
	26 F5			BNE	L	Repeat for next byte
	3F			SWI		Halt

The following instruction sequence uses three index registers; although it is perhaps more straightforward than the previous sequence, it takes more memory bytes and executes more slowly (see Figure 2-6).

ML	MC (hex)			Mnemonics		Comments
	8E 00 28			LDX	#40	Point X to result
	10 8E 00 1E			LDY	#30	Point Y to #2
	CE 00 14			LDU	#20	Point U to #1
	D6 13			LDB	<19	Put N into B
	1C FE			ANDCC	#$FE	Clear carry
L	A6 C0			LDA	,U+	Load next byte of #1
	A9 A0			ADCA	,Y+	Add next byte of #2
	A7 80			STA	,X+	Store result; increment X
	5A F7			DECB		Decrement counter
	26			BNE	L	Repeat for next byte
	3F			SWI		Halt

Either of these instruction sequences can be placed anywhere in memory as long as they do not overlap the data locations. The machine code for each sequence also stays the same, regardless of where it is placed in memory, as long as the data structure is fixed, as shown in Figure 2-5 or Figure 2-6.

Suppose now that the N-byte numbers are stored with the most significant bytes first, the usual way for the MC6809, and suppose that N = 5. When the instruction LDX is executed below, X points to the next word *below* the least significant byte of the first number. Since predecrementing is used in the LDA instruction, we see that this is exactly where we want X to point. Notice also how the index option ",X+" moves down a vector in the previous two examples, whereas the index option ",−X" moves up a vector in this example.

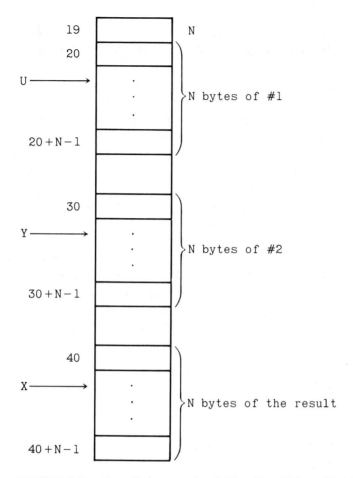

FIGURE 2-6. Data Structure for Adding Two N-Byte Numbers with Three Index Registers

ML	MC (hex)	Mnemonics		Comments
	8E 00 16	LDX	#25	20 + N into X
	C6 05	LDB	#5	Put N into B
	1C FE	ANDCC	#$FE	Clear carry
L	A6 82	LDA	,-X	Next byte of #1 into A
	A9 88 0A	ADCA	<10,X	Add next byte of #2 with carry
	A7 88 14	STA	<20,X	Store result
	5A	DECB		More bytes?
	26 F5	BNE	L	Get next byte
	3F	SWI		Otherwise, halt

ARCHITECTURAL NOTIONS OF ADDRESSING

The particular computer that we are studying, the MC6809, is a one-address computer. Have you thought, perhaps, that a computer that has instructions with two addresses may be better than a one-address computer? In some cases it would, and a three-address computer would be even better, but in other cases it would not. We will compare the static efficiency of a one-address and a three-address computer to help you look beyond the particular machine that we are studying, to understand the general principle of addressing, and at the same time to reassure you that the MC6809 is a good machine for most applications. Next, we will review the detailed fetch/execute cycle to expose some possible ambiguities in the addressing operation of the MC6809. This may help you to understand some very useful addressing techniques. Although these discussions do not show you how to apply specific addressing modes as the previous sections did, they will further your general understanding of addressing and programming.

We might want to add the contents of location 511 to the contents of 512 and put the result into 513. In the MC6809, we would execute the program segment

```
LDA       >511
ADDA      >512
STA       >513
```

The same effect could be obtained in a different computer that had a three-address instruction. The instruction

```
ADD       >511,>512,>513
```

would add the contents of location 511 to that of 512, putting the result into 513. The MC6809 program segment used nine bytes, while this three-address machine might use only seven bytes. The three-address machine is more efficient for this example. However, if we want to add the five numbers in locations 511 to 515 and put the result in 516, the three-address machine must use something like

```
ADD       >511,>512,>516
ADD       >513,>516,>516
ADD       >514,>516,>516
ADD       >515,>516,>516
```

while the one-address MC6809 uses

```
LDA      >511
ADDA     >512
ADDA     >513
ADDA     >514
ADDA     >515
STA      >516
```

A comparison now shows that the three-address machine takes 28 bytes while the one-address MC6809 takes 18. Of course, this computation is very inefficient for the three-address machine but it may represent a more typical computation than the one that the particular instruction directly handles. For a further, but still brief comparison between three-, two-, one- and even zero-address machines, see *Introduction to Computer Organization and Data Structures: PDP-11 Edition,* (H. S. Stone and D. P. Siewiorek, McGraw-Hill Book Company, New York, 1975), Sec. 4.4.

You may have already run into confusing addressing modes. If you haven't yet, we would like to offer the following discussion to help you when you do. Consider the instruction

```
LDX      ,X
```

that loads a register using an address that is calculated using the same register. Is this like a definition of a term that uses the term to define itself? No. It is quite legal and very useful in handling data structures such as linked lists, which you will study in Chapter 6. Let us review the fetch/execute cycle again, with this particular instruction as an example. First, the op code and then the post byte are fetched. The op code is decoded and then the address is calculated. Predecrementing, if needed, is done at this point. Finally, the operation is carried out. Note that the address is calculated using the *old* value in the index register X. Then the two words recalled from that address are put into the index register to become the *new* value of the register. For example, if X contained 100, location 100 contained 0, and location 101 contained 45, then, after the instruction is executed, the X register contains 45.

There are some further ambiguities with the last load instruction, and the corresponding store instruction, when postincrementing is used. For example, with the instruction

```
LDX      ,X++
```

it is not clear whether the load is executed before the + + or after the + +. Note that if the latter is true, the + + would have no effect on the instruction. Indeed, in this machine, the + + is carried out before the operation, in this case a load, so that

```
LDX      ,X++
```

is the same as

```
LDX        ,X
```

For any load instruction involving the same index register for the location of the operand and the location of the result, the general rule is that postincrementing has no effect on the instruction. However, the fact that the postincrementing is carried out before the operation produces an unexpected result in the store counterpart of the load instruction just discussed. For example, with

```
STX        ,X++
```

suppose that X initially contains 373. After the instruction is executed, one will find that 375, rather than 373, has been stored in locations 373 and 374. We conclude this discussion by noting that predecrementing has none of these ambiguities. For example, if X initially contains 373 before the instruction

```
STX        ,--X
```

is executed, then 371 will be stored in locations 371 and 372.

2-6

SUMMARY

In this chapter we looked at the addressing modes in the MC6809. We saw three general themes: the level of addressing, the use of index registers, and the use of relative addressing for position independence.

With the first theme, the main sequence is the immediate, direct, and indirect modes. Generally, they are useful for constant data, constant address but variable data, and variable address, variable data accesses. We also saw inherent and direct page addressing are useful for improving static and dynamic efficiency over direct addressing. Put the most commonly accessed variables in registers, using inherent addressing to access them, and put the next most common variables in page zero, using direct page addressing to access them.

For the second theme, we saw that index registers may be used efficiently to handle addresses that require several accesses, and that index registers may be useful for data structure accesses. Pointer addressing is the fastest and shortest index addressing option and index addressing using 8-bit offsets is available for locations close to that pointed to by the register, while 16-bit offsets are available for other accesses. Pointer addressing is faster than index addressing with an offset, but other instructions may have to be used to move the value of the pointer around in pointer addressing, while index addressing does this within the instruction during the address calculation. We also saw that the accumulators may be used in lieu of an offset, to combine a variable in an index register with a variable in an accumulator to get the effective address. Index registers and their addressing modes provide a lot of power, which we will explore further throughout this book.

With the last theme, the program counter is used as a kind of index register and the same steps used to carry out index addressing are used to carry out relative addressing using the program counter in place of an index register. Although the mechanics are the same, the effect is quite different, and the representation of the address is different. In particular, the address in the instruction using relative addressing is the effective address, not an offset, while the machine code for the instruction uses a relative offset, the amount which must be added to the program counter to get the effective address. This mode is useful in making programs position independent, so that they may be mass produced in ROMs and many different systems can use the same ROM.

This chapter covered the rich collection of addressing modes in the MC6809. These correspond to the modes in most of the other microcomputers, and to most of the useful modes in any computer. Now that you know them, you should be prepared to use them with any instruction in the MC6809 (where they are permitted) as we discuss these instructions in the next chapter. You should know which mode to use, based on our study of the themes above so that you can produce shorter, faster, and clearer programs.

PROBLEMS

1. Write a program that will subtract the N-byte number beginning in location 20 from the N-byte number beginning in location 10, putting the result beginning in location 30. (As is customary throughout the text, multiple byte numbers will be stored higher-order bytes first unless otherwise stated.) The value of N should be placed in location 9. The program should begin in location 40 and be put down in the following format

ML (hex)	MC (hex)	Mnemonics	Comments

    where ML stands for "memory location" and MC stands for "memory contents." The bytes for each instruction may be put down consecutively on the same line in the MC column so that only the location of the first byte of each instruction need be given. You will find it helpful to look at instructions SBCA and ABX in Appendix 2. After you have written this program, write one with the greatest static efficiency and, in the special case of N = 3, write one with the greatest dynamic efficiency. In the last program you will not need to use location 9, which holds the value of the variable N.

2. Find the machine code for the instruction sequence below which adds the byte at location 0 to that of location 1, putting the sum in location 2. Assume that the first byte of the first instruction is placed in location 3.

    ```
    LDA      >0,PCR
    ADDA     >1,PCR
    STA      >2,PCR
    SWI
    ```

    In what sense is this sequence position independent?

3. Show the machine code for the following instructions. For the last instruction, assume that L is at location $117 and that the program counter contains $152 at the time the instruction computes the effective address (i.e., the next instruction begins at $152).

```
LDA  ,X          LDB  <17,X        LDB  A,X
LDA  ,X+         LDB  <-14,Y       LDX  D,Y
LDA  ,--X        LDA  >$6712,X     LDA  <L,PCR
```

4. How many memory reads are needed for the following instructions? How many are fetches and how many are recalls?
(a) LDA [392]
(b) STB [>187,Y]
(c) ADDB [<16,X]

5. Why do some instructions for the MC6809, such as LDY, have two operation code bytes?

6. We normally think of representing memory locations in the MC6809 by the integers 0 through 2**16 − 1. Using the accumulator offset option in the index mode, the contents of the accumulators are treated as 8- or 16-bit two's-complement numbers depending on whether we use A, B, or D. Since the contents of the index register is treated as a 16-bit nonnegative number, explain how this works.

7. Give an instruction sequence that will do the first calculation of Section 2-4 but which does not use any index register, only indirect addressing. You may use locations 35 and 36 to hold the variable address.

8. Give a version for the second example of Section 2-4 which uses self-modifying code (instead of indirect addressing) as discussed in the text.

9. Can the instruction BCC J be replaced by the instruction BVC J if we want to detect signed overflow when N 1-byte signed numbers are added in the second program of Section 2-4?

10. Before the execution of the following sequence, (PC) = 0, (A) = $54, ($0007) = $96, (DP) = 0, and ($0020) = $05. What will be the contents of A after the following sequence is executed?

```
LDA      #5
ADDA     <7
STA      >7
LDA      <$20
SWI
```

This problem should convince you that self-modifying code is, at best, hard to read.

11. Can unsigned overflow occur in the second example of Section 2-4? Explain.

12. Could the designers of the MC6809 have allowed the options +R, ++R, R−, and R−− with the present post byte arrangement? Explain. Could they have added an indirect version of direct page addressing with the present post byte arrangement? Explain.

13. Give the effective address in the following load instructions assuming that (X) = 1000, (B) = $88, and that the contents of locations 397 and 398 are, respectively, 11 and 12. Your answers should be in decimal.
(a) LDA   #112
(b) LDA   <17,X
(c) LDA   <-145,X

(d) LDA   >397
(e) LDA   [397]
(f) LDA   >-603,X
(g) LDA   [>-603,X]
(h) LDA   B,X

An MC6809 microprocessor.

CHAPTER 3

The Instruction Set

In our study of how the computer ticks, we think that you will be motivated to read this chapter because it will describe the actions the computer can do. This is the very essence of the study; this is the chapter that you have been waiting for. It will supply the last ingredient that you need to write programs, so that the computer may magnify your ideas as a lever may your physical capabilities.

In order to learn the possible actions or operations that a computer may execute, you need to keep a perspective. There is a lot of detail. You do need to learn this detail to be able to program the MC6809. But that microcomputer must be viewed as a means to an end, that is, to understand the operations of any computer in general. While you learn the details about programming the MC6809, get the feel of programming by constantly relating one detail to another and questioning the reason for each instruction. When you do this, you will learn much more than the instruction set of a particular computer—you will learn about computing.

We have organized this chapter to facilitate your endeavor to compare and to associate details about different instructions, and to offer some answers to questions that you might raise about these instructions. This is done by grouping similar instructions together and studying the groups one at a time, as opposed to listing instructions alphabetically or by presenting a series of examples and introducing new instructions as needed by each example as we did in Chapter 1. We will present several examples at the end of the chapter, however. Meanwhile, we group similar instructions together into a class and present each class one at a time. As mentioned in Chapter 1, the instructions for the MC6809, as well as any other computer, may be classified as follows:

1. Move instructions.
2. Arithmetic instructions.
3. Logic instructions.
4. Edit instructions.
5. Control instructions.
6. Input/output instructions.

We now examine each class of instructions for the MC6809. This discussion of classes, with sections for examples and remarks, is the outline for the chapter.

At the conclusion of the chapter, you will have all the tools needed to program the MC6809 in machine code. You should be able to write programs on the order of 20 instructions long, and you should be able to write the machine code for these programs. If you have a laboratory parallel to a course that uses this book, you should be able to enter these programs, execute them, debug them, and using this hands-on experience, you should begin to understand computing.

3–1

MOVE INSTRUCTIONS

Behold the humble move instructions, for they labor to carry the data for the most elegant instructions. You might get excited when you find that this computer has a fairly fancy instruction like multiply, or you might be disappointed that it does not have floating-point instructions like the ones most big machines sport. Studies have shown that, depending on the kind of application program examined, between 25 and 40% of the instructions were move instructions, while only 0.1% of the instructions were multiplies. As you begin to understand computing, you will learn to regard these humble move instructions carefully and to use them well.

The instructions of the move class essentially move one or two bytes from memory to a register (or vice versa) or transfer one or more bytes from one register to another within the MPU. The two simplest instructions from this class are the load and store instructions, which have already been examined for accumulators A and B. These instructions may also be used with accumulator D. In the case of D, the effective address in the instruction is for the high byte of D, or accumulator A, while that address plus one is used for the low byte of D, or accumulator B. For example, in the load instruction

```
LDD        >299
```

the contents of A is taken from location 299 while the contents of B is taken from location 300. An exactly parallel situation holds for the store instruction

```
STD        >323
```

where the contents of A is put into location 323 while the contents of B is put into location 324. In addition to D, there are load and store instructions for index registers X, Y, U, and S. They work exactly as described for D.

The transfer and exchange instructions, TFR and EXG, allow the transfer of register R1 to R2 or the exchange of R1 and R2, respectively, where R1 and R2 are any pair of 8- or 16-bit registers. You cannot move data from an 8-bit register to a 16-bit one, or vice versa. The machine code for a TFR or EXG instruction consists of an operation code byte and a post byte. (The op code byte is obtained from the operation code bytes table in Appendix 2, and the post byte is obtained from the transfer/exchange post byte table.) As an example, the instruction

```
TFR        U,Y
```

puts the contents of U into Y and is stored in memory as the two bytes

$1F
$32

The left 4 bits of the post byte indicate the source of the transfer, which is U, and the right 4 bits indicate the destination of the transfer, which is Y.

Since the direct page register has no load instruction, it can be loaded through accumulator A or B with the TFR instruction. For example,

```
LDA        #3
TFR        A,DP
```

puts the value 3 into the direct page register.

The versatile instruction LEA, for load effective address, loads one of the index registers with the effective address in any of the index mode options. For example,

```
LEAX       <19,Y
```

puts the address 19 + (Y) into X, and

```
LEAU        ,X
```

puts the contents of X into U. This last instruction performs the same operation as the instruction TFR X,U. One has to be careful when comparing instructions since they may both make the same "move" but the condition code register may not be changed in the same way for each. For instance, LEAY [,--X] makes the same move as LDY ,--X, but LEAY affects only the Z bit whereas LDY affects Z, N, and V. These condition code bits are used by conditional branch instructions, as we observed in Chapter 2, and it is easy to forget which instruction sets the condition code bits that are being treated by a conditional branch. This program bug is hard to exterminate because the program looks so right that the programmer often concludes that the hardware is malfunctioning.

The TST and CLR instructions are two more examples in the move class of instructions of the MC6809. The clear instruction CLR is used to initialize the accumulators and memory locations with the value zero and, as such, is used to replace instructions such as LDA #0, which can be replaced by CLRA, or the sequence

```
LDA        #0
STA        >345
```

which can be replaced by CLR >345. (Notice again that although CLRA and LDA #0 make the same move, CLRA clears C, whereas LDA #0 does not affect C.) The test instruction TST, sometimes called a "half a load" instruction, is used to adjust the C, V, N, H, and Z bits in the condition code register exactly as a load instruction does, but without actually loading the byte from memory into an accumulator.

The remaining four move instructions for the MC6809 are the push and pull instructions. Incidentally, the word "pop" is used instead of "pull" in many textbooks. The push and pull instructions make the registers U and S *stack pointers* as well as index registers. To understand how these work, we first examine what is called a *stack*. A stack is an abstraction of a stack of letters on your desk. As letters are received they are put on top of the stack; when read, they are removed from the top of the stack. In the computer model, letters become bytes and the memory that stores the stack becomes a *buffer* with a stack pointer as follows. Somewhere in memory, a block of consecutive locations with a low address and high address is put aside for data storage. This block is called a buffer (see Figure 3-1). A register called the stack pointer, say S, points to the top of the stack. If another byte is *pushed* onto the stack, S is decremented by 1 and the byte, from one of the registers, is put into location (S). If a byte is removed or *pulled* from the stack, the byte is transferred to one of the registers and S is incremented by 1. For example, the pull instruction

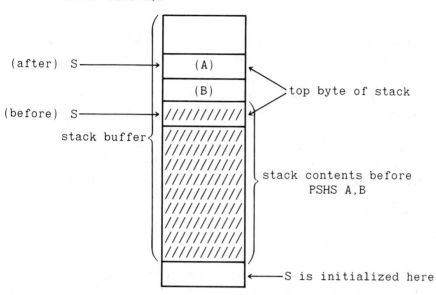

stack change
after PSHS A,B

(after) S———————→ (A)

(B)

top byte of stack

(before) S———————→ ///////////

stack buffer /////////// stack contents before
/////////// PSHS A,B
///////////
///////////
///////////
///////////
///////////
///////////
///////////

←———S is initialized here

FIGURE 3-1. Stack

```
PULS        A
```

performs the same move as

```
LDA         ,S+
```

while the push instruction

```
PSHS        A
```

is the same move as

```
STA         ,-S
```

The PUL and PSH instructions do not, however, affect the bits in the condition code register.

Additionally, any or all of the registers, except S, may be pushed or pulled from the stack for which S is the stack pointer. For example,

```
PSHS        A,B
```

will push B onto the stack and then push A onto the stack (see Figure 3-1).

The instruction

        PULS   A,B

will pull the top byte of the stack into A and then pull the next byte into B. The order always has B pushed before A and A pulled before B, so that PULS A,B is the same as PULS B,A. (See Appendix 2 for the order with the other MPU registers.) The stack pointer S normally points to the top of the stack. If the stack is empty, S points to one byte below the high address of the stack buffer since the first push, in which S is predecremented, must go into the bottom byte of the buffer (see Figure 3-1). The stack pointer U works in exactly the same way as S except that all registers except the U register may be pushed or pulled on this, the *user stack*. The stack pointed to by S is called the *hardware stack*.

As another example, the instruction

        PULS   A,B,X,Y

has the following two bytes of machine code, an op code byte and a post byte. (See the PUSH/PULL post byte table in Appendix 2 to see how the post byte is determined. In particular, since A, B, X, and Y are pulled, the post byte is %00110110 = $36.)

As before, regardless of the order in which A, B, X, and Y are written in the instruction, the bytes are always pulled off the stack in the order A, B, X(high), X(low), Y(high), Y(low).

The hardware stack and the stack pointer S must be used with some care in computers like the MC6809. There is a temptation to use it as an index register, to move it around to different data locations. This is very dangerous. Interrupts, which may occur randomly, save data on the hardware stack, and programs used to aid in the testing and debugging of your program generally use interrupts. Such a program may be very difficult to test and debug because some data in your program may be overwritten in your attempt to test and debug it. On the other hand, this same stack is the best place to save data used by a subroutine, which is not used by other subroutines, as we explain later. The S register is generally initialized once, at the beginning of the program, and thereafter adjusted only by the PSHS and PULS instructions and, perhaps, the LEAS instruction. For example, if the bottom of the stack is at location $3FFF, the instruction initializes the stack at the beginning of the program so that the first push is into location $3FFF. The user's stack and the U register are not so encumbered, so that U is usually used as an index register that has the additional capability of the PSHU and PULU instructions. It may be used as a stack pointer by the user, as the name implies, but the U register is also a good index register in the general sense and would typically be used as such. Once again, however, the hardware stack and the S register must be treated with some care. To see a simple, but typical, use of the stack, suppose that you want to load the direct page register with the number 3 but you do not want to change the values in accumulators A or B because these values are needed later in the program. Assuming that the hardware stack has been initialized, as in instruction (1), we could execute

```
PSHS      A           Save the value in A
LDA       #3
TFR       A,DP
PULS      A           Restore the value in A
```

for this purpose. If we also did not want to change any bits in the condition code register, we could execute

```
PSHS      A,CC        Save the values in A and CC
LDA       #3
TFR       A,DP
PULS      A,CC        Restore values in A and CC
```

This concludes our discussion of the move instructions and we now turn our attention to the arithmetic instructions.

3-2

ARITHMETIC INSTRUCTIONS

The computer is often used to compute numerical data, as the name implies, or to keep books or control machinery. These operations need arithmetic instructions, which we now study. However, you must recall that computers are designed and programs are written to enhance static or dynamic efficiency. Rather than have the four basic arithmetic instructions that you learned in grade school—add, subtract, multiply, and divide—computers have the instructions that occur most often in programs. Rather than the sophisticated divide, we will see the often used increment instruction in a computer. Let us look at them. (In these examples, we use direct addressing. Any addressing mode in Chapter 2 may be substituted for this particular mode.)

We have already discussed the add instructions

```
ADDA      >326
ADDB      >326
ADCA      >326
ADCB      >326
```

The corresponding subtraction instructions

```
SUBA      >326
SUBB      >326
SBCA      >326
SBCB      >326
```

are the obvious counterparts of the add instructions if one remembers to substitute "borrow" for "carry" in the mnemonics.

Arithmetic instructions are really very simple and intuitively obvious, except for the condition code bits. The problem is that the same instruction may be used on unsigned binary data as well as two's-complement data, and the programmer has to keep this distinction straight with the actual use of the instruction. You must remember that addition or subtraction is the same for unsigned as for two's-complement numbers, but the test for overflow is different (see Appendix 1). This test is reflected in the condition code bit that is set after the instruction is over. In the case of subtract instructions, for example,

```
SUBA      >397
```

$C = 1$ if, and only if, there has been an unsigned overflow; that is, (A) − (397) produces a borrow or, when each number is treated as an unsigned number, (A) < (397). [Here (A) and (397) denote the contents of A and the contents of location 397.] Similarly, $V = 1$ if, and only if, a two's-complement (signed) overflow has occurred, that is, when (A) and (397) are treated as two's-complement numbers, (A) − (397) is not in the 8-bit two's-complement range. Note again that the identical subtraction operation is performed regardless of whether the numbers are treated as two's-complement or unsigned numbers.

The add and subtract instructions may also be used with accumulator D. For example,

```
ADDD      >326
```

adds the contents of D with the 2-byte number stored, high byte first, in locations 326 and 327. This instruction then performs the same addition as the sequence

```
ADDB      >327
ADCA      >326
```

The condition code bits H and Z are treated differently by the sequence, however. One of the first instruction sequences at the end of Chapter 1 could have been written

```
LDD        >10
ADDD       >12
STD        >14
SWI
```

for some improvement in static and dynamic efficiency, as well as clarity. The subtract instruction SUBD performs the corresponding 16-bit subtraction. The add with carry and the subtract with carry (or borrow) are used for multiple-byte numbers as seen in earlier examples. Since the instructions ADCD and SBCD are missing, multiple-byte arithmetic must be done one byte at a time rather than using two bytes at a time.

As noted earlier, some arithmetic instructions are included in the instruction set to enhance static and dynamic efficiency. We often add 1 to or subtract 1 from an accumulator or a word in memory, say to count the number of times that something is done. Rather than use an ADDA instruction with an immediate address of #1, a shorter instruction INCA is used for these many instances. The increment and decrement instructions

```
INCA
INCB
INC        >326

DECA
DECB
DEC        >326
```

add or subtract 1 from A, B or a memory location. Looking at Appendix 2, it seems a little puzzling that the carry bit is unaffected by an INC or DEC instruction. However, we needed this same property in the loop examples of Chapter 2 which added two N-byte numbers. The loop counter was decremented and tested for zero, but the carry bit was not affected by the DECB, BNE, LDA, or STA instructions. Thus the carry used with the ADCA instruction is the carry produced by the last execution of that same instruction, and not the DEC, BNE, LDA or STA instructions. Of course, the only time that one should get a carry with the INC instruction is when the contents of the byte is 0 after the instruction is executed. Thus $Z = 1$ is equivalent to $C = 1$ for the INC instruction if the INC instruction was designed to change C.

We may also increment or decrement the 16-bit registers X, Y, U, and S by the LEA instructions, as in

```
LEAY       <1,Y
```

or

```
LEAY        < - 1 , Y
```

Incrementing X or Y in this way sets the condition code bit Z so that it may be tested by some of the conditional branching instructions, but incrementing U and S in this way does not change the condition code bits at all. Note then that X and Y may be used as counters that may be tested but that U or S may not. (The reasons for this are due to the operations of the parent MC6800 microprocessor, and the need to be as similar as possible in the MC6809.) Finally, note that any index addressing mode may be used with LEAX, LEAY, LEAU, and LEAS. You may add any constant to one index register and put the result in the same or another index register with this mode, or you may add the contents of an accumulator (A, B, or D) to an index register and put the result in the same or another index register. Note that addition may be done directly to index registers as well as accumulators. The former uses the LEA instructions and finds its greatest use in computations involving addresses. The latter uses the ADD instructions and finds greatest use in handling the arithmetic required by the end user, as opposed to the arithmetic to handle addresses, which is not visible to the end user.

Negation, subtracting a number from 0, is done often enough that it merits a special instruction. The instructions

```
NEGA
NEGB
NEG        > 327
```

subtract the 8-bit number in A, B, or a memory location from zero, placing the result in the same place as the operand. The bits C, N, Z, and V are set for this subtraction.

There is a multiply instruction MUL which multiplies the unsigned numbers in A and B, putting the result in D. If the numbers in A and B are treated as 8-bit two's-complement numbers, and if the product is known to be in the 8-bit two's-complement range, MUL yields the correct 8-bit signed product in B. (See the problems at the end of the chapter.) For example, if each of the numbers in A and B is a signed number in the 4-bit two's-complement range, MUL gives the 8-bit signed product in B. One may also multiply a signed or unsigned number by two with the arithmetic shift-left instructions

```
ASLA
ASLB
ASL        > 327
```

One may divide a two's-complement number by two with the corresponding arithmetic shift-right instructions

```
ASRA
ASRB
ASR        >327
```

Note that although the MC6809 has a multiply instruction MUL, there is no corresponding general divide instruction. The MUL instruction improves static and dynamic efficiency because it is used quite often by more involved address calculations. Division must be done by a subroutine as we discuss in Chapter 7.

Comparisons are normally made by subtracting two numbers and checking if the result is zero, negative, positive, or a combination of these. The problem with using the subtract instruction to compare a fixed number against many numbers is that the fixed number has to be reloaded in an accumulator or index register each time the subtraction is performed. To streamline this process, a special subtract instruction is included which does not change the contents of the accumulator or index register used. These compare instructions are used to compare the contents of registers A, B, D, X, Y, U, and S with the contents of memory locations in order to give values to the condition code bits C, V, N, and Z. They do not change the value in these registers but otherwise act like a subtract instruction. For example, the instruction

```
CMPA       >327
```

determines bits C, V, N, and Z as though the subtraction (A) − (327) had been done, but without changing the contents of A. With the 16-bit registers, two consecutive bytes from memory are taken in the usual way to determine bits C, V, N, and Z for a 16-bit subtraction. The TST instructions might have been described as a special case of the compare instructions since, for example, TSTA is a 1-byte version of

```
CMPA       #0
```

As another example of the use of the stack, suppose that you want to compare the contents of U with the contents of X. You might be tempted to use

```
CMPU       ,X
```

but remember this instruction compares the contents of U with the contents of the two bytes *pointed to* by X. A correct sequence using the stack is

```
PSHS       X            Put copy of X onto stack
CMPU       ,S++         Compare (U) with copy of X; remove copy of X
```

where we have used "+ +" to remove the copy of X from the stack after it is used.

Finally, there are two special instructions, ABX and DAA. The instruction ABX performs the addition (B) + (X), treating (B) as an unsigned number and putting the result in X. No condition code bits are affected by this instruction. At first glance, one might think that it is the same as

```
LEAX        B,X
```

but remember that when accumulator B is used as offset in the index mode, its contents is treated as a two's-complement number which will frequently yield a different result for the sum (B) + (X). This LEAX instruction also affects the Z bit, whereas ABX does not. The DAA instruction, for decimal adjust in accumulator A, is used when binary-coded decimal numbers are being added. Briefly, two decimal digits per byte are represented with binary-coded decimal, the most significant four bits for the most significant decimal digit and the least significant four bits for the least significant decimal digit. Each decimal digit is represented by its usual 4-bit expansion so that the 4-bit sequences representing 10 through 15 are not used. To see how the decimal adjust works, suppose that the hexadecimal contents of A is $27 and the hexadecimal contents of location 333 is $91. After

```
ADDA        >333
```

is executed, the contents of A will be $B8 and the carry bit will be zero. However, if we are treating these numbers as binary-coded decimal numbers, what we want is $18 in A and the carry bit equal to 1. The sequence

```
ADDA        >333
DAA
```

does just that. The DAA instruction may be used after ADDA or ADCA but may *not* be used with any other instructions such as ADDB, DECA, or SUBA.

The arithmetic instructions of the MC6809, like any computer, implement the most commonly used arithmetic functions. Thus INC is an instruction whereas DIVIDE is not. These instructions are relatively obvious, except for the two's-complement overflow bit V and the carry bit C, which are set for signed and unsigned arithmetic operations. The use of these bits takes some care, as we have tried to indicate.

3-3

LOGIC INSTRUCTIONS

Logic instructions are used to set and clear individual bits in A, B and CC. They are used by compilers, programs that translate high-level languages to machine code, to manipulate bits to generate machine code. They are used by controllers of machinery because bits are used to turn things on and off. They are used by operating systems to control input/output (I/O) devices and to control the allocation of time and memory on a computer. Logic instructions are missing in calculators. That makes it hard to write compilers and operating systems for calculators, no matter how much memory they have. Returning to a problem at the end of Chapter 1, we say that a programmable calculator is not a von Neumann computer because it does not have logic instructions or any efficient replacements for these instructions with combinations of other instructions. [This differentiation may be pedagogically satisfying, but unfortunately, von Neumann's original computer is not a von Neumann computer by this definition. Since we are engineers and not historians, we say that programmable calculators, and von Neumann's original computer, are not (von Neumann) computers in the strictest sense because they cannot support compilers and operating systems efficiently.]

Consider now the logic instructions that make a computer a computer and not a calculator. The most important logic instructions carry out bit-by-bit logic operations on accumulators A or B with a memory location or an immediate value. (See Figure 3-2 for a summary of the common logic operations.) For example, the instruction

```
ANDB        >17
```

carries out a bit-by-bit AND with the contents of B and the contents of location 17, putting the result in B (see Figure 3-3). The two instructions ANDA and ANDCC do the same thing except that ANDCC uses only immediate addressing and the condition code register CC. As an example,

```
ANDCC       #$FE
```

clears the carry bit in the condition code register, that is, puts $C = 0$ leaving the other bits unchanged. This instruction is used only to clear condition code bits and is not used to modify other data bits. The same remarks hold for the OR instructions, ORA, ORB, and ORCC, and for the exclusive OR instructions, EORA and EORB (see Figure 3-3 again). There is no EORCC instruction. While the ANDCC instruction is used to clear bits in the CC register, the ORCC instruction is used to set bits in that register. In addition, the OR and AND

```
   X 0  1        X 0  1        X 0  1          X 0  1
 Y              Y              Y              Y
 0 | 0  0       0 | 0  1       0 | 0  1         1  0
 1 | 0  1       1 | 1  1       1 | 1  0

   X AND Y        X OR Y        X EOR Y       X COMPLEMENT
```

FIGURE 3-2. Common Logic Operations

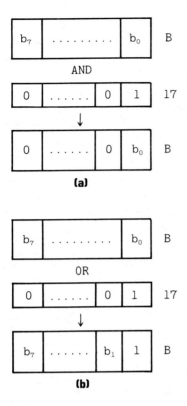

FIGURE 3-3. Results of (a) ANDB >17 and (b) ORB >17.

instructions are used to set or clear control bits in registers used in input/output operations. Consider this example. Suppose that we need to clear bits 0 and 4, set bits 5, 6, and 7, and leave bits 1, 2, and 3 unmodified in accumulator A. The following instructions carry out these modifications.

```
ORA        #$E0        Set bits 5, 6, and 7, leaving others unchanged
ANDA       #$EE        Clear bits 0 and 4, leaving others unchanged
```

The complement instruction COM takes the complement of the bit-by-bit contents of A, B, or a memory location, putting the result in the same place. Finally, the BIT instruction, for bit test, determines the bits as though the AND instruction had been performed with A or B and the contents of a byte from memory. With the BIT instruction, however, the contents of A and B are unchanged. It is to the AND instruction what the CMP instruction is to the SUB instruction; it is used to avert the need to reload the register after the condition code bits are set as in the AND instruction.

Logic instructions are used primarily to set and clear, and to test and change (logically invert) bits in a word. These instructions are used to build operating systems and compilers, and other programs that control resources and format data. These are the instructions that make a computer so much more useful than a programmable calculator.

EDIT INSTRUCTIONS

Edit instructions rearrange bits of data, without generating new bits as an ADD does. Large machines have complex edit instructions, but microcomputers have simple ones. The class of edit instructions generally permute bits within the MPU registers. For example, the arithmetic shift-left instructions

```
ASLA
ASLB
ASL        >327
```

shift all the bits left, putting the most significant bit into the carry bit of the condition code register, and putting a zero in on the right (the same as LSLA) (see Figure 3-4). This, except for overflow, doubles the unsigned or signed number contained in A. The ASR instruction keeps the sign bit unchanged and shifts all other bits to the right, putting the least significant bit into the carry bit (see Figure 3-4). As mentioned in the discussion of the arithmetic class of instructions, ASR divides the original two's-complement number contained in an accumulator or memory location by two (rounding is to the next lowest integer).

The remaining shifts and rotates (e.g., LSR, LSL, ROR, ROL) are easily understood by looking at Figure 3-4. The rotate instructions are used with multiple-byte arithmetic operations such as division and multiplication. For example, the sequence

```
ASLB
ROLA
```

multiplies the unsigned contents of D by two, and the sequence

```
ASRA
RORB
```

divides the signed contents of D by two. Further examples are given in Chapter 7.

The remaining edit instruction, the SEX instruction, is interesting but not quite as much as its name implies. Suppose that you are getting ready to add an 8-bit two's-complement number to a 16-bit two's-complement number. If the 8-bit number is positive, you merely attach eight leading zeros to it and

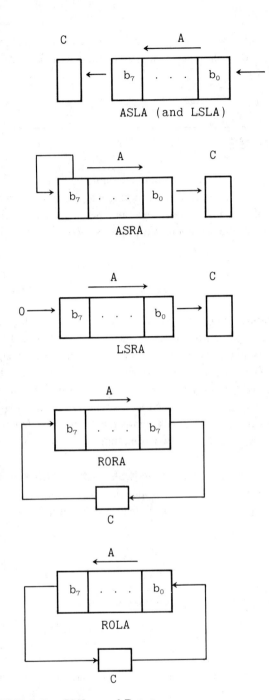

FIGURE 3-4. Shifts and Rotates

perform the addition. If the 8-bit number is negative, you know that the leading bit in its 16-bit two's-complement representation should be a 1 and, after a little thought, you should be able to see that the leading eight bits should all be ones, while the last eight bits remain unchanged. The SEX instruction performs this sign extension of the contents of B into the contents of A:B, putting all zeros in A if the contents of B is positive or putting all ones in A if the contents of B is negative.

Edit instructions are then used to rearrange bits in a word. A common use is to multiply or divide a word by two, but they may be used for more general rearrangements.

3-5

CONTROL INSTRUCTIONS

The next class of instructions, the control instructions, are those that affect the program counter. After the MOVE class, this class composes the most often used instructions. Control instructions are divided into branching instructions and what might be called subroutine instructions. We discuss branching instructions first.

Branching instructions all use relative addressing. For example, the instruction

```
BRA        L
```

for "branch always" will cause the program counter to be loaded with the address L. Corresponding to the branch always instruction is a rather amusing instruction,

```
BRN        L
```

which "branches never" regardless of the location L. It is useful because any branching instruction can be changed to a BRA or BRN instruction just by changing an op code byte. This allows a programmer to choose manually whether a particular branch is taken while he or she is debugging a program.

Conditional branch instructions test the condition code bits. As noted earlier, these bits have to be carefully watched, for they make a program look so correct that you want to believe that the hardware is at fault. The hardware is rarely at fault. The condition code bits are often the source of the fault because the programmer mistakes where they are set, and which ones to test in a conditional branch. The instructions should now be reviewed with regard to how they affect the condition code bits. See the right column of the operation code bytes table in Appendix 2. Note that move instructions generally either change the N and Z bits or change no bits; arithmetic instructions generally change all bits; logic instructions change the N and Z bits; and edit instructions change all bits.

However, there are many exceptions, and these exceptions are precisely the ones that cause mystifying errors. There is sound rationale for which bits are set and the way they are set. Some of that is discussed in this chapter. But most of it is simply learned by experience. We conclude by reminding you that when your program does not work, and you have checked every angle, carefully examine the setting and testing of the condition code bits. Now we look at the testing of these bits in detail.

There are eight simple branching instructions which test only a single bit in the condition code register.

BNE	L	Branches to location L if $Z = 0$
BEQ	L	Branches to location L if $Z = 1$
BPL	L	Branches to location L if $N = 0$
BMI	L	Branches to location L if $N = 1$
BVC	L	Branches to location L if $V = 0$
BVS	L	Branches to location L if $V = 1$
BCC	L	Branches to location L if $C = 0$
BCS	L	Branches to location L if $C = 1$

The letters S and C are used for "set" and "clear" (1 and 0, respectively) in the mnemonics for the branching instructions. (See Appendix 2 to find the op code bytes of these instructions.)

We can illustrate the use of the BNE instruction again by a simple move example which parallels the basic loop examples of Chapter 2. Suppose that we want to move three consecutive bytes from location 20 to location 30. We could use the sequence

```
LDA     <20
STA     <30
LDA     <21
STA     <31
LDA     <22
STA     <32
```

or use

```
        LDB     #3         Initialize B for a 3-byte move
        LDX     #30        Point X to the location of the result
L       LDA     <-10,X     Next byte to be moved into A
        STA     ,X+        Move byte to destination; adjust X
        DECB               Any more bytes to move?
        BNE     L          Branch if Z = 0
```

When three bytes are being moved, the first sequence executes faster than the second and is stored in memory with fewer bytes. However, if ten bytes are to be moved instead of three, the first sequence, expanded for ten bytes, takes many more memory bytes than the second sequence while still executing somewhat faster. We will examine this point again in Section 3-7.

Frequently, two numbers are compared, as in a compare instruction or a subtraction. One would like to make a branch based on whether the result is positive, negative, and so forth. The table below, where R stands for the contents of a register and M stands for the contents of a memory location (or locations), shows the test and the branching statement to make depending on whether the numbers are interpreted as signed numbers or unsigned numbers. (See also the table of branching instructions in Appendix 2.)

Test	Signed	Unsigned
R < M	BLT	BLO (or BCS)
R ≤ M	BLE	BLS
R ≥ M	BGE	BHS (or BCC)
R > M	BGT	BHI

The branch mnemonics for the two's-complement, or signed, numbers case are the ones usually described in mathematical prose, or used in FORTRAN conditional branching statements. For example,

BLT   For "branch if less than"
BLE   For "branch if less than or equal to"

and so forth. The mnemonics for unsigned numbers are offbeat enough to keep you from confusing them with the signed ones, for example,

BLO   For "branch if lower"
BLS   For "branch if lower or the same"
BHI   For "branch if higher"
BHS   For "branch if higher or the same"

Notice that BLO is the same instruction as BCS, and BHS is the same instruction as BCC. Here then is an example of two different mnemonics describing the same instruction, something that is sometimes warranted when the programmer will be using the same instruction with two distinct interpretations. Why not have a mnemonic for each circumstance?

One should consult the instruction set summary in Appendix 2 for a while to make sure that the correct branch is being chosen. For example, you might be tempted on the test $R \geq M$ to take the simple branch BPL for signed numbers instead of BGE. The difficulty with this is that you want the branch test to work even when there is a signed overflow in the subtraction or comparison. But this is just exactly when the sign is incorrect, and when using BPL would not replace BGE. Thus, after a compare or subtract between signed numbers, use BGE rather than BPL. You might also be tempted to use BPL for the unsigned test $R \geq M$. However, if $R = 136$ and $M = 4$, then $N = 1$ after performing the test $R \geq M$. Thus BPL would not take the branch even though $R - M \geq 0$. Thus after a comparison or subtraction between unsigned numbers, use BHS rather than BPL.

Each of the preceding branch statements is represented in memory by an op code byte followed by the 1-byte two's-complement relative offset. All branch statements have "long" branch counterparts where each instruction is prefaced with an L and the offset is a 2-byte two's-complement number. Almost all of the long branch instructions have 2-byte op codes.

Finally, there are some miscellaneous unconditional branch statements

```
JMP
EXG        R , PC        (R can be X, Y, U, S, or D)
TFR        R , PC        (R can be X, Y, U, S, or D)
NOP
```

which are self-explanatory after looking at Appendix 2. Notice that the JMP instruction may use relative addressing as an index mode option and may also use most of the other modes as well.

You may have already written a program where one segment of it is repeated in several places. Have you wished that you knew how to avoid writing it more than once? One possibility is to use the EXG and TFR instructions. Assuming that the segment that you want repeated is at location SUB, you may use

```
LDX        #SUB
EXG        X , PC
```

to get into the segment while, at the end of the segment, you execute TFR X,PC to get back to the main program (see Figure 3-5). Notice how X holds the address of where to return while the program segment is being executed. This technique requires that the index register X be left unchanged in this program segment so that the return to the main program will be executed properly.

This last situation is so commonly encountered in programs that the repeated program segment is given the name *subroutine* and special instructions are used to make the branching to and returning from the subroutine more efficient. For example, if the subroutine begins at location SUB, the instruction

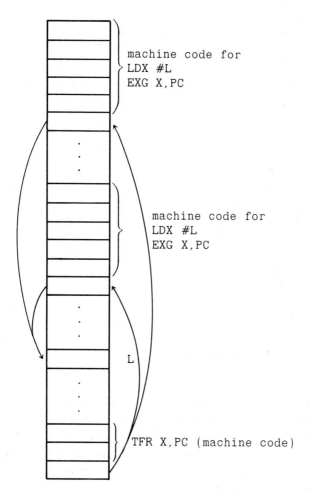

machine code for
LDX #L
EXG X,PC

machine code for
LDX #L
EXG X,PC

L

TFR X,PC (machine code)

FIGURE 3-5. **Executing a Particular Segment of Code Several Times While Writing It Only Once**

```
BSR       SUB
```

(for *branch to subroutine*) causes the PC to be loaded with location SUB *and* the address immediately after the BSR instruction to be pushed onto the hardware stack, low byte first. At the end of the subroutine, the 1-byte instruction RTS (for *return from subroutine*) causes the top two bytes of the hardware stack to be pulled into the PC, high byte first. These two instructions are depicted in Figure 3-6, where the address after the BSR instruction is denoted H:L, the concatenation of the high byte H and low byte L. This address is called the *return address*. Notice how the pair of instructions, BSR SUB and RTS, efficiently get into and return from the subroutine, and do so without tying up

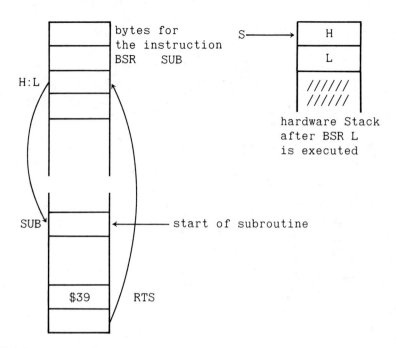

FIGURE 3-6. The BSR and RTS Instructions

any index register. However, for the new pair to work properly, H:L must be on top of the stack at the time the RTS instruction is executed.

There is also a LBSR instruction which uses a 2-byte relative offset to get the effective address, and a JSR instruction which uses the direct, direct page, and index addressing modes for the effective address. Both instructions push the return address onto the stack in the same way that BSR does.

We have covered both the conditional and unconditional branch instructions. We have also covered the jump and related instructions together with subroutine branch and jump instructions. Control instructions provide the means to alter the pattern of fetching instructions, and are the second most common type of instruction. If you use them wisely, they will considerably enhance the static and dynamic efficiency of your program as well as clarify it.

3–6

INPUT/OUTPUT INSTRUCTIONS

The last class of instructions for the MC6809, the input/output or I/O class, is easy to describe because there aren't any! With the MC6809 a byte is transferred between an accumulator and a register in an I/O device through a memory location chosen by hardware. The LDA instruction with that location then inputs a byte from the register of the I/O device to accumulator A, while the STA instruction with that location does the corresponding output of a byte. Other instructions, such as DEC, INC, and CLR, may be used as I/O instructions, depending on the particular device. We look more closely at all of these issues in Chapter 8.

MORE EXAMPLES

To see how some of the instructions are used and to get more practice in dealing with how instructions affect the bits in the condition code register, consider the following problem. We want to add two N-byte, two's-complement numbers where the first is stored beginning in location 20, the second beginning in location 30, and the result is stored beginning in location 40 (see Figure 3-7). All numbers are stored with the most significant bytes first, the value of N is stored in location 19 and signed overflow is indicated by putting 1 in location

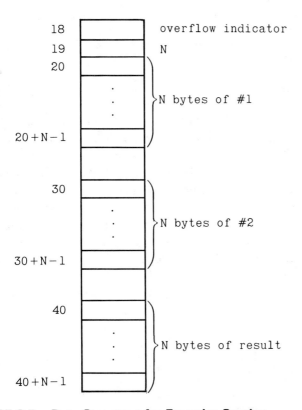

FIGURE 3-7. Data Structure for Examples Section

18, with 0 put there otherwise. This is the same as an earlier example in Chapter 2 except for two things. We are now detecting signed overflow and storing the numbers higher-order bytes first.

The mnemonics for just adding up the N bytes with this data structure are

```
      LDB      <19          Put N into B
      LDX      #20          Point X to high byte of first number
      LEAX     B,X          Position X for low byte of #1
      ANDCC    #$FE         Clear carry
L     LDA      ,-X          Next byte of #1 into A
      ADCA     <10,X        Add next byte of #2 into A
      STA      <20,X        Store result
      DECB                  Decrement counter
      BNE      L            Another byte?
      SWI                   Halt
```

Looking at Figure 3-7, we see that the low byte of the first number is at location $20+N-1$. Executing the sequence

```
   LDB     <19
   LDX     #20
   LEAX    B,X
```

puts the location $20+N$ into X. Because predecrementing is used in the loop with the instruction

```
   LDA     ,-X
```

the byte loaded into A the first time through the loop will be from location $20+N-1$, the second time through from location $20+N-2$ and so forth. This is exactly what we want.

The five statements before the SWI form the basic loop, adding up all N bytes. Notice that the STA instruction puts $V = 0$ and the DECB instruction also affects the V bit so that one cannot determine if signed overflow has occurred by checking the V bit after the loop is completed. One way to modify the program above to detect overflow is to go through the basic loop $N - 1$ times and detect overflow when adding the last, most significant bytes. This is, of course, the only place you have to check for $V = 1$. The new program follows, where we note that N must be at least 2 for the program to work correctly.

```
      CLR      <18          Clear overflow location
      LDB      <19          Put N into B
      LDX      #20          Point X to high byte of first number
      LEAX     B,X          Position X for low byte of #1
      ANDCC    #$FE         Clear carry
      DECB                  N - 1 is now in B
```

```
L       LDA     ,-X         Next byte of #1 into A
        ADCA    <10,X       Add next byte of #2 into A
        STA     <20,X       Store result
        DECB                Decrement counter
        BNE     L           Another byte?
        LDA     ,-X
        ADCA    <10,X       Add the high bytes and check V = 1
        BVC     J           If V = 1, increment location 18
        INC     <18         Set overflow indicator
J       STA     <20,X       Place result
        SWI                 Halt
```

If we look at the instruction CLR more closely, we see that it also puts C = 0. Furthermore, the load and decrement instructions do not affect the carry, so that

```
ANDCC       #$FE
```

may be eliminated. Also, for this particular problem, the instruction

```
LEAX        B,X
```

can be replaced by the 1-byte instruction ABX. This straightforward program, shown below, now takes 33 bytes and works for N ≥ 2.

```
        CLR     <18         Clear overflow and carry
        LDB     <19         N into B
        LDX     #20         Point X to high byte of #1
        ABX                 Position X for LS byte of #1
        DECB                N - 1 into B
L       LDA     ,-X         Next byte of #1 into A
        ADCA    <10,X       Add next byte of #2 into A
        STA     <20,X       Store result
        DECB                Decrement counter
        BNE     L           Another byte
        LDA     ,-X         Load high byte of #1 into A
        ADCA    <10,X       Add high byte of #2 into A
        BVC     J           If V = 1, increment overflow
        INC     <18
J       STA     <20,X       Store high byte of result
        SWI                 Halt
```

The reason that we had to pull the adding of the last, most significant bytes out of the loop is because DECB affects V and STA clears V. To get around this, we can use X as a counter and U as an index register pointing to the result, so that STA ,−U can be replaced by PSHU A.

```
        CLR     <18         Clear overflow; sign extend N to two bytes
        LDX     <18         Put N, extended to two bytes, into X
        LEAU    <40,X       Position U for low byte of result
L       LDA     <19,X       Next byte of #1 into A
        ADCA    <29,X       Add next byte of #2 into A
        PSHU    A           Store result
        LEAX    <-1,X       Decrement counter
        BNE     L           Another byte?
        BVC     J           Signed overflow
        INC     <18         Set overflow indicator
J       SWI                 Halt
```

In the preceding program, the sequence

```
    PSHU    A
    LEAX    <-1,X
    BNE     L
```

does not affect V so that we can add all N bytes in the loop and then check for overflow. While this program takes only 25 bytes, the previous program takes fewer clock cycles each time through the loop and is still faster. One might have noticed that LEAX , − X is shorter and faster than LEAX < − 1,X. As we discuss in Chapter 4 there is another index addressing option which uses only five bits for the offset and, in this situation, would be just as short (two bytes) and one clock cycle faster than LEAX , − X.

Finally, we can go back to the earlier program and save the condition code register as shown below. Notice that we clear the carry using CLRA rather than the 2-byte instruction ANDCC #$FE.

```
        LDB     <19         N into B
        LDX     #20         Point X to #1
        ABX                 Position X for LS byte of #1
        CLRA                Clear carry bit
L       LDA     ,-X         Next byte of #1 into A
        ADCA    <10,X       Add next byte of #2 into A
        TFR     CC,B        Save CC in B
        STA     <20,X       Store result
        DEC     <19         Decrement counter
        BNE     L           Another byte?
        ANDB    #2
        LSRB                Put V into LS bit of B
        STB     <18         Store V in overflow location
        SWI                 Halt
```

After the loop is completed in the above sequence, B contains the contents of the condition code register immediately after the last byte has been added. The instructions

```
ANDB      #2
LSRB
```

put the V bit into the least significant bit of B while putting all other bits to 0. Thus the contents of B equals the value of the signed overflow indicator. This program is only 27 bytes long but is still slower than the first program for larger values of N.

We have been emphasizing finding short programs and have merely pointed out which of these is the fastest. Suppose now that N is fixed at, say, N = 3. Then the program

```
      CLR     <18
      LDA     <22
      ADCA    <32
      STA     <42
      LDA     <21
      ADCA    <31
      STA     <41
      LDA     <20
      ADCA    <30
      BVC     J
      INC     <18
J     STA     <40
      SWI
```

will execute faster than the fastest of the previous examples since DECB and BNE have been eliminated from the addition of each byte. A speed and memory trade-off is clear; for N = 10 this approach would take a very long program compared to the others but would certainly execute faster than any of the others.

At first glance it is not apparent that we can make this last technique work for variable N. However, by putting the previous instructions beginning at location 100, but omitting CLR <18, and by putting the following sequence beginning at location 50, we get a fast but long program for N between 0 and 3.

ML	Mnemonics		Comments
50	LDX	#60	Point X to jump table
53	LDB	<19	N into B
55	ASLB		2 * N into B
56	ABX		2 * N + (X) into X
57	CLR	<18	Clear overflow indicator and carry
58	JMP	[,X]	Jump to entry point
60	address of SWI		
62	address of Last LDA		
64	address of second LDA		
66	address of first LDA		

The locations 60 through 67 serve as a *jump table:* bytes 60 and 61 contain the address of where to "jump" if N = 0, 62 and 63 the address of where to jump if N = 1, and so on. Jump tables are used frequently in more substantial situations. Here they give us a useful example of indirect addressing.

REMARKS

One might wonder why some move instructions, such as LDA, TSTA, and STA, always put V = 0 rather than leaving V unchanged as they do C. The reason is that doing so allows all of the signed branches to work after these instructions as well as after the arithmetic type of instruction. For example, suppose that one wants to look at the contents of some memory location, say 458, and branch to location L if the contents of location 458, treated as a signed number, is greater than 0. The sequence

```
TST       >458
BGT       L
```

does exactly this. If the TST instruction had left V unaffected, we would have had to use the longer sequence

```
          TST       >458
          BMI       J
          BNE       L
J         next instruction
```

or possibly

```
          TST       >458
          ANDCC     #$FD      Put V = 0
          BGT       L
```

A little more experience will show that the designer's choice here is quite reasonable since we will find a more frequent use of signed branches after load instructions than checking for signed overflow as we did in the examples of Section 3-7.

In all of the preceding examples, we have only put down the instruction mnemonics and the addresses. The routine, error prone job of finding the machine code and showing the locations of these bytes in memory has been omitted. We have also omitted calculating the relative offset to the symbolic location L in the BNE L instruction. These are things that an *assembler* will do for us. A crude assembly language version of the program which saved the CC register in B is shown below, where we have omitted the comments.

```
            NAM      ADD
            ORG      50
            LDB      <19
            LDX      #20
            ABX
            CLRA
    L       LDA      ,-X
            ADCA     <10,X
            TFR      CC,B
            STA      <20,X
            DEC      <19
            BNE      L
            ANDB     #2
            LSRB
            STB      <18
            SWI
            END
```

Notice that three new mnemonics have been added. These are not machine instructions; they are *assembler directives,* which provide information to the assembler. For example, the directive NAM, for "name," tells the assembler that your program is starting and that the name of your program is "ADD." The END directive tells the assembler that your program has ended and to disregard further mnemonics. The remaining directive ORG, for "origin," tells the assembler where to start putting the program bytes. In the example above, the instructions will start at location 50 and end at location 76 since the program is 27 bytes long. You could have put any starting point down as long as the instruction bytes did not overlap the data structure. The assembler listing of this program is shown in Figure 3-8. Column one lists the line numbers of the program, column two gives the hex value of the operand of the assembler directive or the memory location of the first byte of the instruction on that line, and column three gives the actual machine code for the instructions. As we can see, the assembler has done the tedious work for us, including calculating the relative offset in the BNE L instruction. In Chapter 4 we will see that the assembler can do much more than just generate the machine code for programs such as the one above.

PROBLEMS

When a program is asked for in the problems below, use the format that is used for the examples in the text.
1. What is the difference between the BLT and BMI instructions? Illustrate the differences with examples.
2. Suppose that the (Y) = 613 and (X) = 918 before *each* of the following instructions is executed. Give the contents of the registers X and Y after each is executed. Selected

```
00001                         NAM    ADD
00002 0032                    ORG    50
00003 0032 D6     13          LDB    <19
00004 0034 8E     001E        LDX    #30
00005 0037 3A                 ABX
00006 0038 4F                 CLRA
00007 0039 A6     82     L     LDA    ,-X
00008 003B A988  0A           ADCA   <10,X
00009 003E 1F     A9          TFR    CC,B
00010 0040 A788  14           STA    <20,X
00011 0043 0A     13          DEC    <19
00012 0045 26     F2          BNE    L
00013 0047 C4     02          ANDB   #2
00014 0049 54                 LSRB
00015 004A D7     12          STB    <18
00016 004C 3F                 SWI
00017                         END
TOTAL ERRORS:    0
TOTAL WARNINGS:    0
```

FIGURE 3-8. Assembler Listing for the Program ADD

memory locations and their contents before each instruction are shown below where all numbers are in decimal. Your answers should also be in decimal.

(a) LEAX ,--X
(b) LDX , ,--Y
(c) LEAX [,Y++]
(d) LDX [,Y++]
(e) LDY ,Y++
(f) LEAY [,Y++]
(g) LEAY [,Y]
(h) LDY [,Y]

ML	MC
611	8
612	9
613	14
614	163
615	31
616	191
.	
.	
.	
3746	12
3747	19
3748	111
3749	210

Explain what will happen if STY ,– –Y or STY [,– –Y] is executed with the same initial conditions for Y and the given memory locations.

3. Suppose that we have an vector of 1-byte signed numbers whose first byte is at location 100 and whose length is at location 99. We want to search through the vector, putting all those numbers that are negative and even into an vector beginning at location 200. Write a program that will do this, keeping the order of the numbers in the second vector the same as the original vector. How would you change the program if you also wanted to put the length of the new vector in location 46?

4. Suppose that we have N 16-bit two's-complement numbers stored beginning at location 50. The two bytes of each number are stored consecutively, high byte first. Write a program that finds the maximum number and puts it in locations 48 and 49, high byte first. The variable N is stored in location 47. How would your program change if the numbers were unsigned? Try to write the program for greatest static efficiency.

5. Give the MC6809 instruction sequences that would carry out the same operation as the following nonexistent MC6809 instructions.
   (a) NEGD
   (b) AAX
   (c) ADX
   (d) INCD
   (e) ASLD

6. Find single instructions, if they exist, that will replace two NOPs, three NOPs, four NOPs and five NOPs (one for each case). Ignore the number of clock cycles.

7. Explain why putting V = 0 in a load instruction makes all of the signed branches work after that instruction.

8. Will a signed branch work after a DEC or INC instruction? Explain. What about unsigned branches?

9. What are the differences between ADDA #1 and INCA?

10. Why doesn't DAA work after an INC, DEC, or ASR instruction?

11. Write an instruction sequence that will compute the number of bits in D which are equal to 1. This number should be in A at the end of the sequence.

12. Write a program that adds the two 3-byte numbers at locations 10 through 12 and 13 through 15, putting the sum in locations 16 through 18. All numbers should be stored high byte first and, when the SWI is encountered, the condition code bits Z, N, V, and C should be set correctly. The program should try to maximize static efficiency.

13. Repeat Problem 12 for two N-byte numbers using the data structure of Figure 3-7. You do not need the overflow indicator shown in this data structure, however.

14. Suppose that you want now to subtract the second number from the first number using the data structure of Figure 3-7. How would the programs in Section 3-7 be modified?

15. Why would you never use the JMP or JSR instructions with program counter relative addressing?

16. In the programs of Section 3-7 that use the data structure of Figure 3-7, how would you use the signed overflow indicator to get the actual sum even if there were overflow?

17. Give a program that adds N 2-byte signed numbers stored in the data structure shown in Figure 3-9. The result is to be a 3-byte sum stored in locations 50 through 52. Can signed overflow occur in this problem?

18. Give a program that adds two N-byte signed-magnitude numbers using the data structure of Figure 3-7. You do not, however, have to detect signed-magnitude overflow.

19. Write a program that adds N 1-byte signed numbers which are stored beginning in location 10. The value of N is stored in location 9. To prevent signed overflow, the sum should be sign extended to two bytes and stored in locations 7 and 8.

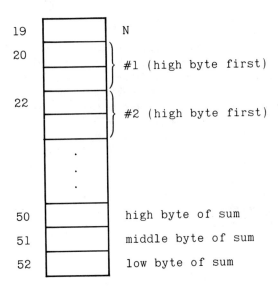

FIGURE 3-9. Data Structure for Adding N 2-byte Signed Numbers

20. Write an instruction sequence that increments the 4-byte number stored with the highest two bytes in X and the lowest two bytes in U.

21. Which pair of instructions, BSR-RTS or EXG-TFR, executes more quickly when used to call and return from a subroutine?

22. Write a program that takes the ith bit from locations 100 through 131 and puts it in the carry bit C. The bits in locations 100 through 131 are labeled as shown below.

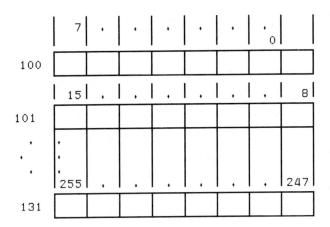

The value of the variable i is contained in location 99. The program should not change any of the data in locations 99 through 131. Begin your program in location 0 and write it so that the number of bytes it takes is within 10% of the minimum possible.

23. Write a program to search a block of N bytes, beginning in location $100, to find the address of the first byte with bits 0, 3, and 5 set and bit 7 cleared. If no byte has these bits set, the address $200 should be used for the answer. The value of N is in location $FF, and the address of the first satisfactory byte is placed in locations $FD and $FE, high byte first.

24. Write a program to set bit 0, clear bit 7, and leave all other bits unchanged in all bytes of a block beginning in location $100. The block has N bytes, with the value of N stored in location $FF.

25. Write an instruction sequence that will take a byte at location L and branch to location L0 if bit 0 is set, branch to location L1 if bit 0 is clear and bit 1 is set, branch to location L2 if bits 0 and 1 are clear and bit 2 is set, and so on for locations L3 through L7.

26. Write a sequence to divide the unsigned contents of A by 8, putting the quotient in A and the remainder in B.

27. Write a program that will find all the prime numbers between 1 and 65,535. The prime numbers should be placed beginning in location 100, high byte first. The number of primes found should be placed in locations 98 and 99, again high byte first.

28. Explain why the MUL instruction works for signed numbers in A and B as long as the product is in the 8-bit two's-complement range ($-128 \leq$ product ≤ 127).

29. Write a program that adds N 2-byte numbers which are stored consecutively, higher-order bytes first, beginning in location 10. The value of N is stored in location 9 and the 2-byte sum is placed in locations 7 and 8. Instead of using accumulator D and ADDD to accumulate the result, use the index register X and LEAX. Are there any limitations to this approach?

An enlargement of the MC68000 microprocessor chip.

CHAPTER 4

Assembly Language for the MC6809

In the examples presented so far, you have probably noticed some real programming inconveniences, such as finding the operation code bytes, computing the addresses (particularly relative addresses), and associating the variable names with their memory locations. Furthermore, if you change the program, much of this routine work may have to be done again. What we have been doing is sometimes called *hand assembly,* in that we generate all of the machine code ourselves. Certainly, hand assembly is appropriate to the understanding of computer fundamentals. Beyond this we need to know hand assembly to *patch* our programs, that is, remove the errors without reassembly. (See Problem 5 at the end of this chapter for an example of patching.) In this chapter we study the assembler and the skill of assembling programs using the computer.

An *assembler* is a program that someone else has written, a program that will help us write our own programs. We describe this program by how it handles a line of input data. The assembler is given a sequence of ASCII characters. (See Appendix 2 for the table of ASCII characters.) The sequence of characters, from one carriage return to the next, is a *line of assembly language code* or an *assembly language statement*. For example,

```
LDA        #$10
```
(1)

is an assembly language statement and, if line (1) is typed as

(space) L D A (space) # $ 1 0 (carriage return)

it would be stored in memory for the assembler as shown below.

$20
$4C
$44
$41
$20
$23
$24
$31
$30
$0D

The *assembly language* program, entered this way in ASCII for each assembly language statement, is called the *source code* for the assembler. The assembler outputs the machine code for each line of assembly language code. For example, for line (1), the assembler would output the bytes $86 and $10, the op code byte and immediate operand of (1), and their locations. The machine code output by the assembler for an assembly language program is frequently called the *object code*. The assembler also outputs a *listing* of the program, which lists each assembly language statement and the hexadecimal machine code that it generates. The assembler listing also indicates any errors that it can detect (*assembly errors*). This listing of errors is a great benefit, since the assembler program tells you exactly what is wrong and you do not have to run the program to detect these errors one at a time as you do with more subtle bugs. If you input an assembly language program to an assembler, the assembler will output the hexadecimal machine code, or object code, that you would have generated by hand (see Figure 4-1). An assembler is a great tool to help you write your programs, and you will use it most of the time from now on.

In this chapter you will look at an example to see how an assembly language program and assembler listing are organized. Then you will look at assembler

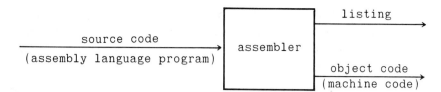

FIGURE 4-1. An assembler has the source code for its input and the listing and object code for its output.

directives, which provide the assembler with information about the data structure and the location of the instruction sequence but do not generate instructions for the computer in machine code. You will see some examples that show the power of these directives. The main discussion will focus on the standard Motorola assembler. (We will also point out the places where the assembler EDTASM+ for the TRS-80 Radio Shack Color Computer differs from the Motorola assembler. These slight differences are discussed in Appendix 4.) Next, the mechanics of a two-pass assembler (the most common kind) are discussed. You will see what can be done, and what is impossible, regarding forward references. Finally, you will briefly study some ideas related to that of the assembler—the loader, compiler, interpreter, and macro assembler.

At the end of this chapter you should be prepared to write programs on the order of 100 assembly language lines. You should be able to use an assembler to translate any program into machine code, and you should understand how the assembler works. Although you may not be able to understand how to write an assembler, you will be prepared from now on to use an assembler as a tool to help you write your programs.

4–1

INTRODUCTORY EXAMPLE AND ASSEMBLER PRINTOUT

We now consider a simple example to introduce you to assembly language programs. Consider a program that obtains the maximum of a sequence of numbers. We will assume that this sequence consists of 16-bit signed numbers stored consecutively in memory, high byte first for each number. This data structure is called a *vector* or (one-dimensional) *array*. The name of the vector will be the location of the first byte of the vector, so that the high byte of the ith number in the vector (i = 0, 1, 2, ...) can be found by adding 2*i to the vector name. Suppose then that Z is a vector of N 16-bit two's-complement numbers beginning in location 50 with N stored in location 47. The ith number will be denoted Z(i) for i = 0 through N − 1. We want a program that finds the maximum of these numbers, putting it in locations 48 and 49.

One possible program for this, following the style of previous examples, is shown below, where only the address of the first byte of the instruction is given in the ML column. We have arbitrarily started the program at address 100, allowing for at most 25 16-bit numbers.

ML	MC		Mnemonics		Comments
64	8E 00 32		LDX	#50	Point X to vector
67	EC 84		LDD	,X	First number into D
69	10 A3 81	LOOP	CMPD	,X++	Compare (D) with next number
6C	2C 03		BGE	JUMP	Do not replace
6E	EC 88 FE		LDD	<-2,X	Put new number for maximum
71	0A 2F	JUMP	DEC	<47	Decrement counter
73	26 F4		BNE	LOOP	Other number to check?
75	DD 30		STD	<48	Store result
77	3F		SWI		Halt

Looking at the preceding program, we certainly would like to use just the mnemonics column with the variable addresses and the labels for the branches and let the assembler generate the other two columns, that is, do what we have been doing by hand. We would also like to be able to use *labels*, also called *symbolic addresses* (or just *symbols*), for the memory locations that hold the values of variables. The meaning of symbolic addresses is explored in greater detail in the next section. We use them in this section to get the main idea of their use before dissecting them carefully. The use of symbolic addresses would allow

```
LDX     #50
DEC     <47
STD     <48
```

all to be replaced by

```
LDX     #Z
DEC     <N
STD     <RESULT
```

respectively. An assembly language version of the program above that does this is shown below.

```
NAM     MAX
OPT     S
ORG     47
```

```
N          RMB     1
RESULT     RMB     2
Z          RMB     50
           LDX     #Z              Point X to the vector Z
           LDD     ,X              Z(0) into D
LOOP       CMPD    ,X++            (D) − Z(i)
           BGE     JUMP            Do not replace if GE
           LDD     < − 2 ,X        Z(i) into D
JUMP       DEC     < N             Decrement counter
           BNE     LOOP            Another number?
           STD     < RESULT        Store result
           SWI                     Halt
           END
```

Putting this assembly language program into the assembler yields the output listing shown in Figure 4-2. Although some new mnemonics have crept in, we can nevertheless see that we do not have to refer to actual addresses, only labels. We can see that we have not had to calculate relative offsets for the branching instructions, and we have not had to find memory locations or machine code. We now look into some of the details.

An assembly language statement takes the following form, where the fields, groups of consecutive locations on a line, are separated by one or more blank spaces:

Label	Operation	Operand	Comment
Field	Field	Field	Field

The label field and the comment field may be empty and, depending on the operation, the operand field may be empty.

Label Field

A label (or symbolic address), if present, *must* begin in the first space and can consist of one to six alphanumeric characters, the first of which is a letter. If an asterisk is in the first space, the whole line is treated as a comment line. Finally, labels that are identical to register labels are not allowed (e.g., A, B, CC, DP, X, Y, U, S, PC, and D). Additionally, PCR is not allowed as a label.

Operation Field

Except for comment lines, this field must consist of an instruction mnemonic or assembler directive (more about these later). The mnemonic must be written with no spaces: CLRA, TSTB, ADDD, and so on.

Operand Field

This field contains the addressing information for the instruction. Although numbers can be used to specify addresses, you will find symbolic addresses

```
00001                             NAM  MAX
00002  002F                       ORG  47
00003                             OPT  S
00004  002F        0001 N         RMB  1
00005  0030        0002 RESULT    RMB  2
00006  0032        0032 Z         RMB  50
00007  0064  8E    0032           LDX  #Z         POINT X TO Z
00008  0067  EC    84             LDD  ,X         Z(0) INTO D
00009  0069  10A3  81   LOOP      CMPD ,X++       (D) — Z(I)
00010  006C  2C    03             BGE  JUMP       DON'T REPLACE IF GE
00011  006E  EC88  FE             LDD  <-2,X      Z(I) INTO D
00012  0071  0A    2F   JUMP      DEC  <N         DECREMENT COUNTER
00013  0073  26    F4             BNE  LOOP       ANOTHER NUMBER?
00014  0075  DD    30             STD  <RESULT    STORE RESULT
00015  0077  3F                   SWI             HALT
00016                             END
TOTAL ERRORS:      0
TOTAL WARNINGS:      0


SYMBOL TABLE

JUMP   0071  LOOP   0069  N       002F  RESULT  0030  Z       0032
```

FIGURE 4-2. Assembler Listing for the Program MAX

generally much easier to use in the operand field. For example, using the symbolic address or label ALPHA, the following addressing modes

>ALPHA	Direct addressing
ALPHA	Relative addressing in branching statements
ALPHA ,PCR	Relative addressing with an 8-bit relative offset
>ALPHA ,PCR	Relative addressing with a 16-bit relative offset
< ALPHA ,X	Index addressing with an 8-bit constant offset
>ALPHA ,X	Index addressing with a 16-bit constant offset
[ALPHA]	Indirect addressing
< ALPHA	Direct page addressing
#ALPHA	Immediate addressing

can now all use symbolic addresses in place of numbers in the previous examples.

The assembler will understand the use of addition, multiplication, and the like, using symbolic addresses. If ALPHA is location 100, the assembler will put in the value 101 if the operand field contains ALPHA + 1. The same notation that we have been using in the examples is valid except that now *expressions* can be used in place of numbers or symbolic addresses for all of those addressing modes that used 8- or 16-bit numbers.

In simplest terms, an *expression* is just the usual algebraic combination of labels, numbers, and the operations $+$, $-$, $/$, and $*$. The evaluation of an expression is, for the Motorola assembler, exactly like FORTRAN. All expressions used in this book will have obvious evaluations so that the exact conventions of FORTRAN will not be needed. A symbolic address, by itself, is a (trivial) expression. Some examples of expressions are

```
JUMP
JUMP*(8+TAB)
((RATE-2)*17)-TEMP
```

One must be careful to have no spaces in the expression or between the expression and any other characters used to identify the addressing mode. (Recall that a space would indicate that what follows is in the comment field.) Thus

```
JUMP ,X
#RATE- 5
# RATE*TEMP
[17+MAX ]
```

all cause assembly errors.

Comment Field

The programmer can insert short comments stating the purpose of each instruction. The comments begin one or more blanks after the operand field and are printed in the assembler listing but are otherwise ignored by the assembler.

In summary, writing an assembly language program is a lot easier than writing machine code by hand. You can use symbolic addresses, letting the assembler determine where to put them and letting the assembler make sure that the instructions have the right operand values. You do have to conform to the rules of the language, however, and you have to spell the mnemonics exactly the way the assembler wants to recognize them. Although it would be nice to be able to just talk to the computer and tell it what you want it to do using conversational English, an assembler can barely understand the mnemonics for the instructions if you write them correctly and carefully. Nevertheless, writing assembly language programs is a lot easier than writing machine coded programs directly in hexadecimal.

4-2

ASSEMBLER DIRECTIVES

Before looking more closely at how the assembler works we describe the simplest *assembler directives*. These are instructions to the assembler which do not result in any actual executable machine coded instructions but are, nevertheless, essential to providing information to the assembler. A number of these will be introduced in this section and are listed in Table 4-1 for your convenience.

TABLE 4-1. Assembler Directives

Mnemonic	Example	Explanation
NAM	NAM PROG	Names the program PROG
END	END	Terminates the assembler program
ORG	ORG $100	Puts the next and following bytes beginning in location $100
EQU	ALPHA EQU $10	Makes the symbol ALPHA have the value $10
FCB	ALPHA FCB $20,$34	Makes the symbol ALPHA have the value of the current location; initializes the current location to the value $20 and the next location to $34
FDB	ALPHA FDB $1234	Makes the symbol ALPHA have the value of the current location; initializes this location to $12 and the next location to $34
FCC	ALPHA FCC 'ABC'	Makes the symbol ALPHA have the value of the current location; initializes the word at this location to the ASCII letter letter ''A,'' the next location to the ASCII letter ''B,'' and the next to ''C''
OPT	OPT S	Specifies assembler options such as this option to request printing the symbol table, a list of the values of all the labels used in the program
RMB	Z RMB 10	Makes the label Z have the value of the current location; increments the location counter by 10
SETDP	SETDP 5	Instructs the assembler to use direct page addressing when addresses are on page 5

Two assembler directives are used to indicate the start and end of the program. For example, the assembler directive NAM (for name) allows you to give a name to your program, and is usually the first line of an assembly language program. The END directive tells the assembler when your program ends, and must be the last line of your program. Each directive appears in the operation field and the directive NAM usually has a name of your choice appearing in the operand field. For the program of Figure 4-2, the name of the program is MAX. Both of these directives should be in every program that you write. (The assembler EDTASM+ for the TRS-80 Color Computer does not use the NAM directive but most assemblers do. To run any of the programs in this book on the TRS-80 Color Computer, eliminate the NAM directive. See also Appendix 4 for a discussion of the differences between EDTASM+ and the Motorola assembler for the other assembler directives.)

If we go back to the example at the beginning of the chapter, we recall that what we wanted was to just write down the mnemonics column and let the assembler generate the memory locations and their contents. There must be some additional information given to the assembler; in particular, you have to tell the assembler where to start putting the program or store the variables. This is the purpose of the ORG (for ORiGin) directive. The mnemonic ORG appears in the operation column and a number (or expression) appears in the operand column. The number in the operand column tells the assembler where to start putting the instruction bytes, or reserved bytes for variables, that follow. For example, if one has

```
ORG        100
LDX        #123
 ,
 ,
 ,
```

the assembler will put the three bytes for LDX #123 in locations 100, 101, and 102, while the bytes for the instructions that follow are put consecutively in locations 103, 104, ... The operand can be described in decimal, hexadecimal, or binary, following Motorola's usual conventions. Thus we could replace the ORG directive above by

```
ORG        $64
```

If there is no ORG directive at the beginning of your program, the Motorola assembler will start at memory location 0. There can be more than one ORG directive in a program. (See Appendix 4 for a discussion on the use of the ORG directive with the Radio Shack assembler EDTASM+.)

In all of our examples, we have set aside memory locations for variables. In the last example, we set aside bytes for N, RESULT, and Z. The way we tell the assembler to do this is with the RMB (reserve memory bytes) directive. Here RMB appears in the operation field and the number in the operand field tells the assembler how many bytes are being reserved. The label in the RMB directive is the variable name which the bytes are being reserved for. The label is given the value of the address of its first, and perhaps only, byte. In the program of Figure 4-2, the label N is given the value 47, RESULT is given the value 48, and Z is given the value 50.

The symbolic address N, which was introduced in Section 4-1, appears to have a split personality, especially for data. The symbol N is being used in two different ways here, as an address and as the value of a variable. The way to understand this is by analogy to a glass of water. When you say "drink this glass," the glass is the container, but you mean to drink the contents of the container. You do not expect the listener to be confused because he would never think of drinking the container. So, too, the symbolic address N stands for the container, which is the location of the variable N, whereas the contents of the container, the word at the address N, is the value of the variable N. If you think hard enough, it is generally clear which is meant. In the instructions

```
LDX      #L
```

or

```
LEAX      <L,PCR
```

the symbolic address L is the address of the variable, which is the container. In the instruction

```
LDA      >L
```

the symbolic address represents the contents in that it is the contents of location L that goes into A. But if you are confused about what is meant, look to see if the symbolic address is being used to represent the container or its contents.

The RMB assembler directive assigns a number to the symbolic address or container. In the preceding example, the container for N has the value 47 because 47 is the address of N. However, the contents of N is not assigned a value, in contrast to a directive FCB discussed later. The contents of N is *undefined,* being the data that happen to be at location 47 at the time the program is started. The RMB directive does not do anything to the value of a variable.

We have covered everything in the program of Figure 4-2 except the labels LOOP and JUMP, which appear in the label field for two machine instructions, not assembler directives. When a label is used with a machine instruction, it is given the value of the address of the first byte of that instruction. Notice that the value of JUMP in Figure 4-2 is $71 from the symbol table. This value is also the address of the op code byte of the DEC <N instruction. Thus the container JUMP is the address $71, while the contents of JUMP are the bits of the op code byte for the DEC instruction.

Looking at other common assembler directives, the EQU directive (for

EQUate) assigns a specific value to a label such as

```
CORE        EQU         17
```

which gives the value 17 to the label CORE. Generally, equates can be used to assign values to containers. Used this way, they are like RMB directives, where the programmer assigns an address to the container, rather than letting the assembler choose the value automatically. The EQU directive enables you to control where variables are stored, as in hand coding, but allows symbolic addresses to be used, as in assembly language coding to improve readability. We will find EQU directives useful in fixing addresses to jump to in monitor programs and in fixing the addresses of I/O devices in Chapter 8. These directives can also be used to replace constants, to improve readability, and to simplify the modification of programs. For example, the instruction

```
    LDA        #$20
```

might load a mask pattern into accumulator A. It can be replaced by the lines

```
MASK        EQU         $20
            .
            .
            .
            LDA         #MASK
```

where the EQU directive is put at the top of the program. Using EQU directives makes the program more readable, and self-documenting to an extent. It also makes it easier to modify the program if a different mask is used. The value of the mask is in the EQU directive near the beginning of the program. If all changeable parts are kept in this area, it is fairly easy to modify the program for different applications by rewriting the EQU statements in this area. With an EQU directive the label field *cannot* be empty and the operand field can be an expression as well as a number. As we shall see later, there is a small restriction on the labels used in an expression of an EQU directive.

The FCB (form constant byte) directive puts the values in the operand field into successive memory locations starting with the next available memory location. A label, if used, is assigned the address of the first value in the operand field. As an example

```
TABLE       FCB         14,17,19,30                             (2)
```

appearing in a program generates four consecutive bytes whose values are 14, 17, 19, and 30 and whose locations are at TABLE, TABLE + 1, TABLE + 2, and TABLE + 3, as shown.

TABLE	$0E
TABLE+1	$11
TABLE+2	$13
TABLE+3	$1E

The actual value of the container TABLE will depend on where it is placed in the program. Note that, in contrast to the RMB directive, this directive assigns values to the container (the address) as well as its contents (the word at that address). Beware, however, that the contents is given this value only when the program is loaded into memory. If the program is rerun without being loaded again, the value of the contents is what was left there as a result of running the program the last time. When rerunning the program, you should check these values and possibly rewrite them before you assume they are the contents specified by the program. [With the Radio Shack assembler EDTASM+, the FCB directive (2) must be written

```
TABLE      FCB      14
           FCB      17
           FCB      19
           FCB      30
```

See Appendix 4 for more details.] The values in the operand field of an FCB directive must be 1-byte numbers, signed or unsigned, and there must be no spaces in the operand field; that is, one cannot use

```
TABLE      FCB      14, 17, 19, 30
```

The FDB (form double byte) directive does exactly the same thing as FCB except that now two bytes are used for each value in the operand field, where, as usual, the high byte is first. For example, the directive

```
TABLE      FDB      14,17,19,30                                   (3)
```

puts the values in memory as shown.

TABLE	$00
	$0E
TABLE+2	$00
	$11
TABLE+4	$00
	$13
TABLE+6	$00
	$1E

[As with the FCB directive, the Radio Shack assembler EDTASM+ must use

```
TABLE      FDB      14
           FDB      17
           FDB      19
           FDB      30
```

in place of (3).]

The FCC (form constant character) directive does exactly the same thing as FCB except that a sequence of ASCII characters are used in the operand field. (See Appendix 2 for a table of ASCII characters and their representations.) The ASCII codes for the characters are now put in the successive memory locations. The most convenient form is

```
LIST       FCC       \Abc,,p\
```

where the backslash"\"encloses all the ASCII characters to be stored, namely, A through p. The backslash can be replaced by any other ASCII character that is not in the string being enclosed.

The last directive that we consider is OPT (option). The operand field is used to specify one or more options, separated by commas, that control the printed listing and a few other capabilities of the assembler. The directive

```
OPT        S
```

tells the assembler to print a *symbol table* at the end of the assembler listing. This table will list each symbol, in alphabetical order, and give the value (of the container) for that symbol. These handy options can specify the length of the lines used in the listing, the number of lines on a page of the listing, the suppression of warning messages, and turning the printer on or off for various parts of the program to prevent listing some sections of the program. (There is no OPT directive for the EDTASM+ assembler, as options are handled in a different way. See Appendix 4 for details. To run any of the programs in this

```
00001                             NAM   SQUARE
00002                             OPT   S
00003                     *
00004                     * THIS PROGRAM SQUARES THE NUMBER N BETWEEN
00005                     * 0 AND 15, RETURNING THE ANSWER AS NSQ.
00006                     *
00007 0000      0001    N     RMB   1
00008 0001      0001    NSQ   RMB   1
00009 0002      00      TABLE FCB   0,1,4,9,16,25,36,49,64,81
00018 000C      64            FCB   100,121,144,169,196,225
00023                     *
00024 0012 8E 0002             LDX   #TABLE POINT X TO TABLE
00025 0015 D6 00               LDB   <N     PUT N INTO D
00026 0017 A6 85               LDA   B,X    PUT N**2 INTO D
00027 0019 97 01               STA   <NSQ   STORE RESULT
00028 0018 3F                  SWI
00029                          END
TOTAL ERRORS:        0
TOTAL WARNINGS:        0


SYMBOL TABLE


N    0000   NSQ    0001   TABLE   0002   %%%%%  %%%  %%%%%  %%%
```

FIGURE 4-3. Assembler Listing for the Program SQUARE

book on the TRS-80 Color Computer, remove the OPT directive as well as the
NAM directive.)

To see how these directives might be used, suppose that we wanted to store
a table of squares for the numbers between 0 and 15. The following program,
using this table, squares the number N, returning it as NSQ. The assembler
listing is shown in Figure 4-3. Notice that only the first byte of each FCB
command is listed. To get a complete listing, replace the OPT S directive with
OPT S,G, where G is for "generate." With the given data structure, the location
of N^2 equals the location TABLE plus N. Thus if X contains the location
TABLE and B contains the value of N, the effective address in the instruction
LDA B,X is the location of N^2.

```
            NAM       SQUARE
            OPT       S
    *
    *  This program squares the number N between 0 and 15,
    *  returning the answer as NSQ.
    *
    N       RMB       1
    NSQ     RMB       1
    TABLE   FCB       0,1,4,9,16,25,36,49,64,81
            FCB       100,121,144,169,196,225
```

```
        LDX      #TABLE      Point X to TABLE
        LDB      <N          Put N into B
        LDA      B,X         Put N**2 into A
        STA      <NSQ        Store result
        SWI
        END
```

Of course, one would never use this program on the MC6809 since the MUL instruction is available. Using the MUL instruction we can write a version of the same program and, at the same time, square the numbers between 0 and 255.

```
        NAM      SQUARE
        OPT      S
*
*    This program squares the number N between 0 and
*    255, returning the answer as NSQ.
*
N       RMB      1
NSQ     RMB      2
        LDB      <N          Put N into B
        TFR      B,A         Copy N into A
        MUL                  The value of N**2 is now in D
        STD      <NSQ        Store two-byte result
        SWI
        END
```

Notice that now NSQ is a 2-byte number. We could still extend the table technique, however, to larger N using the FDB directive. With double bytes storing the value of each squared number, notice that the address of the high byte of N^2 is now in location TABLE plus 2*N.

```
        NAM      SQUARE
        OPT      S
*
*    This program squares the number N between 0 and 20,
*    returning the answer as NSQ.
*
N       RMB      1
NSQ     RMB      2
TABLE   FDB      0,1,4,9,16,25,36,49,64,81
        FDB      100,121,144,169,196,225
        FDB      256,289,324,361,400
        LDX      #TABLE      Point X to TABLE
        LDB      <N          N into B
        ASLB                 2*N into B
        LDD      B,X         N**2 into D
        STD      <NSQ        Store result
        SWI
        END
```

If we extended this table technique to higher and higher N we would need more and more FDB operands and, for $N > 127$, the ASLB instruction would overflow. However, we could still use the preceding table technique by replacing the last six instructions of the program with

```
CLRA
LDB       <N          D now contains N
ASLB
ROLA                  D now contains 2*N
LDD       D,X
STD       <NSQ
SWI
END
```

MECHANICS OF A TWO-PASS ASSEMBLER

Some questions will soon arise about how symbolic addresses can be used without error. These questions have to be answered in terms of forward references, and their answers have to be understood in terms of how an assembler generates its output in two passes. Although we do not study how to write the assembler program, we do want you to get a feeling for how it works so that you can understand how forward references are limited by what a two-pass assembler can do.

How does an assembler work? Looking at the assembly language program below, which finds all the odd, negative, 1-byte integers in the array COLUMN and puts them into the array ODD, we can literally "assemble" the program ourselves. We begin by reading down through the instructions, called a *pass*,

```
          NAM    ODD
          OPT    S
*
*  This program searches the array COLUMN looking
*  for odd, negative, one-byte numbers which then
*  are stored in array ODD. The length of COLUMN
*  is N and the length of ODD is M. The value of
*  M is calculated by the program.
*
          ORG    5
N         RMB    1
```

```
M            RMB    1
COLUMN       RMB    50
ODD          RMB    50
*
             CLR    <M         Initialize M
             LDB    <N         Put N into B
             LDX    #COLUMN    Point X to COLUMN
             LDY    #ODD       Point Y to ODD
*
LOOP         LDA    ,X+        Next number of COLUMN into A
             BPL    JUMP       Go to next number if positive
             BITA   #1         Z = 1 if, and only if, (A) is even
             BEQ    JUMP       Go to next number if even
             STA    ,Y+        Store odd, negative number into ODD
             INC    <M         Increment length of ODD
JUMP         DECB              Decrement counter
             BNE    LOOP       Another number in COLUMN?
             SWI               Halt
             END
```

building a *symbol table,* a list of all the symbolic addresses or labels and their values. The ORG statement tells us to begin assigning bytes with location 5. Thus the label N has the value 5, the label M has the value 6, the label COLUMN has the value 7, and the label ODD has the value 57. The instruction

```
CLR          <M
```

will take two bytes (and we know what they are), the instruction

```
LDB          <N
```

will take two bytes (and we know what they are), and so forth. Similarly, we see that the first byte of instruction

```
LOOP         LDA          ,X+
```

will be at location 118. Thus the symbolic address (the container) LOOP has the value 118. Continuing in this way, we come to

```
BPL          JUMP
```

which takes two bytes in the program. We do not know the second byte of this instruction because we do not know the value of the address JUMP yet. (This is called a *forward reference,* using a label whose value is not yet known.) However, we can leave this second byte undetermined and proceed until we see that the machine code for DECB is put into location 130, thus giving JUMP the value 130. As we continue our pass downward, we can fill in the two bytes for

```
BNE     LOOP
```

because we know the location of the op code byte and the value of LOOP (e.g., 118 − 131 − 2 = −15, so $F1 is the second byte). Scanning through the program again, which is the second pass, we can fill in the two bytes that we could not determine the first time through for the instructions

```
BPL     JUMP
```

and

```
BEQ     JUMP
```

What we have described is a *two-pass assembler*. On the first pass it generates the symbol table for the program and on the second pass it generates the machine code for the program. The assembler listing for the program is shown in Figure 4-4. (Slightly different comments were used for the program shown in this figure.)

We have been using the character "<" to indicate the direct page addressing mode in instructions like

```
LDA     <N
```

In all cases, we assumed that the direct page register had zero in it because the MC6809 was "reset" when it was turned on, which automatically clears the DP register, and we did nothing to change the value in the direct page register in the program. If the symbol "<" is omitted, the assembler will still try to use direct page addressing when possible. Specifically, on the first pass, if the assembler knows the value of N when the instruction

```
LDA     N
```

is encountered, it will automatically use direct page addressing if N is on page zero. If it does not know the value of N yet, or if N is known but is not on page zero, it will then use direct addressing. For example, in the program ODD, if the RMBs are all put after the program, then direct addressing will be used in every instruction for which there is a choice between direct page addressing and direct addressing even though all the labels are on page zero. (See Figure 4-5 where direct addressing has been used for the variables M and N.)

We can also have the assembler treat any other page like it treats page zero above. The directive

```
SETDP     ALPHA
```

```
00001                              NAM   ODD
00002                              OPT   S
00003                       *
00004                       * THIS PROGRAM SEARCHES THE ARRAY COLUMN
00005                       * FOR ODD, NEGATIVE NUMBERS WHICH ARE PUT
00006                       * IN ARRAY ODD. THE LENGTH OF COLUMN
00007                       * IS N AND THE LENGTH OF ODD IS M.
00008                       *
00009  0005                       ORG   5
00010  0005        0001 N         RMB   1
00011  0006        0001 M         RMB   1
00012  0007        0032 COLUMN    RMB   50
00013  0039        0032 ODD       RMB   50
00014                       *
00015                       * BELOW, WE INITIALIZE M TO 0, PUT N INTO B,
00016                       * POINT X TO COLUMN AND POINT Y TO ODD.
00017                       *
00018  006B  0F    06             CLR   <M
00019  006D  D6    05             LDB   <N
00020  006F  8E    0007           LDX   #COLUMN
00021  0072  108E  0039           LDY   #ODD
00022                       *
00023  0076  A6    80   LOOP      LDA   ,X+
00024  0078  2A    08             BPL   JUMP
00025  007A  85    01             BITA  #1    Z = 1 IFF (A) IS EVEN
00026  007C  27    04             BEQ   JUMP
00027  007E  A7    A0             STA   ,Y+
00028  0080  0C    06             INC   <M
00029  0082  5A         JUMP      DECB
00030  0083  26    F1             BNE   LOOP
00031  0085  3F                   SWI
00032                             END
TOTAL ERRORS:      0
TOTAL WARNINGS:      0

SYMBOL TABLE

COLUMN 0007 JUMP    0082 LOOP    0076 M       0006 N       0005
ODD    0039 %%%%%% %%%% %%%%%% %%%% %%%%%% %%%% %%%%%% %%%%
```

FIGURE 4-4. Assembler Listing for the Program ODD

for "set direct page register" assigns a value to the direct page register *for the assembler*. After its use, the assembler will use direct page addressing instead of direct addressing if, on the first pass, it determines that the high byte of the address is equal to that given in the SETDP directive. The expression in the directive cannot use forward referencing and the programmer must make sure

```
00001                                    NAM    ODD
00002                                    OPT    S
00003                           *
00004                           * THIS PROGRAM SEARCHES THE ARRAY COLUMN
00005                           * FOR ODD, NEGATIVE NUMBERS WHICH ARE
00006                           * THEN STORED IN ARRAY ODD. THE LENGTH OF
00007                           * ODD IS M AND THE LENGTH OF COLUMN IS N.
00008                           *
00009 0005                               ORG    5
00010                           *
00011                           * BELOW, WE INITIALIZE M TO 0, PUT N INTO
00012                           * B, POINT X TO COLUMN AND POINT Y TO ODD.
00013                           *
00014 0005  7F    0024                   CLR    M
00015 0008  F6    0023                   LDB    N
00016 000B  8E    0025                   LDX    #COLUMN
00017 000E  108E  0057                   LDY    #ODD
00018                           *
00019 0012  A6    80     LOOP            LDA    ,X+
00020 0014  2A    09                     BPL    JUMP
00021 0016  85    01                     BITA   #1    Z = 1 IFF (A) IS EVEN
00022 0018  27    05                     BEQ    JUMP
00023 001A  A7    A0                     STA    ,Y+
00024 001C  7C    0024                   INC    M
00025 001F  5A           JUMP           DECB
00026 0020  26    F0                     BNE    LOOP
00027 0022  3F                           SWI
00028                           *
00029 0023        0001   N                RMB    1
00030 0024        0001   M                RMB    1
00031 0025        0032   COLUMN           RMB    50
00032 0057        0032   ODD              RMB    50
00033                           *
00034                                    END
TOTAL ERRORS:          0
TOTAL WARNINGS:          0

SYMBOL TABLE

COLUMN 0025  JUMP      001F  LOOP      0012  M          0024      N          00:
ODD      0057  ###### ####  ###### ####  ###### ######  ###### ##
```

FIGURE 4-5. Assembler Listing for the Modified Program ODD

that the actual value in the DP register at execution time equals that given in
the directive. For example, each use of the SETDP directive should be followed
with instructions which put the same page number in the direct page register as
given in the SETDP directive. See the examples of Figures 4-6 and 4-7, noting

```
00001                                      NAM     TEST
00002                                      OPT     S
00003                              *
00004    0000            0001      N        RMB     1
00005    0001            0001      SUM      RMB     1
00006    0002            000A      Z        RMB     10
00007                              *
00008                    0001               SETDP   1
00009    000C    86      01                 LDA     #1
00010    000E    1F      8B                 TFR     A,DP
00011                              *
00012    0010    8E      0002               LDX     #Z
00013    0013    F6      0000               LDB     N
00014    0016    4F                         CLRA
00015                              *
00016    0017    AB      80       LOOP      ADDA    ,X+
00017    0019    5A                         DECB
00018    001A    26      FB                 BNE     LOOP
00019    001C    B7      0001               STA     SUM
00020    001F    3F                         SWI
00021                                       END
TOTAL ERRORS:              0
TOTAL WARNINGS:               0

SYMBOL TABLE

LOOP     0017    N    0000   SUM     0001    Z    0002   %%%%%   %%%
```

FIGURE 4-6. Program Illustrating Use of the SETDP Directive. Compare this listing with Figure 4-7, where the program has been moved to page 1.

particularly that unless the program loads the DP register with 1, the program in Figure 4-7 will not work correctly.

As implied above, the assembler directive SETDP does not generate any machine instruction to actually load the direct page register. This has to be done by an instruction like TFR A,DP, where A contains the desired page number, or by PULS DP, where the top word on the stack has the desired page number. It might seem awkward to have a different instruction to load the direct page register in the microcomputer hardware from the SETDP assembler directive that tells the assembler that the direct page has some value in it. However, there are sound reasons why this must be done. As an example of this, suppose that you load the direct page register with 5 with an instruction at location $100 and then jump to location $2000, while all of the instructions in memory between locations $100 and $2000 use the direct page register with page zero. Thus, at location $100, you might see

```
00001                                    NAM      TEST
00002                                    OPT      S
00003    0100                            ORG      $100
00004                          *
00005    0100         0001    N          RMB      1
00006    0101         0001    SUM        RMB      1
00007    0102         000A    Z          RMB      10
00008                          *
00009                0001                SETDP    1
00010    010C   86   01                  LDA      #1
00011    010E   1F   8B                  TFR      A,DP
00012                          *
00013    0110   8E   0102                LDX      #Z
00014    0113   D6   00                  LDB      N
00015    0115   4F                       CLRA
00016                          *
00017    0116   AB   80       LOOP       ADDA     ,X+
00018    0118   5A                       DECB
00019    0119   26   FB                  BNE      LOOP
00020    011B   97   01                  STA      SUM
00021    011D   3F                       SWI
00022                                    END
TOTAL ERRORS:          0
TOTAL WARNINGS:          0

SYMBOL TABLE
LOOP  0116  N    0100  SUM    0101  Z    0102  %%%%%  %%%%
```

FIGURE 4-7. Program Listing for the Program of Figure 4-6 Moved to Page 1.
Notice the effect of the SETDP directive on the choice of addressing modes.

```
LDA     #5
TFR     A,DP
JMP     $2000
```

and just before the instruction at location $2000 you might see

```
SETDP     5
```

The point is that you do not have to generate a useless instruction to load the direct page register with 5 at location $2000, but you do have to tell the assembler that, after location $2000 until the next SETDP directive, it should assume that the direct page register has 5 in it, and any address between $0500 and $05FF should be coded with direct page addressing rather than direct addressing.

We have also been using the inequality symbols with index addressing to indicate whether the constant offset is to be described with eight or sixteen bits. The MC6809 actually has another choice for the offset which we have not discussed before now because there is no special symbol for it. This is the 5-bit offset option. In this case, one can actually squeeze the offset into the post byte as described in the instruction set summary of Appendix 2. The assembler chooses between the four offset options in exactly the same way that it chooses between direct page and direct addressing. On the first pass, if it knows the values in all the labels used in an expression for the offset, it will choose the shortest possible offset option or, if the expression is zero, it will take the zero offset option, which is pointer addressing. If it does not know some of the labels used in the expression for the offset, the assembler will default to the 2-byte offset option, determining these bytes on the second pass. From now on, we will drop the use of inequality signs in all addressing modes, except the relative mode, letting the assembler choose the appropriate option.

As we have discussed earlier, an assembler does several things for us. It allows us to use instruction mnemonics, labels for variable locations, and labels for instruction locations while still providing the machine code for our program. As we see below, however, we must be careful with forward references when using assembler directives.

The assembler reads your assembly language program twice. In pass one, the symbol table is generated and, in pass two, the symbol table and the tables of the instruction set summary, with the assembly directives added, are used to produce the machine code and assembly listing. On each pass, each line of assembly language is processed before going to the next line so that some undetermined labels may be determined on the second pass. For example, in the program

```
            NAM       TEST
            OPT       S
            ORG       10
*
K           EQU       M+1
M           RMB       2
*
            LDD       M
            ADDD      #K
            STD       M
            SWI
            END
```

the assembler will not determine K on the first pass since the EQU directive makes a forward reference to M, that is, uses a symbol in the expression for K which has not been determined yet. On the second pass, however, the value of K is determined when the EQU line is processed so that the machine code can be filled in for the instruction

```
ADDD        #K
```

Suppose now that we change the program a little bit.

```
             NAM          TEST
             OPT          S
             ORG          10
*
             LDD          M
             ADDD         #K
             STD          M
             SWI
*
K            EQU          M+1
M            RMB          2
*
             END
```

When the second pass is being made for this program, the instruction

```
   ADDD       #K
```

is encountered before the assembler knows the value of K and the program will not assemble correctly. In this program, two levels of forward referencing are encountered. The instruction

```
   ADDD       #K
```

makes a forward reference to K. The label K in turn makes a forward reference to M in

```
K        EQU        M+1
```

since M is not determined on the first pass when ADDD #K is encountered. Usually, it is easy to see which programs with forward referencing are assembled correctly just by examining how the assembler works with that particular program. Notice Figure 4-8 which has the assembler listing for the preceding program. Error 211 is for the ''undefined symbol'' occurring in the next line of assembly language code below the error message.

By now it should be obvious that for correct assembly a label can appear only once in the label field. Multiple occurrences are given an error message.

Looking at the instructions

```
           ▪
           ▪
           BNE          JUMP
           ▪
           ▪
           ▪
JUMP       ADDA         M
           ▪
           ▪
```

```
00001                              NAM     TEST
00002                              OPT     S
00003    000A                      ORG     10
00004                        *
00005    000A    F6    0014        LDD     M
***ERROR         211
00006    000D    C3    0015        ADDD    #K
00007    0010    FD    0014        STD     M
00008    0013    3F                SWI
00009                        *
00010                  0015    K   EQU     M+1
00011    0014          0001    M   RMB     2
00012                        *
00013                              END
TOTAL ERRORS:            1
TOTAL WARNINGS:          0

SYMBOL TABLE

K    0015  M    0014  %%%%% %%%% %%%%% %%%% %%%%% %%%%
```

FIGURE 4-8.   Illustration of Two Levels of Forward Referencing. With the standard Motorola assembler, the error message refers to the instruction immediately after the message. In this case, ERROR 211 indicates that an undefined symbol appears in the instruction ADDD #K.

in a particular program, one might wonder what happens if the location JUMP is more than 127 bytes below the BNE instruction. Does the assembler still proceed, not knowing location JUMP, and then give an error message when it finds that JUMP is beyond the 127-byte range on the second pass? Or does it immediately put in the long branch equivalent

```
    LBNE        JUMP
```

and determine the right 2-byte relative address on the second pass? It might seem reasonable to expect the latter, but the first possibility has been chosen since the latter choice would force all forward branches to be long branches. In other words, the assembler leaves the burden of picking the shortest branching instruction to the programmer. For exactly the same reason, the programmer will want to use the inequality sign "<" with forward references for relative addressing used with other instructions. As an example, you should use

```
    LDA         <L,PCR
```

instead of

```
    LDA         L,PCR
```

when the effective address L is a forward reference which is within 127 bytes of the next byte after the LDA instruction. Otherwise, the assembler will choose the 2-byte relative offset option.

Now let's look at two more examples. Suppose first that we have a vector Z of N 2-byte signed numbers and we want to arrange or sort it in increasing order. The algorithm that we shall use for the first example is given by the following FORTRAN or Pascal sequence. This example is used in the next section to show how high-level languages differ from assembly languages. You may know one or the other language, and this way of expressing the problem is more accurate than describing it in English. Note, moreover, the similarities of most high-level languages such as FORTRAN, PL/I, ALGOL, and Pascal, as suggested by the similarities of the following two programs.

```
      PROGRAM SORT
      DIMENSION Z(10)
      N=10
      DO  1  I = 1,N-1
      DO  1  J = I+1,N
      IF (Z(I) .LE. Z(J))  GO TO 1
      X = Z(I)
      Z(I) = Z(J)
      Z(J) = X
1     CONTINUE
      END
```

```
      PROGRAM SORT ;
      CONST N = 10 ;
      VAR I,J:INTEGER ;
       Z : ARRAY [1..N] OF INTEGER ;
      BEGIN
        FOR I:= 1 TO N-1 DO
          FOR J:= I+1 TO N DO
            IF Z(I) > Z(J) THEN
              BEGIN
                X:=Z(I) ;
                Z(I):=Z(J) ;
                Z(J):=X ;
              END ;
      END [SORT] .
```

This is a rather poor sorting algorithm, and it does not show how the data Z are input or how the sorted data Z are output but, nevertheless, we can use it to illustrate assembly language programming technique. The program listing is shown in Figure 4-9. Notice that the ASL and LSR instructions do exactly what you want them to do for $N \leq 25$. In fact, we could allow N to be as large as 63 by changing the RMB directive for Z to 126. For N beyond 63 the ASLA and ASLB instructions will yield numbers in A and B which will be treated as

```
00001                          NAM   SORT
00002                          OPT   S
00003                    *
00004                    * THIS PROGRAM SORTS THE ARRAY Z OF N TWO-
00005                    * BYTE SIGNED NUMBERS INTO ASCENDING ORDER.
00006                    *
00007 0000        0001  N     RMB   1       N MUST LESS THAN 64
00008 0001        0001  NDEC  RMB   1
00009 0002        0032  Z     RMB   50
00010                    *
00011 0034 8E     0000        LDX   #Z-2 POSITION X FOR Z(0)
00012 0037 96     00          LDA   N
00013 0039 4A                 DECA
00014 003A 97     01          STA   NDEC  NDEC CONTAINS N - 1
00015 003C 4F                 CLRA        PUT I = 0; (A) = I;
00016                    *                 (B) = J
00017 003D 4C           S1    INCA        PUT I = I + 1
00018 003E 1F     89          TFR   A,B   PUT J = I
00019 0040 48                 ASLA        PUT 2*I INTO A
00020                    *
00021 0041 5C           S2    INCB        PUT J = J + 1
00022 0042 58                 ASLB        PUT 2*J INTO B
00023 0043 10AE  85          LDY   B,X   PUT Z(J) INTO Y
00024 0046 10AC  86          CMPY  A,X   Z(J) - Z(I)
00025 0049 2C     07          BGE   S3
00026                    *
00027 004B EE     86          LDU   A,X   EXCHANGE Z(J) AND Z(I)
00028 004D 10AF  86          STY   A,X
00029 0050 EF     85          STU   B,X
00030                    *
00031 0052 54           S3    LSRB        J INTO B
00032 0053 D1     00          CMPB  N
00033 0055 25     EA          BLO   S2
00034 0057 44                 LSRA        I INTO A
00035 0058 91     01          CMPA  NDEC
00036 005A 25     E1          BLO   S1
00037                    *
00038 005C 3F                 SWI
00039                         END
TOTAL ERRORS:          0
TOTAL WARNINGS:          0

SYMBOL TABLE

N  0000  NDEC   0001  S1      003D  S2      0041  S3      0052
Z  0002  RRRRR  RRRR  RRRRRR  RRRR  RRRRRR  RRRR  RRRRRR  RRRR
```

FIGURE 4-9. Assembler Listing for the Program SORT

negative numbers when used in the accumulator offset option of index addressing. Thus the program, as written, will work only for N up to 63.

For the second example, Figure 4-10 gives the listing for the complete assembly language version of the program of Figure 3-8. Notice particularly the use of simple expressions for the offsets in the index addressing mode and

```
00001                         NAM   ADD
00002                   *
00003                   * THIS PROGRAM ADDS THE TWO N-BYTE NUMBERS
00004                   * NUM1 AND NUM2, PUTTING THE RESULT EQUAL TO
00005                   * SUM. SIGNED OVERFLOW IS INDICATED IN
00006                   * OFLOW.
00007                   *
00008                         OPT   S
00009  000A                   ORG   10
00010                   *
00011  000A      0001   OFLOW RMB   1
00012  000B      0001   N     RMB   1
00013  000C      000A   NUM1  RMB   10
00014  0016      000A   NUM2  RMB   10
00015  0020      000A   SUM   RMB   10
00016                   *
00017  002A D6 0B              LDB   N
00018  002C 8E 0016           LDX   #NUM2   POINT X TO NUM2
00019  002F 3A                ABX           POSITION X FOR LSB
00020  0030 4F                CLRA          CLEAR CARRY
00021                   *
00022  0031 A6 82      ADD1   LDA   ,-X
00023  0033 A9 16             ADCA  NUM1-NUM2,X
00024  0035 1F A9             TFR   CC,B
00025  0037 A7 0A             STA   SUM-NUM2,X
00026  0039 0A 0B             DEC   N
00027  003B 26 F4             BNE   ADD1
00028                   *
00029  003D C4 02             ANDB  #2      MASK OFF V BIT
00030  003F 54                LSRB          SHIFT TO LS BIT
00031  0040 D7 0A             STB   OFLOW   SET OVERFLOW
00032  0042 3F                SWI
00033                         END
TOTAL ERRORS:    0
TOTAL WARNINGS:    0

SYMBOL TABLE

ADD1 0031 N       000B NUM1   000C NUM2   0016 OFLOW   000A
SUM  0020 %%%%% %%%% %%%%% %%%% %%%%% %%%% %%%%% %%%%
```

FIGURE 4-10. Assembler Listing for the Program ADD

how, by initializing X to point to the least significant byte of the second number, the assembler chooses the 5-bit constant offset option in the ADCA and STA instructions.

We summarize that, in designating the base for constants, $ is used for hexadecimal, % is used for binary, @ is used for octal, ` for an ASCII character and nothing for decimal. For example,

```
LDA        #`f
```

will load the ASCII code for lowercase "f" into A.

Finally, we mention the special use of the symbol "*" by the assembler. The assembler uses a number called the *location counter* when it is making its two passes. The location counter keeps track of the address that the assembler is at when it is reading the current assembly language statement. The symbol "*" equals the value of that address. We shall have an occasion to use this symbol when we take up macros.

4–4

ASSEMBLERS, LOADERS, COMPILERS, INTERPRETERS, and MACROS

In this section we introduce some cousins of the assembler, which are other programs that convert sequences of (ASCII) characters into machine instructions. The cross-assembler is discussed first, together with loaders. Then we compare assemblers to compilers, and compilers to interpreters. Finally, we discuss macros used in macro assemblers. For the most part, this material is descriptive, almost philosophical, rather than precise and practical. It is important general knowledge and it is included here because the reader who is working laboratory examples can have some time to master the skills of editing and assembling without being encumbered with more competing detail from this text.

The nearest cousin to the assembler is the cross-assembler. A true assembler is a program that runs on a computer that generates machine code for that same computer. It is common for a microcomputer to be too limited to be able to assemble code for itself, particularly for a microcomputer that is used in a laboratory for a university course. Such computers may not have enough memory, or a disk capable of holding the assembler program or the assembly language to be input to this program, or a printer capable of printing the listing. But it is possible to assemble the program on another computer, called the *host* computer, for the microcomputer, which is called the *target machine*. The assembler, in this case called a *cross-assembler*, is written as a program for the host machine and runs on the host machine. Its output is machine code that runs on the target machine.

The capabilities of the host machine can be used to handle the assembly language program. An *editor* is a program on the host that helps you write the program. Editors can be used to write any kind of (ASCII) character data. (This book was written using an editor program.) The cross-assembler is used to generate the machine code for the target machine. The host machine's printer is used to print the listing, and the host machine's disk is used to hold the (ASCII) assembly language program, the program listing, and the machine code output that is to be put into the target machine.

If your microcomputer has an assembler, it will usually also have a *loader*. The loader is a program that takes the object code of the assembler, usually from a tape or disk, and writes it into memory. This step is usually necessary even if the assembler is in the machine that you wish to load your program into. For example, the assembler is typically such a large program that it leaves very little memory available for your program, especially in a small system. Having the assembler output the object code onto a tape or disk and then having the loader load it into memory means that the memory used to hold the assembler can be used for your program since the loader program is quite short compared to an assembler program. Having a separate loader also means that a particular program need only be loaded for each use, as opposed, perhaps, to reassembling it each time it is used with an assemble-then-load procedure. Of course, one might wonder: If the loader is a program, what loads the loader program? For small systems, the answer is that the loader program is usually part of the monitor program, which does not need to be loaded because it is stored once and for all in ROM. In a system in which it is desired to maximize the available RAM, one might have a small program, called a *bootstrap,* whose only purpose is to load the loader. After the program is put in by the loader, the memory space occupied by the loader could be used by the program for data storage. The bootstrap, now occupying only a small amount of memory space, is in ROM.

If you are using a cross-assembler, the machine code can be copied, by hand, from the listing, into the target machine's memory. This can be tedious. Alternatively, a program called a *down-line loader* can be used to read the machine code that was stored on the host machine's disk, through a telephone line or a special cable, into the target machine's memory. The down-line load program can move the machine code from the host to the target machine without much effort on the user's part, and without as much chance for error as when the code is copied by hand from the listing.

Cross-assemblers are in common use as this book is being written. However, they may become relics of yesteryear as new developments take place. Newer microcomputers are very well designed, so that the instruction set and speed of microcomputers is no longer a serious disadvantage to running the assembler program, and semiconductor memory costs are dropping so that many micro-computers may have enough memory to run the assembler program. (An example of this is the TRS-80 Color Computer with EDTASM+.) Although printer and disk costs are also falling, their cost is still too high to put one on each microcomputer. However, it is possible to connect these microcomputers in a laboratory by means of a high-speed link to implement a *local area network*. The computers in this network are called *servers*. A printer attached to this network, with a computer to support it, is a *print server*. A computer that you experiment with is called a *workstation*. With each workstation connected to the print server, each can print a listing when it needs to, provided that the printer is not already in use. One printer can serve about a dozen workstations. This is economical and efficient. The loader for a workstation is part of the software that controls the local area network. Such a local area network is in use here at the University of Texas, serving about 75 students per semester with eight workstations. The time from discovering an error in a program through reassembling the program to eliminate the error, to rerunning the program, is just a few minutes. It takes about ten times longer to use a cross-assembler if the host machine is busy, such as at the end of the semester in a university. This kind of distributed processing, using local area networks, will probably dominate future laboratory work associated with this book.

A simple loader, whether it is in your own microcomputer or is of the down-line variety, loads the program into locations specified by the assembler. A little thought reveals that the loader needs, for each consecutive block of bytes to be loaded, a starting address for the first byte and the number of bytes in that particular block. The format that this information might take is shown in Figure 4-11. Generally, the machine code of a program will be broken up into several blocks, called *records,* each with the format of Figure 4-11. This is to keep the length of each record within a maximum size. If the loader is to transfer control to the loaded program at the end of the loading process, it needs to know when it has reached the end of the program and what the starting address of the program is. The easiest way to do this is to have the last record consist of the

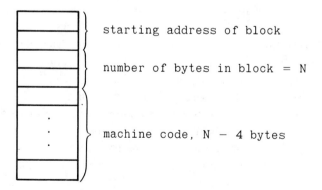

starting address of block

number of bytes in block = N

machine code, N − 4 bytes

FIGURE 4-11. Loader Record

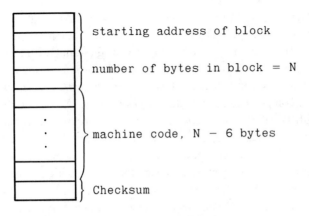

FIGURE 4-12. Loader Record with a Checksum

starting address of block

number of bytes in block = N

machine code, N − 6 bytes

Checksum

starting address followed by an N equal to 0. When the loader encounters this record, it automatically jumps to the starting address of the loaded program.

A byte called the *checksum* is usually included with each block as indicated in Figure 4-12. This byte is formed by adding up all the bytes used to describe that particular block, ignoring carries. After loading, the checksum is computed and compared with the one supplied by the assembler. If any pattern of single errors in the columns has occurred, the two checksums will always be different and an error message can be generated by the loader.

What we have been describing is sometimes called an *absolute* loader since the location of the program is completely specified by the assembler. There is a limitation with an absolute loader. Suppose that you have written a program which uses a standard subroutine from a collection provided by Motorola. You have to copy it physically into your program, perhaps changing the ORG so that it does not overlap with your program, and then assemble the whole package. What you might like to do instead is to be able to assemble your program separately, and then have the loader take your machine code, together with the machine code of any standard subroutines already assembled, and load them all together in consecutive RAM locations so that memory bytes would not be wasted. There are several ways to achieve this. The one that is conceptually the simplest is to have the program and all of the subroutines be position independent. Using program counter relative addressing to replace direct or direct page addressing, we have seen how to do this with a small increase in the number of bytes for our program or subroutines. Assuming that we write our program and subroutines so that they are position independent, our assembler and loader still have to take care of *linking* the program and subroutines. In each subroutine, or in the program, certain symbols would have to be declared as *external*. For example, if we had in our program, DIVIDE would be declared external. In the DIVIDE subroutine, the label DIVIDE would be declared as an *entry* symbol, that is, a label needed by some other subroutine or the program. The *linking* loader, in a manner similar to a two-pass assembler, takes the list of external and entry symbols, calculates the addresses needed at load time, in this example, the 2-byte relative address for DIVIDE in the instruction above, and then inserts the code for the instruction.

We now discuss the difference between an assembler and a compiler. A *compiler* is a program that converts a sequence of (ASCII) characters that are written in a *high-level language* into machine code, or into assembly language that can be converted into machine code. A high-level language is different from an assembly language in two ways. First, a line of a high-level language program will often generate five to a few hundred machine instructions, whereas a line of assembly language will usually generate (at most) one machine instruction. Second, a high-level language is designed to be oriented to the specification of the problem that is to be solved by the program, and to the human thought process, while a program in an assembly language is oriented to the computer instruction set and to the hardware used to execute the program. Consider the program at the end of the preceding section, written in FORTRAN or Pascal. Each line of the program generates many machine instructions or lines of assembly language code. Each high-level language statement is designed to express an idea used in the statement of the problem, and is oriented to the user rather than the machine. The compiler could generate the assembly language program, shown in Figure 4-9, or the machine code produced by this program.

Compilers are used for different purposes than assemblers. Studies have shown that a typical programmer can generate about ten lines of documented, debugged code per day, regardless of whether the program is written in a high-level language or an assembly language. Since a high-level language generates about an order of magnitude more machine instructions per line, a high-level language program should be an order of magnitude shorter (in the number of lines) and an order of magnitude cheaper than an assembly language program that does the same job.

However, a high-level language compiler usually produces inefficient code. For example, an instruction STA LOC1 might be immediately followed by the instruction LDA LOC1 in the compiler output. As the compiler generates code from each line of the program, line by line, the last operation of one line can generate the STA instruction, and the first machine code generated by the next line might be the LDA instruction. The compiler is usually unable to detect such an occurrence and to simplify the code produced by it. Such inefficient code is quite acceptable in a large computer where the slow execution and large memory space needed to store the program are traded against the cost of writing the program. Hardware is cheap and programmers are expensive, so this is a good thing. In a very small computer, which might be put in a refrigerator to control the cooling cycle or keep the time, memory space is limited because the whole computer is on just one chip. Inefficient code is unacceptable here because there is not much room for code and the cost of writing the program is comparatively small. The company that uses high-level languages for small microcomputers will not be able to offer all the features that are crammed into a competitor's product that is programmed in efficient assembly language, or if it offers the same features, its product will cost more because more memory is needed.

Some compilers are called optimizing. They use rules to detect and eliminate the unnecessary operations such as the STA and LDA pair described above. They can be used to generate less inefficient code than that generated by nonoptimizing compilers. But even these optimizing compilers produce some inefficient code. You should examine the output of an optimizing compiler to see just how inefficient it is and you should ignore the claims as to how optimal the code is. Compilers are more powerful, and using them is like driving a car with an automatic transmission, whereas using assemblers is like driving a car with a standard transmission. An automatic transmission is easy to drive and appeals to a wider market. A standard transmission is more controlled and enables you to get the full capabilities out of the machine.

We now consider the differences between the compiler and the interpreter. An *interpreter* is rather like a compiler, being written to convert a high level language into machine code. However, it converts a line of code one line at a time, and executes the resulting code right after it converts it from the high-level language program. A pure interpreter stores the high-level language program in memory, rather than the machine code for the program, and reads a line at a time, interprets it, and executes it. A popular high-level language for interpreters is BASIC, and a program in BASIC appears below, doing the same job as the previous programs in FORTRAN and Pascal.

```
10   FOR I = 1,N-1
20   FOR J = I+1,N
30   IF Z(I) <= Z(J) THEN 70
40   X=Z(I)
50   Z(I)=Z(J)
60   Z(J)=X
70   NEXT J
80   NEXT I
90   END
```

This program looks quite like the FORTRAN program in Section 4-3, but it is stored as is in memory, for a pure BASIC interpreter, and as each line is read from memory, the code for that line is generated as in the assembly language program in Figure 4-9, and that code is executed. Note that lines numbered 30 to 60 are read, interpreted, and executed $N*(N-1)/2$ times while the compiler would read and "interpret" each line just once, executing the machine code $N*(N-1)/2$ times. Interpreters are slow. However, it is easy to change the program in memory and execute it again in an interpreter without having to go through the lengthy process of compiling the code. This saves about one to ten minutes from the time a bug is discovered until it can be corrected and the program rerun. Interpreters are very useful for writing programs that have to be debugged quickly. One of the authors has used a variant of BASIC, BASIC09, sold by Microware, to write programs to test and debug hardware that he has built, writing the programs as he built the hardware. This interpretive language has proved to be a very powerful new tool for building hardware.

Some interpreters are almost compilers. The high-level language is stored in memory almost as written, but some words are replaced by *tokens*. For example, in the preceding program, the word FOR could be replaced by a token $81 (in hexadecimal). All the bytes in the program would be ASCII characters, whose value would be below $7F. The original high-level language can be regenerated from the information in memory, because the tokens can be replaced by their (ASCII) character string equivalents. But as the program is executed, the interpreter can almost use the token $81 as a command, in this case to set up a loop. It does not have to puzzle over what the (ASCII) characters F, O, and R are before it can decide what the line means. These interpreters have the convenience of a pure interpreter, with respect to the ease of changing the program, but they have speeds approaching those of compilers. They are really partly compiler—to get the tokens—and partly interpreter—to interpret the tokens and the remaining characters—and have some of the better features of both. (A BASIC compiler is different, though. It compiles a program, written in BASIC, into assembly language or machine code.)

The last two cousins of the assembler that we examine are the *conditional assembler* and the *macro assembler*. A conditional assembler allows conditional directives such as IFEQ and ENDC. For example, the segment

```
IFEQ      MODE
LDA       #1
STA       LOC1
ENDC
```

inserted in an assembly language program will cause the assembler to include the instructions

```
LDA       #1
STA       LOC1
```

in the program if the value of MODE is equal to zero. If the value of MODE is not equal to zero, these instructions will not be included in the object code for the program. The label MODE is usually defined through an EQU directive, say

```
MODE        EQU        1
```

One of the principal uses of conditional assembly directives is for debugging programs. For example, a number of program segments can be inserted or deleted from a program by just changing the EQU directive defining MODE. There are other conditional directives—IFNE, IFGE, IFGT, IFLE, and IFLT— that can be used instead of IFEQ and, in any of these, the label MODE can be replaced by an expression. All of these directives allow the programmer to control how the program is converted to object code at assembly time.

A program segment or instruction sequence, as we defined it in Chapter 1, is just a sequence of consecutive instructions which is part of a program. A macro assembler is able to generate a program segment, which is defined by a *macro*, when the name of the macro appears in a program. The macro assembler is still capable of functioning just like a regular assembler, generating a machine instruction for each line of assembly language code, but, like a compiler, it is also able to generate many machine instructions from one line of code. The following discussion of how a macro works will show how this can be done.

A frequently used program segment can be written just once, in the macro definition. For example, the macro

```
ABY         MACR
            EXG        X,Y
            ABX
            EXG        X,Y
            ENDM
```

put before the start of the program allows the programmer to use the single mnemonic ABY for the sequence

```
EXG        X,Y
ABX
EXG        X,Y
```

The assembler will insert this sequence each time the macro ABY is used. If the mnemonic ABY is used ten times in the program, the three instructions above will be inserted into the program each time the mnemonic ABY is used. The advantage is clear. The programmer almost has a new instruction that adds the unsigned contents of B to Y, and he or she can use it like the real instruction ABX that actually exists in the machine. The macro is a large-scale instruction. Moreover, macros can be used like high-level language statements. *Structured macros* are used to implement the IF-THEN-ELSE, DO-LOOP, and similar control statements of high-level languages in assembly language. This gives some of the ease of writing high-level languages to assembly language, but retains the tight control over the machine, where it is needed.

The general form of a macro is

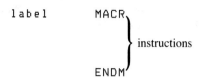

Here the term "label" is the name of the macro that appears in the label field of the MACR directive. It must not be the same as an instruction mnemonic or an assembler directive. The phrases MACR and ENDM are assembler directives indicating the start and the end of the macro. Both appear in the operation field of the instruction. Every time the programmer uses this macro, he or she writes

```
    label          parameters
```

where the label is the name of the macro, which is placed in the operation field, and the parameters are the actual parameters used at that point in the program. The parameter list appears in the operand field without spaces. As an example, the macro

```
MOVE       MACR
           LDD           \0
           STD           \1
           ENDM
```

will move the two bytes at parameter location 0 to parameter location 1. The backslash "\" indicates the presence of a *formal parameter* in a macro, an address or a number whose actual value must be supplied with each use of the macro. There can be up to 36 formal parameters labeled

$$\backslash 0,\ldots,\backslash 9,\backslash A,\ldots,\backslash Z \tag{4}$$

When used in the program, say as

```
    MOVE        Z+3,M
```

the two bytes at locations $Z+3$, $Z+4$ will be moved to locations M, $M+1$. In this example, all the usual rules for choosing between direct and direct page addressing would apply. Additionally, if the actual parameters involve an index mode of addressing, the actual parameters must be enclosed within parentheses as in

```
    MOVE        (3,X),(,Y)
```

for the sequence

```
LDD        3,X
STD         ,Y
```

As implied in the example above, when a macro is used, the actual parameters are inserted in a one-to-one correspondence with the order in (4). Null arguments are specified by the absence of an actual value. For example, if we had written MOVE as

```
MOVE       MACR       \0
           LDD        \2
           STD
           ENDM
```

then all of our uses would have to be written like

```
MOVE       L+3,,M
```

The point here is to use the next unused parameter in (4) when another parameter is needed in a macro. Do not skip any parameters in the sequence 0,...,9,A,...,Z.

There are several further considerations with macros which we take up briefly. Can a macro definition use a macro defined earlier? The answer, using the standard Motorola macro assembler, is yes as long as the "nesting" is limited to three layers. Also, if labels are to be used with macros, then, assuming that the macro will be used more than once during the program, assembler-generated labels must be used. For example, the macro

```
ADD        MACR
           LDX        \0
           LDB        \1
           CLAR
\.0        ADDA       ,X+
           DECB
           BNE        \.0
           ENDM
```

when implemented by

```
ADD        #M,N
```

adds the contents of the N bytes beginning in location M, putting the result in A. The notation "\.n" is used for an assembler-generated label where n is between 0 and 65535. The assembler will generate a new number, preceded by a decimal point, for the label each time the macro is used, but within each expansion of the macro, the label will be given the same number. Each generated label is of the form ".n," where n is between 0 and 65535. Finally, a macro can have conditional directives within its definition. The actual parameters of the macro can then be tested with these directives to determine how the macro is expanded. Most macro assemblers have conditional assembly capabilities.

4–5

SUMMARY

In this chapter we learned that an assembler can help you write much larger programs than you would be able to write by hand coding in machine code. Not only are the mnemonics for the instructions converted into instruction op code bytes, but also symbolic addresses are converted into memory addresses. However, every new powerful tool also has some negative aspects. To use an assembler, you have to spell the mnemonics correctly, and use the symbolic addresses exactly the same way throughout the program. You have to be concerned about the rules of writing a line of assembly language code, and the rules about forward references. But once these are mastered, you can use this powerful tool to help you write larger assembly language programs.

The assembler is just one such tool for converting your ideas into machine instructions. High-level languages can be used, too, using compilers and interpreters to convert your language into the machine's language. High-level languages let you write even larger programs with a similar degree of effort, but they move you away from the machine and it is difficult to extract the full power of the computer when you are no longer in full control. While high-level languages are used extensively to program most computers, especially larger computers, you will find many instances where you will have to program small computers in assembly language in your engineering designs.

PROBLEMS

1. Suppose that your program contains the directives

    ```
    N          RMB        L
    L          EQU        10
    ```

    Will it assemble correctly in every program? Why or why not? Can you say anything about forward references used in expressions in the operand field of an RMB directive?

2. Write an assembly language program that finds the maximum MAX of N 4-byte signed numbers contained in array Z. Your program should have in it the assembler directives

    ```
    N          RMB        1
    MAX        RMB        4
    Z          RMB        80
    ```

and be position independent. How would your program change if the numbers were unsigned?

3. Give the memory locations and contents that the Motorola assembler would give for the assembly language program below. Also, provide a symbol table.

```
              NAM       TEST
*             ORG       50
ADDR          RMB       40
N             RMB       1
M             RMB       1
*
              LDX       #40
              LDB       N
              ASLB
              ABX
              LDY       B,X
              LDB       M
              CLRA
*
LOOP          ADDA      ,Y+
              DECB
              BNE       LOOP
              STA       RESULT
              SWI
*
RESULT        RMB       1
              END
```

4. Write an assembly language version of the jump-table example of Section 3-7. Use N = 3.

5. It is easy to patch a program that has an extra instruction in it. We merely replace that instruction with the number of NOPs equal to the number of instruction bytes removed. However, suppose that CLRA was omitted in the program of Problem 3. How would we fix it without moving the bytes below that instruction?

6. Write an assembly language program that sorts the array Z of N 2-byte signed numbers into ascending order. The algorithm that you should use is given by the following sequence of FORTRAN or Pascal statements.

```
        PROGRAM SORT (INPUT,OUTPUT)
        DIMENSION Z(10)
        N = 10
2       FLAG = 0,
        DO 1 I = 1,N-1
        IF (Z(I+1) ,GE, Z(I)) GO TO 1
        Y = Z(I)
        Z(I) = Z(I+1)
        Z(I+1) = Y
        FLAG = FLAG + 1,
1       CONTINUE
        IF (FLAG ,GE, 1,) GO TO 2
        END
```

```
              PROGRAM SORT ;
              CONST N = 10 ;
              VAR I,Y : INTEGER ;
                 FLAG : BOOLEAN ;
                   Z : ARRAY [1,.N] OF INTEGER ;
              BEGIN
                FLAG := FALSE ;
                REPEAT
                  FOR I := 1 TO N-1 DO
                    IF Z(I+1) < Z(I) THEN
                    BEGIN
                       Y := Z(I) ;
                       Z(I) := Z(J+1);
                       Z(I+1) := Y ;
                       FLAG := TRUE
                    END
                  UNTIL NOT (FLAG)
              END , [SORT]
```

The program should include the assembler directives

```
              ORG          10
N             RMB          1
FLAG          RMB          1
Z             RMB          50
```

with the instructions beginning in location 100.

7. Rewrite the program of Figure 4-9 so that an array Z of any size can be used. You will find it helpful to have the index register X point to Z(I) and index register Y point to Z(J). Use postincrementing by 2 where possible and, to terminate the loops, push the address of the last number Z(N) on the stack and use

```
      •
      •
      CMPX          ,S
      •
      •
      CMPY          ,S
      •
      •
```

to see if you have reached the end of the array.

8. Give a macro MUL10 that multiplies the unsigned contents of D by 10, putting the result in D and setting C if an overflow occurs.

9. Give a macro NEGT that replaces the M-byte number stored at location L with its two's-complement. The call should be of the form NEGT L,M.

10. Write an assembly language program that finds the sum SUM of two N-byte signed-magnitude numbers NUM1 and NUM2. The result should also be in signed-magnitude form. Your program should include the assembler directives

```
              ORG      10
N             RMB      1
NUM1          RMB      10
NUM2          RMB      10
SUM           RMB      10
```

11. Write an assembly language program that adds N 2-byte signed numbers stored in the vector Z. Your program should sign-extend each number as it is being added into the current sum so that the result SUM is a 3-byte signed number. Your program should have the assembler directives

```
              ORG      10
N             RMB      1
Z             RMB      100
SUM           RMB      3
```

Can overflow occur in your program?

12. Write an assembly language program to find the smallest nonzero positive number SPNUM in the array Z of N 2-byte signed numbers. If there are no nonzero positive numbers, the result should be put equal to zero. Your program should have the following assembler directives:

```
              ORG      10
N             RMB      1
Z             RMB      100
SPNUM         RMB      2
```

13. Write an assembly language program that finds the sum of two N-byte signed numbers NUM1 and NUM2, putting the (N + 1)-byte result into SUM.

14. Write a macro WTD that computes the number of bits equal to 1 in accumulator D, putting the number in accumulator B. Try to choose a macro that has the greatest dynamic efficiency.

15. Why does the macro assembler described in the text require labels to begin with a letter or, in the case of assembler-generated labels, a decimal point?

16. Write macros for the following nonexistent MC6809 instructions.
    (a) NEGD
    (b) AAX
    (c) ADX
    (d) INCD
    (e) ASLD

17. Hand assemble the following program, providing the same listing and symbol table that the Motorola assembler would.

```
              NAM      TEST
              OPT      S
              ORG      10
*
K             EQU      M+1
M             RMB      2
*
```

```
          LDA       M
          ADDA      K
          STA       M
          SWI
          END
```

18. Write an assembly language program that finds the sum SUM of two N-byte numbers NUM1 and NUM2 and, when the SWI is encountered, has the condition code bits Z, N, V and C set properly. Your program should have the directives

```
N         RMB       1
NUM1      RMB       20
NUM2      RMB       20
SUM       RMB       20
```

19. Give a macro that increments the 4-byte number stored at the address given to the macro. No registers should be changed by the macro.

20. Write an assembly language program that takes the Ith bit from the vector Z and puts it in the carry bit. The bits are numbered in the vector Z as shown.

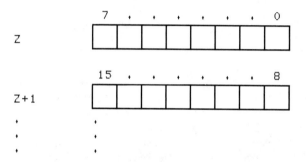

Your program should not change any of the variables and should have the directives

```
I         RMB       2
Z         RMB       8192
```

21. Write a program to search a vector Z of N bytes until a byte is found which has the same bits in positions 0, 3, 5, and 7 as the word MATCH. The address of the first byte found should be placed in ADDR. If no byte is found in Z with a match, $FFFF should be placed in ADDR. Your program should have the directives

```
N         RMB       1
Z         RMB       100
MATCH     RMB       1
ADDR      RMB       2
```

22. Write a program that will find all the prime numbers between 1 and 65,535. The prime numbers should be placed beginning in location 100, high byte first. The number of primes found should be placed in locations 98 and 99, again high byte first. Write your

program for maximum static efficiency and then consider what you might do to improve dynamic efficiency.

23. Rewrite the macro MOVE in the text so that no registers are changed except the CC register, which should be changed exactly like a load instruction.

24. Write a macro XCHG that will exchange two bytes in memory between locations L and M. No registers should be changed by the macro. A typical use would be

```
XCHG      L ,M
```

25. Write a macro XCHG that will exchange N bytes between locations L and M. No registers should be changed by the macro. A typical use would be

```
XCHG      L ,M ,N
```

26. Correct the following assembly language program so that each line would be accepted by the Motorola assembler without an assembler error. Do not change any lines that are already correct. The program replaces each of the N 8-bit two's-complement numbers with the absolute value of the number, rounded down to the next lower even number. For example, $+4$ is replaced with $+4$, -4 with $+4$, -5 with $+4$, $+5$ with $+4$, and so on.

```
NEXTB    MACR                    Macro NEXTB ends loops whose
         DECB                         Counter is in accumulator B
*        BCS      \0
         ORG      $100           Begin program
         LEAX     N ,VECTOR      Point X to VECTOR
         LDB      N              Length of VECTOR into B
LOOP     LD       A ,X+          A vector element into A
         BLO      L1             If negative,
         COM      A              replace with two's-complement
L1       ANDA     #$1            Make contents of A even
         STAA     -1 ,X          Put number back
*        NEXTB                   Macro call to end the loop
         SWI                     End of program
VECTOR   RMB      N
N        EQU      #5             Number of elements in VECTOR
         END
```

27. Correct the following assembly language program so that each line would be accepted by the Motorola assembler without an assembler error. The program takes a sequence STRING of ASCII characters and converts all of the lowercase letters in STRING to uppercase letters while finding the number COUNT of letters that were converted. Do not change any lines that are already correct.

```
         ORG      0
COUNT    RMB      0              Number of characters changed
STRING   FCC      "Abc ,1        String to be converted
BEGIN    FDB      STRING         Starting address of string
S        FCB      STRING-BEGIN   The length of the string
*
```

```
          ORG     #$3000
          LD      A,S              String size into A
LEAY      #COUNT                   Counter address into Y
          LDX     BEGIN            X points to STRING
          CLR     COUNT            Initialize counter
*
LOOP      LDAB    ,X               Get next character
          CMP     #$61             Compare character with "a"
          BLOW    L                If lower, go to L
          CMPB    $7A              Compare character with "z"
          BLS     L                If higher, go to L
          ANDB    #$2              Change by clearing bit 5
COUNT     INC     ,Y               Increment counter
L         STAB    ,X+              Put back letter
          DEC     A                Decrement number left
          BNE     LOOP             Check next character
          SWI
          END
```

28. Write macros that will clear, set and test the ith bit in location L. (As usual, the bits are labeled right to left in each byte beginning with 0.) For example,

```
CLEAR      L,5
```

will clear bit #5 in location L.

29. Using the data structure of Problem 20, write an instruction sequence that will put the carry bit into the ith bit of the data structure. The assembler directives for this sequence should be

```
I          RMB     1
Z          RMB     32
```

The picture above shows an **MC68000** board which contains a monitor program and **32K** of **RAM**. Connected to a power supply and a terminal, the board can be used to test **MC68000** programs that are entered from the terminal.

CHAPTER 5

Subroutines

Subroutines and macros are fantastic tools that will exercise your creativity. Until you learned about macros in Chapter 4, you learned to write programs using the instructions supplied by Motorola in their MC6809 microprocessor. Have you ever wished you had an instruction that executed a floating-point multiply? The MC6809 does not have such powerful instructions, but you can write a subroutine to execute the floating-point multiply operation, and the instruction that calls the subroutine now behaves pretty much like the instruction that you wish you had. Subroutines can call other subroutines as you build larger instructions out of simpler ones. In a sense, your final program is just a single instruction built out of simpler instructions. This idea leads to a methodology of writing programs called *top-down design*. You can also write a macro to execute the floating-point multiply, but the macro repeats the code for the floating-point multiply each time it is used, tending to fill the memory in a small microcomputer. Thus creative new instructions are usually implemented as subroutines where the code is written only once. In fact, macros are commonly used just to call subroutines. In this chapter we concentrate on the use of subroutines to implement larger instructions and to introduce programming methodologies.

To preview some of the ideas of this chapter, consider the following simple subroutine, which adds the contents of the X register to accumulator D.

```
SUB     PSHS    X        Push copy of X onto stack
        ADDD    ,S++     Add copy into D; pop copy off stack
        RTS
```

It can be called by the instruction

```
BSR     SUB
```

Recall from Chapter 3 that the BSR instruction, besides branching to location SUB, pushes the return address onto the hardware stack, low byte first, while the instruction RTS at the end of the subroutine pulls the top two bytes of the stack into the program counter, high byte first. Notice particularly that the instruction

```
ADDD        ,S++
```

in the subroutine above not only adds the copy of the contents of X into D but also pops the copy off the stack so that the return address will be pulled into the program counter by the RTS instruction (see Figure 5-1).

The BSR and RTS instructions are *calling and returning mechanisms* and the PSHS and ADDD instructions are the *program segment* in this subroutine. The X and D registers at the time the BSR is executed contain the *input parameters* and the D register at the time that the RTS is executed contains the *output parameter*. We *pass* these parameters into the subroutine at the beginning of its execution and out of the subroutine at the end of its execution. The value saved on the stack by the PSHS instruction is a *local variable* of the subroutine.

In this chapter we discuss the mechanics of how subroutines are written and, to a much lesser extent, the creative issue of what should be a subroutine and what should not. Echoing the theme of Chapter 1, we want to teach you how to implement your good ideas correctly, so that you will know how to use the subroutine as a tool to carry out these ideas.

This chapter is divided into sections that correspond to each capability that you need to write good subroutines. We first examine the storage of local variables. This discussion gives us an opportunity to become familiar with the stack, so that the later sections are easier to present. We next discuss the passing of parameters and then consider calling by value, reference, and name. We next discuss the techniques for calling subroutines and returning from them. After discussing reentrant and recursive subroutines, we then consider the testing of subroutines and calling routines together with a good set of rules for documenting subroutines. Finally, we present a few examples that tie together the various

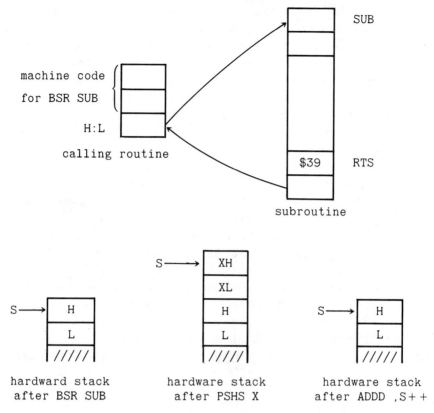

FIGURE 5-1. In this figure, H:L denotes the return address and the contents of X is denoted XH:XL.

concepts that have been presented in the earlier sections, and present some conclusions and recommendations for further reading.

Upon completion of this chapter, you should be able to pick the correct methods to call a subroutine, use local variables in it, and pass parameters to and from it. You should know how to test and document a subroutine and test the routine that calls the subroutine. With these capabilities, you should be ready to exercise your imagination creating your own subroutines for larger programs.

5-1

LOCAL VARIABLES

In this section we offer a mechanism that will help you write much clearer programs. The main asset to clarity is the modularization of a program into smaller segments. Think small, and the relationships within your program will be clearer. The problem with programs that are not so modularized is that a change to correct a bug in one part of the program may cause a bug in another part. If this propagation of errors explodes cancerously, your program becomes useless. The way to squelch this propagation is to divide the program into segments and to control the interaction between the segments with standard techniques. The main source of uncontrolled interaction is the storage of data for different segments. In this section we introduce you to the tools to break up a program into segments and to store efficiently the data needed by these segments. In a later section on testing, we will examine the interaction between segments.

A *program segment* is a sequence of instructions that are stored one after another in memory as part of your program. An *entry point* of the segment is any instruction of the segment that can be executed after some instruction which is not in the segment. An *exit point* of the segment is any instruction that can be executed just before some instruction that is not in the segment. Figure 5-2 shows the flowchart of a program segment with multiple entry and exit points. For simplicity, however, you may think of a segment as having one entry point, which is the first instruction in the segment, and one exit point, which is the last instruction in the segment.

For the purpose of this discussion we assume that the program segment has information passed into it by its *input parameters* (or *input arguments*), and the

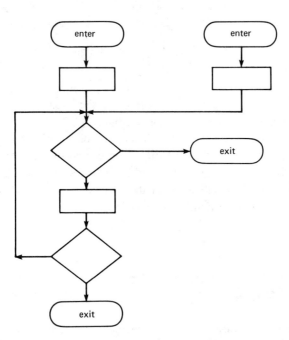

FIGURE 5-2.   Program Segment with More than One Entry Point and More than One Exit Point

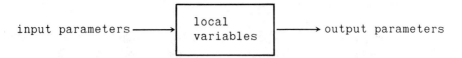

input parameters ⟶ local variables ⟶ output parameters

FIGURE 5-3. Representation of a Program Segment in Terms of Local Variables and Parameters

results of its computation are passed out through its *output parameters* (or *output arguments*). Any variables used in the segment for its computation which are not parameters are called *local variables*. Figure 5-3 shows the program segment as a box with the parameters and variables that relate to it. Some of the parameters may be *global variables*, variables that are, or can be, used by all program segments. (In the MC6809, global variables are most efficiently stored on page zero and accessed by direct page addressing.) If you have learned about sequential machines, the input parameters are like the inputs to the sequential machine, the local variables are like the internal states of the machine, and the output parameters are like the outputs of the machine. As a sequential machine can describe a hardware module without the details about how the module is built, one can think about the input and output parameters and local variables of a program segment without knowing how it is written in assembly language. Indeed, one can think of them before the segment is written.

Consider the following example. Suppose that we have two vectors V and W, each having two 1-byte elements (or components) V(1), V(2) and W(1), W(2). We want to compute

$$V(1)*W(1) + V(2)*W(2) \tag{1}$$

which is an example of the dot product of V and W used in physical applications. The input parameters are the components of V and W and the one output parameter is the dot product. If the components of V and W are assumed to be 1-byte unsigned numbers, we might, for convenience, assume that V and W are contained in X and Y with components 1 and 2 contained, respectively, in the high and low bytes of each register. If we assume that the 2-byte dot product is placed in accumulator D at the end of the segment, it is clear that we will have to store one of the products in (1) somewhere while we are computing the second product in accumulator D. This 2-byte term that we save is a local variable for the program segment we are considering. It may also be convenient to place copies of the vectors somewhere for easy access during the calculation. These copies would also be local variables. We will continue this example below to show how local variables are stored in a program segment.

We first consider the lazy practice of saving local variables as if they were global variables, stored in memory and accessed with direct page or direct addressing. For example, assuming that the directive

TEMP   RMB   2

is in the program, one could use the two locations TEMP and TEMP+1 to store one of the 2-byte local variables for the dot product segment. This is a bad practice for several reasons. With this technique, memory will be taken up by local variables of various program segments; but such data will hardly ever be used, thus increasing the memory requirements for our program and data. If we try to get around this by using TEMP for various program segments, essentially making TEMP a global variable, we introduce the possibility of using TEMP over again by one segment before its value is completely used by another segment, something that can lead to the propagation of errors between segments discussed earlier. This can be seen by looking at the "coat hanger" diagram of Figure 5-4. A horizontal line represents a program segment, and a break in it represents a call to a subroutine. The diagonal lines represent the subroutine call and its return. Figure 5-4 illustrates a program segment using TEMP to store a variable to be recalled later. Before the recall, however, TEMP has been changed by subroutine B, which is called by subroutine A, which itself is called by the program segment. This case is difficult to debug because each subroutine will work correctly when tested individually but will not work with the given program segment. This technique also makes it hard to document the meaning of the local variable for the various program segments using TEMP and generally makes the program less clear. The remainder of this section deals with how local variables can be stored on the stack, and how they can be handled by the assembler.

The Motorola MC6809 has a stack and instructions with addressing modes to use it to store local variables. Recall from Chapter 2 that index addressing using the stack pointer can access data in the stack and can push or pull data from the stack. For example,

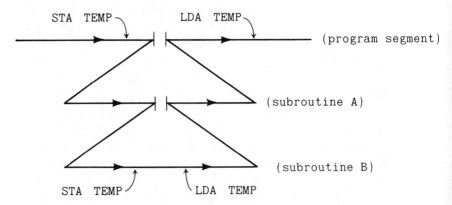

FIGURE 5-4. This figure illustrates how a subroutine can change the value of a global variable before a program segment has completed using it.

```
LDA         2,S
```

reads the third word on the stack, and

```
CLR         ,-S
```

will push a zero word on top of the stack. Recall from Chapter 3 that some special instructions are available for use on the stack. The instruction LEAS can be used to move the stack pointer; as an example,

```
LEAS        2,S
```

pops two words from the stack. The instructions PSHS and PULS can push or pull one or more registers from the stack. For example, the instruction

```
PULS        A,X
```

will first pull a word from the stack, putting it in accumulator A, and then pull two words from the stack, putting the first in the high byte of X and the second in the low byte of X. As we shall see, these instructions make it easy for you to store local variables on the stack.

The MC6809 also has a U index register that is called the user stack. While the designers call it a stack, it is just too useful as an index register to waste as a stack pointer. It is really as powerful as the X register, in that instructions that load or store U are shorter than those that load or store the Y register, and the PULU and PSHU instructions can be used as multiple load or store instructions analogous to

```
LDA         ,U+
```

or

```
STA         ,-U
```

Although some programmers use the U register to store local variables, it is generally too valuable to waste for that function, and the S register, which points to what we will be calling the *stack*, is quite adequate.

The stack is said to be *balanced* in a segment if, when we leave the segment, the number of words pulled from the stack after entry to the segment is equal to the number pushed, and at no time during execution of the segment are there more words pulled than have been pushed. We will also say in this case that the segment is *balanced*.

A simple two- or three-line program segment can be used to replace some instructions that are missing from the instruction set. The one used at the beginning of the chapter is an example of this which also illustrates the idea of balancing the stack. Suppose that we want to add the contents of the X register to accumulator D. The segment below does this in two instructions.

```
PSHS     X
ADDD     ,S++
```

The first instruction obviously pushes a copy of the contents of X onto the stack. The second adds this copy from the stack into accumulator D and then pops the copy from the stack. This technique can be used to compare the contents of index registers with each other and create a number of other instructions which are missing from the MC6809 instruction set. Note that in this segment the net number of words pushed, two, equals the net number of words pulled and that at no time do we pull more words than we push.

We offer a general and simple rule for balancing the stack in a program segment so that the segment will be balanced. Push all the local variables of the segment on the stack at the entry point, and pull all of the local variables off the stack at the exit point, and do not push or pull words from the stack anywhere else in the program segment except for two- or three-line segments used to implement missing instructions as just described. While an experienced programmer can easily handle exceptions to this rule, it is quite sound and we recommend it to you. In the following sections, our program segments will be balanced unless otherwise noted and we will usually follow this rule, only occasionally keeping local variables in registers.

We now look more closely at this rule to show how local variables can be bound, allocated, deallocated, and accessed using the stack. *Binding* means assigning an address (the actual address used to store the variable) to a symbolic name for a variable. *Allocation* of a variable means making room for that variable in memory, and *deallocation* means removing the room for that variable. *Accessing* is the process of finding that variable which, for local variables, will be on the stack. An input parameter supplies a value to be used by the program segment. While input parameters are usually not changed by the program segment, local variables and output parameters that are not also input parameters generally need to be *initialized* in the program segment. That is, before any instruction reads a value from them, a known value must be written in them. A local variable or output parameter is usually initialized immediately after the entry point of the program segment.

Local variables are bound in two steps. The symbolic address is converted to a number which is an offset that is used in index addressing with the stack pointer. This is done by the assembler before the program is run. The binding is completed when the program is running. There, the value in the stack pointer S, at the time the instruction is executed, is added to the offset to calculate the actual location of the variable, completing the binding of the symbolic address to the actual address used for the variable. This two-step binding is the key to reentrant and recursive subroutines, as we discuss in a later section.

We will allocate local variables in a balanced program segment using the LEAS and PSHS instructions, which make room for the local variables, and deallocate the variables using the LEAS and PULS instructions, which remove the room for the local variables. We will bind and access local variables in a couple of ways to illustrate some alternative techniques that you may find useful. First, to access local variables, we use explicit offsets from the stack pointer, reminiscent of the programming that you did in the first three chapters. Then we use the SET assembler directive, and finally we use the ORG and RMB directives to do the first step of the binding of local variable names to offsets for the stack pointer. This allows symbolic names to be used to access these local variables, taking advantage of the assembler to make our program clearer.

Let's now look at our dot product example, where we will denote the copies of X and Y that are placed on the stack LOCV and LOCW. The first term of the dot product (1), which will also be placed on the stack, will be denoted TERM.

```
PSHS    X,Y      Allocate and initialize LOCV and LOCW
LEAS    -2,S     Allocate room for Term
LDA     2,S      First component of LOCV into A
LDB     4,S      First component of LOCW into B
MUL              The value of first term is now in D
STD     ,S       Store first term in TERM
LDA     3,S      Second component of LOCV into A
LDB     5,S      Second component of LOCW into B
MUL              Calculate second term
ADDD    ,S       Add in TERM; dot product is now in D
LEAS    6,S      Deallocate local variables; balance stack
```

Notice how the simple rule for balancing the stack has been used in this segment. If the stack pointer were changed in the interior of the segment, offsets for local variables would change, making it difficult to keep track of them. As it is now, we have to determine the offsets from the stack pointer for each local variable. The local variable TERM occupies the top two bytes, the local variable LOCV occupies the next two bytes, and the local variable LOCW occupies the next two bytes. Keeping track of these local variables without using symbolic addresses is very similar to what you did in the first three chapters. But the assembler can keep track of them for you, so that you can use symbolic addresses for local variables in the same way that you did in Chapter 4 for global variables. Using appropriate symbolic names, you can make the program much clearer and avoid making trivial mistakes.

There are three ways to bind names to locations relative to the stack pointer using the EQU, SET, and RMB assembler directives. The EQU directive turns out to be almost identical to the SET directive, but the latter is slightly better if labels need to be reused. We will discuss the use of the SET directive and the RMB directive.

The SET directive can be used to define the values of a symbolic address just like the EQU directive except that the value of the symbolic address can be changed elsewhere in the program by using another SET directive. Knowing that TERM is on top of the stack, we can bind the value of the name TERM to the location 0,S using the SET assembler directive and using TERM,S to access it. Note that you bind the name of the container TERM to 0,S and not the contents of TERM to 0 with the SET directive. That is, we use 0 wherever we see TERM, and we use it in calculating the address with TERM as an offset in index addressing with the S register. Similarly, we can bind LOCV to 2,S and LOCW to 4,S. Also, the number of bytes needed for the local variables in the LEAS instructions to allocate and deallocate the local variables can be set to a value when local variables are being defined. The initialization of these variables is changed a bit to make NBYTES easier to use but the effect is the same. The program segment to calculate the dot product can now be rewritten as follows.

```
TERM    SET     0
LOCV    SET     2
LOCW    SET     4
NBYTES  SET     6
*
        LEAS    -NBTYES,S       Allocate space for local variables
        STX     LOCV,S          Copy of V into LOCV
        STY     LOCW,S          Copy of W into LOCW
        LDA     LOCV,S          First component of LOCV into A
        LDB     LOCW,S          First component of LOCW into B
        MUL                     First term of dot product into D
        STD     TERM,S          Put first term into TERM
        LDA     LOCV+1,S        Second component of LOCV into A
        LDB     LOCW+1,S        Second component of LOCW into B
        MUL                     Second term of dot product into D
        ADDD    TERM,S          Add first term into D to get dot product
        LEAS    NBYTES,S        Deallocate space for local variables
```

Note that the statements are quite readable without the comments, although good comments are still valuable. The EQU directive can be used in place of the SET directive, but the symbolic names cannot be used again with different values when the EQU directive is used. This technique, where the SET directives are put right before the allocation of local variables for each program segment, serves as a comment to clarify the program, and encourages you to use local variables freely and give them meaningful names.

As described above, this technique requires the programmer to calculate the values for the various labels and calculate the value for NBYTES. If the segment is changed for some reason, adding or deleting a variable requires a new set of calculations. This can be avoided as illustrated below.

```
TERM      SET      0
LOCV      SET      TERM+2
LOCW      SET      LOCV+2
NBYTES    SET      LOCW+2
*
          .
          .
          .
```

With this use of the SET directive, each new local variable is defined in terms of the local variable just previously defined plus the number of bytes for that local variable. Insertion or deletion of a local variable in a segment now requires changing only two lines, a convenience if the number of local variables gets large.

Another technique, using the RMB directive, plays a trick on the assembler. The technique uses the RMB directive to bind the local variables partially with the stack pointer S, using the location counter and the ORG directive to modify the location counter. Recall that

```
ALPHA       RMB        2
```

will normally allocate two words for the variable ALPHA. The location counter is used to bind addresses to labels like ALPHA as the assembler generates machine code. The location counter, and hence the address bound to the label ALPHA, corresponds to the memory location where the word associated with the label ALPHA is to be put. An RMB statement, with a label, binds the current value of the location counter to the label (as the name of the container, not the contents), and adds the number in the RMB statement to the location counter. This will bind a higher address to the next label, allocating the desired number of words to the label of the current directive. Note that

```
ALPHA       RMB        0
```

will bind the current location counter to the label ALPHA, and add zero to the location counter so that the location counter is unchanged. (The asterisk * can also be used to do this, but we have had enough trouble with the asterisk to recommend against using it in assembly language programs unless absolutely necessary.) Also, recall that the ORG directive can set the location counter to any value. These can be used as shown in the following example.

```
LCSAVE    RMB      0      Save current value of location counter
          ORG      0      Set the location counter to zero
TERM      RMB      2      First term of dot product
LOCV      RMB      2      Copy of input vector V
LOCW      RMB      2      Copy of input vector W
```

```
NBYTES   RMB       0          Number of bytes needed for local variables
         ORG       LCSAVE     Restore location counter
*
           ‚
           ‚
           ‚
```

You can reset the location counter to zero many times, and you should do this
before each group of RMB directives that are used to define local storage for
each program segment. These RMB statements should appear first in your
program segment. Each set should be preceded by a directive such as

```
LCSAVE   RMB       0
```

to save the location counter using LCSAVE, an

```
ORG       0
```

directive to set the location counter to 0, and each set should be followed by a
directive such as

```
ORG       LCSAVE
```

to set the origin back to the saved value to begin generating machine code for
your program segment. The pair

```
ORG       0
  ‚
  ‚
  ‚
ORG       LCSAVE
```

can be replaced by

```
RMB       − *
  ‚
  ‚
  ‚
RMB       LCSAVE − *
```

which avoids the use of the ORG statement. (This can be useful if one is using
EDTASM+ with the TRS-80 Color Computer. See Appendix 4.)

It is easy to insert or delete variables without making mistakes, using this
technique, because the same line has the variable name and its length, as
contrasted with the last technique using the SET directive. The number of bytes
needed to store the local variables is also automatically calculated with this
technique. You do, however, have to write three more lines of code with this
technique and the same name may not be used over again in another RMB

directive, for this will define the same name several times and generate an error message. You have to invent some kind of convention in naming variables to avoid this problem, but that is not too difficult to do.

The final concept that we introduce here is that of nested local variables. Suppose that a program segment B is entirely contained in a program segment A. We say that B is *nested* in A. An instruction inside B may need to access a local variable that is allocated and bound for all of segment A. There are two techniques that can be used to access the variable in B that is defined for A. These are the extended local access and stack marker access techniques described below.

The idea of the *extended local access* technique assumes that there is a way to fix the location of the desired variable over one or more allocations of local variables. The following example shows how this can work. The program segment below is the whole segment A discussed above, and the segment B is the segment from label SD to label ENDB inclusive. In segment B, there is a load instruction that needs to get at local variable SC of segment A. The offset that you need is obviously the number of words allocated at the entry to segment B plus the relative offset from that position to the position of the desired variable. Using the SET directive approach, and defining the sizes of each allocation with SET directives, the offset is SC + SIZEB and the address is SC + SIZEB,S.

```
SA      SET     0           SA, SB, and SC are each one word
SB      SET     1           Local variables of segment A
SC      SET     2
SIZEA   SET     3           Number of words allocated for segment A
        LEAS    -SIZEA,S    Local variable allocation for segment A
        .
        .       (segment A instructions)
        .

SD      SET     0           SD and SE are each one word local
SE      SET     1           Variables in segment B
SIZEB   SET     2           Number of words allocated for segment B
        LEAS    -SIZEB,S    Local variable allocation for segment B
        .
        .       (segment B instructions)
        .
        LDA     SC+SIZEB,S  Get local variable SC from A
        .
        .       (segment B instructions)
        .
ENDB    LEAS    SIZEB,S     Deallocate local variables for B
        .
        .       (segment A instructions)
        .
ENDA    LEAS    SIZEA,S     Deallocated local variables for A
```

We can use the dot product calculation to illustrate this further. In the version below, the outer segment A copies vectors into the stack where the inner segment B calculates the dot product. The dot product is placed in D by segment B and left there by A.

```
VV        SET       0                          Input vector
WW        SET       2                          Input vector
SIZEA     SET       4
*
STARTA    LEAS      -SIZEA,S                   Start of segment A
          LDD       #$1234
          STD       VV,S
          LDD       #$5678
          STD       WW,S
*
TERM      SET       0
SIZEB     SET       2
*
STARTB    LEAS      -SIZEB,S                   Start of segment B
          LDA       VV+SIZEB,S
          LDB       WW+SIZEB,S
          MUL
          STD       TERM,S
          LDA       VV+1+SIZEB,S
          LDB       WW+1+SIZEB,S
          MUL
          ADDD      TERM,S
ENDB      LEAS      SIZEB,S                    End of segment B
*
ENDA      LEAS      SIZEA,S                    End of segment A
```

The stack marker technique uses an index register to provide a reference to local variables of outer segments. Just before a program segment allocates its variables, the old value of the stack pointer is transferred to a register. Just after the local variables are allocated, the value in this register is put into a local variable for the inner segment. It is called a *stack marker* because it marks the location of the stack that was used for the local variables of the outer program segment. It is always in a known position on the stack (in this case, on the very top of the stack), so it is easy to find. See the following example, where the inner program segment can access the local variables of the outer segment by loading the stack marker into any index register, and using index addressing to get the variable. Note that the stack marker is deallocated together with the other local variables at the end of the program segment.

```
SMA       SET       0                Stack marker
SA        SET       2                SA, SB, and Sc are each one word
SB        SET       3                Local variables of segment A
SC        SET       4
```

```
SIZEA    SET      5              Number of words allocated for A
         TFR      S,X            Save stack marker
         LEAS     -SIZEA,S       Allocation of local variables for A
         STX      SMA,S          Put stack marker on the stack
                  ,
                  ,    (segment A instructions)
                  ,
SMB      SET      0              Stack marker
SD       SET      2              SD and SE are each one word local
SE       SET      3              Variables of segment B
SIZEB    SET      4              Number of words allocated for B
         TFR      S,X            Save stack marker
         LEAS     -SIZEB,S       Allocation of local variables for B
         STX      SMB,S          Put marker on stack
                  ,
                  ,    (segment B instructions)
                  ,
         LDX      ,S             Get stack marker for B
         LDA      SC,X           Get local variable SC from A
                  ,
                  ,    (segment B instructions)
                  ,
ENDB     LEAS     SIZEB,S        Deallocate stack marker, local variables
                  ,
                  ,    (segment A instructions)
                  ,
ENDA     LEAS     SIZEA,S        Deallocate stack marker, local variables
```

Using the same segments A and B as we used above for the dot product calculation with extended local access, we can illustrate the stack marker technique further as follows.

```
MARKA    SET      0              Stack mark for segment A
VV       SET      2              Input vector
WW       SET      4              Input vector
SIZEA    SET      6
*
STARTA   TFR      S,X            Start for segment A
         LEAS     -SIZEA,S
         STX      MARKA,S
         LDD      #1234
         STD      VV,S
         LDD      #5678
         STD      WW,S
*
MARKB    SET      0              Stack mark for segment B
TERM     SET      2
SIZEB    SET      4
*
STARTB   TFR      S,X
```

```
            LEAS      -SIZEB,S
            STX       MARKB,S
            LDA       VV,X
            LDB       WW,X
            MUL
            STD       TERM,S
            LDA       VV+1,X
            LDB       WW+1,X
            MUL
            ADDD      TERM,S
ENDB        LEAS      SIZEB,S        End of segment B
*
ENDA        LEAS      SIZEA,S        End of segment A
```

Either the extended local access or the stack marker access mechanisms can be used in cases where program segments are further nested. Consider a program segment C with SIZEC local variables that is nested in segment B and needs to load accumulator A with the value of SA, a local variable of segment A. Using extended local access as in the first example, the following instruction will accomplish the access.

```
    LDA      SIZEC+SIZEB+SA,S
```

Using the stack marker of the second example, the following instructions will access the variable.

```
    LDX      ,S        Get to segment B
    LDX      ,X        Get to segment A
    LDA      SA,X      Access local variable SA
```

The extended local access mechanism appears to be a bit simpler for smaller assembly language programs because it takes fewer instructions or directives. The stack marker mechanism seems to be preferred in compilers because the compiler program has less to "remember" using this approach than using the other, where the compiler has to keep track of the sizes of each allocation of local variables, particularly if a subroutine is called by many program segments that have different numbers of local variables. It is not unreasonable to expect a large program to have 20 levels of nesting. Because the stack marker to the next outer segment is always on top of the stack, the compiler does not have to remember where it is. In fact, the labels for stack markers are not really necessary for access at all, their only real use being for allocation and deallocation of the local variables. With two good mechanisms, you will find it easy to use one of them to handle nested program segments to many levels.

This section introduced the idea of a local variable and the techniques for storing local variables on the Motorola MC6809. Local variables can be used in any program segment. They are especially easy to use in the MC6809, because the LEAS instructions are able to allocate and deallocate them, the index addressing mode using the stack pointer is useful in accessing them, and the SET or RMB directives are very useful in binding the symbolic names to offsets to the stack pointer. These techniques can be used within subroutines, as we discuss in the remainder of this chapter. They can also be used with program segments that are within macros or those that are written as part of a larger program. The nested program segments can be readily handled too, using either the extended local access or stack marker technique to access local variables of outer program segments.

5-2

PASSING PARAMETERS

We now examine how parameters are passed between the subroutine and the calling routine. We do this because an assembly language programmer will have frequent occasions to use subroutines written by others. These subroutines may come from other programmers which are part of a large programming project, or they may be subroutines that are taken from already documented software, such as assembly language subroutines from a FORTRAN or Pascal support package. They may also come from a collection of subroutines supplied by the manufacturer in a user's library. In any case, it is necessary to understand the different ways in which parameters are passed to subroutines, if only to be able to use the subroutines correctly in your own programs or, perhaps, modify them for your own specific applications.

In this section we examine six methods used to pass parameters to a subroutine. We illustrate each method with our dot product example of Section 5-1. The simplest method is to pass parameters in registers as we did in our earlier examples. This is considered first; then the passing of parameters by global variables is discussed and discouraged. We then consider passing parameters on the stack and after the call, which are the most common methods used by high-level languages. We then discuss the rarely used method of passing parameters by putting them immediately above the subroutine itself, and the technique of passing parameters using a table, which is widely used in operating system subroutines.

The first method is that of passing parameters through registers, which is preferred when the number of parameters is small. We will also use this method to illustrate the idea of a calling sequence. Suppose that the *calling routine*, the program segment calling the subroutine, puts a copy of the vector V into X and a copy of the vector W into Y, where, as before, the high byte of the register contains the first component of the vector and the low byte contains the second component. Both components of each vector are 1-byte unsigned numbers.

Assuming that the dot product is returned in accumulator D, a subroutine DOTPRD which performs the calculation is shown below.

```
*               SUBROUTINE DOTPRD
*
*               LOCAL VARIABLES
*
TERM     SET    0                First term of dot product
LOCX     SET    2                Copy of the vector in X
LOCY     SET    4                Copy of the vector in Y
NBYTES   SET    6
*
DOTPRD   LEAS   -NBYTES,S        Allocate space for local variables
         STX    LOCX,S           Place copy of X into LOCX
         STY    LOCY,S           Place copy of Y into LOCY
         LDA    LOCX,S           First component of LOCX into A
         LDB    LOCY,S           First component of LOCY into B
         MUL                     First term of dot product into D
         STD    TERM,S           Place first term into local variable
         LDA    LOCX+1,S         Second component of LOCX into A
         LDB    LOCY+1,S         Second component of LOCY into B
         MUL                     Second term of dot product into D
         ADDD   TERM,S           Add first term into D to get dot product
         LEAS   NBYTES,S         Deallocate space for local variables
         RTS
```

The instructions

```
LDX    V           Put the copy of V into X            (2)
LDY    W           Put the copy of W into Y
BSR    DOTPRD      Call the subroutine
STD    DTPD        Place result
```

in the calling routine cause the subroutine to be executed. [We have assumed that component $V(1)$ is in location V and that component $V(2)$ is in location $V+1$. A similar assumption is made for W.] Notice that the values in A and B have been changed by the subroutine since an output parameter is being returned in D. The sequence of instructions in the calling routine that handles the placement of the input and output parameters is termed the *calling sequence*. In our calling sequence we have, for convenience, assumed that copies of the global variables V and W are put into X and Y for input parameters to DOTPRD while the output parameter in D is copied into the global variable DTPD. These three global variables could just as easily have been local variables for the calling routine. In general, then, the calling sequence is the program segment in the calling routine that loads the parameters, calls the subroutine, and unloads the parameters.

To emphasize that a calling sequence is in no way unique, suppose that the calling routine has vectors which are local variables on the stack, labeled LV and LW as offsets to the stack pointer. To compute the dot product between LV and LW, the calling routine could execute

```
LDX        LV,S        Copy or LV into X              (3)
LDY        LW,S        Copy of LW into Y
BSR        DOTPRD
STD        LDP,S       Store dot product in LDP
```

where we have assumed that it puts the dot product of LV and LW into another local variable LDP. We have, for simplicity, omitted the binding, allocation, and deallocation of the local variables of the calling routine. The point of this second example is to stress that any calling sequence for the subroutine DOTPRD must load copies of the vectors that it wants the dot product of into X and Y and then call DOTPRD. It must then get the dot product from D to do whatever it needs to do with it. From a different point of view, if you were to write your own version of DOTPRD, but one that passed parameters in exactly the same way, your version could not directly access the global variable V used in the calling sequence (2). If it did, it would not work for the calling sequence (3).

Parameters are passed through registers for most small subroutines. The main limitation with this method of passing parameters is that there are only three 16-bit registers (you do not pass parameters in the stack pointer S), a few 8-bit registers, and a few condition code bits. Although this limits the ability of the MC6809 to pass parameters through registers, you will, nevertheless, find that many, if not most, of your subroutines will use this simple technique.

The next technique we discuss is that of passing parameters through global variables. We include it because it is used in small microcomputers like the MC6805, but we discourage you from using it in larger machines like the MC6809. It is easy to make mistakes with this technique, so much so that most experienced programmers avoid this method of passing parameters when other techniques are available. Figure 5-5 shows a coat-hanger diagram that illustrates how incorrect results can occur when parameters are passed with global variables. Notice in particular how subroutine B writes over the value of the global variable passed by the calling routine to subroutine A so that subroutine A may not have the value intended by the calling routine when it performs the load instruction.

In assembly language, global variables are defined through an RMB directive that is usually written at the beginning of the program. These variables are usually stored on page zero so that direct page addressing may be used to access them. Assuming that the directives

```
V          RMB         2
W          RMB         2
DTPD       RMB         2
```

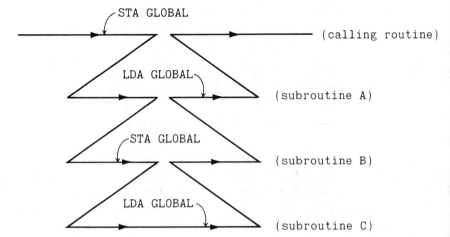

FIGURE 5-5. This figure illustrates how a subroutine (B) can change a global variable being passed to another subroutine (A) before that subroutine has used it.

are written somewhere in the program, the following subroutine does the previous calculation, passing the parameters through these locations. Note that we use local variables in this subroutine as discussed in Section 5-1.

```
*            SUBROUTINE DOTPRD
*
*            LOCAL VARIABLES
*
TERM    SET    0              First term of the dot product
NBYTES  SET    2
*
DOTPRD  LEAS   -NBYTES,S      Allocate space for local variables
        LDA    V              First component of V into A
        LDB    W              First component of W into B
        MUL                   First term of dot product into D
        STD    TERM,S         Save first term
        LDA    V+1            Second component of V into A
        LDB    W+1            Second component of W into B
        MUL                   Second term of dot product into D
        ADDD   TERM,S         Dot product into D
        STD    DTPD           Place dot product
        LEAS   NBYTES,S       Deallocate local variables
        RTS
```

The subroutine, as written, uses the memory locations for V, W, and DTPD to pass the parameter values to the subroutine. If the calling routine wants to compute the dot product of its local variables LV and LW, putting the result in LDP, the following calling sequence could be used.

```
LDD      LV,S
STD      V              Place copy of LV into V
LDD      LW,S
STD      W              Place copy of LW into W
BSR      DOTPRD
LDD      DTPD           Get result
STD      LDP,S          Place result in local variable LDP
```

Notice that the calling routine's local variables are copied into global variables V and W before execution and copied out of the global variable DTPD after execution. Any other calling sequence for this version of DOTPRD must also copy the vectors that it wants to compute the dot product of into V and W, call the subroutine, and then get the dot product from DTPD. Note also that the last LEAS instruction of the subroutine could be omitted in the program segment if we replaced the ADDD instruction with

```
ADDD     ,S++           Dot product into D; deallocate local variable
```

We now consider the very general and powerful method of passing parameters on the stack. We illustrate the main idea, interpreting it as another use of local variables, as well as a technique that makes and erases "holes" in the stack, and we consider variations of this technique that are useful for very small computers and for larger computers like the MC68000.

Input and output parameters can be passed as if they were local variables of the program segment that consists of the calling sequence that allocates, initializes, and deallocates the local variables around the subroutine call. In this mode the parameters are put on the stack before the BSR or JSR. For our particular dot product example, the calling sequence might look like the following.

```
LOCV     SET      0         Input parameter copy of the vector V
LOCW     SET      2         Input parameter copy of the vector W
LOCDP    SET      4         Output parameter copy of dot product
PSIZE    SET      6         Number of bytes for parameters
*
         LEAS     -PSIZE,S  Allocate space for parameters
         LDD      V         Copy global variable into D
         STD      LOCV,S    Store in parameter LOCV,S
         LDD      W         Copy global variable into D
         STD      LOCW,S    Store in parameter LOCW,S
         BSR      DOTPRD
         LDD      LOCDP,S   Get output parameter
         STD      DTPD      Place output in global variable
         LEAS     PSIZE,S   Deallocate space for parameters
```

For simplicity, we have assumed that the values of the input parameters come from global variables V and W, and the output parameter is placed in the global

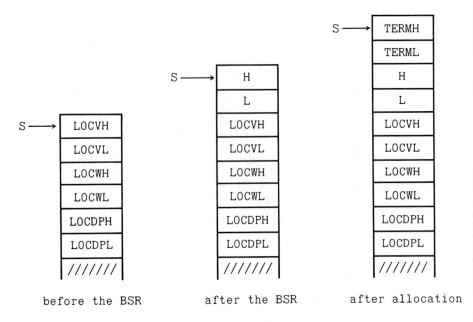

before the BSR	after the BSR	after allocation

H: suffix used to denote high byte of 2-byte number
L: suffix used to denote low byte of 2-byte number
H:L: denotes the return address

FIGURE 5-6. Location of Parameters Passed on the Hardware Stack. Notice that the value of LOCDP is not determined until the end of the subroutine.

variable DTPD. All of these global variables could, however, just as well have been local variables of the calling routine. The idea is exactly the same. The stack is as shown in Figure 5-6 immediately after the BSR instruction. The dot product subroutine can now be written as shown.

```
*               SUBROUTINE DOTPRD
*
*               LOCAL VARIABLES
*
TERM      SET      0           First term of the dot product
NBYTES    SET      2
*
*               PARAMETERS
*
RADDR     SET      2           Return address
LOCV      SET      4
LOCW      SET      6
LOCDP     SET      8
*
DOTPRD    LEAS     -NBYTES,S   Allocation for local variables
          LDA      LOCV,S
          LDB      LOCW,S
```

```
          MUL
          STD       TERM,S            Copy first term into local variables
          LDA       LOCV+1,S
          LDB       LOCW+1,S
          MUL       TERM,S
          ADDD      LOCDP,S           Dot product into D
          STD       NBYTES,S          Place dot product in output parameter
          LEAS                        Deallocate local variables
          RTS
```

Notice several things about the way this version of the subroutine is written. We do not need the local variables to hold copies of V and W as we did in the earlier versions since the copies are already on the stack as parameters where we can access them using the extended local access technique described in Section 5-1. Because the number of parameters and local variables is small, and because each is equal to two bytes, we can easily calculate the stack offsets ourselves, particularly if we use a dummy parameter RADDR for the return address. Notice particularly how we have redefined the labels LOCV, LOCW, and LOCDP in the subroutine with the SET directive to avoid adding an additional offset of 4 to each parameter to account for the number of bytes in the return address and the local variables.

Suppose now that we write the subroutine in the following way.

```
*         SUBROUTINE DOTPRD
*
*         LOCAL VARIABLES
*
TERM   SET  0                         First term of the dot product
NBYTES SET  2
*
*         PARAMETERS
*
LOCV   EQU  0
LOCW   EQU  2
LOCDP  EQU  4
PSIZE  EQU  6                         Number of bytes for parameters
*
DPTPRD LEAS  -NBYTES,S                Allocation for local variables
       LDA   LOCV+NBYTES+2,S
       LDB   LOCW+NBYTES+2,S
       MUL
       STD   TERM,S                   Copy first term into local variable
       LDA   LOCV+NBYTES+3,S
       LDB   LOCW+NBYTES+3,S
       MUL
       ADDD  TERM,S                   Dot product into D
       STD   LOCDP+NBYTES+2,S         Dot product into output parameter
       LEAS  NBYTES,S                 Deallocate local variables
       RTS
```

When EQU is used in this way, the additional offset of NBYTES + 2 is needed to access the parameters to account for the local variables and the return address. No SET or EQU directives are needed in the calling sequence, however, since EQU is a global definition; that is, the labels LOCV, LOCW, LOCDP, and PSIZE are fixed, respectively, at 0, 2, 4, and 6 throughout the program. The calling sequence for this case might be the following:

```
LEAS    -PSIZE,S        Allocate space for parameters
LDD     V               Get copy of V
STD     LOCV,S          Put copy in parameter location
LDD     W               Get copy of W
STD     LOCW,S          Put copy in parameter location
BSR     DOTPRD
LDD     LOCDP,S         Get value of dot product
STD     DTPD            Put in global location
LEAS    PSIZE,S         Deallocate space for parameters
```

Putting the additional offset of NBYTES + 2 in the subroutine, which is written only once, makes the calling sequence, which may be written many times, more straightforward. However, keeping the EQU directives with the subroutine as shown will force 2-byte offsets for parameter accesses in all of the calling sequences placed before the subroutine. For this reason, the EQU tables for subroutines might be placed at the beginning of a program to improve the static efficiency of the calling sequences. One could also force 1-byte offsets by using "<" before the expressions that access the parameters, as in

```
LDA     <LOCW+NBYTES+2,S
```

This, however, would still not get the 5-bit offset for those local variables that would be accessed with offset expressions in the range from zero to fifteen.

The reader should recognize that in this method of passing parameters, the calling sequence is just another instance of a balanced program segment, with local variables that are the parameters to the subroutine. Variables are copied from the calling routine to the parameter locations and back so that the subroutine will have a precise place to find them. Compare this to the earlier example where parameters were passed by global variables, and review the discussion after that example.

There is another way to think of this technique which some students have found to be more concrete. You can think of "holes in the stack." To pass an argument out of the subroutine, such as LOCDP, you create room for it in the calling routine. The instruction

```
LEAS    -PSIZE,S
```

creates a hole for this output parameter, among other things, and the subroutine puts some data in this hole. Conversely, the input parameters LOCV and LOCW are used up in the subroutine and leave holes after the subroutine is completed. These holes are erased by the instruction

```
LEAS      PSIZE,S
```

Some readers may appreciate the generality of the idea of parameters as local variables of the calling sequence, whereas others may prefer the more concrete technique of providing holes and removing holes for input and output parameters.

One could also have used the U register as a stack for passing parameters. For example, the analogous subroutine for the last example would be obtained by replacing S by U in the calling sequence and the subroutine and dropping the additional offset of 2 everywhere in the subroutine. As with the stack pointer S, one also needs to initialize the user's stack pointer U in the program before the subroutine is used. Although this method of using U avoids a lot of fuss with the return address on the stack and is clearer, the U register is generally too useful to tie up as a stack pointer, as we observed earlier in this chapter. However, in a computer with more registers, such as the MC68000, this technique becomes quite attractive to use with registers like U.

The reason that the stack mode of passing arguments is recommended is that it is very general. Since registers are quite limited in number and are useful for other functions, it is hard to pass many parameters through registers. You can pass as many arguments to or from a subroutine as you will ever need using the stack. Compilers often use this technique. It is easier to use a completely general method in a compiler, rather than a kludge of special methods that are restricted to limited sizes or applications. The compiler has less to worry about and is smaller because less code in it is needed to handle the different cases. This means that many subroutines that you write for high-level languages such as ALGOL, Pascal, or Ada may require you to pass arguments by the conventions that it uses. Moreover, if you want to use a subroutine already written for such a language, it will pass arguments that way. It is a good idea to understand thoroughly the stack mode of passing parameters. You may be forced to use it someday.

We now consider another very common method of passing arguments. They can be put after the BSR or equivalent instruction. This way, they look rather like addresses that are put in the instruction just after the op code. There are two variations of this technique, which are discussed below.

In the first alternative, the parameters are placed after the BSR or JSR instructions in what is called an *in-line argument list*. Looking at Figure 5-7, we see that the return address, which is pushed onto the hardware stack, points to where the parameters are located. When parameters are passed this way, sometimes referred to as *after the call*, the subroutine has to increment the return address appropriately to jump over the parameter list. If this is not done, the MPU would, after returning from the subroutine, try to execute the parameters

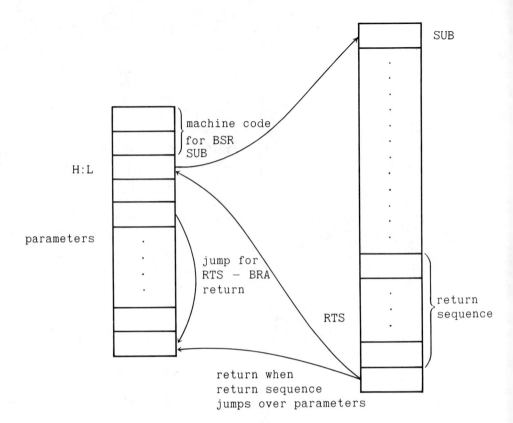

FIGURE 5-7. Parameters Passed After the Call

as though they were instructions. For our dot product example, assume that the parameter list looks as follows:

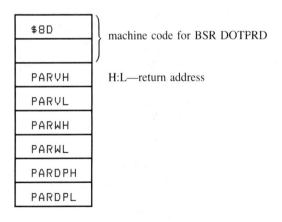

where we have added the suffix H and L for the high and low bytes of the values of the given parameters. Notice that the subroutine must skip over the six bytes in the parameter list when it returns to avoid "executing the parameters." The following subroutine does this.

```
*           SUBROUTINE DOTPRD
*
*           LOCAL VARIABLES
*
TERM        SET    0              First term of the dot product
NBYTES      SET    2
*
*           PARAMETERS
*
PARV        SET    0              Copy of vector V
PARW        SET    2              Copy of vector W
PARDP       SET    4              Dot product of V and W
PSIZE       SET    6
*
DOTPRD      PULS   X              Return address into X
            LEAS   -NBYTES,S      Allocation for local variables
            LDA    PARV,X
            LDB    PARW,X
            MUL
            STD    TERM,S         Copy first term into local variable
            LDA    PARV+1,X
            LDB    PARW+1,X
            MUL
            ADDD   TERM,S         Dot product into D
            STD    PARDP,X        Place dot product in output parameter
            LEAS   NBYTES,S       Deallocate local variables
            JMP    PSIZE,X
```

Notice that the return address is pulled into X before the local variables are allocated and that the labels for the parameters are now used as offsets with X. In particular, the label PSIZE used in the JMP instruction automatically allows the proper return. If we make the assumption that the global variables V, W, and DTPD are moved to and from the parameter list, a calling sequence would look as follows:

```
PARV        SET    0
PARW        SET    2
PARDP       SET    4
*
            LDD    V              Copy of V into D
            STD    PARV+L,PCR     Place copy in parameter list
            LDD    W              Copy of W into D
```

```
              STD       PARW+L,PCR      Place copy in parameter list
              BSR       DOTPRD
       L      RMB       6
              LDD       PARDP+L,PCR     Get value of dot product
              STD       DTPD            Place in global variable
```

The second alternative permits the return from the subroutine to be simply an RTS instruction without modifying the return address saved by the BSR instruction. The trick is to put a BRA instruction in front of the argument list to branch around the list as shown below (see also Figure 5-7).

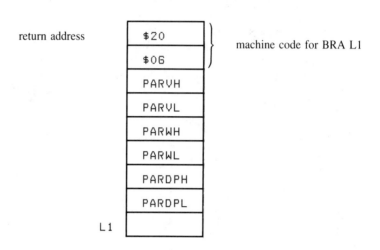

One should note that this technique generally takes more bytes of code than doing the correction within the subroutine since each call requires an additional two bytes. To account for the BRA instruction, the labels for the parameters have to be increased by 2 so that the subroutine is now written as follows.

```
*             SUBROUTINE  DOTPRD
*
*             LOCAL  VARIABLES
*
TERM          SET       0              First term of the dot product
NBYTES        SET       2
*
*             PARAMETERS
*
PARV          SET       2              Copy of vector V
PARW          SET       4              Copy of vector W
PARDP         SET       6              Dot product of V and W
*
DOTPRD        LDX       ,S             Return address into X
              LEAS      -NBYTES,S      Allocation for local variables
```

```
        LDA      PARV,X
        LDB      PARW,X
        MUL
        STD      TERM,S          Copy first term into local variable
        LDA      PARV+1,X
        LDB      PARW+1,X
        MUL
        ADDD     TERM,S          Dot product into D
        STD      PARDP,X         Place dot product in output parameter
        LEAS     NBYTES,S        Deallocate local variables
        RTS
```

The calling sequence for this version would have the BRA instruction added as shown below.

```
PARV    SET      0
PARW    SET      2
PARDP   SET      4
*
        LDD      V               Copy V into D
        STD      PARV+L,PCR      Place copy in parameter list
        LDD      W               Copy W into D
        STD      PARW+L,PCR      Place copy in parameter list
        BSR      DOTPRD
        BRA      L1
L       RMB      6
L1      LDD      PARDP+L,PCR     Get value of dot product
        STD      DTPD            Place in global variable
```

The typical use of passing parameters after the call assumes that all of the arguments are either constant addresses or constant values. They are often just addresses. The addresses are not modified, although the data at the addresses can be modified. In particular, one will always be modifying the data at the addresses where output parameters are placed. Calling sequences for this situation are particularly simple, as we show below for our dot product example.

```
        BSR      DOTPRD
        FDB      ADDRV           Address for V
        FDB      ADDRW           Address for W
        FDB      ADDRDP          Address for dot product
```

We emphasize that these addresses are constants for each place in the program. At another place in the program the addresses would generally be different constants. A dot product subroutine for this calling sequence is shown below.

```
*       SUBROUTINE DOTPRD
*                           ʹ
*       LOCAL VARIABLES
*
```

```
TERM    SET    0
NBYTES  SET    2
*
DOTPRD  PULS   X                       Return address into X
        LEAS   -NBYTES,S               Allocate space for local variables
        LDY    ,X++                    Point Y to V
        LDU    ,X++                    Point U to W
        LDA    ,Y
        LDB    ,U
        MUL                            First term of dot product into D
        STD    TERM,S                  Place first term in local storage
        LDA    1,Y
        LDB    1,U
        MUL                            Second term of dot product into D
        ADDD   TERM,S                  Dot product into D
        STD    [,X]                    Place dot product
        LEAS   NBYTES,S                Deallocate space for local variables
        JMP    ,X                      Return
```

Because programs are usually in ROM in microprocessor applications, parameters passed after the call must be constants or constant addresses. In these cases, calling sequences and subroutines like the ones shown just previously would be used.

Passing parameters in an in-line argument list is often used in FORTRAN programs. A FORTRAN compiler passes the addresses of parameters, such as the parameters in the example above. Like the stack method, this method is general enough for FORTRAN, and it is easy to implement in the compiler. In assembly language routines, this method has the appeal that it looks like an "instruction," with the op code replaced by the calling instruction and the addressing modes replaced by the argument list.

The next technique is used in a few cases. The parameters can be put in the area of memory that can be easily addressed by program counter relative addressing. A good place to put the parameters is just above the subroutine itself. In this situation the calling routine must place the parameters before the entry point of the subroutine, as shown in Figure 5-8. Assuming that the parameters are placed as shown there, we can rewrite our subroutine as follows.

```
*       SUBROUTINE DOTPRD
*
*       PARAMETERS
*
PARV    RMB    2                       Copy of vector V
PARW    RMB    2                       Copy of vector W
PARDP   RMB    2                       Dot product of V and W
*
*       LOCAL VARIABLES
*
TERM    SET    0
```

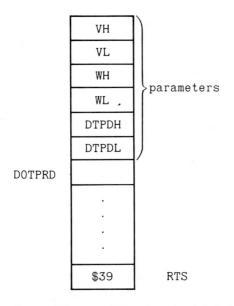

parameters

DOTPRD

$39   RTS

H: suffix used to denote high byte of 2-byte number
L: suffix used to denote low byte of 2-byte number

FIGURE 5-8.   Parameters Passed Before the Subroutine Entry Point

```
NBYTES   SET      2
*
DOTPRD   LEAS     -NBYTES,S      Allocation for local variables
         LDA      PARV,PCR
         LDB      PARW,PCR
         MUL                     First term of DP into D
         STD      TERM,S         Store in local variable
         LDA      PARV+1,PCR
         LDB      PARW+1,PCR
         MUL                     Second term into D
         ADDD     TERM,S
         STD      PARDP,PCR      Place dot product
         LEAS     NBYTES,S       Deallocate local variables
         RTS
```

A typical calling sequence might be

```
LDX      V                Copy of V into X
STX      PARV             Place copy into parameter
LDX      W                Copy of W into X
STX      PARW             Place copy into parameter
BSR      DOTPRD
LDX      PARDP            Get dot product
STX      DTPD             Copy into global variable
```

Notice that if the subroutine is to be position independent, program counter relative addressing must be used when the parameters are accessed.

This technique, passing parameters before the called subroutine, has several disadvantages. One outstanding disadvantage in microcomputers is that the program code, and thus the subroutine, may well be in read-only memory. The parameter area will be close to the subroutine, and thus will be in ROM, rather than in RAM, so that one cannot write the parameters into the ROM holding the subroutine. An additional disadvantage will be shown when we look at reentrant coding requirements in a later section.

We now consider the technique of passing parameters via a table. The argument list, which is in-line when parameters are passed after the call, can be a table stored anywhere in memory. If many parameters are passed in the same way to many different subroutines, it is sometimes convenient to put all of these parameters in a table and pass the address of the table through an index register. This is essentially the same idea as passing parameters after the call; one is now just combining the individual in-line argument lists into one table. For our example, suppose that one uses a table whose address is passed in X and which looks like

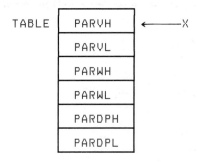

where, as before, the suffixes H and L stand for the high and low bytes of the 2-byte parameters PARV, PARW, and PARDP. The subroutine can be rewritten for this case as follows.

```
*          SUBROUTINE DOTPRD
*
*          PARAMETERS
*
PARV       SET       0
PARW       SET       2
PARDP      SET       4
*
*          LOCAL VARIABLES
*
```

```
TERM      SET       0
NBYTES    SET       2
*
DOTPRD    LEAS      -NBYTES,S
          LDA       PARV,X
          LDB       PARW,X
          MUL                       First term into D
          STD       TERMS,S
          LDA       PARV+1,X
          LDB       PARW+1,X
          MUL                       Second term into D
          ADDD      TERM,S          Dot product into D
          STD       PARDP,X         Place dot product
          LEAS      NBYTES,S        Deallocate local variables
          RTS
```

where a possible calling sequence is

```
PARV      SET       0
PARW      SET       2
PARDP     SET       4
*
          LDX       #TABLE          Table address into X
          LDD       V               Copy V into D
          STD       PARV,X          Place copy into table
          LDD       W               Copy W into D
          STD       PARW,X          Place copy into table
          BSR       DOTPRD
          LDD       PARDP,X         Get value of dot product
          STD       DTPD            Place in global variable
```

Somewhere in the program, the bytes for TABLE would be set aside with

```
TABLE     RMB       6
```

One could eliminate the SET directives in the subroutine and the calling sequence by using EQU directives with the TABLE description, for example,

```
TABLE     RMB       6
PARV      EQU       0
PARW      EQU       2
PARDP     EQU       4
```

This technique, passing parameters by a table, is quite common in operating system subroutines such as those used in the operating systems MDOS and FLEX that can be used with the MC6809. One thing that an operating system does is control a floppy disk in a way that is transparent to the user. The number of parameters needed to control a disk can be very large, so that the table can serve as a place to keep all the parameters while only the address of the table is sent to the subroutine.

In this section we considered ways to pass arguments to and from subroutines. The register technique is best for small subroutines that have just a few arguments. The stack technique is best for larger subroutines because it is the most general. The in-line argument list that passes parameters after the call is suitable for most applications and is used in FORTRAN subroutines, and the table technique is commonly used in operating system subroutines. The techniques that pass parameters in global variables and that put them before the subroutine entry point were covered for completeness, but their use was discouraged.

5-3

PASSING ARGUMENTS BY VALUE, REFERENCE, AND NAME

Computer science students, as opposed to electrical engineering students, study the passing of parameters in high-level language subroutines on a different level than that used in the preceding section. We include this section to explain that level to you. On the one hand, this level is very important if, say, you are writing or using a subroutine that is used by a high-level language program and that subroutine has to conform to the properties discussed below. On the other hand, the differentiation between some of the characteristics discussed below is rather blurry in assembly language programs.

The most important characteristic of a parameter is whether you pass the value of the parameter to the subroutine, or the address of the parameter to the subroutine. In the example used throughout Section 5-2, values of the vectors and the dot product usually were passed to and from the subroutine rather than the addresses of these arguments. (The one exception was in the discussion of passing parameters after the call, where constant addresses were passed in the argument list.) If the value of a parameter is passed, we say the parameter is passed or called *by value*. Output parameters passed by value are also said to be passed or called *by result*. If the address of the parameter is passed, the parameter is passed by reference or by name as we describe below.

The passing of parameters by value is completely general, but could be time consuming. Consider a simple example where the string STRING of ASCII characters, terminated by an ASCII carriage return ($0D), is passed one character at a time into the subroutine, and the string is up to 100 characters long. Clearly, a lot of time would be used copying the characters into parameter locations. Were there enough registers, we would have to load 100 bytes into registers before calling the subroutine. A hundred bytes would be moved to global memory using the global technique, or 100 bytes would be pushed on the stack using the stack technique. Obviously, it is more efficient to pass an address rather than these values. For this case, the address would be the address of the first character of the string, or the label STRING itself.

The characteristics of passing parameters by addresses have been differentiated into two types, depending on whether the value of the argument is considered to be fixed or whether it may change. The differentiation becomes important when the variable is actually a subroutine or function that returns a value, or an input register that receives data from the outside world rather than an ordinary variable in memory. In these cases the variable could change during the execution of the subroutine, unlike the ordinary variable in memory, which would change only if the subroutine itself changed it. We will confine this discussion to changes made by the subroutine itself.

If the value of the parameter is not supposed to change during the execution of the subroutine, the parameter is called by *reference*, but if it is allowed to change, the parameter is called by *name*. If a parameter is called by reference, it remains the same throughout the execution of the subroutine. The subroutine may not change it, except when it is an output parameter, where the subroutine may store a value in the given location. If an input parameter is called by reference, it is effectively evaluated when the subroutine is called and it is evaluated just once. If a parameter is called by name, however, it can be changed by the subroutine as the subroutine proceeds, or it could be changed by the outside world. It has to be evaluated each time it is used because it could change. The value that a call by name parameter has is not consistent throughout the subroutine, and the value at any given time depends on what has happened to the parameter.

You might observe that a parameter called by reference is handled in a more dynamically efficient way, since the parameter is evaluated just once. The value remains dependably constant as the subroutine is executed. This is desirable for many applications. The call by name method is more flexible since you can change the value, but it is more prone to error since the parameter may have to be evaluated each time that it is used, and is thus less dynamically efficient since each evaluation takes time.

When we use a call by value or a call by reference for an input parameter, that parameter is copied or evaluated once and does not change, as an input parameter, during the subroutine. This has implications even in simple subroutines. Suppose that we have a subroutine which exchanges two variable values Z and W, as in

Z into T
W into Z
T into W

where T is a local variable of the subroutine. If we should now want to exchange H(J) and J, where H(J) is the Jth element of the vector H, the sequence

J into T

H(J) into J

T into H(J)

will be different from

H(J) into T

J into H(J)

T into J

if, in the first sequence, we allow the value of H(J) to change to reflect the change of J. If we had passed Z and W by reference, using index registers X and Y, one can see that both sequences would yield the same result. To implement the first sequence to reflect the change in J, one uses a call by name. This allows the input parameter to change each time it is used in the subroutine. A simple example of call by name occurs when you rewrite the SORT program of Chapter 4 as a subroutine, passing the address of the vector through X and the value of N through B. Because one is recalculating the values of the vector elements during the subroutine, it becomes a call by name rather than a simple call by reference. For further reading we suggest the book by Peterson listed in Section 5-9.

Call by name is also useful when the parameters themselves are subroutines as, for example, in a subroutine that integrates the function f between 0 and 1. In this case, the function f is the name of a subroutine that is supplied to the integration subroutine and it is reevaluated each time a new point of f is needed for the subroutine calculation. For example, the call to f may supply a starting point and an increment delta. The nth call to the subroutine returns the value of the function f(x) at x = starting point + (n − 1)*delta. This continues until the calling routine changes the value of the starting point. Each call to f inside the integration subroutine returns a different value for f even though the input parameters to f are the same. This, then, is an example of call by name.

In this section we have described the types of information that are passed about parameters. The most important distinction is whether a value is passed (a call by value) or whether an address is passed (a call by reference or, possibly, a call by name).

5-4

CALLING AND RETURNING MECHANISMS

The MC6809 provides several mechanisms to call a subroutine and return from it. The standard subroutine uses BSR, or the equivalent instruction, to call the subroutine, and RTS, or the equivalent instruction, to return from it. We have used this mechanism in the earlier sections of this chapter. However, there are the SWI and RTI instructions that can be used for the software interrupt handler, the LDX #RETURN and TFR X,PC instructions that can be used to call and return from a program segment that is very much like a subroutine, and the EXG X,PC instruction that can flip-flop between two program segments called coroutines. In the spirit of showing design alternatives, we will survey these techniques, pointing out some advantages and disadvantages of each approach.

As we proceed, we will discuss several related important topics. We will look at hardware interrupts and at the fork and join mechanisms used in timesharing. These important topics are best covered in this section on calling and returning mechanisms.

The BSR-RTS mechanisms are the most commonly used to call and return from subroutines. However, there are alternatives to both the calling and returning mechanisms. The alternatives to the returning mechanism are discussed first; then the alternatives to the calling mechanism are discussed.

The alternative to the returning mechanism can be used to improve greatly the clarity of your programs. A significant problem in many programs that call subroutines occurs when the subroutine alters the contents of a register, but the writer of the calling routine does not think it does. The calling routine puts some number in that register, before calling the subroutine, and expects to find it there after the subroutine returns to this calling routine. It will not be there. Two simple solutions to this problem come to mind. One is to assume all subroutines will change any register, so the calling routine will have to save and restore any values in registers that it wants to save. The other is to assume that the subroutine will save and restore all registers except those used for output parameters. The latter solution is generally more statically efficient because any operation done by a subroutine requires instructions that are stored just once, where the subroutine is stored, whereas any operation done in the calling routine requires instructions to be stored at each place that the subroutine is called. Suppose that a subroutine is called ten times. Then the former solution needs ten pairs of program segments to save and restore the register values. The later solution requires only one pair of segments to save and restore the registers. Because of this, the MC6809 was designed to save efficiently the registers at the beginning of the subroutine, using a PSHS instruction, and to restore them at the end of the subroutine, using a PULS instruction. Moreover, the PULS instruction can also pull the program counter as it pulls the values of the other registers from the stack. The PULS instruction that pulls the program counter is an alternative to the RTS instruction.

Consider the following simple example to add the contents of the register X to that of register Y without altering any register except Y. If we use

```
SUB    TFR    X,D
       LEAY   D,Y
       RTS
```

then the register D and the Z bit are changed. However, if we save CC and D first, we get the desired subroutine.

```
SUB     PSHS    D,CC            Save D and CC
        TFR     X,D
        LEAY    D,Y             (X) + (Y) into Y
        PULS    CC,D,PC         Restore CC, D; return
```

Notice particularly how

```
PULS            CC,D
RTS
```

have been combined into

```
PULS            CC,D,PC
```

This technique for saving registers can be used to save all the registers used in a subroutine that do not return a result of the subroutine. Obviously, if X, Y, and the direct page register are changed, then

```
PSHS            DP,X,Y
```

would be used at the beginning of the subroutine, and

```
PULS            DP,X,Y,PC
```

would be used at the end of the subroutine.

The extended local access of local variables can be used with this technique. Consider the body of the subroutine after the PSHS instruction and before the PULS instruction as a program segment. The local variables are allocated just after the PSHS instruction that saves registers, and are deallocated just before the PULS instruction that returns to the calling routine. You now look at the saved register values as local variables of an outer program segment that includes the PSHS and PULS instruction. Using extended local access, you can read these registers and write into them, too. This allows you to output data in a register, even if the data are saved.

As an example of this, let's look at the preceding example again, now using saved registers as local variables of an outer program segment.

```
REGCC   SET     0
REGD    SET     1
REGX    SET     3
REGY    SET     5
SUB     PSHS    CC,D,X,Y
        LDD     REGX,S          Get caller's X value
        ADDD    REGY,S          Add to caller's Y value
```

```
STD        REGY,S              Place result in caller's location
PULS       CC,D,X,Y,PC
```

Note that this idea was expanded earlier to cover the passing of arguments on the stack. The basic idea is that you just have to know where the data are, relative to the current stack pointer S, in order to access it. Thus you can access the saved registers or the caller's local variables, or the caller's saved registers, just as easily as you can access your own local variables. You are really using the extended local access technique regardless of the variations.

Other return mechanisms were discussed in Section 5-2. We now consider variations of the calling mechanism.

Although BSR is the most efficient instruction to call subroutines, its 8-bit offset limits it to call subroutines within -128 to $+127$ locations of the instruction after that BSR instruction. The LBSR instruction can be used for subroutines that are outside that range. Both instructions are position independent. This means that if the BSR or LBSR instruction and the subroutine itself are in the same ROM, the subroutine will be called correctly wherever the ROM is placed in memory. The JSR instruction using direct or indirect addressing does not have this property and, because of this, should be avoided except for one case.

The one exception is where the subroutine is in a fixed place in memory. A monitor or debugging program is a program used to help you step through a program to find errors in it. These programs are often in ROM at fixed addresses in memory to allow the reset mechanism (that is executed when power is first turned on) to work correctly. Calling a subroutine of the monitor program from outside of the monitor program should be done with a JSR instruction, using direct or indirect addressing, because, wherever the calling routine is assigned in memory, the subroutine location is fixed in absolute memory, not relative to the address of the calling routine. The simple statement that all subroutines must be called using BSR or LBSR to make the program position independent is wrong in this case.

A variation of the calling mechanism uses computed addresses, computed in an index register, say X, and loaded from there into the program counter using

```
JSR        ,X
```

One place where this calling mechanism is used is to call a subroutine with many entry points. In this situation we need to have a standard means to call these different entry points which does not change if the subroutine is modified. If this is not done, a subroutine modification to fix a bug may cause a change in the calling routine because the entry point it used to jump to is now at a different location. This is another example where fixing an error in one part of a program can propagate to other parts of the program, making the software very difficult to maintain. The solution is to have standard places to call which contain the appropriate jumps to the correct entry points. The standard places are at the beginning of the subroutine so that their locations will not be affected by changes in the subroutine. These places contain LBRA instructions which jump to the proper entry point. The LBRA instructions are always the same length regardless of whether or not the entry point can be reached by a BRA. When LBRA instructions are used, the standard places to jump are always some multiple of three bytes from the beginning of the subroutine.

An example will make this clearer. Suppose that we have a subroutine SUB with three entry points, SUB0, SUB1, and SUB2. The layout of the subroutine is shown below

```
SUB       LBRA      SUB0
          LBRA      SUB1
          LBRA      SUB2
SUB0      ....
          .
          .
          .
SUB1      ....
          .
          .
          .
SUB2      ....
          .
          .
          .
          RTS
```

If one wants to call subroutine SUB at its ith entry point, then, assuming that the value of i is in accumulator B, the following calling sequence can be used.

```
PSHS      B
ASLB
ADDB      ,S+           Multiply contents of B by 3
LDX       #SUB
JSR       B,X           Jump to ith entry point
```

Notice that the machine code for the calling sequence stays the same regardless of internal changes to subroutine SUB. If SUB is on a ROM chip, a program could use SUB by using an EQU directive to define the label SUB at the beginning of the program, where the address in the EQU directive is the address of where the ROM chip is placed in memory. Calling sequences like the one above could then be used for any of the entry points in SUB. If a change to SUB is made, say to correct some errors in the code on the chip, only the relative offset needs to be changed in the LBRA instructions to account for changes in the entry points. No changes in the external program are necessary if the address SUB stays the same. Even if the address SUB changes, one only needs to change the EQU directive defining SUB and reassemble the program. This technique is really easy to implement, and limits the interaction between program segments so that changes in one segment do not propagate to other segments. A variation of this technique uses indirect addressing and addresses instead of LBRA instructions. For example, if the layout of SUB has the LBRA instructions replaced by

```
SUB       FDB       SUB0
          FDB       SUB1
          FDB       SUB2
```

then a calling sequence that corresponds to (4) is

```
ASLB                Multiply contents of B by 2
LDX       #SUB
JSR       [B,X]     Jump to ith entry point
```

This variation works well for a subroutine that must be at a fixed place in memory since fewer bytes are used with FDBs than LBRA instructions; however, the technique does not yield a position independent subroutine. Although we described this technique and its variation as useful for a subroutine with several entry points, either works equally well for distinct subroutines.

Now we consider some variations of subroutines. The first is the SWI handler. A *handler* is really just a subroutine that is used to "handle" an interrupt, and the SWI instruction is a software interrupt. We also consider the program segment that keeps the return address in a register rather than on the stack, and a related idea, that of the coroutine.

The ubiquitous *software interrupt* instruction SWI pushes all the registers onto the hardware stack, except S, and then loads the program counter with the contents of locations $FFFA and $FFFB. (The E bit in the CC register is also set *before* the pushes, whereas the I and F bits are set after the pushes.) The following sequence produces the same effect as the SWI instruction except for differences in the way bits in the CC register are set.

```
          PSHS      CC,A,B,DP,X,Y,U,PC
          LEAU      RET,PCR             Get return address
          STU       10,S                Place return address
          JMP       [$FFFA]
RET                 (next instruction)
```

The subroutine at the address contained in $FFFA and $FFFB is called the *SWI handler*. A handler must end in an RTI instruction rather than an RTS instruction since all registers are pushed onto the stack with the SWI instruction. The RTI instruction at the end of an SWI handler does the same thing as the instruction

The SWI instruction differs from the BSR instruction in that the address of the handler is obtained indirectly through the implied address $FFFA. This makes the SWI instruction shorter, in this case 1-byte long.

When you are debugging a program, you can use a program called a *debugger* or a *monitor* to help you debug the program that you are writing. You may want to display the values in some of the registers or memory locations, or to insert some data into some of the registers or memory locations. As used with most debug programs, the SWI handler is a routine in the debug program that displays a prompt character, such as ''*,'' on the terminal and waits for the user to give commands to display or change the values in registers or memory locations. This can be used to display or change any amount of data, or even to modify the program. This SWI instruction is called a *breakpoint*.

A typical monitor program inserts a breakpoint at the start of an instruction by replacing the op code byte with an SWI instruction. The address of the replaced op code byte, as well as the byte itself, are kept in a part of RAM that the monitor uses for this purpose. The program now runs until it encounters the SWI breakpoint. Then the registers might be displayed together with a prompt for further commands to examine or change memory or register contents. It is indispensable that the SWI instruction be 1-byte long to be used as a breakpoint. If you tried to put breakpoints in the program with a LBSR instruction, you would have to remove three bytes. If your program had a branch in it to the second byte being removed, unfathomable things may begin to happen! The problem in your program would be even harder to find now. However, if the single word SWI instruction is used, this cannot happen and the SWI handler call can be made to help you debug the program. One limitation of breakpoints is that the program being debugged must be in RAM. It is not possible to replace an op code in ROM with an SWI instruction. Programs already in ROM are therefore more difficult to debug.

Early in this book, we said that the SWI instruction was to be used at the end of each program. This instruction is really a breakpoint. You cannot turn off a microcomputer at the end of a program, but you can return to the debug program, in order to examine the results of your program. The ''halt'' instruction is just a return to the debug program.

The SWI2 and SWI3 instructions do essentially the same thing as the SWI instruction except that the program counter is loaded from different consecutive addresses, ($FFF4, $FFF5 for SWI2 and $FFF2, $FFF3 for SWI3) and the interrupt bit I is not set. These instructions also happen to be two words long rather than one. The handlers, whose addresses are put there, are used in lieu of subroutines for very commonly used operations needing to save all of the registers. For example, operating system subroutines frequently use these instructions.

The SWI2 and SWI3 instructions can be used to *emulate* other instructions. Emulation means getting exactly the same result, but perhaps taking more time. This technique is often used in minicomputers that are sold in different models that have different costs and speeds. The faster, more expensive model may have an instruction such as floating-point add that is implemented on the slower, cheaper model as SWI2. The same program can be run in both the cheaper and more expensive models. When such an op code is encountered in more expensive models, it results in the execution of the instruction. In cheaper models it results in calling a handler to emulate the instruction. In a sense, the instructions SWI2 and SWI3 are wildcard instructions because they behave a bit like instructions, but are really calls to software handlers. The DEC PDP-11 uses these types of instructions, which they call *trap* instructions, to emulate some instructions in cheaper models that are implemented in hardware in more expensive models.

We digress for a moment to discuss *hardware interrupts*. These are handlers that are called up by an I/O device when that device wants service. An I/O hardware interrupt can occur at any time, and the main program will stop as if the next instruction were an SWI instruction. When the handler has finished, the RTI instruction is executed. This causes the main program to resume exactly where it left off. One exception, the *reset interrupt*, occurs when the reset pin on MC6809 has a low signal put on it. The program counter is then loaded with the contents of locations $FFFE and $FFFF. The reset pin can be put in a circuit such that the pin is put low whenever the power is turned on, thus allowing the microprocessor to start running its program stored in ROM. The hardware interrupt is not all that magical. It is merely a handler that is called by I/O hardware by putting the appropriate signal on some pin of the MC6809. This hardware is outside the direct control of the program that you are writing.

We now consider a program segment that behaves like a subroutine, but the return address is saved in a register rather than on the stack. Although it is not widely used with the MC6809, it is an alternative to be considered, it is used in some form in other computers (such as the TMS 9900), and it leads to the coroutine that is a very interesting alternative. The address is calculated in a register, such as X, and then transferred to the program counter, as in the computed JSR discussed earlier. However, one can also use the pair of instructions EXG X,PC and JMP ,X for a subroutine call and return, respectively, where X contains the computed return address. The appeal of this pair of instructions is that one does not have the return address pushed on top of the stack. This is useful if the purpose of the subroutine is to push or pull some words onto or from the stack. The standard BSR-RTS mechanism leaves the return address on the stack in the way.

As an example, suppose that we want a subroutine to allocate ten words on the stack and initialize them to the value zero. This subroutine can be written

```
INITL    LDA      #10
INIT1    CLR      ,-S
         DECA
         BNE      INIT1
         JMP      ,X
```

where a calling sequence is

```
LEAX     INITL,PCR
EXG      X,PC
```

However, if the subroutine called in this way calls another subroutine in the same way, one has the problem of saving two return addresses. Further nesting of these subroutines makes this problem even more difficult. The stack, of course, automatically saves return addresses for any depth of nesting when one uses the normal BSR-RTS mechanism. For the most part, then, the call and return with EXG X,PC and JMP ,X is limited to subroutines that do not call other subroutines.

The coroutine is not well known, but is an excellent technique for certain applications. Besides, it is interesting and challenging. We consider a particularly simple coroutine mechanism in this section. We will extend this idea at the end of the section. The calling program splits into two parts, which are called *coroutines*. The coat-hanger diagram of Figure 5-9 illustrates the idea of a coroutine. It does this by calling a program segment in one of the ways discussed above used to call a subroutine or handler. That program segment then returns to the main routine, somewhat like a return from a subroutine, but keeping track of the location where the subroutine ended execution. The main routine will then call the subroutine by resuming the subroutine exactly where it left off. The subroutine will be executed until it returns to the main routine, and when it does it will keep track of the location where it stopped. The subroutine and main routine will ping-pong control back and forth in this way until finally the subroutine returns to the main routine in the normal way, not leaving behind any reference to its return address. You should observe that the main program and the subroutine are really equal in stature between the first call and the last return. They are coroutines rather than a main program and a subroutine.

main routine

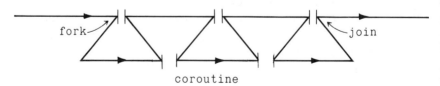

coroutine

FIGURE 5-9. The Forking and Joining of Coroutines

We offer an example of a coroutine that uses the EXG X,PC instruction to swap control between the coroutines. The X index register is reserved to contain the saved program counter of the other routine. In this example we will evaluate the inner product of V and W, returning the result in accumulator D, where, as before, V(1), V(2), W(1), and W(2) are all 1-byte unsigned numbers. We first show this evaluation in a subroutine using global variables V and W.

```
SUB     LDA     V
        LDB     W
        MUL
        PSHS    D
        LDA     V+1
        LDB     W+1
        MUL
        ADDD    ,S++
        RTS
```

In this subroutine the input arguments are passed through an inflexible mechanism (which is through global variables but could as well be any other mechanism). It would be nice to use the flexible and powerful addressing modes of the MC6809 to get the arguments in different ways each time the routine is called. The solution is to return (temporarily) to the main routine each time that a variable is needed, so that the main routine can use possibly different addressing modes to get the data. The subroutine is first modified to use the X register to hold the return address, and is then modified to return to the calling routine to get the input arguments, V(2) and W(2) [V(1) and W(1) can be obtained just before the routine is executed, so there is no reason to return to the main program to get these again]. In particular, the coroutine is

```
COROUT  MUL
        PSHS    D
        EXG     X,PC        Return to main routine to get V(2),W(2)
        MUL
        ADDD    ,S++
        TFR     X,PC
```

and the main routine would look like

```
        LDA     V
        LDB     W
        LEAX    COROUT,PCR
        EXG     X,PC
        LDA     V+1
        LDB     W+1
        EXG     X,PC
```

You can verify that the main routine executes its first four instructions, then the routine COROUT executes its first three, then the main routine executes its last three, then the routine COROUT executes its last three. When COROUT executes its last instruction, the address of the next instruction is not saved in X, but a normal exit is used. The main routine continues below the last EXG instruction listed in the preceding example.

The preceding example could use other addressing modes to get the arguments. For example, the following sequence could be used with COROUT.

```
LDA     ALPHA,S
LDB     #$D1
LEAX    COROUT,PCR
EXG     X,PC
LDA     GETA,S
LDB     GAMMA
EXG     X,PC
```

In this example, different modes of addressing could be used to get the input parameters used in the calculation of the dot product. The common part of the calculation is put in the coroutine COROUT and the varying part that differs each time the calculation is done can be left in the main program as shown in the two examples above. This is especially useful when routines are written to implement high-level language statements such as in BASIC interpreters or in the support packages used for FORTRAN or Pascal.

Coroutines are also used for other purposes. In I/O programming for high-level languages, the high-level language needs local variables and the I/O control program needs local variables. But these are not like local variables that are destroyed upon each exit from the program segment and reallocated and initialized on each entry to the segment, rather they have to be kept from one execution to the next. Look at the preceding example. The two words pushed on the stack in COROUT have to be there while control returns to the main program and when control returns back to COROUT, so that the first product will be correctly added to the second product. It is not possible to reinitialize the local variable saved on the stack when the second part of COROUT is executed. Similarly, I/O routines need this kind of retained local variable. In the programming language C, this kind of local variable is called a static storage variable. In our context, we might call it a *coroutine local variable*.

Coroutines are also used in time sharing. Different programmers write the main and subroutine programs above (but they do not share data and they operate independently of each other). Control passes from one to the other. Each user appears to have a computer that is operating at about half the speed of the real computer in this simple example. The principal advantage, though, is that with one program running, any I/O operation makes the processor wait for its completion. Time sharing allows another coprocess to begin execution when the other is held up by a wait for an I/O operation.

Finally, coroutines are used to write loosely coupled programs. The same programmer can write two routines such as main and COROUT above that are allowed to run rather independently of each other, as in time sharing. For example, one program could list a program on the printer while the other could be used to edit a different program. This way, the user does not have to sit around and wait while a slow printer prints the program. The operation of creating the two independent coprocesses is called *fork*ing and the operation of putting the two parts back together is *join*ing (see Figure 5-9).

In this section we have considered the subroutine and its alternatives. The subroutine is most often called by the BSR or LBSR instruction, but is occasionally called using the JSR instruction with direct or index addressing to achieve position independence. The RTS may be included in the PULS instruction when registers are saved and restored to make the subroutine transparent regarding the alteration of registers. The SWI and RTI instructions call and return from handlers, which are like subroutines but which are also like user-defined machine instructions. The hardware interrupt is a handler that is initiated by a hardware signal rather than a program call. The EXG X,PC instruction may be used to make a program segment work like a subroutine, saving the return address in the index register, and it may be used to implement a particularly simple kind of coroutine. With these tools, you are ready to modularize your programs into subroutines or equivalent program segments, so that each subroutine is more compact and easier to understand, and so that interactions between these subroutines are carefully controlled to prevent unnecessary propagation of errors.

5-5

REENTRANT AND RECURSIVE SUBROUTINES

Having considered interrupts and having studied methods of argument passing, we can now describe a very useful property of subroutines, that of being *reentrant*. A subroutine is reentrant if it can be interrupted, used by the interrupt handler, and then continue correctly with its original calculation after the interrupt handler has returned control to the subroutine. To be reentrant a subroutine generally cannot use global variables and all local variables must be kept on the stack or in registers. Let's now try to see why this general rule is true.

Suppose that the dot product of two vectors passed in X and Y is written as shown below, where the value of the dot product is returned in accumulator D.

```
*        SUBROUTINE DOTPRD
*
*        LOCAL VARIABLES
```

```
*
TERM    RMB   2                          First term of dot product
LOCX    RMB   2                          Copy of the vector in X
LOCY    RMB   2                          Copy of the vector in Y
*
DOTPRD  STX   LOCX,PCR                   Place copy of X into LOCX
        STY   LOCY,PCR                   Place copy of Y into LOCY
        LDA   LOCX,PCR                   First component of LOCX into A
        LDB   LOCY, PCR                  First component of LOCY into B
        MUL                              First term of dot product into D
        STD   TERM,PCR                   Place first term into local variable
        LDA   LOCX+1,PCR                 Second component of LOCX into A
        LDB   LOCY+1,PCR                 Second component of LOCY into B
        MUL                              Second term of dot product into D
        ADDD  TERM,PCR                   Add first term into D to get dot product
        RTS
```

Notice that the local variables TERM, LOCV, and LOCW have all been put into memory like global variables. This prevents DOTPRD from being reentrant for the following reason. If an interrupt occurs and the interrupt handler uses DOTPRD, the values in the local variables can be written over making the result of the original calculation invalid when the interrupt handler returns control to DOTPRD. Notice that if we put these local variables on the stack, as we did originally in Section 5-2, this problem does not occur because new copies of these local variables are kept on the stack when DOTPRD is used in the interrupt handler. Had we wanted to, we could also have kept the local variable TERM in the register U by changing several of the instructions. This version of DOTPRD would also be reentrant because the contents of U are saved on the stack when an interrupt occurs and restored when the handler is finished. This example then illustrates one important principle. You must put local variables on the stack or in registers to get reentrant subroutines.

If one can see why DOTPRD above is *not* reentrant, one should be able to see why passing parameters through global variables or before the subroutine entry point lead generally to subroutines that are not reentrant. Passing the parameters through registers, after the call, on the stack or in a table will generally yield reentrant subroutines if local variables are stored on the stack or in registers. When passing parameters in a table, however, it is tacitly assumed that the interrupt handler uses a different table from that being used by the interrupted subroutine. Although passing parameters after the call leads to subroutines that are reentrant, one should take care to notice that subroutines that call a subroutine, and pass parameters to that subroutine after the call, are not themselves generally reentrant. (See the problems at the end of the chapter.)

A subroutine is *recursive* if it calls itself. For example, consider the following subroutine, which computes $1 + 2 + \ldots + (A)$.

```
SUM        CMPA      #1
           BEQ       S1
           PSHS      A
           DECA
           BSR       SUM
           ADDA      ,S+
S1         RTS
```

Recursive subroutines can push many bytes on the stack before they return. The effect of this is that much more memory is used by the subroutine than is indicated by the number of bytes used to store the instructions because local variables and return addresses are being pushed on the stack with each recursive call. It takes little imagination to find a better nonrecursive subroutine to replace the one above. We will, however, have a more natural example of a recursive subroutine in Chapter 6.

The virtue of being reentrant is quite important, and fairly easy to achieve in the MC6809. It is important because a subroutine that you write today may be just the one that you need at a later time as a subroutine called from within an interrupt handler. If it is not reentrant, and you do not know that, then at some time, according to Murphy's law, you will be executing your subroutine when an interrupt occurs, and the interrupt handler will use the same subroutine. That bug is very hard to find. It is better to write all your subroutines as reentrant routines. Recursion is a nice idea. Some elegant programs have recursive subroutines. However, in microcomputers we prefer to avoid recursion because it uses up memory by storing return addresses and local variables on the stack. In effect, the stack is used like a primitive counter to count executions of the subroutine.

In our examples and problems, we will generally require all subroutines to be not only statically efficient and position independent, but also reentrant.

5-6

TESTING

One of the major uses of subroutines is to modularize a program so that each module is manageably small and testable. We discuss this very important idea in this section. First, a bit of philosophy is spun about top-down design and reasons for it. We present an example to show how this technique is used. The notion of a driver and a stub are then discussed to show some tools for top-down design and testing.

The introduction to this chapter suggested that the subroutine was a kind of machine instruction that you write to your own specifications. These subroutines are called by routines that can themselves be subroutines, building up your entire program. This gives you a design philosophy of writing programs. Instead of immediately banging away writing code, you should think of the program that you want to write as a new instruction that you want to add to the instruction set.

Just as you would like an instruction to be described to you, you then describe this new instruction without writing any code. The basic parts of the description are the input and output parameters, their sizes and restrictions, and the algorithm that the instruction executes. The algorithm can be a mathematical equation, a FORTRAN, Pascal, or other high-level language description of the calculation that you want to do, or it can be a word description. As a FORTRAN or Pascal program, the algorithm should be interpreted with some degree of freedom. You should say: "Do this program, or any other program that gets the same outputs for the same inputs, but you do not have to do it exactly the same way as this program does it." As a word description, it should be accurate enough for some impartial judge to determine if a particular program is or is not an implementation of the description. Naturally, there must be at least one way to carry out the description. This defines the new instruction.

The main specification is broken into smaller components, one level down. Each component becomes a subroutine, or at least a program segment. It should be a subroutine if it is used many times in the larger component. This improves static efficiency. If it is used just once, it may be a subroutine to simplify testing, or it may be just a program segment. In either case, the new smaller components should be described just like the original definition of the program was described. Identify local variables, input and output variables, and the algorithm that the smaller component executes. This is continued until the smallest unit of execution, the machine instruction, is defined. It is, of course, necessary to "land" on existing instructions at this level of decomposition, lest you have to design a new microcomputer to implement these desired instructions.

The programming of such a design can mirror the design philosophy. The first step is usually to write the main program as a series of subroutine calls to the next lower-level components, but these components are first written as *stubs*. A stub is a subroutine that you write in lieu of the subroutine that does the component's work. About all that a stub is supposed to do is to let you know that it is executed. In a high-level language, a stub may be a print statement that prints the line "COMPONENT A IS EXECUTED." It may also allow the programmer to read some of the input parameters and to enter some of the output parameters that are used in the main program to alter its sequencing of operations. In assembly language, the easiest thing to do is to put breakpoints at the start of subroutines. The main program can then be executed and the sequence of calls to the subroutines can be observed and verified. Again, as in high-level language programs, the breakpoint can be used to examine input parameters and set output parameters of the subroutine that are used to alter the control of the main program. Stubs can be used at lower levels, just like at this level, after the stub at the higher level is converted to a working subroutine.

Stubs allow you to check the logic of the main routine in terms of lower-level components before the lower-level components are even written.

We now demonstrate these ideas with an example. The following algorithm has been used to evaluate the speed and accuracy of various BASIC and Pascal compilers on different microcomputers because it is a nice but simple mixture of additions and multiplies. (An algorithm used to measure performance is called a *benchmark*.) As mentioned earlier, we will specify the problem and algorithm with a high-level language. Although it is unnecessary, we will use both FORTRAN and Pascal, so that most readers will be able to use one of the languages to understand the problem and algorithm. We write the program first in FORTRAN and then in Pascal.

```
       PROGRAM NAME(INPUT,OUTPUT)
       PRINT 10
10     FORMAT ('Enter N')
       READ 20,AN
20     FORMAT (F10.4)
       PRINT 30
30     FORMAT ('Enter C')
       READ 20,C
       S = 0.
       DELTA = 0.
       DO 40 I = 1,INT(AN)
       DELTA = DELTA + C
40     S = S + DELTA * DELTA
       PRINT 50,DELTA,S
50     FORMAT ('DELTA = ',F10.4,' S = ',F10.4)
       END

       PROGRAM 'Name';
       VAR c,delta,n,s:REAL;
       BEGIN WRITELN('Enter N') ; READLN(n) ;
         WRITELN('Enter C') ; READLN(c) ;
         S := 0. ;
         delta := 0. ;
         FOR I := 1 TO INT(n) DO
         BEGIN
           delta := delta + c ;
           s := s + delta * delta
         END ;
         WRITELN ('Delta = ',delta,' s = ',s)
       END.
```

Analyzing the algorithm, we detect the need for subroutines to carry out program segments that will be used more than once. A program segment to input a floating-point number is used more than once, so it will be a subroutine. We will call it FPIN for "floating-point input." Other parts of the program will be coded simply as program segments in this example, although some could be coded as subroutines to facilitate testing them, as we will describe below. We derive the need for subroutines as indicated in the following diagram.

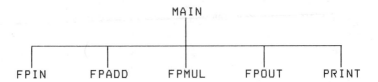

Here FPIN is the floating-point input subroutine, FPADD is the floating-point add subroutine, FPMUL is the floating-point multiply subroutine, FPOUT is the floating-point output subroutine, and PRINT is a subroutine to print ASCII character strings like 'Enter N'.

Upon writing the main program, we need to determine the way that variables will be stored and arguments passed. Variables of the MAIN program will be stored as local variables, and will be four bytes long. The arguments will be called by reference and will be passed through the X register. The first portion of the main program will look this way:

```
        ORG     0
MSIZE   SET     $4000           Maximum size of available memory
C       SET     0
DELTA   SET     C+4
N       SET     DELTA+4
SS      SET     N+4
SIZE    SET     SS+4
S1      FCC     'Enter N'
        FCB     $0D             Carriage return
S2      FCC     'Enter C'
        FCB     $0D             Carriage return
MAIN    LDS     #MSIZE-SIZE     Initialize stack; allocation for LVs
        LEAX    S1,PCR          Get address of message 'Enter N'
        BSR     PRINT           Print it out
        LEAX    N,S             Address of local variable N
        BSR     FPIN            Read in N
        LEAX    S2,PCR          Get address of message 'Enter C'
        BSR     PRINT           Print it out
        LEAX    SS,S            Address of local variable SS
        BSR     FPIN            Read in C
                .
                .
                .
```

A stub for a subroutine such as FPIN would be coded as

```
FPIN    RTS
```

and an SWI instruction (breakpoint) would be inserted in place of the RTS instruction when the program is debugged. The breakpoint would permit the programmer to examine the contents of the X register to see where the result is to be stored, and then to insert manually the value of the number being input, such as N or C, using a command in the debug program to change the contents of memory locations.

The FPIN subroutine can be analyzed just like the MAIN program. We can determine that a subroutine will be needed to input an ASCII character that represents a number, since that operation will be used many times, and that the FPADD and FPMUL subroutines needed for MAIN will also be called within FPIN. As in the analysis of MAIN, we can write FPIN as a routine using stubs for the ASCII character input, FPADD, and FPMUL subroutines.

This example will be considered in Chapter 7. Some of the subroutines in it will be coded and can be used if you wish to run this program in the laboratory.

The opposite approach to building the main module first is to write the smallest module (lowest-level subroutine) first. You can write a *driver* to test this subroutine before the next higher-level subroutine is designed. A driver merely feeds the subroutine its arguments, calls it up, and takes the output arguments from it. In a high-level language, a driver will often consist of one or more INPUT statements to let you set up inputs to the subroutine, the subroutine call, and one or more PRINT statements to print the values of the output parameters. In assembly language programs, breakpoints are set before and after the subroutine calling sequence. When the breakpoint is executed before the subroutine calling sequence, the input parameters are set by the programmer using the breakpoint handler. A breakpoint after the subroutine calling sequence is used to display the output parameters. A driver can be used to test the subroutines, at the lowest level or at higher levels. It allows you to verify that a module performs to the specifications which you set for that module.

The size of a module can be important. We demonstrate this with an analogy to a mathematical problem. Compare the solution of a problem with one unknown, such as

$$2*Y = 11$$

with a problem with three unknowns, such as

$$3*X + 2*Y + Z = 17$$
$$X - Y - Z = -3$$
$$2*X + 3*Y - Z = -4$$

Solving three equations with one unknown is much easier than solving an equation with three unknowns, as the example above suggests. This analogy suggests that a module to be tested should have one unknown. It should not be so large that there are several unknowns, but it should have one unknown. Although the question of what an unknown is is not well defined in this discussion (because a mature programmer may have no difficulty with a segment of code that baffles a novice programmer, and a known to one programmer may be an unknown to another), it is important to try this approach. Our experience with a course on interfacing is that those students who used this "divide-and-conquer" approach could complete a laboratory assignment in three to four hours, whereas those students who wanted to solve for all unknowns at one time spent over 30 hours trying to complete the assignment.

Testing a module with a driver should be done with considerable thought. On the one hand, one test of a module is almost always inadequate. You do not want a program that works for only one set of values and "blows up" for other sets. At the other extreme, a simple addition program, adding two 32-bit numbers, has 2^{64} different possible inputs. To test all possibilities would be longer than you can wait! So you have to test some reasonable and judicious set of input parameter values. Typically, one tests the endpoints of each range. In an ADD subroutine, test inputs that just produce acceptable results, that just produce overflow, and that just produce zero. This sort of approach would usually be considered adequate for testing most modules using a driver.

This section presented a few ideas that are useful in writing large programs that can be reliably tested. The idea of top-down design is to understand the problem thoroughly before you begin writing code, and to write the main program first before the subroutines are coded. This permits you to define the subroutines, as the main program was defined, before you start testing them. Top-down design has been demonstrated to be faster to program and debug, especially for large programs. The idea of a subroutine, and a driver for testing it, was also introduced. This technique is very valuable for writing programs for interfacing to I/O hardware. It makes it possible to test parts of the hardware and software in a simple environment before the parts are combined. These concepts show how subroutines are indispensable for testing large programs and programs that interface to I/O hardware.

5-7

DOCUMENTATION

We begin this section with a list of coding techniques which, hopefully, will make your programs or subroutines more readable. The emphasis here is on clarity rather than efficiency.

1. Use meaningful labels which are as short as possible.

2. Explain what the labels mean if they are used as variables. This would usually be done in the program or subroutine header.
3. One should try to write code so that the program flow is progressively forward except for loops. This means that one should avoid using unconditional jumps or branches in any way that breaks up the forward flow of the program.
4. Keep segments short, probably 20 instructions or less. If not commented in some way, at least use an ''*'' to break up the code into segments for the reader.
5. Straightforward code is better than shorter, tricky code.
6. Including lucid, meaningful comments is the best way to make your program clear. Either a comment line or a comment with an instruction is acceptable, but it is probably best to use complete lines of comments sparingly. Do not make the sophomore mistake of ''garbaging up'' your program with useless comments, such as explaining what simple instructions do.
7. With subroutines, always give a typical calling sequence if parameters are being passed on the stack, after the call or in a table. This is virtually the only direct way that the programmer has of indicating the order and size of parameters being passed to or from the subroutine. In addition, always indicate how registers are changed in a subroutine.

Finally, one should consider attaching a flowchart with each subroutine as part of the documentation. Flowcharts are particularly useful for detailing complex control sequences. For example, the rather impenetrable sequence

```
        CMPY    #11708
        BEQ     L1
        BMI     T1
        CMPB    #3
        BEQ     L2
        CMPB    #6
        BEQ     L3
        BRA     L4
T1      TSTA
        BMI     L5
        BRA     L6
```

becomes more fathomable when displayed as part of the subroutine flowchart shown in Figure 5-10.

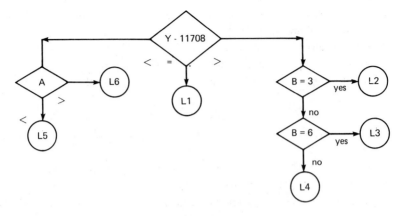

FIGURE 5-10. Flowchart for Example Control Sequence

FURTHER EXAMPLES AND DISCUSSION ON SUBROUTINES

We now look at several examples to illustrate the ideas discussed in the earlier sections. This section offers a slightly different perspective on some of the topics that were discussed in detail in earlier sections.

The first example illustrates a FORTRAN oriented subroutine and the use of macros to generate the calling sequence. The specification of the subroutine IFSUB is to behave like the FORTRAN statement

```
IF(ALPHA) THEN 10,20,30
```

or the Pascal statement

```
IF(ALPHA < 0) THEN GOTO 10
ELSE IF (ALPHA =0) THEN GOTO 20
ELSE GOTO 30.
```

The variable ALPHA is a 4-byte two's complement number, and this parameter is called by reference and passed in an in-line argument list. The 4-byte number beginning at address ALPHA is stored with the most significant bytes first. The high-level language statements with labels 10, 20, and 30 will be the assembly language addresses L10, L20, and L30. These addresses will also be passed in the in-line list after the address for ALPHA. The subroutine is to save and restore all registers that are used in it except the condition code register. The calling sequence for this subroutine is

```
        LBSR    IFSUB
        FDB     ALPHA
        FDB     L10
        FDB     L20
        FDB     L30
```

(A general calling sequence using a macro will be introduced below.) The subroutine, following the algorithm suggested by the flowchart shown in Figure 5-11, is shown below. Note that the LDD instruction sets the N and Z condition code bits that can be tested by the BMI/BPL and BEQ/BNE instructions. Because V is put equal to zero by LDD, all of the signed branches work also. (Do not, however, use the unsigned branches, such as BHI, BLO and so forth after a load instruction.)

```
*           SUBROUTINE IFSUB
*
*    IFSUB transfers program control to address ARG2 if
*    the 4-byte signed number at address ARG1 (called by
*    reference) is negative, to address ARG3 if zero
*    and to address ARG4 if strictly positive.
*    All registers except CC are unchanged. The calling
*    sequence is
*
*
*           BSR     IFSUB
*           FDB     ARG1,ARG2,ARG3,ARG4
*
IFSUB    PSHS    D,X,Y           Save registers used
         LDX     6,S             Return address into X (skip six bytes)
         LDY     ,X              Address of 4-byte number into Y
         LDD     ,Y              Get most significant two bytes
         BLT     LESS            If less than 0, go to ARG2
         BNE     GREAT           If not zero, go to ARG4
         LDD     2,Y             Least significant two bytes into D
         BNE     GREAT           If not zero, go to ARG4
         LDX     4,X             ARG3 into X
         BRA     EXIT            Put X into return address and exit
LESS     LDX     2,X             ARG2 into X
         BRA     EXIT            Put X into return address and exit
GREAT    LDX     6,X             ARG4 into X
EXIT     STX     6,S             Put X into return address
         PULS    D,X,Y,PC        Restore registers and return
```

Note the simplicity of the flowchart in Figure 5-11 and how it clarifies this program. Note that the requirement to save and restore all registers used in the subroutine is easy to carry out. The addresses to be jumped to are simply put in the place where the return address is stored, and the registers, including the program counter, are restored. Because this subroutine is rather simple, we

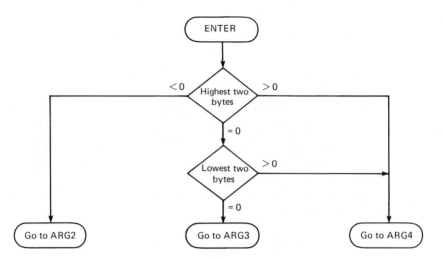

FIGURE 5-11. Flowchart for Subroutine IFSUB

dispensed with using labels for offsets from X to identify parameters. This also eliminated the SET directives to define these labels.

To conclude the first example, we show how to use a macro to write the calling sequence. Any subroutine that requires four arguments, each of which is a 2-byte constant, can be called using the following macro.

```
CALL      MACR
          LBSR      \0
          FDB       \1,\2,\3,\4
          ENDM
```

The call to the subroutine above would be

```
CALL      IFSUB,ALPHA,L10,L20,L30
```

Observe that this macro will expand into code that is essentially the same as the calling sequence for the subroutine that was given earlier. Also note how this assembly language statement looks almost like the FORTRAN statement

```
IF(ALPHA) 10,20,30
```

Again, this macro can be used with any subroutine that needs four 2-byte constant arguments. You can also use conditional assembly commands to write a macro that can handle a variable number of arguments. (See the problems at the end of this chapter.)

In our second example we want to return the value of one of 256 bits stored consecutively in bytes 0 through 31, where bits 0 through 7 are in the first byte, bits 8 through 15 are in the second byte, and so on. The numbering of bits within any particular byte is always right to left and, assuming that the input argument i is passed on the stack, the value of the ith bit will be returned in C.

To improve static efficiency, at perhaps the expense of clarity, we will make the subroutine balance the stack for the calling sequence. This means that the calling sequence will not have the customary instructions at the end to delete the local variables used to pass the parameters. The subroutine will do that. Assuming that the value of i is in accumulator B and that the ith bit is put into the least significant bit of A, the calling sequence is

```
PSHS    B
LBSR    GETBIT
ROLA
```

and the subroutine would appear as follows.

```
*          SUBROUTINE GETBIT
*
*    GETBIT gets the ith bit from byte locations 0 to
*    31, putting it into the C bit. GETBIT changes
*    registers CC, D, X, and Y. Assuming that the value
*    of i is in A and that we branch to L1 if the ith
*    bit is 1, the calling sequence is
*
*          PSHS    A
*          BSR     GETBIT
*          BCS     L1
*
GETBIT  PULS    Y          Return address into Y
        LDB     ,S         Value of i into B
        LSRB               Divide contents of B by 8; B contains
        LSRB               the byte number of the byte holding
        LSRB               the ith bit
        LDX     #0         Point X to vector of bits
        LDA     B,X        Byte containing ith bit into A
        PULS    B          Value of i into B; balance stack
        ANDB    #7         Get bit position in word containing ith bit
*
LOOP    LSRA               Get ith bit into C
        DECB
        BPL     LOOP
*
        JMP     ,Y         Return
```

Notice that the calling sequence in the subroutine header is not the same one that was used earlier. Any calling sequence is suitable for the header as long as it shows the order of the parameters, how the parameters are loaded and unloaded, and how the stack is being balanced. In this subroutine we have passed one of the input parameters through a global variable, namely, the table of bits at locations 0 through 31. Even though we have used a global variable here, the subroutine is still reentrant because the calling routine does not change it. (See the problems at the end of the chapter.) Note that the carry bit is the easiest register to pass a 1-bit result. It is often used to indicate an error by setting the carry if an error is found and clearing the carry if no error is found. Notice that the program counter was pulled from the stack into Y at the beginning of the subroutine and JMP ,Y is used to exit the subroutine. Letting the subroutine balance the stack is more statically efficient than the technique suggested in the section on passing parameters because the calling sequence is shortened. For example, if the subroutine had not balanced the stack, the calling sequence would be something like

```
PSHS    B
LBSR    GETBIT
ROLA              Rotate C into LS bit of A
LEAS    1,S       Balance stack
```

If the subroutine is called ten times, the LEAS instruction at the end of the calling sequence is omitted at a savings of 20 bytes. However, this method is not as clear as the one introduced in the section on passing parameters, and it should not be used except where static efficiency is most important.

The next example that we present uses the SWI3 instruction to emulate a multiply instruction. We want a multiply instruction that works something like the ADDD n,S instruction, but instead multiplies the unsigned 16-bit value in D with the unsigned 16-bit value at locations n,S and n+1,S and leaves the unsigned 16-bit integer product in D. If the product is correct, the carry is cleared, but if it is in error because the real product is larger than sixteen bits, the carry is set. The SWI3 instruction will be used with the calling sequence

```
SWI3
FDB         n
```

which calls the SWI3 handler shown in Figure 5-12. To call this handler, the address of the first instruction is put in locations $FFF2 and $FFF3. (See Appendix 4 to see how to do this with the TRS-80 Color Computer.) The handler works this way. If the number in D is denoted a:b, the number at n,S is denoted c and the number at (n+1),S is denoted d, the product is determined as shown below.

$$
\begin{array}{rcc}
 & a & b \\
* & c & d \\
\hline
 & (b & * & d) \\
(a & * & d) \\
(b & * & c) \\
(a & * & c) \\
\hline
\end{array}
$$

$\longleftarrow \qquad \longrightarrow$

(keep only this part)

An overflow occurs for the handler if:

1. The bytes a and c are nonzero.
2. The high bytes of the products a * d or b * c are nonzero.
3. The addition of the low bytes of a * d and b * c with the high byte of b * d produces a carry.

These conditions are tested and, if they occur, the carry is returned set; otherwise, the carry is returned cleared and the 2-byte product is returned in D.

The SWI3 handler is shown in Figure 5-12. It uses the register values that are automatically saved by the execution of the SWI3 instruction as parameters. The condition code register is on top of the stack, accumulators A and B are one byte and two bytes below the top of the stack, and the program counter is ten bytes below the top of the stack. Equate statements are used to let the programmer use register names as offsets to the stack pointer. The output is in A and B, and these bytes on the stack are used to save the product that will be returned to the calling routine. The input values of A and B are saved in the Y register. This makes it convenient to add the high byte of b * d to the low bytes of a * d and b * c, and to reload the input parameters from Y into D each time they are needed.

Except for the loading of the input values, the calculation of a * d and of b * c is identical—they are multiplied, the low byte is added to the value of A that is saved on the stack, and the high byte of the product is examined to see if it is zero. Therefore, the two computations are "factored" into a subroutine UPDATE for static efficiency. Note that inside UPDATE, the saved registers are accessed with an offset of 2, as the saved value of A is accessed by ACCA + 2,S. This offset accounts for the return address of the subroutine UPDATE and is another example of the use of extended local access.

Thinking about the SWI3 handler, consider the issue of classifying the mode being used. Is the result being passed by registers or on the stack? To the calling routine, the technique is clearly passing in registers, but within the handler, the technique appears to be the same as passing on the stack. Which is it? Well, it really does not matter. The main reason for classification of techniques is not to generate questions to confound the student on the final exam, but to open up the world of alternatives to him or her in a well structured way so that they can be comprehended.

Our last example provides another illustration of how one uses labels when parameters are being passed on the stack and when local variables are being used in the subroutine. We begin with a simple version of DOTPRD.

```
*                    SUBROUTINE DOTPRD
*
*    DOTPRD computes the dot product of vectors V and W
```

```
*    which have two 1-byte unsigned components. The
*    vectors V and W and the dot product DTPD are passed
*    by reference. Assuming that the address of V is in
*    X, the address of W is in Y, and the address of
*    DTPD is in U, the calling sequence is
*
*              PSHS      X,Y,U
*              BSR       DOTPRD
*              LEAS      6,S
*
*    Registers A, B, CC, X, and Y are changed.
*
*                        LOCAL VARIABLES
*
TERM          SET       0                   First term of the dot product
NBYTES        SET       2
*
*                        PARAMETERS
*
RADDR         SET       2                   Return address
ADDRV         SET       4                   Address of V
ADDRW         SET       6                   Address of W
ADDRDP        SET       8                   Address of DTPD
*
DOTPRD        LEAS      -NBYTES,S           Allocation for local variables
              LDX       ADDRV,S             Point X to V
              LDY       ADDRW,S             Point Y to W
              LDA       ,Y+
              LDB       ,Y+
              MUL
              STD       TERM,S              First term into local variabale
              LDB       ,X
              LDA       ,Y
              MUL
              ADDD      TERM,S              Dot product into D
              STD       [ADDRDP,S]          Dot product into output parameter
              LEAS      NBYTES,S            Deallocate local variables
              RTS
```

Since each parameter or local variable is two bytes long, we computed the values of the labels ourselves, as this is easier than putting in the additional information to let the assembler do it. This method effectively includes the calculations that would be done using extended local access for the parameters. Notice how the use of generic symbols (symbols that do not refer to specific addresses or offsets in the subroutine) V, W, and DTPD makes the description of the subroutine and calling sequence clearer.

Using extended local access for the parameters, the subroutine can be written as shown in Figure 5-13. The extended local access version needs an additional offset of 2 to account for the return address. As it is written, the labels for the

```
*              SWI3       HANDLER
*
* This handler multiplies the 16-bit unsigned number a:b in D by
* the 16-bit unsigned number c:d at n,S. If the higher two bytes
* of the product are zero, C is cleared upon return and the
* 2-byte product returned in D; otherwise, C is returned set.
* Registers A and B are changed. The call to the subroutine is of
* the form
*
*              SWI3
*              FDB        n
*
CCR       EQU      0                   Condition code register
ACCA      EQU      1                   Accumulator A
PCTR      EQU      10                  Return value of PC
NBYTES    EQU      12
*
          TFR      D,Y                 Save D in Y
          LDX      PCTR,S              Get return address
          LDD      ,X++                n into D; adjust return address
          STX      PCTR,S              Place return address
          LEAX     D,S                 Position X for c:d
          TST      NBYTES,X            Is c equal to zero?
          BEQ      GOOD
          TST      ACCA,S              Is a equal to zero?
          BEQ      GOOD
          BSR      ERROR               a*c <> 0; set C and return
GOOD      TFR      Y,D                 Put b in B
          LDA      NBYTES+1,X          Put d in A
          MUL                          b*d into D
          STD      ACCA,S              Save b* d on stack
*
          TFR      Y,D                 Put c into A
          LDB      NBYTES+1,X          Put d into B
          BSR      UPDATE
          TFR      Y,D                 Put b into B
          LDA      NBYTES,X            Put c into A
          BSR      UPDATE
          RTI
*
UPDATE    MUL
          TSTA
          BEQ      CONT
ERROR     LDA      CCR+2,S
          ORA      #1                  Set carry
          STA      CCR+2,S
          RTS
CONT      ADDB     ACCA+2,S
          STB      AAAC+2,S
          BCS      ERROR               Set carry if overflow
          RTS
```

FIGURE 5-12. SWI3 Handler

```
*                   SUBROUTINE DOTPRD
*
* DOTPRD computes the dot product of vectors V and W which have
* two 1-byte unsigned components. The vectors V and W and the dot
* product DTPD are passed by reference. Assuming that the address
* of V is in X, the address of W is in Y, and the address of DTPD
* is in U, the calling sequence is
*
*                   PARAMETERS
*
ADDRV     SET       0                    Address of V
ADDRW     SET       2                    Address of W
ADDRDP    SET       4                    Address of DTPD
PSIZE     SET       6                    Size of parameter list
*
*         LEAS      -PSIZE,S
*         STX       ADDRV,S
*         STY       ADDRW,S
*         STU       ADDRDP,S
*         BSR       DOTPRD
*         LEAS      PSIZE,S
*
* Registers A, B, CC, X and Y are changed.
*
*                   LOCAL VARIABLES
*
TERM      SET       0                    First term of the dot product
NBYTES    SET       2
*
DOTPRD    LEAS      -NBYTES,S                Allocation for local variables
          LDX       ADDRV+NBYTES+2,S         Point X to V
          LDY       ADDRW+NBYTES+2,S         Point Y to W
          LDA       ,X+
          LDB       ,Y+
          MUL
          STD       TERM,S                   First term into local variable
          LDB       ,X
          LDA       ,Y
          MUL
          ADDD      TERM,S                   Dot product into D
          STD       [ADDRDP+NBYTES+2,S]      Place dot product
          LEAS      NBYTES,S                 Deallocate local variables
          RTS
```

FIGURE 5-13. Subroutine DOTPRD

parameters are the same in the subroutine and the given calling sequence, but if the labels are used in different ways in other parts of the program, the SET directives must be repeated with each use of the calling sequence. If one wanted to keep the subroutine from changing any registers, we could put

```
PSHS        CC ,D ,X ,Y
```

at the beginning of DOTPRD, replace RTS with

```
PULS        CC ,D ,X ,Y ,PC
```

and replace each occurrence of NBYTES + 2 with NBYTES + 9. This, of course, is just using another level of extended local access to save registers as described in Section 5-4. We again remind the reader that with a simple subroutine, using extended local access is more work. However, if you imagine a subroutine with ten parameters and ten local variables, this method becomes very helpful.

For completeness, the subroutine is rewritten in Figure 5-14 using stack markers. Notice that an additional offset of 2 is required to access the parameters because of the return address. In this simple subroutine, we did not need to make room on the stack for the subroutine stack marker because it was kept in X. We also could have eliminated the STX instruction for the same reason. However, in a more complicated subroutine, we might have needed X for something else than just holding the stack marker. In this situation, we would replace an instruction such as

```
LDY         ADDRV + 2 ,X
```

with

```
LDY         0 ,2
LDY         ADDRV+2 ,Y
```

If the calling sequence uses the same set of labels for the parameters as used by DOTPRD, then, as noted earlier, the set directives will typically have to be repeated as part of the calling sequence. Finally, it is also possible to use stack markers and not change any registers. (See the problems at the end of this chapter.)

These examples bring together some of the key ideas that were introduced in this chapter. We saw different alternatives to subroutines, different ways to pass parameters, and different uses of local variables. Although the earlier sections strove to simplify the concepts, real subroutines use a mixture of these concepts that are hard to classify. However, classifying all of the mixtures is unnecessary since knowing the different basic techniques lets you choose one, or a mixture of ones, to tackle your problem.

```
*                    SUBROUTINE DOTPRD
*
* DOTPRD computes the dot product of vectors V and W which have
* two 1-byte unsigned components. The vectors V and W and the dot
* product DTPD are passed by reference. Assuming that the address
* of V is in X, the address of W is in Y, and the address of DTPD
* is in U, the calling sequence is
*
*                    PARAMETERS
*
SMCS        SET         0               Stack marker for calling sequence
ADDRV       SET         2               Address of V
ADDRW       SET         4               Address of W
ADDRDP      SET         6               Address of DTPD
PSIZE       SET         8               Size of parameter list
*
*           TFR         S,D
*           LEAS        -PSIZE,S
*           STD         SMCS,S
*           STX         ADDRV,S
*           STY         ADDRW,S
*           STU         ADDRP,S
*           BSR         DOTPRD
*           LEAS        PSIZE,S
*
* Registers A, B, CC, X, Y, and U are changed.
*
*                    LOCAL VARIABLES
*
SMSUB       SET         0               Stack marker for subroutine
TERM        SET         2               First term of the dot product
NBYTES      SET         4
*
DOTPRD      TFR         S,X             Stack marker for parameters
            LEAS        -NBYTES,S       Allocation for local variables
            STX         SMSUB,S         Place stack marker
            LDY         ADDRV+2,X       Point Y to V
            LDU         ADDRW+2,X       Point U to W
            LDA         ,Y+
            LDB         ,U+
            MUL
            STD         TERM,S          First term into local variable
            LDB         ,Y
            LDA         ,U
            MUL
            ADDD        TERM,S          Dot product into D
            STD         [ADDRDP+2,X]    Place dot product
            LEAS        NBYTES,S        Deallocate local variables
            RTS
```

FIGURE 5-14. Subroutine DOTPRD

SUMMARY AND FURTHER READING

This chapter introduced the subroutine. It was dissected into parts to show alternative techniques for each part. Local variables were studied along with alternatives for accessing local variables of nested program segments. Calling and returning mechanisms were studied and the principal one, using BSR and RTS, was shown to have several alternatives, including ones that save the registers and restore them efficiently. Alternatives such as SWI and EXG X,PC were studied, and the coroutine was introduced. We then turned to the techniques that are used to pass arguments. The register, global, stack, in-line argument list, before the subroutine entry point, and table techniques were considered. We then considered the idea of reentrancy and recursion. We considered the really powerful ideas of top-down design and of testing using drivers. We considered the issues important to documentation, and then we brought these ideas together with some examples.

The reader may wish to pursue some of the topics in more detail. Coroutines are discussed in the last chapter of *Microcomputer Interfacing* (Harold S. Stone, Addison-Wesley Publishing Co., Inc., Reading, Mass., 1982), and stack markers are used extensively in Chapter 5 of *Programming Microprocessor Interfaces for Control and Instrumentation* (Michael Andrews, Prentice-Hall, Inc., Englewood Cliffs, N.J., 1982). The book *Computer Organization and Assembly Language Programming* (James Peterson, Academic Press Inc., New York, 1978) contains a deeper discussion of calling parameters by reference and by name.

You should now be able to write subroutines, call them, and pass arguments to them in an effective manner. You should be prepared to use them in the following chapters to manipulate data structures, perform arithmetic, and interface to I/O hardware. Moreover, you should know how to approach a problem using top-down design, or how to test a module with a driver. The need for the last two techniques is not apparent to the student who writes a lot of small programs and never faces the problem of writing a large program. When he or she does face that problem without the tools that we have introduced, inefficiencies and chaos generally will be the result. We introduced these techniques early and suggest that you use them whenever you can do so, even if they are not absolutely needed.

PROBLEMS

1. Is the subroutine of Figure 5-15 reentrant? Is it position independent? Indicate the changes necessary, if any, to make it have both these properties. Can you make any changes in the subroutine as it is now written to save instructions?

```
*                           SUBROUTINE CVBTD
*
* CVBTD takes the 16-bit unsigned number in D and converts
* it to five ASCI decimal digits at the address passed in X,
* most significant digits first. Registers A, B, CC, X, and Y
* are changed.
*
            DPT         S
*
K           FDB         10000
            FDB         1000
            FDB         100
            FDB         10
            FDB         1
*
* We subtract as many multiplies of each power of ten as we can
* from D without getting a carry. The number obtained, after
* ASCII conversion, becomes the ASCII decimal coefficient of
* that power of 10.
*
CVBTD       LDY         #K                  Point Y to constants
            LEAS        -1,S                Allocated space for local variable
CBD1        CLR         ,S                  Initialize counter
CBD2        SUBD        ,Y
            BCS         CBD3
            INC         ,S                  Increment counter
            BRA         CBD2
*
CBD3        ADDD                            Restore remainder
            ,Y
*
            PSHS        A
            LDA         1,S                 Get counter
            ADDA        #$30                ASCII conversion
            STA         ,X+
            PULS        A
*
            LEAY        2,Y                 Point Y to next constant
            CMPY        #K+10
            BNE         CBD1
            PULS        A,PC                Balance stack and return
```

FIGURE 5-15. Subroutine CVBTD

2.   Write a reentrant, position independent subroutine SEARCH which finds the number of
      times NUM that the integer K appears in the vector Z of length N and precision 1.
      Assuming that the address of Z is in X, the value of K is in A, the value of N is in B,
      and the value of NUM is to be placed in A, the parameters are passed on the stack with
      the calling sequence

          PSHS   A,B,X

```
LEAS      -1,S          Hole for NUM
BSR       SEARCH
PULS      A             Put NUM into A
LEAS      4,S           Balance stack
```

Registers A, B, and X are changed.

3. Do the same thing as in Problem 2, assuming that the input parameters are passed after the call in the same order while the parameter NUM is returned on the stack as before. Provide an example of a calling sequence.

4. One reason for not passing output parameters after the call is the following. A subroutine that calls another subroutine and has some parameters passed back to it after the call will not always be reentrant. Explain why this is so. Are there similar restrictions on input parameters?

5. Write a reentrant, position independent subroutine COMPAR that subtracts the M-byte number at the location contained in X from the M-byte number at the location contained in Y, returning the C, N, V, and Z bits properly. The value of M is to be passed in accumulator B.

6. We have talked about global variables and local variables for subroutines. There is a type of variable, called a dynamic local variable, which is stored on the stack and is used by more than one subroutine or by the subroutine and the main program. Looking at the example below, we see that SUB2 uses the variable that the main program pushes on the stack. Can SUB2 be reentrant? What are the problems with using dynamic local variables?

```
                          .
                          .
                          .
Main        LDA       #1
            PSHS      A
            BSR       SUB1
            LDA       ,S+
            .
            .
            .
            SWI
SUB1        .
            .
            .
            BSR       SUB2
            .
            .
            .
            RTS
SUB2        LDA       4,S
            INCA
            STA       4,S
            .
            .
            .
            RTS
```

7. Give a recursive subroutine SUB that adds the N 1-byte numbers in the vector Z, assuming that the address of Z is passed in X, the value of N is passed in B, and the sum is returned in A.

8. Give an example of passing output parameters after the call where the program can still be stored in ROM.

9. How would you write IFSUB if it were to be placed in a ROM? (See Section 5-8.)

10. Is subroutine GETBIT reentrant? Are global variables being used to pass parameters in GETBIT? (See Section 5-8.) Rewrite GETBIT so that no registers are changed except CC.

11. Suppose that parameters are being passed in a table to a subroutine SUB, and that an interrupt handler uses subroutine SUB and the *same* table to pass its parameters to SUB. What sort of restrictions can be placed on the parameters so that SUB will still be reentrant?

12. Write a subroutine WAIT that delays the number of seconds contained in A and then returns. You may assume that the clock cycle is 1 microsecond.

13. Provide a position independent reentrant subroutine to go with the header below. The effective use of labels for offsets on the stack is encouraged.

```
*                    SUBROUTINE DOTPRD
*
*    DOTPRD computes the dot product of two 2-component
*    vectors V and W, where all components are 1-byte
*    unsigned numbers. The vectors V and W, as well as
*    the dot product DTPD, are passed by reference on
*    the stack with the calling sequence
*
*         LDX      #V         Address of V into X
*         LDY      #W         Address of W into Y
*         LDU      #DTPD      Address of DTPD into U
*         PSHS     X,Y,U
*         BSR      DOTPRD
*         LEAS     6,S
*
*    Overflow is not detected by DOTPRD and no registers,
*    except CC, are changed.
```

14. Repeat Problem 13 but eliminate the instruction LEAS 6,S from the calling sequence so that the subroutine balances the stack.

15. Write a position independent reentrant subroutine MUL10 that multiplies the unsigned contents of D by 10, putting the result in D and returning the C bit equal to 1 if an overflow occurs. Only registers D and CC should be changed.

16. Write a subroutine WTD that computes the number of bits equal to 1 in accumulator D, putting the number in accumulator B. Only registers D and CC should be changed.

17. Give a position independent reentrant subroutine INCM that increments the N-byte number whose address is passed in X. The address of N is passed in Y. No registers should be changed by INCM.

18. Write a subroutine to search an N-byte vector Z until a byte is found that has the same bits in positions 0, 3, 5, and 7 as the word MATCH. The address of Z is passed in X, the address of MATCH is passed in Y, the value of N is passed in B and the address of the first byte found with a match is placed in U. If no byte is found in Z with a match, $FFFF should be placed in U.

19. Write a subroutine XCHG that will exchange N bytes between locations L and M. The addresses L and M and the address of N are passed after the call with the calling sequence

```
BSR     XCHG
FDB     L
FDB     M
FDB     ADDRN       Address of N
```

No registers should be changed by XCHG.

20. Is a recursive subroutine reentrant? Explain why or why not. You may wish to consider the following example.

```
SUM     CLRA
        TST     COUNT
        BEQ     S1
        ADDA    COUNT
        DEC     COUNT
        BSR     SUM
S1      RTS
```

21. Why does one need an EQU directive if the assembler has a SET directive?

22. Write an instruction sequence that produces the same moves as the instruction SWI and, in addition, sets the bits in the CC register the same way.

23. Write a subroutine INITL that initializes ten bytes on the stack to zero and uses BSR INITL as it calling sequence.

24. A version of DOTPRD that passes parameters on the stack is shown below. A typical calling sequence is

```
LOCV    SET     0           Input parameter copy of V
LOCW    SET     2           Input parameter copy of W
LOCDP   SET     4           Number of bytes for parameters
PSIZE   SET     6
*
        LEAS    -PSIZE,S
        LDD     V           Copy global variable into X
        STD     LOCV,S      Store in parameter LOCV,S
        LDD     W           Copy global variable into X
        STD     LOCW,S      Store in parameter LOCW,S
        BSR     DOTPRD
        LDD     LOCDP,S     Get output parameter
        STD     DTPD        Output into global variable
        LEAS    PSIZE,S
```

A student looking for shortcuts decides that STD DTPD can be eliminated from the calling sequence if STD LOCDP,S inside the subroutine is replaced with STD DTPD. Explain why this will not work.

```
*           SUBROUTINE DOTPRD
*
```

```
*              LOCAL VARIABLES
*
TERM      SET      0              First term of the DP
NBYTES    SET      2
*
*              PARAMETERS
*
RADDR     SET      2              Return address
LOCV      SET      4
LOCW      SET      6
LOCDP     SET      8
*
DOTPRD    LEAS     -NBYTES,S      Allocation
          LDA      LOCV,S
          LDB      LOCW,S
          MUL
          STD      TERM,S         Save first term
          LDA      LOCV+1,S
          LDB      LOCW+1,S
          MUL
          ADDD     TERM,S         Dot product into D
          STD      LOCDP,S        Put into output parameter
          LEAS     NBYTES,S       Deallocate local variables
          RTS
```

25. Write a macro CALL to call a subroutine with from zero to four 2-byte arguments. It pushes the arguments on the stack, copying them from global variables, and balances the stack. For example,

```
CALL      SUB1
```

will result in

```
BSR       SUB1
```

while

```
CALL      SUB2,ALPHA,BETA
```

results in

```
LDD       BETA
PSHS      D
LDD       ALPHA
PSHS      D
BSR       SUB2
LEAS      4,S
```

Use NARG, which is set by the assembler to the number of arguments in the macro you are currently expanding, and the conditional directive IFGE which inserts the code to the next ENDC if the operand of IFGE is positive.

26. Rewrite the stack marker version of DOTPRD so that no registers are changed (see Figure 5-14).

27. Discuss the advantages of passing parameters on the stack versus passing them after the call.

28. How would the calling sequence (4) be modified if the subroutine SUB replaced the LBRA instructions with

```
SUB       FDB       SUB0-SUB
          FDB       SUB1-SUB
          FDB       SUB2-SUB
```

What are the advantages of doing this, if any?

29. Indicate how you would change the last dot product segment of Section 5-1 so that all of the accesses to TERM use the address TERM,X. From this, conclude how all local variables can be accessed from the stack marker using negative offsets.

30. Write a subroutine to test whether a 2-byte number N is prime. The number N should be passed by reference in X and the carry bit should be returned set if N is prime.

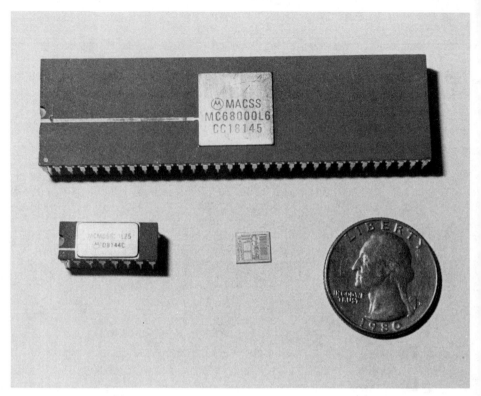

This picture shows the sizes of the **MC68000** microprocessor and Motorola's **64K** dynamic RAM. The small chip between the quarter and the **64K** dynamic RAM is the actual **MC68000** "chip." While it is roughly the same size as its **RAM** counterpart, the large number of extra pins needed by the **MC68000** force it to be put in a bigger package.

CHAPTER 6

Elementary Data Structures

And on the eighth day, he saw that there was confusion within the programs that he had written, so he created data structures. . . . Our programmer, playing god in his little world within his computer, soon finds that there are endless alternatives to the ways that data are stored, and that there is disorder. This introduction points out hyperbolically that the discovery of data structures happens as the programmer matures from novice to expert. You may think that this chapter is rather irrelevant to programming, especially in microcomputers. But wait until your eighth day. Before you get into a crisis due to the general disarray of your data, and then convince yourself of the need for data structures, we want you to have the tools needed to handle that crisis. In this chapter we cover the data structures that are most useful in microcomputer systems.

The first section discusses what a data structure is in more detail. Indexable structures, including the frequently used vector, are discussed in the second section. The third section discusses sequential structures, which include the string and the stack structures. The linked list is briefly discussed next, only to give you an idea of what it is, while the conclusions summarize the chapter with recommendations for further reading on data structures.

At the end of this chapter, you should be able to use simple data structures, such as vectors and strings, with ease. You should be able to handle deques and their derivatives, stacks and queues, and you should know a linked list structure when you see one. This chapter should provide you with the tools that you need to handle most of the problems that cause confusion when storing data in your microcomputer programs.

WHAT A DATA STRUCTURE IS

In previous chapters we described a data structure as the way data are stored in memory. While this description was adequate for those earlier discussions, we now want to be more precise. A *data structure* is the way data are stored *and* accessed. This section expands on this definition.

A data structure is an abstract idea that is used as a reference for storing data. It is like a template for a drawing. For example, a vector is a data structure that we have used since Chapter 2. Several sets of data can be stored in a vector in the same program and the same "template" is used to store each set. You may write or see a program that uses vectors that have five 1-byte elements. While writing another program, you may recognize the need for a vector that has five 1-byte elements and, by using the same template or data structure that you used earlier, you can quickly copy appropriate parts of the old program to handle the vector in your new program. Moreover, another program may need a similar structure that has ten 1-byte elements, or three 2-byte elements or even a vector whose elements are themselves vectors. Rather than having a different template around for each possible vector, you will, with some understanding, be able to modify a program that handles a vector with five 1-byte elements to handle these other cases, too. In a sense, data structures are elastic templates that can be stretched to accommodate different sizes.

We have used the analogy with a template to describe how data are stored in a data structure. The description of a data structure is completed when we describe how the data of the structure can be read or written, that is, *accessed*. A simple example will make this clear. A vector Z of N 1-byte elements can be stored in consecutive bytes of a buffer created with the directive

```
Z       RMB        20
```

This buffer, beginning at location Z, will allow N to be as large as 20. By pointing X to the first byte of the buffer,

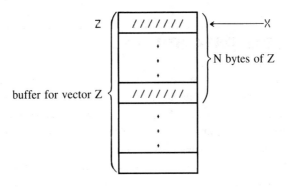

we can easily access any byte of the vector. For instance,

```
LDX       #Z
LDA       3,X
```

will read the fourth byte of the vector into accumulator A. Suppose however, that our N bytes were not stored in a buffer but were stored on a tape which, when read, moves forward one byte. The constraint here is that we can access only the "current" byte on the tape. This situation is exactly analogous to a person sitting at a terminal typing characters to be input to a computer. To remind us of this, the data structure of N consecutive bytes which can be accessed only at some "current" position is called a *string*. Of course, once a string is put into memory by storing it in consecutive bytes of a buffer, it can be accessed like a vector. This distinction becomes important in applications. Is one accessing a string in memory, or accessing a string from a terminal or some other hardware device? Thus the programmer should consider what data structure is appropriate for the application, which includes considering the constraints which are placed on accessing that structure.

The data structure, as we observed in Chapter 2, affects both static and dynamic efficiency. Besides the compactness and speed of the program itself, the compactness of the data may be affected by the structure used to store it. In a small microcomputer with 128 bytes of RAM, a program may not work at all if the data are stored in a structure that requires 200 bytes of RAM, but it may work if the correct data structure is used and that structure requires only 100 bytes of RAM. Using the right data structure can also improve clarity because the techniques to access the structure for a particular program may be more transparent than with a less appropriate structure.

INDEXABLE DATA STRUCTURES

We have already used the vector data structure, which is the most common example of an indexable data structure. A *vector* is a sequence of *elements* (or components), each of which is labeled by a number called an *index*. The indexes of successive elements are successive integers, and each element is represented by the same number of bytes. The number of bytes representing each element of the vector is termed its *precision,* the number of elements in the vector is its *length,* and the index of the first element is its *origin* (or *base*). For example, a vector Z with N elements would usually have its element labeled with i denoted $Z(i)$, where i runs between the origin and the (origin + N − 1). For an origin of 1, the elements are labeled $Z(1)$, ..., $Z(N)$ while, for an origin of 0, the elements are labeled $Z(0)$, ..., $Z(N-1)$. If the origin is understood, we refer to the element $Z(i)$ as the ith element.

Vectors stored in memory are stored in buffers, putting successive elements in successive memory locations. If the elements of the vector have more than one byte of precision and represent integers or addresses, we have adopted the convention that the elements are stored most significant bytes first. (This is also the convention followed by Motorola.) A buffer to hold the vector Z is established with the assembler directive

```
Z       RMB       20
```
(1)

With this directive, we have a buffer that will hold a vector of up to twenty 1-byte elements, a vector of up to ten 2-byte elements, a vector of up to five 4-byte elements, and so on. Although the directive (1) establishes the buffer to hold the vector, it does not specify the origin, precision, or the length of the vector stored in the buffer. Any element of a vector can be accessed and, to access the ith element, the programmer must know the precision and origin of the vector. For example, if Z has an origin of 1 and a precision of 1, then $Z(i)$ can be loaded into A with the following sequence, assuming that the value of i is in B.

```
LDX       #Z        Point X to Z              (2)
DECB                i − 1 into B
LDA       B ,X      Z(i) into A
```

If the precision is 2 and the origin still 1, the following sequence puts the ith element of Z into D, assuming that the value of i is initially in B.

```
LDX       #Z        Point X to Z
DECB                i − 1 into B
ASLB                2*(i − 1) into B          (3)
LDD       B ,X      Z(i) into D
```

The origin is 1 for Z in the segments (2) and (3). It seems obvious by now that, for assembly language programming, an origin of 0 has a distinct advantage since the DECB instruction can be eliminated from segments (2) and (3) if Z has an origin of 0. This is why most assembly language programs use 0 for the origin, sometimes called *zero-origin indexing*. Unless stated otherwise, we will assume an origin of 0 for all of our indexable data structures. Accessing the elements of vectors with higher precision is straightforward and left to the problems at the end of the chapter.

A *list* is similar to a vector except that each element in the list may have a different precision. Lists are stored in memory in buffers just like vectors, successive elements in successive memory locations. Like a vector, there is an origin and a length and each element of the list can be accessed. However, you cannot access the ith element of a list by the simple arithmetic computation used for a vector. Consider the following example of a list L which consists of 30 bytes for a person's name, followed by 9 bytes for his social security number, followed by 45 bytes for his address, and another 10 bytes for his telephone number. This list then has four elements, which we can label L(0), L(1), L(2), and L(3), and whose precisions are 30, 9, 45, and 10, respectively. Assuming that the label L is used for the address of the first byte of the list, we can load the jth byte of L(2) (the address) into A with the sequence

```
LDX        #L+39      Point X to L(2)                                (4)
LDA        A,X        jth byte of L(2) into A
```

where we have also assumed that the value of j is initially in accumulator A. While the segment (4) seems simple enough, remember that we have had to compute the proper offset to add to L in order to point X to L(2). For simple lists, such as this example, this is not much of a problem and the programmer may elect to do it "in his head." However, suppose that the list had 50 elements instead of 4. The programmer could do the calculation once for each element at assembly time by constructing the vector of offsets

```
OFFSET         FCB         0,30,39,84
```

The jth byte of the ith element of L could be put into accumulator A with the following segment, assuming that the value of j is initially in A and the value of i is in B.

```
LDX        #OFFSET    Point X to the vector of offsets
LDB        B,X        Offset for L(i) into B
LDX        #L         Point X to the List L
LEAX       B,X        Point X to L(i)
LDA        A,X        jth byte of L(i) into A
```

This looks better than (4), but what if the list had 100 elements? Although the calculation for the table of offsets is beginning to look unpleasant, another problem has crept in. The programmer now has to remember the association of list indexes with the attributes that he wants to access. In our example above, we could add the person's height, weight, high school graduated from, and so on. Remembering the index for the telephone number would now be too much. Our experience with local variables suggests another approach. For our example list we can create labels for the offsets to avoid remembering the sizes of each element.

NAME	EQU	0	Name of person	
SSN	EQU	NAME + 30	Social security number	
ADDRSS	EQU	SSN + 9	Address of person	(5)
TN	EQU	ADDRSS + 45	Telephone number	
NBYTES	EQU	TN + 10	Number of bytes in the list	

To get the jth byte of the telephone number into accumulator A, one could use the following segment, assuming that j is initially contained in A.

```
LDX     #L        Point X to list
LEAX    TN,X      Point X to telephone number
LDA     A,X       jth byte of telephone number into A
```

Notice that with the EQU directives of (5) we do not need the vector of offsets and thus save the memory needed to store that vector. Notice also that once X points to the element of L representing the telephone number, accessing the bytes for the telephone number is exactly like accessing the elements of a 10-byte vector of 1-byte elements. What makes this technique work is that it is easier to associate labels with attributes rather than numbers with attributes, particularly since the order of the list elements is usually unimportant. Notice that the EQU statements (5) not only let the programmer use labels for offsets, but let the assembler calculate the offsets instead of the programmer.

An *array* is a vector whose elements are vectors, each of which has the same length and precision. By taking the first vector to be of length 1 we see that a vector is a special case of an array. For us, it suffices to consider an array as the usual two-dimensional matrix pattern of elements of the same precision

AR(0,0),	AR(0,1),	AR(0,2), ...
AR(1,0),	AR(1,1),	AR(1,2), ...
AR(2,0),	AR(2,1),	AR(2,2), ...
.	.	.
.	.	.
.	.	.

where, as before with vectors and lists, it is convenient to start indexing the rows and columns from 0. If we consider our array to be a vector of rows, the data structure is called a *row major* array. If we consider it to be a vector of columns, the data structure is called a *column major* array. For example, if the

AR(0,0)	AR(0,0)
AR(0,1)	AR(0,1)
AR(0,2)	AR(0,2)
AR(0,3)	not used
AR(0,4)	not used
AR(1,0)	AR(1,0)
AR(1,1)	AR(1,1)
AR(1,2)	AR(1,2)
AR(1,3)	not used
AR(1,4)	not used
.	.
.	.
.	.
AR(4,4)	not used

FIGURE 6-1.   Storing the 5 by 5 Array of 1-byte Numbers by Rows and Embedding a 2 by 3 Array in It

precision of each array element is one byte and if the array is a row major array (e.g., stored by rows), then, assuming that the m by n array AR is embedded in a 5 by 5 array as shown in Figure 6-1, the address of AR(i,j) is given by

$$\text{address of } AR(i,j) = i * 5 + j + \text{address of } AR(D,D) \tag{6}$$

Notice that the address of AR(i,j) does not depend on m and n when it is stored as shown in Figure 6-1. The formula (6) can easily be modified for arrays with higher-precision elements, where one can use the MUL instruction to compute array addresses. For instance, if the precision of each element of AR is two bytes, if i and j are in accumulators A and B, respectively, and if AR is the address of the first byte of the array, the following segment puts AR(i,j) into accumulator D.

```
LDX      #AR         Point X to the array AR
PSHS     B           Save j
LDB      #5          Number of columns into B
MUL                  i*5 into D
ADDB     ,S+
ADCA     #0          (i*5) + j into D
```

```
ASLB
ROLA                              2*((i*5) + j) into D
LDD           D,X                 AR(i,j) into D
```

In this segment, multiplication by two for the contents of D is done by

```
ASLB                                                             (7)
ROLA
```

Multiplication by powers of two can be done by repeating (7). A further example of accessing arrays is shown in Figure 6-2 where the subroutine ZTRANS computes the transpose ZT of an m by n matrix Z of 1-byte elements stored by columns.

A *table* is a vector of identically structured lists. For example, one might have a table of lists where each list is exactly like the list example just discussed, one for each person in the table. Index addressing can be used to access any particular list in the table and used again, as done earlier, to access any particular element of the list. For instance, the directive

```
NUM           EQU          100                  Number of lists in the table
TABLE         RMB          NUM*NBYTES
```

creates a buffer for 100 of the lists defined by (5). The address of the first byte of the buffer is TABLE. If we want to put the location of the first byte of the telephone number of the ith person into Y, where i runs between 0 and 99, we could use the following segment, assuming that i is contained in B.

```
LDY           #TABLE           Point Y to buffer holding the table
LDA           #NBYTES          Number of bytes per list into A
MUL                            NBYTES * i into D
LEAY          D,Y              Point Y to ith list
LEAY          TN,Y             Point Y to telephone number in ith list
```

This discussion has examined indexable data structures. Each element of an indexable data structure can be accessed and, furthermore, some form of indexing can be used for the access. The simple, but very useful, vector was easy to access because the address of the ith element, assuming a zero origin, is obtained by adding i*(precision) to the address of the vector. A list is like a vector, but has fewer restrictions, in that elements can be of any precision. Arrays and tables are just mixtures of these two structures. These indexable structures are used often in a microcomputer like the MC6809, because they are so easy to handle with the index addressing options and the multiply instruction of this machine.

```
*                      SUBROUTINE ZTRANS
*
* ZTRANS computes the transpose ZT of an M by N matrix Z of 1-
* byte numbers where each matrix is inserted in the corresponding
* positions of a 5 by 5 matrix stored by columns. Assuming that
* the address of the matrix Z is in X, the address of its
* transpose ZT is in Y, the value of M in A, and the value of N
* in B, the parameters are passed on the stack with the calling
  sequence
*
*            PSHS   A,B,X,Y
*            BSR    ZTRANS          Balance the stack
*            LEAS   6,S
*
* Registers A, B, X, Y, and U are changed.
*
*                    PARAMETERS
*
RA           SET    0               Return address
M            SET    RA+2            Number of rows of Z
N            SET    M+1             Number of columns of Z
ADDRZ        SET    N+1             Address of Z
ADDRZT       SET    ADDRZ+2         Address of ZT
*
* The inner loop below takes the bytes of the matrix by rows,
* inserting them in the column of its transpose. X points to the
* next row of the matrix to be transferred, U points to the next
* byte of the current row to be transferred, and Y points to the
* column of the transpose getting the transfers. The contents of
* B will be the current column byte receiving the transfer.
*
ZTRANS       LDX    ADDRZ,S         First row address into X
             LDY    ADDRZT,S        First column address into Y
*
STR1         CLRB                   First column byte
             LEAU   ,X+             First row byte
*
STR2         LDA    ,U
             STA    B,Y             Transfer
             LEAU   5,U             Next row byte
             INCB                   Next column byte
             CMPB   N,S
             BNE    STR2            Finish current row
*
             LEAY   5,Y             Next column
             DEC    M,S
             BNE    STR1            Finish all rows
             RTS
```

FIGURE 6-2.   Subroutine ZTRANS

SEQUENTIAL DATA STRUCTURES

We now consider sequential data structures. The ubiquitous string, which you met earlier, and various deques, including the stack, are sequential structures. The key characteristic of sequential structures is that there is a current location, or top or bottom, to the structure, and access to the data in this structure is limited to this location.

Strings can be accessed at a current location, which can be moved as the string is accessed. If the current location is a memory word whose address is stored in the index register X, the string can be accessed by an instruction

```
LDA        ,X
LDA        ,X+
```

or

```
LDA        ,-X
```

Strings can be variable or constant. A buffer is used to hold a variable string which, in particular, can have a variable length. In a program with string manipulations, the length of a particular string can change in the program (up to the size of its buffer) in contrast to a vector of, say, 2-byte numbers which has a constant length throughout most programs. Constant strings can be created in memory with assembler directives like

```
STRING    FCC       /This is a string/                        (8)
```

This string can appear in the program area as a constant to be displayed on a terminal or to be printed on a printer. It is often in the program area because it may be stored in ROM together with the program. To preserve position independence, the address of the string is put in an index register using program counter relative addressing as in

```
LEAX      STRING,PCR
```

With this instruction, the address of the first character of STRING will be put into X regardless of where the ROM containing the program is placed in memory.

Strings of characters are frequently input and output from a terminal using a buffer. To discuss this, we first need to make some remarks about how single characters are input and output between a terminal and the MPU. Suppose that we have written two subroutines, INCH (for "input character") and OUTCH (for "output character"), for communicating with a terminal. Specifically,

```
LBSR        INCH
```

waits for a key to be depressed at the terminal and, when depressed, returns to the calling routine with the ASCII code of the key depressed in A. The instruction

```
LBSR        OUTCH
```

displays the ASCII contents of accumulator A on the terminal screen. In particular, since the ASCII code is only seven bits long, the most significant bit in A will be ignored. All ASCII symbolic characters will be displayed, while other characters, such as carriage return ($0D) and line feed ($0A), will move the screen cursor in the usual way. (The remaining ASCII characters are used for different purposes and are displayed differently on different terminals. They are usually input from the terminal keyboard by holding down a "control" key and pressing one of the other keys. These characters will not be needed in this discussion.) Implicit in the subroutine OUTCH is a segment of code that will wait until the previous character is displayed on the terminal before the current character in A is displayed. The exact details of INCH and OUTCH are not important at this point and will be taken up in Chapter 8.

Inputting or outputting a single character is easy with INCH or OUTCH. Using buffers, we can input or output strings of ASCII characters almost as easily. For example, we could display the constant string (8) on the terminal beginning at the current cursor position with the segment

```
        LDB    #16          Number of characters in STRING into B
        LDX    #STRING
LOOP    LDA    ,X+          Next character of STRING into A          (9)
        LBSR   OUTCH
        DECB
        BNE    LOOP
```

The preceding segment assumes that the programmer will count the number of characters in the string. This can be avoided by adding

```
LENGTH        EQU        *-STRING
```

after the definition of STRING and replacing LDB #16 with LDB #LENGTH in the sequence (9). We can also input a string of characters from the terminal, terminated by an ASCII carriage return ($0D), with the program segment

```
        LDX    #BUFFER      Point X to the buffer to hold the string
AGAIN   LBSR   INCH
        CMPA   #$0D         Is the character input a carriage return?
        BEQ    OUT
        STA    ,X+          Place character in buffer
        BRA    AGAIN
OUT     RTS
```

The string is stored in a buffer labeled BUFFER established with the directive

```
BUFFER          RMB          100
```

which allows BUFFER to hold up to 100 characters.

Another type of sequential data structure is the deque, which we now discuss. A special case of the deque is the stack, which we used extensively in Chapter 5. Our stacks have also been indexable since both the U and S registers can be used as index registers as well as stack pointers. Nevertheless, when these stack pointers are used only with push and pull instructions, they become true sequential structures.

A *deque* is a generalization of a stack. It is a data structure that contains elements of the same precision, and there is a top element and a bottom element. Only the top and bottom elements can be accessed. *Pushing* an element onto the top (or bottom) makes the old top (or bottom) the next-to-top (or next-to-bottom) element and the element pushed becomes the new top (or bottom) element. *Popping* or *pulling* an element reads the top (or bottom) element, removes it from the deque, and makes the former next-to-top (or next-to-bottom) element the new top (or bottom) element (see Figure 6-3). You start at some point in memory and allow bytes to be pushed or pulled from the bottom as well as the top. In our discussion, we will first assume that all of memory is available to store the deque elements, and then we will consider the more practical case where the deque is confined to a buffer rather than all of memory.

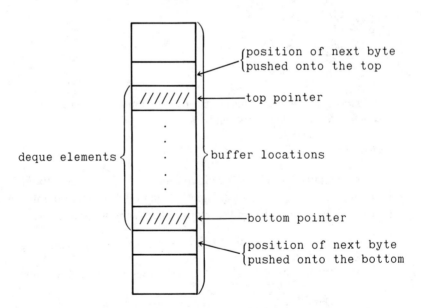

FIGURE 6-3. Deque Data Structure when the Bottom Pointer Points to the Bottom of the Deque

A deque can use registers to point to its top and bottom elements. Any of the registers X, Y, or U can be used to point to the top of the deque and, if location L is where one wants the first possible push on the top to go, one initializes the top pointer with

```
LDR        #L + 1
```

where R is one of the registers X, Y, or U. A push from accumulator B onto the top of the deque then corresponds to

```
STB        , - R
```

while a pull from the top into B corresponds to

```
LDB        , R +
```

Since the first byte pushed onto the bottom should go into location $L + 1$, the bottom pointer should be initialized with

```
LDR        #L
```

A push on the bottom from B would correspond to

```
STB        , + R
```

while a pull into B from the bottom becomes

```
LDB        , R -
```

Because these options are not available on the MC6809, one can use

```
LEAR       1 , R
STB        , R
```

and

```
LDB        , R
LEAR       - 1 , R
```

respectively, for the push and pull operations with B and the bottom of the deque. It is more statically and dynamically efficient, however, to have the bottom pointer work a bit differently from the top one. For example, if the bottom pointer points one byte *below* the bottom of the deque, the push and pull between B and the bottom can be implemented with

```
STB        , R +
```

and

```
    LDB          , − R
```

respectively. The bottom pointer is initialized, for this case, by

```
    LDR          #L + 1
```

Using a bottom pointer this way for deques produces another change. Offsets from the bottom pointer into the deque, besides being negative, are off by one from the corresponding offsets for the top pointer. If the data structure you are using is a deque and, additionally, allows the elements of the deque to be accessed from the bottom pointer with offsets, you will have to remember this if you use this type of bottom pointer.

As we have thus far described a deque, it can build outward from some location L and, with any number of bytes set aside for it, can overflow either the top or bottom of the buffer. It can also underflow if a pull is made when the deque is empty. There is also a more subtle situation, the contents of a deque can move upward or downward in memory without changing its size. For example, if one repeatedly pushes onto the top and pulls from the bottom, the deque moves upward in memory without changing the number of bytes it contains. If the deque is to be confined to a buffer, we need a way to implement the push and pull operations with the top and bottom of the deque so that the buffer will not overflow unless the number of deque elements exceeds the size of the buffer. To do this, we think of the buffer as being wrapped around a drum as shown in Figure 6-4. When a byte is pushed into the top byte of the deque buffer, the next byte pushed onto the "top of the deque" is actually put into the bottom byte of the buffer. A similar implementation is used for pulling from the top and pushing and pulling with the bottom. As an example, if we use a buffer with 50 bytes to hold the deque, we would have the directive

```
DEQUE        RMB          50
```

at the start of our program. If accumulator A contains the number of elements in the deque and if X and Y are the top and bottom pointers, we would initialize the deque with

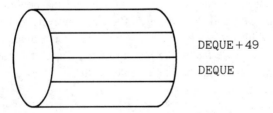

DEQUE + 49

DEQUE

FIGURE 6-4.   Buffer for a Deque Wrapped on a Drum

```
PSHDTB      MACR
            CMPA        #50
            LBEQ        ERROR                   Go to error routine
            CMPX        #DEQUE                  Pointer on top?
            BNE         \.0
            LDX         #DEQUE + 50
\.0         INCA
            STB         - X
            ENDM


PULDTB      MACR
            TSTA
            LBEQ        ERROR                   Go to error routine
            DECA
            CMPX        #DEQUE + 50             Pointer at the bottom?
            BNE         \.0
            LDX         #DEQUE
\.0         LDB         , X +
            ENDM
```

FIGURE 6-5.   Macros for Pushing and Pulling B from the Top of the Deque

```
CLRA                        Initialize deque count to 0
LDX         #DEQUE          First push onto top into DEQUE + 49
LDY         #DEQUE          First push onto bottom into DEQUE
```

Pushing and pulling bytes between B and the top of the deque could be done with the macros PSHDTB and PULDTB shown in Figure 6-5. The index register X points to the top of the deque, while the index register Y points one byte below the bottom of the deque. Similar macros can be written for pushing and pulling bytes between B and the bottom of the deque. In this example, if the first byte pushed is onto the top of the deque, it will go into location DEQUE + 49, whereas, if pushed onto the bottom, it will go into location DEQUE. Accumulator A keeps count of the number of bytes in the deque and location ERROR is the beginning of the program segment that handles underflow and overflow in the deque.

One would normally not tie up two index registers and an accumulator to implement a deque as we have done above. The pointers to the top and bottom of the deque and the count of the number of elements in the deque would normally be kept in memory together with the buffer for the deque elements. The macros for this implementation are easy variations of those shown in Figure 6-5. (See the problems at the end of the chapter.)

A *queue* is a deque where elements can only be pushed on one end and pulled on the other. We can implement a queue exactly like a deque but now only allowing, say, pushing onto the top and pulling from the bottom. The queue is a far more common sequential structure than the deque because the queue

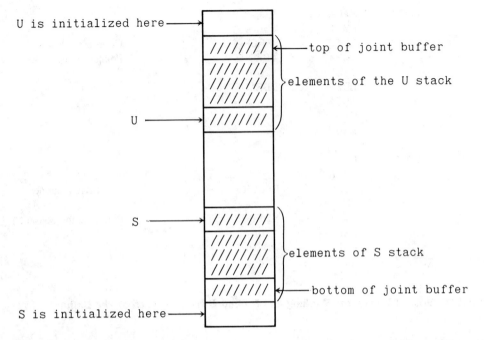

FIGURE 6-6. Two Back to Back Stacks where PSHU A Corresponds to STA ,+U and PULU A Corresponds to LDA ,U —

models requests waiting to be serviced on a first-in first-out basis. Another very common variation of the deque, which is close to the queue structure, is the *shift register* or *first-in first-out buffer*. The shift register is a full deque that only takes pushes onto the top, and each push on the top is preceded by a pull from the bottom. If the buffer for the shift register holds N bytes, then, after N or more pushes, the bottom byte of the shift register is the first in among the current bytes in the shift register, the next-to-bottom is the second in among the current bytes, and so on. If all pushes into the shift register are from accumulator B, only one macro and one pointer are needed to implement this data structure. (See the problems at the end of the chapter.) Although these two sequential structures are more common than the deque, we have concentrated on the deque in our discussion to illustrate the differences between accessing the top and bottom of these sequential structures with the MC6809.

We now look more closely at the two stack pointers on the MC6809. The U stack is, like the S stack, designed to push and pull from the top. If we wanted to use both as stack pointers, we would have to set aside two buffers for each stack, say 512 bytes for each. If the U stack pushed and pulled from the bottom, we could have put these 512-byte buffers back to back as shown in Figure 6-6. The advantage of this scheme is immediately evident. If there is room left on the U stack, the S stack can keep pushing into the buffer of the U stack, and vice versa. The chances of stack overflow for either stack is thus decreased and, with presumably a little extra effort in hardware, the MC6809 could be made to detect a stack overflow. For example, if the U and S stack contents become equal, an interrupt could occur at the end of the push instruction being executed, causing the program counter to be loaded with the contents of, say, locations $FFEE and $FFEF. The interrupt handler could then do whatever the programmer wanted when the combined stacks have overflowed. Notice that if the U stack is to push and pull from the bottom in the most natural way, its indexing options would be preincrementing $(, + U)$ and postdecrementing $(,U-)$ instead of predecrementing $(, -U)$ and postincrementing $(,U+)$, respectively. Due to these shortcomings of the use of the U register to implement a user stack and to the need to use the U register as an index register, we generally discourage using the U register as a stack pointer.

One of the motivations for having the back to back stacks of Figure 6-6 is that the probability of a stack overflow for either stack is decreased. This same motivation prompts us to look again at the way we might store multiple strings. For example, suppose in a program that we are going to need five variable strings, which we label STG0, STG1, STG2, STG3, and STG4. We can set aside 300 bytes for each string with the directives

```
STG0        RMB         300
STG1        RMB         300
STG2        RMB         300
STG3        RMB         300
STG4        RMB         300
```

With these disjoint buffers for different strings, a string that is temporarily larger than its buffer size cannot use available locations from the other buffers. For example, if STG0 becomes longer than 300 bytes, it will overwrite STG1 even if STG1 is only 10 bytes long. To try to get the same flexibility that is obtained with back to back stacks, one might use a single buffer which is implemented in a circular fashion like the buffer pictured in Figure 6-4. This single buffer would be established with

```
ADDR0       RMB         2          Address of string 0
ADDR1       RMB         2          Address of string 1
ADDR2       RMB         2          Address of string 2
ADDR3       RMB         2          Address of string 3          (10)
ADDR4       RMB         2          Address of string 4
END4        RMB         2          Address of first character after string 4
BUFFER      RMB         1500       Buffer to hold the five strings
```

where the six addresses are necessary to keep track of the five strings. For example, the difference between the variables ADDR4 and ADDR3 is the length of string 3 if this difference is positive; otherwise, the length is 1500 plus this difference. Storing the strings in the buffer would be handled much like accessing the deque discussed earlier. If a new string is being inserted into the location for string 2, the bytes for strings 3 and 4 may have to be shifted to accommodate the new string 2.

In a given application, we would, with disjoint buffers for each string, try to set the buffer sizes in such a way that the strings would overflow their respective buffers with small probability. This might require more memory than we could afford. Putting all the strings in one buffer may allow us to cut the buffer size down to what we have available. Whether the tradeoff between buffer size and the byte shuffling needed to keep the strings in the one buffer is worth it will then depend on the application. One situation where such an approach has been used is in text processing. In the course of deleting strings of text from a particular document, the person doing the text processing may discover that he has inadvertently deleted a string that he wanted to keep. For this reason, many text processing programs maintain one buffer as in (10) to hold, say, the last five deleted strings. These strings are maintained on a first-in first-out basis, so that the user can, with the appropriate command, retrieve any one of the last five strings deleted. To maintain the strings in a first-in first-out basis, one now keeps the six addresses themselves in a shift register. We leave the details for this to the problems at the end of the chapter.

In this section we have studied the sequential structures which are commonly used in microcomputers: the string and the variations of the powerful deque, the stack, queue, and shift register. As you have seen, they are easy to implement on the MC6809.

6–4

LINKED LIST STRUCTURES

The last structure that we discuss is the powerful linked list structure. Because its careful definition is rather tedious and it is not as widely used in microcomputer systems as the structures discussed in the previous sections, we examine this structure in the context of a concrete example, a data sorting problem. Suppose that we have a string of ASCII letters, say,

$$t\ c\ x\ a\ b\ u\ f \tag{11}$$

where we want to print the letters of the string in alphabetical order.

We will store this string of letters in a data structure called a *tree*, using a linked list data structure to implement the tree. The reason that we do not want to store the letters in consecutive bytes of memory as, say, a vector, but in a linked list implementation of a tree, is that, stored as a vector, the time to find a particular letter grows linearly with the number of letters in the string. If the letters were files of data, searching for a particular file could take days if the number of files is large. Organized as a linked list implementation of a tree, the search time grows logarithmically with the number of files so that searching for that same file could be done in seconds. Large collections of data are typically stored in some manner to improve the time to search them, and the linked list implementation of a tree is a common way to do this.

We first describe the tree using the algorithm to generate its graph. The first letter in the string is put at the *root* of the tree (see Figure 6-7), while the second letter is put at the left or right *successor* node of the root, depending on whether it is alphabetically before or after the letter at the root. Successive letters begin at the root node, going left or right to successor nodes in the same way as the second letter until an empty node is found. The new letter is placed at this empty node. We recommend that you work through the characters in the string above, and build up the tree shown in Figure 6-7 using the foregoing rule.

As you have just seen, it is fairly easy to generate the graph of the tree. We now describe how to store the tree in memory using a *linked list* structure. After each letter in the string, append two integers where the first is the string index of the letter for the left successor and the second is the string index of the letter for the right successor. (String indexes, as usual, begin at 0, so that 0 is the string index for t, 1 is the string index for c, and so on.) The symbol NS indicates no successor of that type. (See Figure 6-8 for the linked list representation of the tree.) This linked list structure contains identically structured lists, such as the first three bytes, t,1,2. The list index of each list is identical to the string index of the letter in the list so that the list t,1,2 is the 0th list in the linked list. Each list has three elements, a letter and two links. Although the elements of each list are the same precision in this example (each is one byte), the precisions are generally different, from one bit to hundreds of bits per element. The links in this example are equal to the indexes of the lists that

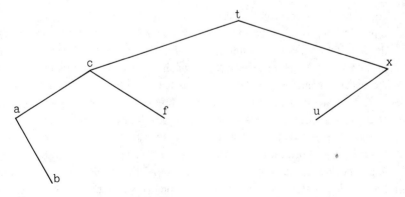

FIGURE 6-7. Picture of the Tree Representing the String (11)

t
1
2
c
3
6
x
5
NS
a
NS
4
b
NS
NS
u
NS
NS
f
NS
NS

FIGURE 6-8. Linked List Representation of the Tree Shown in Figure 6-7. The symbolic contents of each byte is shown rather than the usual hexadecimal contents.

contain the left and right successors. For the top list, which is the 0th list and represents the root of the tree, the left successor of the root is the letter c, and the list that contains the letter c is the list with index 1, so that the first link of the 0th list is 1. The right successor of the root of the tree is the letter x, and the list that contains x is the list with index 2, so the second link of the 0th list is 2. You are invited to verify that the other lists, which are identical in form to the 0th list, have the same relationship to the tree that the 0th list has.

Once the linked list is formed, the tree can be scanned to print the letters in order by an algorithm pictured in Figure 6-9. The idea behind the algorithm is this. Starting at the root, wrap a cord around the outside of the tree and print each node's letter (except "NS"), as you pass under its *crotch*. Its crotch is the part between the branches to its successors or, if it does not have successors, the crotch is the part between where the successors would be connected. (Try this out on Figure 6-9.) Although a human being can visualize this easily, a computer has a hard time working with pictures. This algorithm can be implemented in a computer using the elegantly simple rule:

1. Process the tree at the left successor node.
2. Print the letter. (12)
3. Process the tree at the right successor node.

In processing the root node, you process the tree containing nodes c, a, b, and f first, then print the letter t, then process the tree containing x and u last. Before you print the letter t, you have to process the tree containing the nodes c, a, b, and f first, and that processing will result in printing some letters first. In processing the tree containing c, a, b, and f, you process the tree containing a and b, then print the letter c, then process the tree containing f. Again, before you print the letter c, you have to process the tree containing a and b first, and that will result in some printing. In processing the tree containing a and b, you process the "null" tree for the left successor node of letter a (you do nothing), then you print the letter a, then you process the tree containing b. In processing the tree containing b, you process the "null" tree, you print the letter b, then you process the "null" tree. After you print the letter c, you will process the tree containing f and then process the tree containing x and u after printing the letter t. Try this rule out on the tree, to see that it prints out the letters in alphabetical order.

The flowchart in Figure 6-10 shows the basic idea of the rule (12) as a subroutine. The calling sequence sets LINK to 0 to process list 0 first. If LINK is NS, nothing is done; otherwise, we process the left successor, print the letter, and process the right successor. Processing the left successor requires the subroutine to call itself, and processing the right successor requires the subroutine to call itself again so that this subroutine is recursive, as discussed in Chapter 5. (To read the flowchart of Figure 6-10 correctly, the operation RETURN means to return to the place in the flowchart after the last execution of TRESRT.)

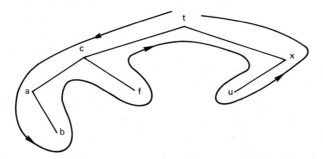

FIGURE 6-9. Algorithm for Scanning the Tree from the Left

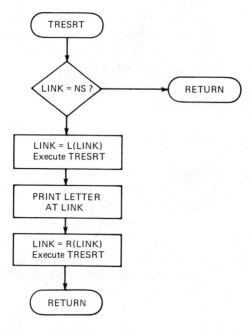

L(LINK) — Link to left successor of LINK
R(LINK) — Link to right successor of LINK

FIGURE 6-10. Flowchart for Scanning Tree from the Left

The subroutine itself is shown in Figure 6-11. It simply implements the flowchart, with some modifications to improve static efficiency. First, the index register X is pointed to the 0th list, so that LINK can be input as a parameter in accumulator B. This link value is multiplied by three to get the address of the character of the list, the link value is multiplied by three with one added to get the link to the left successor, and multiplied by three with two added to get the link to the right successor. The subroutine computes the value 3 * LINK and saves this value on the stack. In processing the left successor, the saved value is recalled and one is added. The number at this location, relative to X, is put in B and the subroutine is called. To print the letter, the saved value is recalled and the character at that location is passed to the subroutine OUTCH, which causes the character to be printed. The saved value is pulled from the stack (since this is the last time it is needed) and two is added. The number at this location relative to X is passed in B as the subroutine is called again. A minor twist is used in the last call to the subroutine. Rather than doing it in the obvious way, with a BSR TRESRT followed by an RTS, we simply do a BRA TRESRT. The BRA will call the subroutine, but the return from that subroutine will return to the caller of this subroutine. This is a technique that you can always use to improve static efficiency. You are invited, of course, to try out this little program.

```
*                 SUBROUTINE TRESRT
*
* TRESRT scans the linked list TREE from the left, putting out
* the characters in alphabetical order. The address of TREE is
* passed in X with the calling sequence
*
*         LDX       #TREE
*         CLRB                  Put LINK to 0
*         BSR       TRESRT
*
* Registers A and B are changed. Subroutine OUTCH is used to print
* the ASCII contents of accumulator A at the terminal.
*
NS        EQU       $FF
*
TRESRT    CMPB      #NS
          BNE       T1
          RTS
T1        PSHS      B            Get link to left successor
          ASLB
          ADDB      ,S
          STB       ,S           Save 3*(B) on stack
          INCB                   3*(B) + 1 into B
          LDB       B,X          Left successor link into B
          BSR       TRESRT
          LDA       ,S           Recover 3*(B)
          LDA       A,X
          JSR       OUTCH        Put out next character
          PULS      B            Recover 3*(B) from stack, remove from stack
          ADDB      #2
          LDB       B,X          Link to right successor into B
          BRA       TRESRT
```

FIGURE 6-11. Subroutine TRESRT

The main idea of linked lists is that the list generally has an element that is the number of another list, or it has several elements that are numbers of other lists. (This number is more often the absolute address of the list rather than a relative list number that was used in the example above.) The number, or *link*, allows the program to go from one list to a related list, such as the list representing a node to the list representing a successor of that node, by loading a register with the link element. The register is used to access the list. This is contrasted to the table, which is a vector of lists. In a table, one usually accesses one list (row) after the list (row) above it was accessed. In a linked list, one can use any link from one list to go to another list. By providing appropriate links in the list, the programmer can easily implement an algorithm that requires going from list to list in a particular order. Compare the implementation of the tree structure above using a linked list with one using a simple table where the nodes are put down successively by levels. Not only must offsets be calculated to go from node to successor node, but gaps will be left in the table where the tree has no successors and testing for the end of the search will be quite messy. Even constructing this table from the string will be difficult. However the program can be written in a simple and logical form with a linked list, using the power of the data structure to take care of many variations. In the example above, nodes that have no left successor or nodes that have no right successor are handled the same way as nodes that have two successors. While links can simplify the program, as we have just discussed, additional links can speed up a program by permitting direct access to lists that are linked via several link-list-link-...-link-list steps. Linked lists can simplify the program as well as speed it up, depending on how the designer uses them.

This final section briefly introduced the linked list structures. These are very useful in larger computers, although rarely seen in microcomputers, in our experience. Nevertheless, they are well known to be useful in artificial intelligence applications so that you may expect to see them used in the near future in robots and pattern recognition devices. You should read further material on these powerful structures.

6-5

SUMMARY AND FURTHER READING

This chapter has presented the data structures that are most commonly used in microcomputers. Although many programmers have written millions of lines of code without knowing about them, they help you to create order in a maze of possible ways to store data, they allow you to copy, or almost copy, the code needed to access the structures, and they allow you to save memory by using a better structure.

To show how your knowledge of data structures can save memory in a small computer, consider the storage and access of a mathematical array of ten rows by ten columns of 1-byte numbers, where 96 of the numbers are zero (this is called a sparse array). A natural way to store this data is in an array, but that array would take 100 memory locations and most would contain zeros. It is more efficient to store the four numbers of the sparse array in a table that stores the nonzero elements of the array, where the first column of the table is the row number, the second is the column number, and the third is the data in that row and column. This could be done in only twelve bytes. Knowledge of data structures can enable you to make a program work in a limited amount of memory which may not be possible otherwise.

This chapter only scratches the surface of this fertile area of study. If you study computer science, you will probably take a whole course on data structures, as well as meeting this material in other courses on database systems and compiler design. It is your best single course to take from the computer science area of study. Many textbooks are available for these courses, and you can use practically any of them to expand your comprehension of data structures. We suggest one of the earliest books, *Fundamental Algorithms,* Vol. I, *The Art of Computer Programming,* 2nd Ed. (D. Knuth, Addison-Wesley Publishing Co., Inc., Reading, Mass., 1973), for your reading.

From reading this chapter, you should be able to handle any form of the simple data structures that are likely to be met in microcomputer programming, and you should be able to handle the various types of sequential structures. You should also be able to recognize the linked list structures. But most important, you should be prepared to put some order in the way your programs handle data.

PROBLEMS

For the indexable data structures below, you may assume that the origin is zero.

1. What are the limitations on the precision and length of the vector Z which are accessed by program segments (2) and (3)? How would you change these segments for a vector Z with length 500?

2. Write a subroutine READV that returns the ith element of a vector V at the address ADDRI. The precision of V is M. Assuming that the address of V is in X, the address ADDRI is in Y, the value of i is in B, and the value of M is in A, the parameters are passed on the stack with the calling sequence

```
PSHS     A ,B ,X ,Y
LBSR     READV
LEAS     6 ,S
```

No registers are changed by READV.

3. Write a subroutine WRITEV that writes the M bytes at the address in Y into the ith element of the vector V of precision M. The address of V is passed in X and the values of i and M are passed in A and B, respectively. Indicate which registers are changed by WRITEV.

4. Write a subroutine READL that reads the ith element of the list L into the vector Z. The vector OFFSET contains the 1-byte offsets for the list L. The parameters are passed on the stack with the calling sequence

```
LDB      #17          Value of i into B
LDX      #L           Address of list into X
LDY      #Z           Address for ith vector into Y
LDU      #OFFSET      Address of offset vetor into U
PSHS     B ,X ,Y ,U
LBSR     READL
LEAS     7 ,S         Balance stack
```

No registers are changed by READL.

5. Consider the vector of 32 bytes in locations 0 through 31. Assume that the bits in this vector are labeled 0 to 255 beginning with the first byte in the vector and going right to left within each particular byte. Write a subroutine SETBIT which will set the ith bit in this vector assuming that the value of i is passed on the stack with the calling sequence

```
LDA      #56        Value of i into A
PSHS     A          Place parameter
BSR      SETBIT
LEAS     1,S        Balance stack
```

No registers are changed by SETBIT.

6. Write a subroutine STRBIT that will store the binary-valued variable FLAG in the ith bit of the vector in Problem 5. The value of FLAG and i are passed on the stack with the calling sequence

```
LDA      FLAG       Value of FLAG into A
LDB      #77        Value of i into B
PSHS     A,B        Place parameters
BSR      STRBIT
LEAS     2,S
```

Are the subroutines that you have written for this and Problem 5 reentrant?

7. Write a subroutine DISPLY, using OUTCH, which will display a vector with the structure of Problems 5 and 6 as an array of 0's and 1's of size 8 by 32. The bits of the vector must be displayed left to right, 32 consecutive bits per row. You may assume that the address of the vector is passed after the call with the sequence

```
BSR      DISPLY
FDB      VECTOR
```

8. Give two macros PSHDBB and PULDBB to go with those of Figure 6-5 which will push and pull the contents of accumulator B with the bottom of the deque.

9. One would not usually tie up two index registers and an accumulator to implement a deque. Rewrite the four macros and the initialization sequence to push and pull bytes from B and the top and bottom of the deque when the deque is stored in memory as

```
COUNT    RMB    1       Deque count
TPOINT   RMB    2       Top pointer
BPOINT   RMB    2       Bottom pointer
DEQUE    RMB    50      Buffer for the deque
```

Here, COUNT contains the number of elements in the deque and TPOINT and BPOINT contain, respectively, the addresses of the top and bottom of the deque. The macros should not change any registers except for B, which will be changed by the pull macros.

10. Assuming that the location of the deque and the error sequence are fixed in memory, how would you change the macros of Figure 6-5 so that the machine code generated is independent of the position of the macro? How would you change these macros if the size of the deque was increased to 400 bytes?

11. Do you see how you can avoid keeping a counter for the deque? For example, can you check for an empty or full deque without a counter? What about a queue?

12. Assume that a shift register is established in your program with

```
SHIFTR      RMB      100      Buffer memory
POINT       RMB      2        Pointer to SHIFTR
```

Write a macro to put bytes into the shift register from B and pull them out into A. If less than 100 bytes have been pushed into the shift register, how can you access the first byte put in?

13. Write the subroutines and macros necessary to maintain five strings in a buffer in a first-in first-out basis. Your implementation should include a branch to location OFLOW if an overflow of the buffer to hold the strings occurs.

14. Write a subroutine that reads in a string of ASCII lowercase letters, terminated by a carriage return, and then forms the linked list shown in Figure 6-8. You should write the subroutine so that the input letters are accessed as a string. For example, do not store them in a buffer to use them later. Your subroutine may use the subroutine INCH.

15. What is the limitation on the number of characters in the tree for the subroutine of Figure 6-10? How would you change the subroutine to allow for 250 characters?

16. Write the subroutine that corresponds to TRESRT but which now scans the tree from the right, printing the characters out in reverse alphabetical order.

17. Write a subroutine to add M 4-byte numbers which corresponds to the following header.

```
*                      SUBROUTINE ADD4
*
* ADD4 adds the M 4-byte numbers pointed to by Z placing
* the result in SUM. All parameters are passed on the
* stack with the sequence
*
* LDB       M                Value of M into B
* LEAX      Z,PCR            Address of Z into X
* LEAY      SUM, PCR         Address of SUM into Y
* PSHS      B,X,Y
* BSR       ADD4
* PULS      B,X,Y            Balance stack
```

18. Write a position-independent reentrant subroutine to go with the header below.

```
*                      SUBROUTINE INSERT
*
* INSERT inserts the string STG into string TEXT at
* the first occurrence of the ASCII letter SYMBOL. No
* insertion is made if SYMBOL does not occur in TEXT.
* The parameters are passed on the stack with the
* sequence
*
* LDA       SYMBOL           ASCII symbol into A
* LDB       LSTG             Length of STG into B
* LDX       #STG             Address of STG into X
* PSHS      B,X
* LDB       LTEXT            Length of TEXT into B
* LDX       #TEXT            Address of TEXT into X
* PSHS      A,B,X
* BSR       INSERT
```

Notice in the calling sequence above that the subroutine is balancing the stack.

19. Write a macro PRINT that will print a constant string of characters at the terminal using OUTCH. A typical use of PRINT would be

```
PRINT        (Print this at the terminal)
```

which would display "Print this at the terminal" beginning at the current cursor position.

20. Write a subroutine that will take a string of characters, terminated by a carriage return, from the keyboard using INCH and place them at the address passed in index register X. Assuming that the input string is called NAME, write a macro INPUT for the calling sequence for this subroutine which would look like

```
INPUT        NAME
```

The macro INPUT should work for *any* name you supply in the macro which has a buffer defined by

```
NAME        RMB        50
```

21. Write an MC6809 assembler program able to assemble programs having the following specifications.
   (a) The operations will only be LDA, ADD (for ADDA), STA, SWI, FCB, and END.
   (b) At most six labels can be used, each of which is exactly three uppercase letters long.
   (c) Only direct addressing can be used with instructions and only hexadecimal numbers used with the FCB directive.
   (d) The input line will have a fixed format: label (3 characters), space, instruction mnemonic (3 characters), space, address (3 characters or 2-digit hexadecimal number prefixed with a $). There are no comments or carriage returns and, if a label is missing, it is replaced by 3 spaces.
   (e) The program will have from 1 to 10 lines, ending in an END directive.
   (f) The source code has no errors (i.e., your assembler does not have to check errors). The origin is always zero.

Your assembler will have the source code prestored as a character array TEXT, 10 rows by 11 columns, and will generate an object code string OBJ up to 30 bytes long. No listing will be generated. The assembler should be able to at least assemble the following two programs.

```
        LDA ABB              ALP FCB $01
        ADD BAB              GAM FCB $00
            BBA              DEL FCB $04
                             BET FCB $03
    ABB FCB $01              LDA ALP
    BAB FCB $02              ADD BET
    BBA FCB $00              ADD DEL
        END                  STA GAM
                             SWI
                             END
```

Since no errors occur, you can check some op codes for just one letter, but you have to check all letters of a label. A two-pass assembler is required. On the first pass, just get the lengths of each instruction or directives and save the labels and their addresses in a list. End pass one when END is encountered. On pass two, put the op codes and addresses in the string OBJ.

22. Write an input subroutine to go with the assembler of Problem 21. It should take up to ten lines of assembly language from the terminal, each line terminated by a carriage return, and form the table for the assembler. The table should be placed at the address passed in X.

23. Write a macro MOVE that will move a string of ASCII characters, terminated by a carriage return, from location L to location M with

```
MOVE        L,M
```

No registers should be changed by MOVE.

24. Write a macro CMPSTG that compares two strings of ASCII characters at locations L and M, assuming that each string is terminated by a carriage return. The macro call

```
CMPSTG      L,M
```

should return the Z bit set if the two strings are equal.

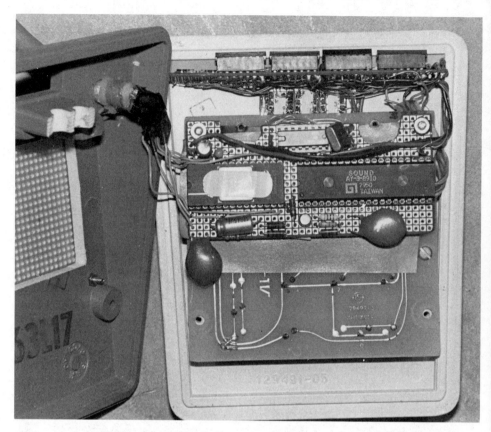

The complete **MC68705** microcomputer system shown fits into the bottom of a small keyboard case. The **LED** display (upper right part of the board), **MC68705** (left center), and the **AY-3-8910** sound chip (right center) control the lights of a bingo display, generate sound effects and music for the game, and monitor the keyboard for commands for the bingo numbers called out. Numbers can be used in small computers, too.

CHAPTER 7

Arithmetic Operations

This chapter deals with the number crunching issues of how one writes program segments to evaluate algebraic formulas and how one writes subroutines for multiple-precision integer arithmetic, floating-point arithmetic, and conversion between different bases.

In the first section we discuss ways to convert integers between number systems, such as binary and decimal. These techniques are needed when you input numbers from a terminal keyboard and output numbers to a terminal display. A full comparison of these techniques is made, something that you should try to do in writing your own subroutines for any purpose, namely, examine all the possibilities and select the best one for your situation. The second section fills in the details concerning signed and unsigned integer arithmetic which have not been taken up in the examples of earlier chapters. In particular, multiple-precision multiplication and division are covered in this section. The third section deals with floating-point arithmetic. This material should be understood by anyone who expects to use a microprocessor in a control application where the numerical details of the control algorithm will be an important aspect of the overall design. Even if one will eventually only program in a high-level language, this background will be helpful in understanding why the same program, run on different machines, can yield different numerical results which, at times, might be critical. The final section presents a technique to write program segments that evaluate algebraic formulas. The operations in the formulas are assumed to be supplied by subroutines so that the evaluation of the formula becomes a sequence of subroutine calls. The actual variables used in the formula could be integers, floating-point numbers, or any other type of variable that the subroutines have been written to handle.

After reading this chapter, you should be able to write a sequence of subroutine calls to evaluate any algebraic formula. You should be able to convert integers from one base to another and write subroutines to carry out any multiple-precision arithmetic operation. You should understand the principles of floating-point arithmetic to the point that you could write subroutines for the usual floating-point operations. You should also be able to use available floating-point software, such as the Motorola MC6839 floating-point ROM chip, after reading the software documentation.

Further reading is recommended at the end of the chapter to help you write subroutines to implement floating-point operations or handle arithmetic in other number systems.

7-1

INTEGER CONVERSION

A microcomputer frequently communicates with the outside world through ASCII characters. For example, the subroutines INCH and OUTCH discussed in Chapter 6 allow the MPU to communicate with a terminal and this communication is done with ASCII characters. When numbers are being transferred between the MPU and a terminal, they are almost always decimal numbers. For example, one may input the number 3275 from the terminal keyboard, using the subroutine INCH, and store these four ASCII decimal digits in a buffer. The contents of the buffer after the digits are input would be as shown.

$33
$32
$37
$35

While each decimal digit can be converted to binary by subtracting $30 from its ASCII representation, the number 3275 still has to be converted to binary (e.g., $0CCB) or some other representation, if any numerical computation is to be done with it. One also has to convert a binary number into an equivalent ASCII decimal sequence if this number is to be displayed on the terminal screen. For example, suppose that the result of some arithmetic computation is placed in accumulator D. This result will usually be in binary, say, $0CCB. The equivalent decimal number, in this case 3275, must be found and each digit converted to ASCII before the result can be displayed on the terminal screen. We focus on the ways of doing these conversions in this section.

One possibility is to do all of the arithmetic computations with binary-coded-decimal (BCD) numbers, where two decimal digits are stored per byte. For example, the BCD representation of 3275 in memory would be

$32
$75

Going between the ASCII decimal representation of a number and its equivalent BCD representation is quite simple, involving only shifts and the AND operation. With the MC6809, it is a simple matter to add BCD numbers using the ADDA or ADCA with the DAA instruction. Subtraction of BCD numbers on the MC6809 must be handled differently from the decimal adjust approach because the subtract instructions do not correctly set the half-carry bit H in the CC register. (See the problems at the end of the chapter.) For some applications, addition and subtraction may be all that is needed so that one may prefer to use just BCD addition and subtraction. There are many other situations, however, which require more complex calculations, particularly applications involving control or scientific algorithms. For these, the ASCII decimal numbers are converted to binary because binary multiplication and division is much more efficient than multiplication and division with BCD numbers. Thus we convert the input ASCII decimal numbers to binary when we are preparing to multiply and divide efficiently. However, depending on the MPU and the application, BCD arithmetic may be adequate so that the conversion routines below are not needed.

We consider conversion of unsigned integers first, discussing the idea in general and then giving examples of conversion between decimal and binary representations so that you can see the principle in some detail. A brief discussion of conversion of signed integers concludes this section. The conversion of numbers with a fractional part is taken up in Section 7-3.

An unsigned integer N less than b^m has a unique representation

$$N = c_{m-1}*b^{m-1} + c_{m-2}*b^{m-2} + \cdots + c_1*b + c_0 \tag{1}$$

where $0 \le c_i < b$ for $0 \le i \le m - 1$. The sequence $c_{m-1}, \ldots, c_0$ is called an *m-digit base-b representation* of N. We are interested in going from the representation of N in one base to its representation in another base. There are two common schemes for this conversion that are based on multiplication, and two schemes that are based on division. Although one of the division schemes is taught in introductory logic design courses, and you are likely to select it because you know it well, it does not turn out to be the most efficient to implement in a microcomputer. We look at all the schemes in general, and then give examples of each to find the most promising one.

The two multiplication schemes simply carry out (1), doing the arithmetic in the base that we want the answer in. There are two ways to do this. Either evaluate expression (1) as it appears, or else nest the terms as shown.

$$N = (\cdots(0 + c_{m-1})*b + c_{m-2})*b + \cdots + c_1)*b + c_0 \qquad (2)$$

The other two schemes involve division. Notice from (1) that if you divide N by b, the remainder is c_0. Dividing the quotient by b again yields c_1 and so forth until one of the quotients becomes 0. In particular, if one has a base-r representation of N and wants to go to a base-b representation, division of N by b is done in base-r arithmetic. You are probably familiar with this technique because it is easy to go from a decimal representation to any base with it using a calculator since the calculator does decimal arithmetic. The other scheme using division simply divides the number N, assumed to be less than b^m, by b^{m-1} so that the quotient is the most significant digit c_{m-1}. Dividing the remainder by b^{m-2} produces the next most significant digit, and so on. We will also consider these schemes below. Which of these four schemes is best for microcomputers? We now look more closely at each for conversion between decimal and binary bases.

Consider first the multiplication scheme that evaluates formula (1) directly. Suppose that N_4, . . . , N_0 represent five decimal digits stored in a buffer pointed to by X. Assume that these five decimal digits have been put in from the terminal using INCH so that each digit is in ASCII. Then

$$N_4*10^4 + N_3*10^3 + \cdots + N_0*10^0 \qquad (3)$$

is the integer that we want to convert to binary. To carry out (1) we can store constants

```
K        FDB        10000,1000,100,10,1
```

and then multiply N_4 times (K):(K + 1), N_3 times (K + 2):(K + 3), and so on, adding up the results and putting the sum in D. The subroutine shown in Figure 7-1 does just that, indicating an overflow by returning the carry bit equal to 1. The multiplication scheme in Figure 7-1 takes advantage of the fact that the assembler can convert 10^4 through 10^0 into equivalent 16-bit binary numbers

```
*                     SUBROUTINE CVDTB
*
* CVDTB puts the unsigned equivalent of five ASCII decimal digits
* at the location in X into D. C is set if there is an overflow.
* Registers A, B, CC, X, and Y are changed.
*
K         FDB       10000,1000,100,10,1
*
SUM       SET       0                   Current sum
PP        SET       SUM+2               Partial product
LAST      SET       PP+2                End of table address
OFLOW     SET       LAST+2              Overflow indicator
DD        SET       OFLOW+1             Decimal digit
NBYTES    SET       DD+1                Number of bytes for local variables
*
CVDTB     LEAS      -NBYTES,S           Space for local variables
          LEAY      K+10,PCR            End of table address into Y
          STY       LAST,S
          LEAY      K,PCR               Point Y to constants
          CLR       SUM,S
          CLR       SUM+1,S             Initialize sum
          CLR       OFLOW,S             Initialize overflow
*
C1        LDA       ,X+                 Next ASCII digit into A
          SUBA      #$30                ASCII to binary
          STA       DD,S                Save decimal digit
*
          LDB       1,Y                 Low byte of next constant
          MUL
          STD       PP,S                Save partial product
*
          LDA       DD,S                Restore decimal digit
          LDB       ,Y++                High byte of constant
          MUL
          ADDB      PP,S                Add in partial sum
          ADCA      #0                  Propagate carry
          BEQ       C2                  No overflow if (A) = 0
          INC       OFLOW,S             Increment overflow
*
C2        TFR       B,A
          LDB       PP+1,S              New product term into D
          ADDD      SUM,S               Add to current sum
          STD       SUM,S               Update sum
          BCC       C3
          INC       OFLOW,S
C3        CMPY      LAST,S              Is Y at the end of the table?
          BNE       C1
*
          ROR       OFLOW,S             Overflow into carry
          LDD       SUM,S               Sum into D
          LEAS      NBYTES,S            Balance stack
          RTS
```

FIGURE 7-1. Conversion from Decimal to Binary by Multiplication

using the FDB directive. Notice that the overflow location will be incremented at most once in this subroutine since $2^{17} > 99999$. Thus the instruction

```
ROR      OFLOW,S
```

will set the C bit correctly for the return since the remaining three instructions in the subroutine do not affect C.

Looking at the second multiplication conversion scheme applied to our present example, we rewrite the decimal expansion formula (3) as

$$((((0 + N_4)*10 + N_3)*10 + N_2)*10 + N_1)*10 + N_0 \tag{4}$$

Doing our calculations iteratively from the inner pair of parentheses, we can get the same result as before without storing any constants. A subroutine that does this is shown in Figure 7-2. As with the previous subroutine, overflow can occur only once, either with the last call to MUL10 or with the addition of N_0 to the sum, so that the carry bit is returned correctly with the instruction

```
ROR      ,S+
```

This instruction also balances the stack before the return. In this subroutine, there is only one local variable, except for a short sequence to save the low byte of the sum, so that the binding process can be omitted. If we compare the two subroutines, we see that the second one has the clear edge in terms of lines of code or static efficiency, particularly if you consider the ten bytes used by the FDB directive in the first subroutine. Furthermore, if one wanted to convert a 10-digit decimal number to a 32-bit binary number, the difference in the static efficiencies of these two multiplication techniques would become even more pronounced. For example, a 40-byte table of constants would be needed for the analog of the subroutine of Figure 7-1, an increase of 30 bytes which is not needed by the corresponding analog of the subroutine of Figure 7-2. The clear winner then between these two subroutines is the one in Figure 7-2. Finally, one can modify each subroutine to take the ASCII decimal digits directly from the terminal, using the subroutine INCH, effectively accessing the digits as a string of characters rather than a vector. (See the problems at the end of the chapter.)

The remaining two techniques use division. The second division technique that divided by different numbers each time, getting the most significant digit first, suffers from the same malady as the first multiplication scheme. A lot of numbers have to be stored in a table and that reduces static efficiency. The other division scheme, getting the least significant digits first, is the one most commonly taught in introductory courses on logic design. Although it is better than the last division scheme, it is going to be less useful on the MC6809 than the multiplication schemes because this microcomputer has no decimal divide

```
*                      SUBROUTINE CVDTB
*
* This subroutine converts the five ASCII decimal digits stored
* at the location contained in X into an unsigned 16-bit number
* stored in D. The carry bit is set if overflow occurs. Registers
* A, B, CC, X, and Y are changed.
*
CVDTB    LDY      #5            Initialize counter
         CLRA
         CLRB                   Initialize sum, a register variable in D
         PSHS     A             Clear overflow
*
C1       PSHS     B             Save low byte of sum
         LDB      ,X+           Get next ASCII digit
         SUBB     #$30          ASCII to binary conversion
         ADDB     ,S+           Add digit to current sum
         ADCA     #0            Propagate carry
         BCC      C3
         INC      ,S            Set overflow
C3       LEAY     -1,Y          Decrement counter
         BEQ      C2
         BSR      MUL10         Multiply (D) by 10
         BCC      C1
         INC      ,S            Set overflow
         BRA      C1
C2       ROR      ,S+           Overflow into carry bit, balance stack
         RTS
*
*                      SUBROUTINE MUL10
*
* Subroutine MUL10 multiplies the unsigned contents of D by 10,
* returning the answer in D. Assuming that the original contents
* of D is less than (2**17)*10, the carry bit is set if there is
* an overflow
*
MUL10    PSHS     D
         ASLB
         ROLA                   2*(D) into D
         ASLB
         ROLA                   4*(D) into D
         ADDD     ,S++          5*(D) into D
         ASLB
         ROLA                   10*(D) into D
         RTS
```

FIGURE 7-2. Conversion from Decimal to Binary by Multiplication

instruction, and the divide routine will take up memory and be slow. Thus the best scheme for conversion from decimal to binary is the multiplication scheme that uses the nesting formula (2) to avoid the need to store all the powers of 10.

Let's apply the division techniques to another common problem, that of converting a binary number into ASCII decimal digits to be output to a terminal. In particular, suppose that we want to convert the unsigned 16-bit number in D into five ASCII decimal digits.

Consider the division scheme that generates the most significant digit first. We could again have a table of constants in the subroutine with the directive

```
K        FDB        10000,1000,100,10,1
```

Looking at the expansion (1) we see that N_4 is the quotient of the division of (D) by (K):(K + 1). If we divide the remainder by (K + 2):(K + 3), we get N_3 for the quotient, and so forth. These quotients are all in binary, so that a conversion to ASCII is also necessary. The subroutine CVBTD of Figure 7-3 essentially uses this technique except that the division is carried out by subtracting the largest possible multiple of each power of ten which does not result in a carry. Notice that the usual return sequence in CVBTD has been replaced by

```
PULS     D,X,PC       Deallocate local variables; return
```

since the registers D and X are changed by the subroutine anyway.

The technique used by the subroutine of Figure 7-3 has the same difficulties as the one in Figure 7-1, larger numbers require a larger table of constants. We now look at the other division scheme. For example, if the contents of D is divided by 10, the remainder is the binary expansion of N_0. Dividing this quotient by 10 yields a remainder equal to the binary expansion of N_1, and so on. The subroutine that carries out this algorithm is shown in Figure 7-4. It uses another subroutine DIV10, which is not shown, but which can be written easily after reading the next section.

Suppose that we wanted to convert a 16-bit unsigned binary integer in D to the equivalent decimal number using the best multiplication technique, in particular, the one that used (2) instead of (1). Write the binary expansion of the number b_{15}, . . . , b_0 in D as

$$(\cdots (0*2 + b_{15})*2 + \cdots + b_1)*2 + b_0$$

and assume that the equivalent five decimal digits are to be placed at the address passed in X, with one decimal digit stored per byte in binary. (We can convert each digit to ASCII later, if necessary.) After initializing the result to 0, we can see how to build up the equivalent decimal number iteratively from the innermost parentheses above by repeating the following steps.

```
*                    SUBROUTINE CVBTD
*
* CVBTD converts the unsigned binary contents of D into five
* ASCII decimal digits which are placed at the address passed
* in X.
*
K          FDB      10000,1000,100,10,1
*
* Below, for each power of 10, we subtract it as many times as
* possible from D without causing a carry. The number obtained,
* after ASCII conversion, becomes the ASCII decimal coefficient
* of that power of 10. Registers X, Y, CC, and D are changed.
*
LAST       SET      0                    Address for end of table
COUNT      SET      LAST+2               Decimal count
SAVEA      SET      COUNT+1              Location to save A
NBYTES     SET      SAVEA+1              Number of bytes for local variables
*
CVBTD      LEAS     -NBYTES,S            Locations for local variables
           LEAY     K+10,PCR
           STY      LAST,S
           LEAY     K,PCR                Point Y to constants
*
CVB1       CLR      COUNT,S
CVB2       SUBD     ,Y
           BLO      CVB3
           INC      COUNT,S
           BRA      CVB2
*
CVB3       ADDD     ,Y++                 Restore D; point Y to next constant
*
           STA      SAVEA,S
           LDA      COUNT,S              Decimal coefficient into A
           ADDA     #$30                 ASCII conversion
           STA      ,X+                  Output next ASCII digit
           LDA      Restore A
           SAVEA,S
*
           CMPY     LAST,S
           BNE      CVB1
           PULS     D,Y,PC               Deallocate local variables; return
```

FIGURE 7-3. Conversion from Binary to Decimal by Division

1. Multiply the five decimal digits pointed to by X by 2.
2. Add 1 to the five decimal digits pointed to by X if $b_n = 1$.

Recall, however, that the preceding operations must be done in decimal. For this, it is more convenient to output our digits in BCD rather than one decimal

```
*                       SUBROUTINE CVBTD
*
* CVBTD converts the unsigned contents of D into an equivalent
* 5-digit ASCII decimal number at the location passed in X.
* Registers A, B, CC, and X are changed. The subroutine DIV10
* is used which divides the top two bytes on the stack by 10,
* returning the remainder in B, and replacing the top two
* bytes with the quotient.
*
CVBTD      PSHS    D           Save number being converted
           LDB     #5
           LDA     #$30        ASCII 0 into A
CVB1       STA     ,X+
           DECB
           BNE     CVB1
*
CVB2       LBSR    DIV10
           ADDB    ,-X         ASCII conversion
           STB     ,X
           TST     1,S         Test quotient
           BNE     CVB2
           TST     ,S          Test quotient
           BNE     CVB2
           PULS    D,PC        Balance stack and return
```

FIGURE 7-4   Conversion from Binary to Decimal by Division

digit per byte since we can take advantage of the DAA instruction. In particular, notice that in the subroutine of Figure 7-5, the carry bit in loop CBD2 equals b_n the first time through, while the next two times through, the loop completes the doubling in decimal of the BCD contents of the three bytes pointed to by X. The conversion of the BCD number to ASCII, if desired, is straightforward. (See the problems at the end of the chapter.)

Conversion of signed numbers is straightforward once the foregoing techniques are understood. This conversion can be done strictly by the formula that defines the signed number, as done above for unsigned numbers, or the signed number can be expressed as a sign and a magnitude, and the magnitude can be converted as before because it is an unsigned number. The idea of conversion is quite general. You can convert to base-12 or from base-12 using any of these ideas. You can convert between the time in a week expressed in days of the week, hours, minutes, and seconds and the time of the week in seconds represented in binary. This type of conversion is similar to going between a binary sector number and a disk track/sector number, something that becomes important if you are involved in writing disk controller programs. Conversion can be met in unexpected places and, with the techniques of this section, you should be able to handle any integer conversion problem.

```
*
*
* CVBTD converts the 16-bit unsigned number in D to an equivalent
* 6-digit decimal number stored at the address passed in by the
* calling routine in X. The decimal digits are stored in BCD.
* Registers A, B, and CC are changed.
*
CVBTD   PSHS    D           Save number to be converted
*
        CLR     ,X
        CLR     1,X
        CLR     2,X         Initialize decimal number
*
        LDA     #16
        PSHS    A           Save count
*
CBD1    ASL     2,S
        ROL     1,S         Put next bit in C
        LDB     #2          3-byte decimal addition
*
CBD2    LDA     B,X         Get ith byte
        ADCA    B,X
        DAA                 Double in decimal
        STA     B,X
        DECB
        BPL     CBD2
*
        DEC     ,S
        BNE     CBD1
*
        LEAS    3,S         Balance stack
        RTS
```

FIGURE 7-5. Conversion from Binary to Decimal by Multiplication

7-2

INTEGER ARITHMETIC

Multiple-precision arithmetic is very important with 8-bit microcomputers since the range of integers specified by a single byte, whether signed or unsigned, is too small for most applications. We have covered multiple precision addition and subtraction of both signed and unsigned integers in the examples of earlier chapters. This section is devoted to completing the discussion of multiple-precision integer arithmetic with an examination of the multiple-byte compare, negate, division and multiplication operations. We begin with the negate operation.

Double-precision arithmetic is fairly convenient on the MC6809 because there are the ADDD and SUBD instructions. However, other double-precision arithmetic instructions such as NEGD are absent. This instruction, if implemented, would subtract the contents of D from 0, putting the result in D and setting the condition code bits N, Z, V, and C appropriately. The NEGD instruction, if implemented, could be used when you wanted to subtract the number in accumulator D from the two bytes in memory at location L, putting the result in accumulator D. For this, either

```
SUBD    L
NEGD
```

or

```
NEGD
ADDD    L
```

puts the proper 16-bit number in D. To implement NEGD, we could use the 6-byte sequence

```
PSHS    D
CLRA
CLRB
SUBD    ,S++
```
(5)

Not only does it put the same number into D as NEGD would, it also sets the bits N, Z, V, and C in exactly the same way. Recalling that the result of NEGD is the two's-complement representation of the negative of the contents of D, we can also get the same 16-bit number in D by complementing every bit in D and then adding 1 to the result. This yields the 5-byte sequence

```
COMA
COMB
ADDD    #1
```
(6)

The carry bit at the end of (6) is the complement of the one at the end of (5). The other bits, N, Z, and V, are set identically by (5) and (6). We can get a still shorter sequence for NEGD by noticing that (6) is the same as

```
NEGA
NEGB
```
(7)

except that 1 is always added to A whether a carry is generated by adding 1 to B in (6) or not. Since NEGB sets C if the contents of B is nonzero, we can cancel the addition of 1 to A by NEGA in (7), except when the contents of B is 0, by using

```
        NEGA
        NEGB                                                    (8)
        SBCA      #0
```

The 4-byte sequence (8) is the shortest sequence to implement NEGD. Notice, however, that (8) does not set Z and C in the same way as (5).

A straightforward multiple-precision negate subroutine is shown in Figure 7-6 for negating M-byte numbers. The algorithm implemented by the subroutine subtracts the M-byte number from 0, replacing the M-byte number with the result. The N, V, and C bits are set correctly upon return, but the Z bit is not. You are invited to write M-byte versions of (6) and (7) to see if you can improve on the static or dynamic efficiency of the subroutine of Figure 7-6. (See the problems at the end of the chapter.)

A multiple-precision comparison is tricky in almost all microcomputers if you want to correctly set all of the condition code bits so that, in particular, all of the conditional branch instructions will work after the comparison. The subroutine of Figure 7-7 shows how this can be done for the MC6809.

We now look at multiple-precision multiplication. The MC6809 is a fairly unique 8-bit microprocessor in that it has the MUL instruction that multiplies 8-bit unsigned integers. To see the advantages of the MUL instruction, look at the subroutine BINMUL of Figure 7-8, which does exactly the same multiplication as MUL. Neglecting the clock cycles for the BSR and RTS instructions, BINMUL takes between 182 and 219 clock cycles to execute the multiplication. This illustrates the general observation that operations done in hardware are 10 to 100 times faster than the same operations done in software.

```
*                  SUBROUTINE NEGM
*
* NEGM subtracts the M-byte number at the address in X from 0,
* putting the result at the same address. The value of M is
* contained in B, 0 < M < 256. Only CC is changed.
*
NEGM    PSHS    A,B,X
        ABX
        CLRA                    Clear carry
*
NEG1    LDA     #0
        SBCA    ,-X
        STA     ,X
        DECB
        BNE     NEG1
*
        PULS    A,B,X,PC
```

FIGURE 7-6.   M-byte Negation Subroutine

```
*                        SUBROUTINE COMPAR
*
* COMPAR subtracts the M-byte number at the location in X from
* the M-byte number at the location in Y, returning the C, N, V,
* and Z bits correctly. The value of M is passed in accumulator
* B, 0 < M < 128. Registers X, Y, U, A, B, and DP are unchanged.
*
COMPAR    PSHS     A,B,DP,X,U
*
          DECB                          Initialize offset
          LDU      #0                   Initialize U for Z = 1
          CLRA                          Clear carry
*
C1        LDA      B,Y
          SBCA     B,X
          TFR      CC,DP
          BEQ      C2
          LDU      #1                   Set U for Z = 0
C2        DECB
          BPL      C1
*
          TFR      DP,CC
          LEAX     ,U                   Set Z bit correctly
          PULS     A,B,DP,X,U,PC
```

FIGURE 7-7.   M-byte Compare Subroutine

```
*                        SUBROUTINE BINMUL
*
* BINMUL multiplies the two unsigned numbers in A and B, putting
* the product in D. Registers A, B, and CC are changed.
*
BINMUL    PSHS     A,X          Save first number and X
          CLRA
          LDX      #8
*
LOOP      ANDCC    #$FE         Clear carry
          BITB     #1
          BEQ      SHIFT
          ADDA     ,S           Add first number
SHIFT     RORA
          RORB
          LEAX     -1,X
          BNE      LOOP
*
          LEAS     1,S          Balance stack
          PULS     X,PC
```

FIGURE 7-8.   8-bit Unsigned Multiply Subroutine

```
*                    SUBROUTINE MULT
*
* MULT multiplies the 1-byte unsigned integer in A with the M-byte
* unsigned integer whose address is passed in X. The value of M is
* passed in B, while the address for the (M+1)-byte product is
* passed in Y. Registers B and CC are changed.
*
MULT     PSHS    A,B        Save M and 1-byte number
         LEAY    B,Y        Point Y to LSB of product
         CLR     ,Y         Initialize product
         LEAX    B,X        Position X for LSB of M-byte number
*
MULT1    LDA     ,-X        Next byte of M-byte number into A
         LDB     ,S         1-byte number into B
         MUL
         ADDB    ,Y         Add in previous product term
         ADCA    #0         Propagate carry
         STD     ,-Y
         DEC     1,S        Decrement counter
         BNE     MULT1
*
         PULS    D,PC       Balance stack; return
```

FIGURE 7-9.   1-byte by M-byte Unsigned Multiply Subroutine

To do multiple-precision multiplication, one can extend BINMUL in a straightforward way or else take advantage of the MUL instruction. The latter would probably always be the choice, particularly if dynamic efficiency is important. A subroutine that uses MUL and multiplies an unsigned 1-byte number by an M-byte one is shown in Figure 7-9. The general M-byte by N-byte case is handled by the subroutine in Figure 7-10. For the subroutine of Figure 7-9, notice that one does not have to worry about a carry out of accumulator A after the instruction

```
ADCA        0
```

since the contents of A can be no larger than 254 from the earlier MUL instruction. A comparison of this subroutine with the corresponding extension of BINMUL is suggested as a problem at the end of this chapter.

Turning to the division of unsigned integers, the subroutine of Figure 7-11 divides the unsigned contents of B by the unsigned contents of A, returning the quotient in B and the remainder in A. To understand better the division subroutine of Figure 7-11, let's look more closely at binary division, where, for simplicity, we consider just 4-bit numbers. To divide 6 into 13, we can mimic the usual base-10 division algorithm,

```
*                   SUBROUTINE MULT
*
*  MULT multiplies the M-byte unsigned number whose address is passed
*  in X with the N-byte unsigned number whose address is passed in Y.
*  The value of M and N are passed in A and B, respectively, while the
*  result is placed at the address passed in U by the calling routine.
*  Registers X, Y, U, A, CC, and B are changed.
*
M          SET     0
N          SET     M+1
MCOUNT     SET     N+1
NCOUNT     SET     MCOUNT+1
XBYTE      SET     NCOUNT+1
SAVEU      SET     XBYTE+1
NBYTES     SET     SAVEU+2
*
MULT       LEAS    -NBYTES,S     Holes for local variables
           STA     M,S
           STB     N,S
*
           ADDA    N,S           M + N into A
           DECA
M1         CLR     A,U           Initialize result
           DECA
           BPL     M1
*
           LDA     M,S
           STA     MCOUNT,S
           LEAX    A,X           Position X for lowest-order byte
           LEAU    A,U           Initialize U
*
M2         LDB     N,S
           STB     NCOUNT,S
           LEAY    B,Y           Position Y for lowest-order byte
           LEAU    B,U           Position U for current LS output byte
           LDA     ,-X
           STA     XBYTE,S
*
M3         LDA     XBYTE,S
           LDB     ,-Y           Next Y-byte
           MUL
           ADDD    ,--U
           STD     ,U+
*
           BCC     M5
           STU     SAVEU,S
           LEAU    -1,U
M4         INC     ,-U           Propagate carry
           BEQ     M4
           LDU     SAVEU,S
```

FIGURE 7-10. M-byte by N-byte Unsigned Multiply Subroutine

```
*
M5         DEC      NCOUNT,S
           BNE      M3
*
           LEAU     -1,U          Position U for next X-byte
           DEC      MCOUNT,S
           BNE      M2
*
           LEAS     NBYTES,S      Balance stack
           RTS
```

FIGURE 7-10. (cont.)

```
*                   SUBROUTINE DIVIDE
*
* This subroutine divides the 1-byte unsigned number in B by the
* 1-byte unsigned number in A, putting the quotient in B and
* the remainder in A. Registers A and B are changed.
*
DIVIDE     PSHS     A,X           Save divisor and X
           CLRA
           LDX      #8            Initialize counter
*
LOOP       ASLB
           ROLA
           CMPA     ,S
           BLO      JUMP
           SUBA     ,S
           INCB
*
JUMP       LEAX     -1,X          Decrement counter
           BNE      LOOP
           LEAS     1,S           Pop divisor
           PULS     X,PC          Restore X and return
```

FIGURE 7-11. 8-bit Unsigned Divide Subroutine

$$
\begin{array}{r}
10 \\
110\,\overline{)\,1101} \\
110 \\
\hline
001 \\
000 \\
\hline
001
\end{array}
$$

getting a quotient of 2 with a remainder of 1. We can put everything in a 4-bit format if we rewrite the preceding computation as

$$
\begin{array}{r}
0010 \\
0110\,\overline{)\,0001101} \\
0000 \\
\hline
0011 \\
0000 \\
\hline
0110 \\
0110 \\
\hline
0001 \\
0000 \\
\hline
0001
\end{array}
$$

Another way of doing the bookkeeping of this last version is to first put all zeros in the nibble A and put the dividend in nibble B so that the contents of A:B looks like

which we will think of as our initial 8-bit *state*. Next, shift the bits of A:B left, putting 1 in the rightmost bit of B if the divisor can be subtracted from A without a carry, putting in 0 otherwise. If the subtraction can be done without a carry, put the result of the subtraction in A. Repeat this shift-subtract process three more times to get the remainder in A and the quotient in B.

The 8-bit case is identical to the above except that A and B become bytes, our state A:B becomes sixteen bits, and there are eight shifts instead of four. If accumulator D holds the sixteen bits, the shift left on D can be done with

```
ASLB
ROLA
```

which always puts a zero in the rightmost bit of B. If the divisor can be subtracted from A without a carry, one needs to execute

```
INCB
```

and perform the subtraction from A. The complete subroutine is shown in Figure 7-11. You should be able to see how to adapt this subroutine for, say, dividing two unsigned 16-bit numbers or an unsigned 16-bit number by an 8-bit one. (When the dividend and the divisor are of different lengths, one has to check if a 1 has been shifted out when the state is shifted left and, if so, the divisor should be subtracted from the remainder part of the state. See the problems at the end of the chapter.)

We now discuss briefly the multiplication and division of signed integers with a special look at the multiplication of 8-bit signed integers. Using the usual rule for the sign of the product of two signed numbers, we could extend the multiplication subroutines of this section in a straightforward way to handle signed integers. Extending the subroutines for division in this way is also straightforward after recalling that the sign of the remainder is the same as the sign of the dividend and that the sign of the quotient is plus if the signs of the dividend and divisor are equal; otherwise, it is minus.

There are also algorithms to multiply n-bit signed integers directly. We leave the details of this to the references noted at the end of the chapter because it is quite easy to modify any of the subroutines that we have presented for unsigned integers to work for signed integers. We illustrate the technique by showing how to modify the results of the MUL instruction to obtain an 8-bit signed multiply. Suppose that M and N are 8-bit signed integers with two's-complement representations $a_7, \ldots, a_0$ and $b_7, \ldots, b_0$, respectively. If M is in A and N is in B, the MUL instruction multiplies

$$(M + a_7 * 2^8) * (N + b_7 * 2^8) \tag{9}$$

putting the result in D. For example,

$$M = - a_7 * 2^7 + a_6 * 2^6 + \cdots + a_0 * 2^0$$

so that

$$M + a_7 * 2^8 = a_7 * 2^7 + a_6 * 2^6 + \cdots + a_0 * 2^0$$

is the *unsigned* integer in A and, similarly, $N + 2^8$ is the unsigned integer in B. Since (9) equals

$$M*N + a_7*N*2^8 + b_7*M*2^8 + a_7*b_7*2^{16} \tag{10}$$

we see that modifying the contents of D to get M*N requires subtracting the two middle terms of (10) from D if they are nonzero. [The last term of (10), if nonzero, does not appear in D and can be ignored.] The following macro, SGNMUL, makes this adjustment in D, where we note that to subtract 2^8*N or 2^8*M from D, we need only subtract N or M from accumulator A.

```
SGNMUL      MACR
            PSHS      A ,B
            MUL
            TST       1 ,S
            BPL       \ ,0
            SUBA      ,S
\ ,0        TST       ,S
            BPL       \ ,1
            SUBA      1 ,S
```

```
\.1        LEAS     2,S
           ENDM
```

The macro SGNMUL then is like an instruction which multiplies the signed contents of accumulator A times the signed contents of accumulator B, putting the result in D. The Z bit is not set correctly by SGNMUL, however.

We have completed our examination of multiple-precision arithmetic for both signed and unsigned integers. With the techniques developed in this section and in the examples of the earlier chapters, you should be prepared to handle any arithmetic calculation with signed or unsigned integers.

7-3

FLOATING-POINT ARITHMETIC AND CONVERSION

We have been concerned exclusively with integers and, as we have noted, all of the subroutines for arithmetic operations and conversion from one base to another could be extended to include signs if we wish. We have not yet considered arithmetic operations for numbers with a fractional part. For example, the 32-bit string $b_{31}, \ldots, b_0$ could be used to represent the number x, where

$$x = b_{31}*2^{23} + \cdots + b_8*2^0 + \cdots + b_0*2^8 \qquad (11)$$

The notation $b_{31} \ldots b_8.b_7 \ldots b_0$ is used to represent x, where the symbol "." called the *binary point,* indicates where the negative powers of 2 start. Addition and subtraction of two of these 32-bit numbers, with an arbitrary placement of the binary point for each, is straightforward except that the binary points must be aligned before addition or subtraction takes place and the specification of the exact result may require as many as 64 bits. If these numbers are being added and subtracted in a program (or multiplied and divided), the programmer must keep track of the binary point and the number of bits being used to keep the result. This process, called *scaling,* is used on analog computers and was used on early digital computers. In most applications, scaling is so inconvenient to use that most programmers use other representations to get around it.

One technique, called a *fixed-point* representation, fixes the number of bits and the position of the binary point for all numbers represented. Thinking only about unsigned numbers for the moment, notice that the largest and smallest nonzero numbers that we can represent are fixed once the number of bits and the position of the binary point are fixed. For example, if we use 32 bits for the fixed-point representation and eight bits for the fractional part as in (11), the largest number that is represented by (11) is about 2^{24} and the smallest nonzero number is 2^{-8}. As one can see, if we want to do computations with either very large or very small numbers (or both), a large number of bits will be required with a fixed-point representation. What we want then is a representation that uses 32 bits but gives us a much wider range of represented numbers and, at the same time, keeps track of the position of the binary point for us just like the fixed-point representation does. This idea leads to the floating-point representation of numbers, which we discuss in this section. After discussing the floating-point representation of numbers, we examine the arithmetic of floating-point representation and the conversion between floating-point representations with different bases.

We begin our discussion of floating-point representations by considering just unsigned (nonnegative) numbers. Suppose that we use our 32 bits $b_{31}, \ldots , b_0$ to represent the numbers

$$S*2^E$$

where S, the *significand*, is of the form

$$b_{23}.b_{22} \ldots b_0$$

and 2^E, the *exponential* part, has an exponent E, which is represented by the bits $b_{31}, \ldots , b_{24}$. If these bits are used as an 8-bit two's-complement representation of E, the range of the numbers represented with these 32 bits goes from 2^{-151} to 2^{127}, enclosing the range for the 32-bit fixed-point numbers (11) by several orders of magnitude. (To get the smallest exponent of -151, put all of the significand bits equal to 0, except b_0 for an exponent of $-128 - 23 = -151$.)

This type of representation is called a *floating-point* representation because the binary point is allowed to vary from one number to another even though the total number of bits representing each number stays the same. Although the range has increased for this method of representation, the number of points represented per unit interval with the floating-point representation is far less than the fixed-point representation which has the same range. Furthermore, the density of numbers represented per unit interval gets smaller as the numbers get larger. In fact, in our 32-bit floating-point example, there are $2^{23} + 1$ uniformly spaced points represented in the interval from 2^n to 2^{n+1} as n varies between -128 and 127.

Looking more closely at this same floating-point example, notice that some of the numbers have several representations; for instance, a significand of $1.100 \ldots 0$ and an exponent of 6 also equals a significand of $0.1100 \ldots 0$ and an exponent of 7. Additionally, a zero significand, which corresponds to the number zero, has 256 possible exponents. To eliminate this multiplicity, some form of standard representation is usually adopted. For example, with the bits $b_{31}, \ldots , b_0$ we could standardize our representation as follows. For numbers greater than or equal to 2^{-127} we could always take the representation with b_{23} equal to 1.

For the most negative exponent, in this case -128, we could always take b_{23} equal to 0 so that the number zero is represented by a significand of all zeros and an exponent of -128. Doing this, the bit b_{23} can always be determined from the exponent. It is 1 for an exponent greater than -128 and 0 for an exponent of -128. Because of this, b_{23} does not have to be stored, so that, in effect, this standard representation has given us an additional bit of precision in the significand. When b_{23} is not explicitly stored in memory but is determined from the exponent in this way, it is termed a *hidden bit*.

Floating-point representations can obviously be extended to handle negative numbers by putting the significand in, say, a two's-complement representation or a signed-magnitude representation. For that matter, the exponent can also be represented in any of the various ways that include represention of negative numbers. Although it might seem natural to use a two's-complement representation for both the significand and the exponent with the MC6809, one would probably not do so, preferring instead to adopt one of the standard floating-point representations.

We now consider the essential elements of the proposed IEEE standard 32-bit floating-point representation. The numbers represented are also called *single-precision* floating-point numbers and we shall refer to them here simply as *floating-point numbers*. The format is shown below.

31	30	23	22	0
s	e		f	

In the drawing, s is the sign bit for the significand, and f represents the 23-bit fractional part of the significand magnitude with the hidden bit, as above, to the left of the binary point. The exponent is determined from e by a *bias* of 127, that is, an e of 127 represents an exponent of 0, an e of 129 represents an exponent of $+2$, an e of 120 represents an exponent of -7, and so on. The hidden bit is taken to be 1 unless e has the value 0. The floating-point numbers given by

$$(-1)^s * 2^{e-127} * 1.f \qquad \text{for } 0 < e < 256 \qquad (12)$$
$$0 \qquad \text{for } e = 0 \text{ and } f = 0$$

are called *normalized*. (In the IEEE proposed standard, an e of 255 is used to represent $\pm$ infinity together with values which are not to be interpreted as numbers but are used to signal the user that his calculation may no longer be valid.) The value of 0 for e is also used to represent *denormalized* floating-point numbers, namely,

$$(-1)^s * 2^{-126} * 0.f \qquad \text{for } e = 0, f \neq 0$$

Denormalized floating-point numbers allow the represention of small numbers with magnitudes between 0 and 2^{-126}. In particular, notice that the exponent for the denormalized floating-point numbers is taken to be -126, rather than -127, so that the interval between 0 and 2^{-126} contains $2^{23} - 1$ uniformly spaced denormalized floating-point numbers.

Although the format above might seem a little strange, it turns out to be convenient because a comparison between normalized floating-point numbers is exactly the same as a comparison between 32-bit signed-magnitude integers represented by the string s,e,f. This means that a computer implementing signed-magnitude integer arithmetic will not have to have a separate 32-bit compare for integers and floating-point numbers. In larger machines with 32-bit words, this translates into a hardware savings, while in smaller machines, like the MC6809, it means that only one subroutine has to be written instead of two if signed-magnitude arithmetic for integers is to be implemented.

We now look more closely at the ingredients that floating-point algorithms must have for addition, subtraction, multiplication, and division. For simplicity, we focus our attention on these operations when the inputs are normalized floating-point numbers and the result is expressed as a normalized floating-point number.

To add or subtract two floating-point numbers, one of the representations has to be adjusted so that the exponents are equal before the significands are added or subtracted. For accuracy, this *unnormalization* always is done to the number with the smaller exponent. For example, to add the two floating-point numbers

$$2^4 * 1.00 \ldots 0$$
$$+ \ 2^2 * 1.00 \ldots 0$$

we first unnormalize the number with the smaller exponent and then add as shown.

$$2^4 * 1.000 \ldots 0$$
$$+ \ 2^4 * 0.010 \ldots 0$$
$$2^4 * 1.010 \ldots 0$$

(For this example and all those that follow, we give the value of the exponent in decimal and the 24-bit magnitude of the significand in binary.) Sometimes, as in adding,

$$2^4 * \quad 1.00 \ldots 0$$
$$+ \ 2^4 * \quad 1.00 \ldots 0$$
$$2^4 * 10.00 \ldots 0$$

the sum will have to be *renormalized* before it is used elsewhere. In this example

$$2^4 * 10.00 \ldots 0$$

goes to

$$2^5 * 1.00 \ldots 0$$

in the renormalization step. Notice that the unnormalization process consists of repeatedly shifting the magnitude of the significand right one bit and incrementing the exponent until the two exponents are equal. The renormalization process after addition or subtraction may also require several steps of shifting the magnitude of the significand left and decrementing the exponent. For example,

$$
\begin{array}{r}
2^4 * 1.0010 \ldots 0 \\
- \ 2^4 * 1.0000 \ldots 0 \\
\hline
2^4 * 0.0010 \ldots 0
\end{array}
$$

requires three left shifts of the significand magnitude and three decrements of the exponent to get the normalized result

$$2^1 * 1.000 \ldots 0$$

With multiplication, the exponents are added and the significands are multiplied to get the product. For normalized numbers, the product of the significands is always less than 4, so that one renormalization step may be required. The step in this case consists of shifting the magnitude of the significand right one bit and incrementing the exponent. With division, the significands are divided and the exponents are subtracted. With normalized numbers, the quotient may require one renormalization step of shifting the magnitude of the significand left one bit and decrementing the exponent. This step is required only when the magnitude of the divisor significand is larger than the magnitude of the dividend significand. With multiplication or division it must be remembered also that the exponents are biased by 127 so that the sum or difference of the exponents must be rebiased to get the proper biased representation of the resulting exponent.

In all of the preceding examples, the calculations were exact in the sense that the operation between two normalized floating-point numbers yielded a normalized floating-point number. This will not always be the case, as we can get overflow, underflow, or a result that requires some type of rounding to get a normalized approximation to the result.

For example, multiplying

$$
\begin{array}{r}
2^{56} * 1.00 \ldots 0 \\
* \ 2^{100} * 1.00 \ldots 0 \\
\hline
2^{156} * 1.00 \ldots 0
\end{array}
$$

yields a number that is too large to be represented in the 32-bit floating-point format. This is an example of *overflow,* a condition analogous to that encountered with integer arithmetic. Unlike integer arithmetic, however, *underflow* can occur, that is, we can get a result that is too small to be represented as a normalized floating-point number. For example,

$$
\begin{array}{r}
2^{-126} * 1.010 \ldots 0 \\
- \ 2^{-126} * 1.000 \ldots 0 \\
\hline
2^{-126} * 0.010 \ldots 0
\end{array}
$$

yields a result that is too small to be represented as a normalized floating-point number with the 32-bit format.

The third situation is encountered when we obtain a result that is within the normalized floating-point range but is not exactly equal to one of the numbers (12). Before this result can be used further, it will have to be approximated by a normalized floating-point number. Consider the addition of the following two numbers.

$$
\begin{array}{r}
2^2 * 1.00 \ldots 00 \\
+ \ 2^0 * 1.00 \ldots 01 \\
\hline
2^2 * 1.01 \ldots 00(01)
\end{array}
$$

least significant bits of the significand

The exact result is expressed with 25 bits in the fractional part of the significand so that we have to decide which of the possible normalized floating-point numbers will be chosen to approximate the result. *Rounding toward plus infinity* always takes the approximate result to be the next larger normalized number to the exact result while *rounding toward minus infinity* always takes the next smaller normalized number to approximate the exact result. *Truncation* just throws away all the bits in the exact result beyond those used in the normalized significand. Truncation rounds toward plus infinity for negative results and rounds toward minus infinity for positive results. For this reason, truncation is also called *rounding toward zero.* For most applications, however, picking the closest normalized floating-point number to the actual result is preferred. This is called *rounding to nearest.* In the case of a tie, the normalized floating-point number with the least significant bit of 0 is taken to be the approximate result. Rounding to nearest is the default type of rounding for the proposed IEEE floating-point standard. With rounding to nearest, the magnitude of the error in the approximate result is less than or equal to the magnitude of the exact result times 2^{-24}.

One could also handle underflows in the same way that one handles rounding. For example, the result of the subtraction

$$2^{-126} * 1.0110 \ldots 0$$
$$- \ 2^{-126} * 1.0000 \ldots 0$$
$$\overline{2^{-126} * 0.0110 \ldots 0}$$

could be put equal to 0, and the result of the subtraction

$$2^{-126} * 1.1010 \ldots 0$$
$$- \ 2^{-126} * 1.0000 \ldots 0$$
$$\overline{2^{-126} * 0.1010 \ldots 0}$$

could be put equal to

$$2^{-126} * 1.0000 \ldots 0$$

More frequently, all underflow results are put equal to 0 regardless of the rounding method used for the other numbers. This is termed *flushing to zero*. The use of denormalized floating-point numbers appears natural here, as it allows for a gradual underflow as opposed to, say, flushing to zero. To see the advantage of using denormalized floating-point numbers, consider the computation of the expression

$$(Y - X) + X$$

If $Y - X$ underflows, X will always be the computed result if flushing to zero is used. On the other hand, the computed result will always be Y if denormalized floating-point numbers are used. The references mentioned at the end of the chapter contain further discussions on the merits of using denormalized floating-point numbers. Implementing all of the arithmetic functions with normalized and denormalized floating-point numbers requires additional care, particularly with multiplication and division, to ensure that the computed result is the closest represented number, normalized or denormalized, to the exact result. It should be mentioned that the proposed IEEE standard requires that a warning be given to the user when a denormalized result occurs. The motivation for this is that one is losing precision with denormalized floating-point numbers. For example, if during the calculation of the expression

$$(Y - X) * Z$$

$Y - X$ underflows, the precision of the result may be doubtful even if $(Y - X) * Z$ is a normalized floating-point number. Flushing to zero would, of course, always produce zero for this expression when $(Y - X)$ underflows.

The process of rounding to nearest, hereafter just called *rounding*, is straightforward after multiplication. However, it is not so apparent what to do after addition, subtraction, or division. We consider the addition/subtraction case and leave division to the problems at the end of the chapter. Suppose, then, that we add the two numbers

$$\begin{array}{rl} & 2^0 \quad * \ 1.0000 \ldots 0 \\ + & 2^{-23} * \ 1.1110 \ldots 0 \\ \hline \end{array}$$

After unnormalizing the second number, we have

$$\begin{array}{rl} & 2^0 * 1.0 \ldots 00 \\ + & 2^0 * 0.0 \ldots 01 \ (111) \\ \hline & 2^0 * 1.0 \ldots 01 \ (111) \end{array}$$

(The enclosed bits are the bits beyond the 23 fractional bits of the significand.) The result, when rounded, yields

$$2^0 * 1.0 \ldots 010$$

By examining a number of cases, one can see that only three bits need to be kept in the unnormalization process, namely,

g	r	s

where g is the *guard* bit, r is the *round* bit, and s is the *sticky* bit. When a bit b is shifted out of the significand in the unnormalization process,

$$\begin{array}{r} b \rightarrow g \\ g \rightarrow r \\ s \ OR \ r \rightarrow s \end{array} \tag{13}$$

Notice that if s ever becomes equal to 1 in the unnormalization process, it stays equal to 1 thereafter or "sticks" to 1. With these three bits, rounding is accomplished by incrementing the result by 1 if

$$\begin{array}{rl} & g = 1 \text{ and } r \text{ OR } s = 1 \\ \text{or} \quad & g = 1 \text{ and } r \text{ AND } s = 0 \text{ and the least significant} \\ & \text{bit of the significand is 1} \end{array} \tag{14}$$

If adding the significands or rounding causes an overflow in the significand bits (only one of these can occur), a renormalization step is required. For example,

$$2^0 \quad * \; 1.1111 \ldots 1$$
$$+ \; 2^{-23} * 1.1110 \ldots 0$$

becomes, after rounding,

$$2^0 * 10.0 \ldots 0$$

Renormalization yields

$$2^1 * 1.0 \ldots 0$$

which is the correct rounded result and no further rounding is necessary.

Actually, it is just as easy to save one byte for rounding as it is to save three bits, so that one can use six rounding bits instead of one, as follows.

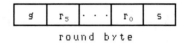

round byte

The appropriate generalization of (13) can be pictured as

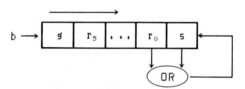

while (14) is exactly the same as before with r replaced by $r_5 \cdots r_0$.

The rounding process for addition of numbers with opposite signs (.e.g, subtraction) is exactly like that above except that the round byte must be included in the subtraction and renormalization may be necessary after the significands are subtracted. In this renormalization step, several shifts left of the significand may be required where each shift requires a bit b for the least significant bit of the significand. It may be obtained from the round byte as shown below. (The sticky bit may also be replaced by zero in the process pictured without altering the final result. However, at least one round bit is required.)

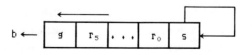

After renormalization, the rounding process is identical to (14). As an example,

$$2^0 \quad * \; 1.0000 \ldots 0$$
$$- \; 2^{-23} * 1.1110 \ldots 0$$

becomes

$$2^0 * 1.0 \ldots 00 \qquad \text{round byte}$$
$$- \; 2^0 * 0.0 \ldots 01 \; (11100000)$$
$$\overline{2^0 * 0.1 \ldots 10 \; (00100000)}$$

which, after renormalization and rounding, becomes

$$2^{-1} * 1.1 \ldots 100$$

Subroutines for floating-point addition and multiplication are given in Appendix 3. To illustrate the principles without an undue amount of detail, the subroutines are given only for normalized floating-point numbers. Underflow is handled by flushing the result to zero and setting an underflow flag, and overflow is handled by setting an overflow flag and returning the largest possible magnitude with the correct sign. These subroutines do not conform to the IEEE standard but, nevertheless, illustrate the basic algorithms, including rounding. The procedure for addition is summarized in Figure 7-12, where one should note that the addition of the significands is an addition of signed-magnitude numbers.

One other issue with floating-point numbers is conversion. For example, how does one convert the *decimal* floating-point number $3.45786 * 10^4$ into a binary

---

1. Attach a zero round byte to each significand and unnormalize the number with the smaller exponent.
2. Add significands of operands (including the round byte).
3. If an overflow occurs in the significand bits, shift the bits for the magnitude and round byte right one bit and increment the exponent.
4. If all bits of the unrounded result are zero, put the sign of the result equal to + and the exponent of the result to the most negative value; otherwise, renormalize the result, if necessary, by shifting the bits of the magnitude and round byte left and decrementing the exponent for each shift.
5. If underflow occurs, flush the result to zero and set the underflow flag; otherwise, round the result.
6. If overflow occurs, put the magnitude equal to the maximum value and set the overflow flag.

FIGURE 7-12. Procedure for Floating-Point Addition

floating-point number with the IEEE format? One possibility is to have a table of binary floating-point numbers, one for each power of ten in the range of interest. One can then compute the expression

$$3*10^4 + 4*10^3 + \cdots + 6*10^{-1}$$

using the floating-point add and floating-point multiply subroutines. One difficulty with this approach is that accuracy is lost because of the number of floating-point multiplies and adds that are used. For example, for eight decimal digits in the decimal significand, there are eight floating-point multiplies and seven floating-point adds used in the conversion process. To get around this, one could write $3.45786*10^4$ as $.345786*10^5$ and multiply the binary floating-point equivalent of 10^5 (obtained again from a table) by the binary floating-point equivalent of $.345786$. This, of course, would take only one floating-point multiply and a conversion of the decimal fraction to a binary floating-point number.

Converting the decimal fraction into a binary floating-point number can be carried out in two steps.

1. Convert the decimal fraction to a binary fraction.
2. Convert the binary fraction to a binary floating-point number.

Step 2 is straightforward so we concentrate our discussion on step 1, converting a decimal fraction to a binary fraction.

Converting fractions between different bases presents a difficulty not found when integers are converted between different bases. For example, if

$$f = a_1*r^{-1} + \cdots + a_m*r^{-m} \qquad (15)$$

is a base-r fraction, then it can happen that when f is converted to a base-s fraction,

$$f = b_1*s^{-1} + b_2*s^{-2} + \cdots$$

that is, b^i is not equal to 0 for infinitely many values of i. (As an example of this, expand the decimal fraction .1 into a binary one.) Rather than try to draw analogies to the conversion of integer representations, it is simpler to notice that multiplying the right-hand-side of (15) by s yields b_1 as the integer part of the result, multiplying the resulting fractional part by s yields b_2 as the integer part, and so forth. We illustrate the technique with an example.

Suppose that we want to convert the decimal fraction .345786 into a binary fraction so that

$$.345786 = b_1 2^{-1} + b_2 2^{-2} + \cdots$$

Then b_1 is the integer part of $2*(.345786)$, b_2 is the integer part of 2 times the fractional part of the first multiplication, and so on for the remaining binary digits. More often than not, this conversion process from a decimal fraction to a binary one does not terminate after a fixed number of bits, so that some type of rounding must be done. Furthermore, assuming that the leading digit of the decimal fraction is nonzero, as many as three leading bits in the binary fraction may be zero. Thus, if one is using this step to convert to a binary floating-point number, probably 24 bits after the leading zeros should be generated with the 24th bit rounded appropriately. Notice that the multiplication by 2 in this conversion process is carried out in decimal so that BCD arithmetic with the DAA instruction is appropriate here much like the CVBTD subroutine of Figure 7-5.

The conversion of a binary floating-point number to a decimal floating-point number is a straightforward variation of the process above and is left as an exercise.

This section covered the essentials of floating-point representations, arithmetic operations on floating-point numbers, including rounding, overflow, and underflow, and the conversion between decimal floating-point numbers and binary floating-point numbers. After reading this section, you should be able to use the MC6839 floating-point ROM chip, or any similar device like a floating-point coprocessor, after reading the application notes or data sheets for the device. This should make it easy for you to use floating-point numbers in your assembly language programs whenever you need their power.

7-4

FROM FORMULAS TO SUBROUTINE CALLS

The preceding section has provided us with the techniques to write subroutines to carry out the usual arithmetic operations on floating-point numbers, namely, $+$, $-$, $*$, and $/$. We could, with further study, write a whole collection of subroutines that would carry out the functions which we would meet in engineering, such as $\sin(x)$, $\cos(x)$, $\log(x)$, $(x)^{1/2}$, y^z, and so on. In a given application, we might have to write a program segment to evaluate a complicated formula involving these operations, for example,

$$z = (x + 2*y)/(\sin(u) + w) \tag{16}$$

This section examines a general technique to write such a program segment.

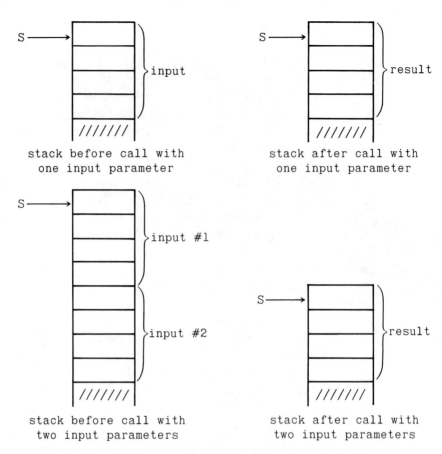

FIGURE 7-13. Passing Parameters on the Stack for Operations with One or Two Operands

For simplicity, we will assume that all operands are single-precision floating point numbers (four bytes) and that the subroutines are written so that the values of the operands are pushed on the stack before the subroutine call with only the result on top of the stack after the return. (See Figure 7-13 and notice particularly that the subroutine for an operation with two operands leaves only the result on top of the stack.) To place these parameters on the stack, we will assume that a macro PUSH has been written which pushes the 4-byte number at address ADDR onto the stack, low byte first, with

```
PUSH        ADDR
```

Similarly, we will assume that a macro PULL has been written so that

```
PULL        ADDR
```

will pull a 4-byte number off the stack, high byte first, and place it at the address ADDR. Assuming that the variables x, y, u, w, and z are at addresses ADDRX, ADDRY, ADDRU, ADDRW, and ADDRZ, respectively, and that the constant 2 is at address ADDR2, we can.evaluate (16) with the following program segment.

```
PUSH    ADDRX
PUSH    ADDR2
PUSH    ADDRY
BSR     FPMUL
BSR     FPADD
PUSH    ADDRU                    (17)
BSR     SIN
PUSH    ADDRW
BSR     FPADD
BSR     FPDIV
PULL    ADDRZ
```

In this segment, FPMUL, FPADD, and FPDIV are subroutines to multiply, add, and divide floating-point numbers, while SIN is a subroutine to calculate the sine of an input floating-point number. The movement of the stack is shown after each operation in Figure 7-14, where the symbols for the values of the variables are used to indicate the contents of each 4-byte block on the stack.

How does one write segment (17) to evaluate formula or expression (16)? The method comes from the work of the Polish logician Jan Lucasiewicz, who

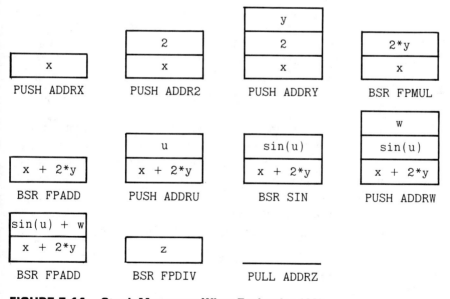

FIGURE 7-14. Stack Movement When Evaluating (16)

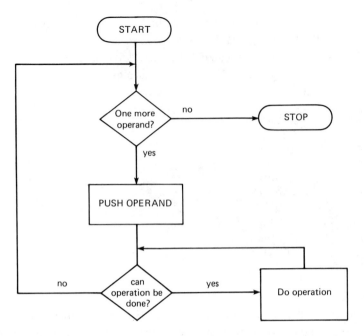

FIGURE 7-15. Algorithm for Writing a Formula in Polish Notation

investigated ways of writing expressions without using parentheses. With his technique, referred to as *Polish notation*, one would write (16) as

$$z = x \ 2 \ y * + u \ \sin w + / \tag{18}$$

Notice that when we read (18) from left to right, each variable name corresponds to a PUSH in (17) and each operation corresponds to a subroutine call. Going between (17) and (18) is easy. The flowchart in Figure 7-15 shows a simple algorithm to write the segment for any expression. You are, of course, invited to try it out!

There is another useful way to display a formula by parsing it into its basic operations using a tree. This tree will be the same one that we used in Chapter 6. Moreover, the technique to write a program segment to evaluate the formula from its tree representation will be virtually the same one that we used to scan the tree from the left in Chapter 6. Any operation with two operands, such as $+$, has a tree with two branches and nodes whose values are the operands for the operation. For example, the result of $x + y$ and $x * y$ are represented by the trees

If the operation has only one operand, the operation is displayed as a tree with only one branch. For example, sin(u) and sqrt(x) (for "square root of x") have trees

If your formula is more complicated than those shown above, you just plug in the results of one tree where the operand appears in the other tree. For instance, if you want the tree for sqrt(x + y), just substitute the tree for x + y into the node for example,

The tree for the formula (16) is shown in Figure 7-16. Notice how the formula is like a projection onto a horizontal line below the tree and how the tree can be built up from the bottom following the "plug in" technique just described.

The reader is invited to find these *parsing trees* for the formulas given in the problems at the end of the chapter. Note that a parsing tree is really a good way to write a formula because you can see "what plugs into what" better than

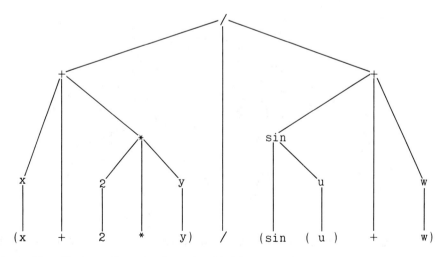

FIGURE 7-16.   Finding a Parsing Tree for (16) from the Bottom-Up

if you write the formula in the normal way. In fact, some people use these trees as a way to write all of their formulas, even if they are not writing programs as you are, because it is easier to spot mistakes and to understand the expression. Once the parsing tree is found, we can write the sequence of subroutine calls in the following way. Draw a string around the tree as shown in Figure 7-17. As we follow the string around the tree, a subroutine call or PUSH is made each time we pass a node for the last time or, equivalently, pass the node on the right. When a node with an operand is passed, we execute the macro PUSH for that operand. When a node for an operation is passed, we execute a subroutine call for that operation. Compilers use parsing trees to generate the subroutine calls to evaluate expressions in high-level languages. The problems at the end of the chapter give you an opportunity to learn how you can store parsing trees the way that a compiler might do it, using techniques from the end of Chapter 6, and how you can use such a tree to write the sequence of subroutine calls the way a compiler might.

You may consider this technique as a way to handle formulas of any complexity, with ease and accuracy. It makes writing these program segments for the MC6809 very easy, and it makes checking the correctness easy, too. This technique can be used with any system that uses a stack to hold intermediate results, say a computer that has a zero-address instruction set as described at the end of Chapter 2.

As a second example, we consider the benchmark calculation that was shown in the section on testing in Chapter 5. The inner loop of the program evaluated the consecutive expressions

$$\text{delta} = \text{delta} + c$$

$$s = s + (\text{delta} * \text{delta})$$

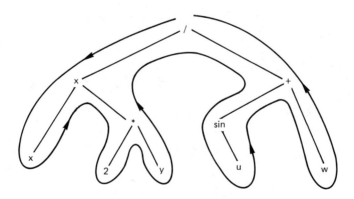

FIGURE 7-17.   Algorithm to Write a Sequence of Subroutine Calls for (16)

These can be described by the trees

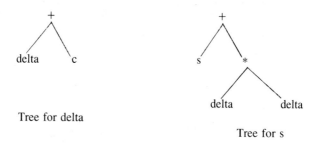

Tree for delta

Tree for s

The subroutine calls for these consecutive expressions are shown below assuming that the 4-byte floating-point numbers c, s, and delta are at addresses ADDRC, ADDRS, and ADDRDL, respectively.

```
PUSH    ADDRDL
PUSH    ADDRC
BSR     FPADD
PULL    ADDRDL
PUSH    ADDRS
PUSH    ADDRDL
PUSH    ADDRDL
BSR     FPMUL
BSR     FPADD
PULL    ADDRS
```

The example above is easy to work through once you have studied the example for (16). Note, however, that a lot of pushing and pulling is done between the variable locations and the stack. Seven of the ten macros or subroutines merely move data to or from the stack, and three do arithmetic operations. It might be more efficient to use another technique for simple problems like this one. For this reason, the MC6839 ROM floating-point chip was implemented with two methods for passing parameters. One method is through registers and can be used in simple problems like this one. The other method passes the arguments on the stack as we have been doing. The stack method then is available for more complicated situations and offers a completely general technique for evaluating expressions.

In this section you learned how to write a program segment of subroutine calls to evaluate any formula. A complex expression like that used to get the roots of a quadratic equation can be handled easily. Short, uncomplicated expressions can be handled with ease this way also, although you may find it more convenient to use a more efficient, but less general method.

SUMMARY AND FURTHER READING

This chapter covered the techniques you need to handle integer and floating-point arithmetic in a microcomputer. We discussed the conversion of integers between any two bases and then discussed signed and unsigned multiple-precision arithmetic operations that had not been discussed in earlier examples. Floating-point representations of numbers with a fractional part, and the algorithms used to add and multiply floating-point numbers, were discussed next together with the problems of rounding and conversion. The IEEE standard floating-point format was used throughout these discussions. We ended with the use of the stack for holding the arguments for arithmetic subroutines, and showed how you can write a sequence of subroutine calls to evaluate any formula.

You should now be able to write subroutines for signed and unsigned arithmetic operations, and you should be able to write and use such subroutines that save results on the stack. You should be able to convert integers from one representation to another, and write subroutines to do this conversion. You should be able to write numbers in the IEEE floating-point representation, you should understand how these numbers are added or multiplied and how errors can accumulate. After reading the data sheet on the Motorola MC6839, you should be able to use this ROM to perform standard arithmetic operations on floating-point numbers.

Further reading on the proposed IEEE floating-point standard can be found in the four expository papers contained in the journal *Computer* (March 1981, Volume 14, Number 3). The version described there is Draft 8.0 and is the version implemented in the Motorola MC6839 ROM chip. The *MC6839 Floating-point User's Manual* (Motorola Inc., Schaumburg, Ill., October 1981) contains a nice summary of the features of the proposed standard. We also recommend *Introduction to Arithmetic for Digital Systems Designers* (S. Waser and M. Flynn, CBS College Publishing, New York, 1982) for further information about arithmetic operations in microcomputers, including a detailed analysis of floating-point operations.

PROBLEMS

1. Rewrite the subroutine of Figure 7-2 so that, using INCH, the digits can be input from the terminal as a string. A carriage return should terminate the input string so that zero through five digits can be put in. (The empty sequence should be treated as zero.) Your subroutine should do the same thing as the one in Figure 7-2 as long as the number of digits put in is five or less.

2. Rewrite the subroutine of Figure 7-5 so that OUTCH can be used to output the decimal digits to the terminal. In particular, use a macro that can replace the DAA instruction, now storing only one digit per byte.

3. Write a subroutine using INCH that will input up to six ASCII decimal digits, terminated by a carriage return, and place the equivalent 6-digit BCD number at the address passed in X.

4. Write a subroutine that will output the 6-digit BCD number pointed to by X to the terminal. The subroutine, using OUTCH, should display the equivalent 6-digit decimal with leading zeros suppressed.

5. Using the subroutine OUTCH, write another subroutine OUTBCD that puts out the BCD contents of accumulator A to the terminal at its current cursor position.

6. Write a macro that will replace the DAA instruction when two base-13 digits are stored per byte.

7. How would you rewrite the subroutines of Figures 7-2 and 7-3 if you did not want any registers changed by the subroutines except those used to pass output parameters?

8. Write a subroutine that divides the unsigned contents of B by the unsigned contents of A, putting the quotient in B and the remainder in A. The technique used should be the same as that used in the subroutine CVBTD of Figure 7-3, that is, subtract the contents of A from B as many times as possible without causing a carry. The number obtained is the quotient, while the number remaining after the subtraction is the remainder. How does this subroutine compare with the one given in Figure 7-11 in terms of static and dynamic efficiency?

9. Provide the divide subroutine DIV10 used by the subroutine of Figure 7-4. Be careful here because the extension of the subroutine of Figure 7-11 to this case requires an extra step beyond the obvious changes needed for a 16-bit dividend.

10. Modify the subroutine of Figure 7-6 so that the Z flag is returned correctly for an M-byte negate.

11. Write M-byte negate subroutines that are M-byte versions of sequences (6) and (8). Are either of these better than the one given in Figure 7-6?

12. Write a subroutine that multiplies the unsigned 16-bit number in X with the unsigned 16-bit number in Y, returning the product in X:Y.

13. Write a subroutine that multiplies the signed contents of the number in X with the signed contents of the number in Y, returning the product in X:Y. You need only modify the output of the subroutine of Problem 12 in a simple way.

14. Write a subroutine that divides the unsigned contents of Y by the unsigned contents of A, putting the quotient in Y and the remainder in A. (Be sure to read the comment for Problem 9.)

15. Another version of subroutine COMPAR is shown below. Is it correct? If not, change it so that it is correct.

```
COMPAR    PSHS    A,B
          LDA     #$FF
          PSHS    A
          DECB
          CLRA
*
COMP1     LDA     B,Y
          SBCA    B,X
          TFR     CC,A
          BEQ     COMP2
```

```
          ANDA      #$FB        Put Z = 0
          STA       ,S
COMP2     DECB
          BPL       COMP1
          ANDA      ,S+         Get correct Z
          TFR       A,CC
          PULS      A,B,PC
```

16. Modify the macro SGNMUL so that the Z flag is correctly set at the end of the macro.
17. Extend the subroutine BINMUL so that it handles the same calculation as the subroutine of Figure 7-9. Which subroutine has the greatest static efficiency?
18. Which has the greatest dynamic efficiency? Give a subroutine MULT that multiplies the M-byte signed number, whose address is passed in X, with the 1-byte signed number whose value is passed in A. The product is to be put at the address passed in Y by the calling routine. The value of M is passed in B, and no registers other than CC are changed by the subroutine.
19. Give a subtract adjust macro for accumulator A assuming that the instructions SUBA and SBCA set the half-carry bit correctly.
20. Since the half-carry is not set correctly by the instructions SUBA and SBCA, how do you subtract multiple byte BCD numbers? Explain.
21. How would you modify the subroutine of Figure 7-10 so that no registers are changed? Only one additional instruction is needed.
22. Write a subroutine to take a decimal fraction .xyz . . . from the terminal and convert it to the closest 16-bit binary fraction at the address in X. The decimal fraction can have up to five decimal digits terminated by a carriage return. Write another subroutine that does the reverse operation.
23. Write a subroutine to convert a single-precision binary floating-point number pointed to by X to a decimal floating-point number that is displayed on a terminal screen.
24. Give an example that shows that the round bit r can not be eliminated, that is, give an example that shows that it really is not superfluous.
25. Give an example of the addition of two floating-point numbers, each with a magnitude less than or equal to 1, that results in the biggest possible rounding error. Repeat the problem for multiplication.
26. Write the PUSH and PULL macros used in Section 7-4. These macros should use subroutines in such a way that their use is as statically efficient as possible.
27. Give a sequence of subroutine calls for the following formula.

$$z = sqrt((17 + (x/y))*(w - (2*w/y)))$$

Provide a parsing tree for this formula and show assembly language statements (FCB directives, etc.,) for the storage of the parsing tree for z so that Problem 28 can be done. Use the linked list structure discussed at the end of Chapter 6.

28. Write a program that will read the data structure of Problem 27 (or any similar formula tree stored in a linked list structure) and then write an assembly language source program (in ASCII) for the subroutine calls needed to evaluate the formula.
29. Give the parsing trees needed to evaluate efficiently the formula

$$z = (4x^2 + y^2)^{1/2} + (y^2/2x)*ln([2x + (4x^2 + y^2)^{1/2}]/y)$$

Assume that you have subroutines to evaluate a square root and a natural logarithm. To do an efficient calculation, you should evaluate the common subexpression first. Show how the formulas

$$delta = delta + c$$
$$s = s + (delta * delta)$$

can be more efficiently evaluated by passing arguments through registers instead of on the stack as was done in the text.

31. Write a subroutine ADD that adds the top two floating-point numbers on the stack, returning the answer on the stack as indicated in the text. For this problem you should use a subroutine from the MC6839 floating-point ROM. See the user's manual for that chip for details. Set up the floating-point control block (FPCB) for affine closure, rounding to nearest, single-precision, and to normalize denormalized numbers. (Hint: The return address for subroutine ADD has to be temporarily pulled into an index register X, the pointer to the FPCB has to be pushed, and you must jump to the subroutine at the address equal to the ROM starting address +$3F. The byte below this JSR instruction must be 0. You return from the subroutine ADD by the instruction JMP ,X.)

32. Write a program to make your microcomputer a simple four-function calculator, using the MC6839 floating-point ROM chip. Use the subroutines in the chip to convert between ASCII and binary and to evaluate all the functions. Your calculator should use Polish notation and should only evaluate +, −, *, and /, inputting data in the form of up to eight decimal digits and decimal point (e.g., 123.45, 1234567.8, 12., and so forth). You will need to consult the user's manual for the details on the MC6839 subroutines.

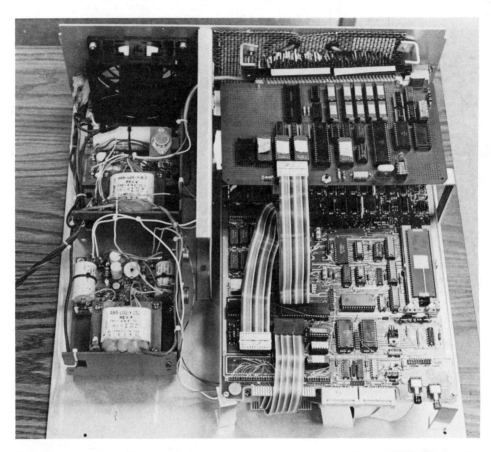

The above picture shows a dual microprocessor system with an **MC6809** (on the right-hand side of the upper board) and an **MC68000** (on the right-hand side of the lower board). The left-hand part of the unit is the power supply. The system was developed to assist conventional visual **EEG** analysis and can accept up to eight **EEG** channels in real time.

CHAPTER 8

Input and Output

An *input routine* is a program segment that inputs words from the outside world into the computer, and an *output routine* is a program segment that does the reverse, it outputs words from the computer to the outside world. Clearly, a computer that does not have input and output routines, and the hardware to carry out these routines, would be useless regardless of its power to invert matrices or manipulate great quantities of data. Until now, we have implied that you should avoid knowing the details of these routines, although you've used them. For example, in Chapters 6 and 7 you used the routine INCH to input an ASCII character from a terminal and OUTCH to output an ASCII character to a terminal. Even though we have left the discussion of input and output until the end of this book, it is really simple and should pose no problem to the reader. In fact, it is really quite satisfying to learn exactly what happens when the otherwise mystical input/output routines such as INCH and OUTCH are executed.

In this chapter we describe how the basic input and output operations are implemented in hardware and executed in software, using a simplified model of the hardware. After discussing the use of buffers in input and output we describe an integrated circuit, the Asynchronous Communications Interface Adapter, that can be used in the INCH and OUTCH routines that you used in Chapters 6 and 7. We next discuss synchronization mechanisms, the ways that are used to transfer data between the MPU and the outside world when the data are available or needed. At the end of this chapter you should be able to understand how basic input and output operations are performed, and be able to read input and output routines that use simple synchronization mechanisms. You should be able to write the simple INCH and OUTCH subroutines that were used in Chapters 6 and 7. References that discuss input/output are noted at the end of the chapter. They can be consulted for information on how to write input/output routines that use the more complex synchronization mechanisms.

8-1

INPUT AND OUTPUT HARDWARE

In this section we introduce a simplified model of the hardware that is used by input/output routines. We also discuss simple input and output ports that will be used in later sections. This discussion is intended to provide enough background for the later sections of this chapter.

Recall from Chapter 1 that a computer is divided into its major components, which are the controller, data operator (arithmetic/logic unit), memory, and input/output unit, and that the microprocessor (MPU) is generally the controller and data operator in a 40-pin integrated circuit package (see Figure 8-1). Since it is not easy to connect the microprocessor to the other two units through just 40 pins, some pins are used for different functions during the execution of different instructions. Input and output instructions use the same pins as load and store instructions with memory, but the action of input and output instructions on input/output hardware is a bit different than the action of load and store

microcomputer

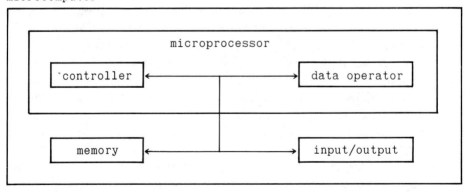

FIGURE 8-1. Simplified Diagram of a Microcomputer

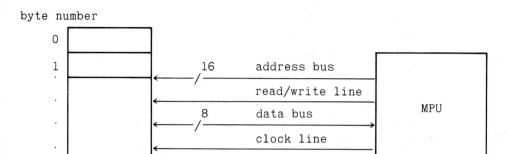

FIGURE 8-2.   A Memory and Its Connection to the MPU. The notation " $\overset{16}{/}$ " indicates a bus with 16 lines.

instructions on memory. In many microcomputers, different instructions are used for memory reads or writes than for input or output operations, even though essentially the same pins are used for each instruction. However, in microprocessors such as the Motorola MC6809, the load instruction is used to input data as well as to read data from memory, and the store instruction is used to output data as well as to store data in memory. We will review from Chapter 1 how the load and store instructions work on memory, and then discuss how the input/output instruction works on an input/output hardware device.

The memory and microprocessor are connected by address, data, and control lines. The Motorola MC6809 in particular has sixteen address lines (the address bus), eight data lines (the data bus), and control lines that include a clock line and a read/write line (see Figure 8-2). Each address, data, or control line has a signal that is a (logical) one if the voltage is above a certain threshold level, and a (logical) zero if the voltage is below that level. The voltages corresponding to a (logical) one and a (logical) zero are also termed *high* and *low* signal, respectively. The clock signal is alternately low and high repetitively in a square wave and the clock signal between high-to-low transitions is called a clock cycle. In each clock cycle, the microprocessor can read a word from memory by putting the address of the word to be read on the address bus and putting the read/write line to high throughout the clock cycle. The memory will put the word on the data bus by the end of the clock cycle, and the processor will copy the word on the data bus into some internal memory register. The microprocessor can also write a word into memory at a particular address in one clock cycle by putting the address on the address bus, the word to be written on the data bus, and making the signal low on the read/write line throughout the clock cycle. At the end of the clock cycle, the microprocessor will write the word on the data bus into the location in memory that is on the address bus. The microprocessor will read instructions into its controller and read data into its data operator or write data from its data operator back into memory using these two basic operations of reading and writing.

The output operation uses the same address, data, and control lines as the write operation. Some addresses in memory are chosen to be *output ports* and they correspond to a hardware component called an *output device,* which has *output lines* connected to the outside world. For example, location $0000 may be an output port, and a hardware output device will be built to output data for that port. Whenever the microprocessor writes data into location $0000, such as in the instruction

```
STA        $0000
```

the data written are put on the output lines of the device. These data are stored in the output hardware and are continuously available on the output lines until another word is output to this port. The change in the output lines occurs at the end of the last clock cycle of the STA $0000 instruction. In short, an output port is just a word in the microcomputer memory whose stored bits are available to the outside world on the lines that come from the output of the device.

The input operation uses the same address, data and control lines as the read operation. Some addresses in memory are chosen as *input ports,* and they correspond to a hardware component called an *input device* that has *input lines* coming from the outside world. For example, location $0000 may be an input port, and a hardware input device will be built to input data from that port. Whenever the microprocessor reads data from location $0000, as in the instruction

```
LDA        $0000
```

the signals on the input lines of the input device will be read into the microprocessor just like a word read in from memory. Note that an input operation ''takes a snapshot'' of the data fed into the input device at the end of the last clock cycle of the load instruction

```
LDA        $0000
```

and is insensitive to the data values before or after that point in the last clock cycle. In short, an input port is just a word in memory that always has the value of the signals that are connected to the input of the device. The word read by an input instruction is the value of the input signals on the input lines at the end of the clock cycle that the port is read.

In a sense, the basic input and output devices trick the microcomputer. The microcomputer thinks it is reading or writing a word in its memory at some address. However, the designer of the microcomputer has selected that address as an input or an output port, and built hardware to input or output data that are read from or written into that port. By means of the hardware, the designer tricks the microcomputer into inputting data when it reads a word at the address of an input port, or into outputting data when it writes data into the word at the address of an output port.

You can build a basic input or output device and connect it to your computer with little effort if the computer provides access to its address, data, read/write and clock lines. Let's look first at how an output device is connected. The basic hardware used to build an output port is an address decoder and an output register. The output register could be connected to eight light emitting diodes (LEDs) so that a particular LED is lit if the corresponding output register bit is one (see Figure 8-3). The register copies the data on its input lines whenever the signal on the CLK input changes from low to high. The data in the register are constantly output to turn the LEDs on if the corresponding bit is one. The address decoder must be designed to provide a low-to-high transition at the end of the clock cycle when, and only when, the port address is on the address bus and the read/write line is low. For instance, an 18-bit input OR gate, whose inputs are connected to the address bus, the read/write line, and the complemented clock line will serve as a decoder for a port address $0000. It will provide the low-to-high transition at the end of the last clock cycle of the instruction

```
STA        $0000
```

See Figure 8-4, where the clock signal, the negated clock signal, the read/write

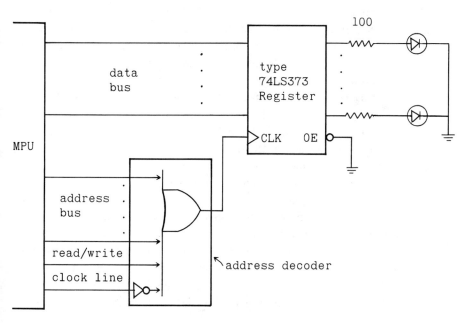

FIGURE 8-3.   Simple Output Device

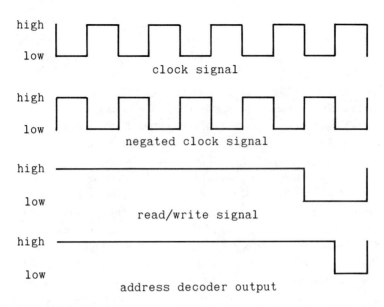

clock signal

high

low

negated clock signal

high

low

read/write signal

high

low

address decoder output

FIGURE 8-4. Signals for Output Port at Location $0000 During the Five Clock Cycles of STA $0000. Direct addressing is assumed for this figure.

line, and the output of the address decoder are depicted. Notice, in particular, that the output of the address decoder goes from low to high at the end of the last clock cycle of the STA instruction. In the previous four clock cycles of the STA instruction, the output of the address decoder has stayed high. (Assuming that direct addressing is being used, the perceptive reader may wonder about the fourth clock cycle in the STA instruction since the first three clock cycles were used to fetch the 3-byte instruction from memory. For example, what address is on the address bus when no byte is being fetched or recalled from memory? This is an example of a *null* cycle and, in such cycles, the MPU automatically puts $FFFF on the address bus and puts the read/write line to read. Since the two bytes at $FFFE and $FFFF are used for the reset address, these two bytes are always in ROM and no read occurs from an input/output register. The value on the data bus during this read is ignored by the MPU. Handling null cycles in this way ensures that random addresses will not get on the address bus during a null cycle.)

The input device is similar to the output device but, in place of the register, uses hardware that responds to read commands at the port address. Referring to Figure 8-5, the 74LS244 *bus driver* is designed to copy the data on the input lines onto the data bus whenever the output from the 17-bit OR gate is 0. The OR gate has the address bus and negated read/write line connected to it so that the output of the OR gate will be 1 until the last cycle of the instruction

```
LDA        $0000
```

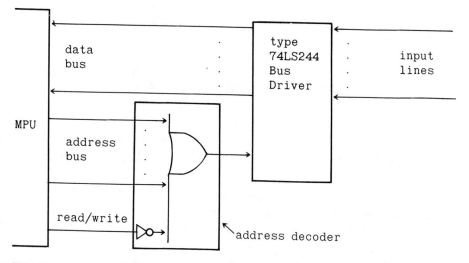

FIGURE 8-5. Simple Input Port at Location $0000

(see Figure 8-6). The byte on the data bus at the end of this clock cycle is the byte put into accumulator A. The MPU then effectively takes a "snapshot" of the input lines at this instant.

Frequently, a system will have 64K bytes of RAM in its memory unit even though some of the RAM locations will not be used. This comes about, for example, when one uses eight 64K-bit RAM chips for components of the memory section. Since one does not want to read from memory at the address of an input port, each input port address must be blocked off by hardware in

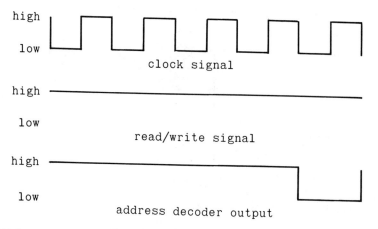

FIGURE 8-6. Signals for the Input Port at $0000 During the Five Clock Cycles of LDA $0000. Direct addressing is assumed for this figure.

the memory unit. We leave the details of this to the references at the end of the chapter.

Both the input device and the output device are very simple, and can be added to any microcomputer in a matter of an hour or so, provided that the address, data, clock, and read/write lines are accessible.

THE USE OF BUFFERS WITH INPUT AND OUTPUT

Input or output of a single word is simple, but we often need to input or output a string of characters, an array of numbers, or a program consisting of many words. This section reviews how buffers are used in these situations.

The simplest and most common situation occurs when one is inputting or outputting a string of bytes. To output a string of bytes to the simple output device of the preceding section, the bytes in the buffer holding the string are moved successively to the output device, where they are displayed by the LEDs. Conversely, to input a string of bytes that is on the input lines of the simple input device, the bytes are stored in consecutive locations of a buffer used for holding strings.

As an example, suppose that the social security number 568-42-7081 is to be output to the LED display. Let's assume that the output of each character will be in ASCII so that the LED display will show $35 for the decimal digit 5, $37 for the decimal digit 7, and so on. This string of bytes could be created in memory by the assembler directive

```
SSN        FCC        "568-42-7081"
```

so that the contents of the buffer holding this string would be as shown.

To output this string to the LED display, we can execute the following sequence.

```
LDX        #SSN        Point X to the buffer
LDB        #11         Number of bytes into B
```

```
L       LDA         ,X+             Get next byte
        STA         $0000           Output to display
        DECB                        Decrement counter
        BNE         L               Another byte?
```

Assuming that direct addressing is used for the STA instruction, a character is output to the LED display every sixteen clock cycles, probably much too fast for any type of useful display. Although one could easily add an arbitrary delay in this loop to display each character as long as desired, we content ourselves here with illustrating the simple use of a buffer for outputting this string.

A string of bytes from the simple input device can be stored in a buffer in a similar manner. For example, if the buffer is created in memory with the assembler directive

```
BUFFER          RMB         200
```

200 bytes can be read from the input device of the preceding section with the following sequence.

```
        LDX         #BUFFER         Point X to buffer
        LDB         #200            Number of bytes into B
L       LDA         $0000           Get next byte
        STA         ,X+             Place in buffer
        DECB                        Decrement counter
        BNE         L               Another input?
```

In this sequence, the values on the input lines are being read every sixteen clock cycles. Assuming that a clock cycle takes 1 microsecond, this sequence might be useful in situations where a function of time is being sampled every 16 microseconds and the eight bits on the data lines of the input device represent a quantization of the sampled values of the function. Almost always, however, this type of application would require a delay in the loop to get the desired interval between the samples. This sequence does, however, illustrate the use of a buffer to hold an input string.

Arrays or vectors can be used with buffers to input or output many numbers in a similar way. Queues are implemented in buffers to input or output data when the program needs them in the same order that they are input or when the device needs them in the same order that they are provided by the program, but at different times than they are provided. We shall give an example of this in Section 8-4. Generally, data structures are used to maintain order in the data that are being transferred between the MPU and an input/output device.

INTEGRATED CIRCUIT CHIPS FOR INPUT/OUTPUT DEVICES

In this section we show how an integrated circuit chip, the Motorola 6850 Asynchronous Communications Interface Adapter (ACIA), is set up to work with the INCH and OUTCH subroutines used in Chapters 6 and 7. The behavior of the chip is described, and its unusual characteristics are explained.

When microcomputers first became available, the input/output devices were built using the simple hardware described in the preceding section. This resulted in microcomputers that were about the same size and the same cost as minicomputers that were entirely built from small-scale integrated circuits, so there was no great advantage to putting only the controller and data operator on a large-scale integrated circuit. We even recall some news articles that predicted the demise of the microcomputer because of this shortcoming. Recalling Mark Twain's well-known remark, the announcement of its demise was premature.

The first microcomputers were followed soon after by the first large-scale input/output chips. It became possible to build an entire computer with only five chips and the cost of a microcomputer was dramatically reduced. One of the first such chips was the ACIA that we discuss below. These chips required new programming techniques that were often misunderstood, so that the chips were considered badly designed or worse. One has to understand that these large-scale chips have to be sold in great volume to recover their design cost, and therefore have to be designed to work in a wide variety of situations to be useful to a lot of different users. The result is that they have to be initialized in software to tailor them to a specific machine requirement, and they have to be tested in software to synchronize to the data as they are available or as they are needed. The initialization software is usually easy to implement but difficult to explain. We will try to give you a feeling for the initialization sequence but we will leave many of the details to the references.

The ACIA is a serial interface chip. That means that it converts the 8-bit word in the computer to a series of bits on a single line, or vice versa. Transmitting words over a single line is slower than a parallel bus used in a computer, but is cheaper and easier to use for connections to a terminal or any other device that is physically more than several feet away from the MPU. We will assume that our input/output device is a terminal which is connected by a pair of lines to the MPU (one for serial input data and one for serial output data) and that the ACIA is used to send and receive data from this terminal with the INCH and OUTCH subroutines.

The ACIA has two ports on the same chip, a *transmitter* that sends serial data out to the terminal, and a *receiver* that receives serial data from the terminal (see Figure 8-7). Each part has a data register that connects to a shift register. In the case of the transmitter, when a word is put in the transmitter data register, the ACIA will then put the word into the transmitter shift register, where it is shifted out serially, one bit at a time. Putting words into the transmitter data register from the MPU is done in exactly the same way that words were put out to the simple output device. The receiver section is essentially a simple input device where the MPU can read the word that is in the receiver data register. The incoming bits are shifted into the receiver shift register serially and, when one full word is shifted in, the word is put in the receiver data register, where it can be read into the MPU in the same way that the MPU did with the simple input device.

The chip also has an output register called a *control register*. The bits in the control register determine how the transmitter and the receiver will work and are usually written once at the beginning of the program in an initialization

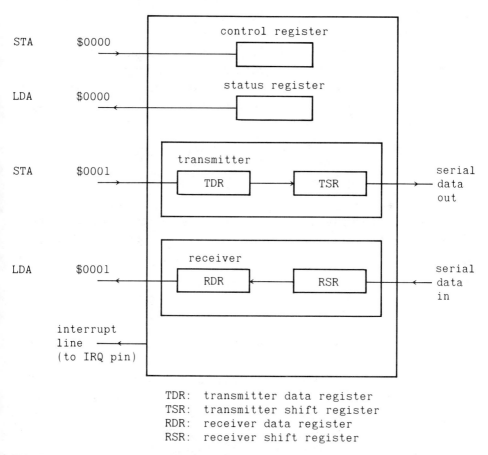

TDR: transmitter data register
TSR: transmitter shift register
RDR: receiver data register
RSR: receiver shift register

FIGURE 8-7. An ACIA Chip (MC6850)

segment. For example, when a word is written into the control register, the following things are determined.

1. The type of parity is fixed. If a parity bit is added to the words being sent or received, the ACIA will add a parity bit to the data word being transmitted using the type of parity specified (e.g., even or odd parity) or, for a received word, take off the parity bit to get the actual word sent and check to see if a parity error occurred.
2. The number of data bits sent per word is chosen. The choice here is between seven and eight bits so that one might choose seven bits if a word is only used for ASCII characters. In this case, the most significant bit of the word is ignored.
3. The choice is made whether the transmitter section can cause a hardware interrupt or not. A similar choice is also made for the receiver section. (We will discuss more carefully later how these sections cause interrupts.)
4. There are other choices, which include how the hardware detects the serial data, but we will not discuss these any further.

Every time one changes one of these choices, or initializes the ACIA at the start of a program, $03 must be stored in the control register to indicate that a *reset* of the ACIA is taking place. The next word written into the control register then selects from the preceding possibilities. For example, if the control register is at location $0000, then

```
LDA     #$03
STA     $0000          Reset the ACIA
LDA     #$15
STA     $0000
```

chooses, among other things, eight data bits, no parity bits, and keeps the receiver and transmitter from causing interrupts. This sequence can be shortened to

```
LDD     #$0315         Reset the ACIA
STA     $0000
STB     $0000
```

The ACIA also has an input register called a *status register*. Different bits in the status register indicate different types of status of the ACIA. Figure 8-8 shows the three bits in the status register that we will use in this chapter. (The remaining bits are used to indicate different types of error conditions, including, for example, a parity error in a received word.) The receiver ready bit is set whenever there is a word in the receiver data register that has not been read by the MPU. Whenever a word is read from the receiver data register, this bit is cleared until a new word is put in that register from the receiver shift register.

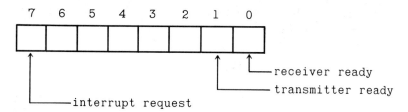

FIGURE 8-8. Status Register of the ACIA

The transmitter ready bit is set whenever the transmitter data register has put its contents into the transmitter shift register to be put out over the serial line, that is, when the transmitter is ready to accept another word to be sent to the terminal. The transmitter ready bit is cleared after a word has been written into the transmitter data register. The interrupt request bit is set whenever the receiver or transmitter has given a hardware interrupt signal to the MPU, a topic we discuss more fully in the next section.

Although it sounds illogical, only two port addresses are used for the four registers. Following the example in the preceding section, we might use locations $0000 and $0001. In this case, if you write a word into location $0001, it will be written in the transmitter output port and, subsequently, it will be shifted out serially to the terminal. If you read a word from location $0001, the word that you read will be from the receiver data register, that is, the last word that was put into the receiver data register from the receiver shift register. The same address is used for both because you should never have to read the word that you send to the terminal (if you have to, you can keep a separate copy of it in a memory word) and you should not be allowed to write a word into the input port. Similarly, writing into location $0000 writes a word into the control register and reading from location $0000 reads the values in the status register. We will use the label ACIASC for the address of the status/control registers and ACIAD for the address of the transmitter and receiver data registers so that

```
LDD     #$0315
STA     ACIASC
STB     ACIASC
```

is the initialization sequence used earlier. Moreover,

```
STA     ACIAD
```

will put a word out to the terminal and

```
LDA     ACIAD
```

will read a word into accumulator A that has come into the ACIA from the terminal. At the beginning of the program, we use the EQU directives to specify the addresses ACIASC and ACIAD as, for example,

```
ACIASC     EQU      $0000
ACIAD      EQU      $0001
```

This is really very simple, isn't it? Well, there is a bit more to input/output programming. Although we have not dealt with all of the details of the address decoder, the control register, and the initialization of the ACIA, we have discussed enough to understand the following section, which covers the synchronization mechanisms used for sending and receiving data. It is also fairly simple. At this point you should understand the initialization of an ACIA and be able to send and receive a word from it. If a terminal is connected to the ACIA, the data words that you send and receive will be in ASCII code, as discussed in Chapters 6 and 7. We look at the specific subroutines for that purpose, INCH and OUTCH, in the next section.

8-4

SYNCHRONIZATION MECHANISMS

We have discussed the use of buffers, assuming that the input/output device is so fast that it will be ready to move a word to or from the computer every time that the computer is ready to input or output a word. But that is rarely the case. For instance, consider the situation where a computer, with a clock rate of 1 million cycles per second, is controlling a terminal that can type ten characters per second. The computer will have to have at least 100,000 clock cycles between sending successive characters to the terminal! Programming the fast computer, you might get the feeling that controlling the input/output device is rather like coaxing a stubborn mule to move. At the other extreme, some input/ output hardware is actually much faster than the computer, and techniques are used to circumvent the slow computer to get data into or out of memory at a very fast rate. These techniques, where the computer is slowed down to handle data from a slow device or where the computer is circumvented to match the speed of a very fast device, are referred to as *synchronization mechanisms,* and are discussed in this section.

The six synchronization mechanisms include two, the real-time and gadfly mechanisms, for slow devices, another two, the polled interrupt and vector interrupt techniques, for devices that perform input and output at unpredictable times, and the final two, direct memory access and context switching, for faster devices. We will concentrate our discussion on the first two mechanisms and a simplified interrupt model. Our examples for this discussion will all use the ACIA. We then conclude this section with a brief description of the other two synchronization mechanisms.

Real-time synchronization uses natural or fabricated delays in the program to match the delays in the input/output device. Consider a program like that in Section 8-2 to output a social security number to a terminal that can print up to ten characters per second. If there is a subroutine SUB that does something useful, such as invert a matrix or assemble a program, and takes at least a tenth of a second, the following program will output the characters to the terminal through the ACIA using real-time synchronization.

```
        LDD     #$0315      Initialization sequence for ACIA port
        STA     ACIASC
        STB     ACIASC
        ,
        ,
        ,
        LDX     #SSN        Point X to SSN                      (1)
        LDB     #11         Number of characters into B
L       LDA     ,X+
        STA     ACIAD       Put out next character
        LBSR    SUB         Delay at least one-tenth of a second
        DECB
        BNE     L
```

It is rarely possible to find a subroutine such as SUB that does something useful and fits the timing requirements of the input/output device. Moreover, such a subroutine can make the program difficult to debug since changes in the subroutine will affect the timing in the input/output part of the program. In particular, SUB can be working correctly, while changes in it could lower its execution time to less than one-tenth of a second, so that the segment (1) no longer works correctly. Consequently, one often writes a program segment, called a *delay loop*, that merely wastes time. Assuming that we have 1 million clock cycles per second, a delay loop that takes a tenth of a second is shown below. The LEAY and BNE instructions in this loop take 5 and 3 microseconds, respectively (see Appendix 2). Since this 8-microsecond loop is executed 12,500 times, the program segment delays the execution of the next instruction by slightly more than 100,000 microseconds. It could be put in the program above, in place of the LBSR SUB instruction, to make a self-contained program to output the social security number.

```
        LDY     #12500
L1      LEAY    -1,Y
        BNE     L1
```

Real-time synchronization has the advantage that it requires no extra hardware beyond the simple input or output port discussed in Section 8-1. However, it is quite wasteful if the computer is made to "twiddle its thumbs" in a delay loop and, even if a useful subroutine can be found to provide the delay, the synchronized program becomes difficult to debug. Nevertheless, one of the authors has written many of these real-time synchronization segments, for example, in a very simple microcomputer program that controls a television channel selector and in a program that formats a floppy disk.

A step above real-time synchronization is gadfly synchronization. This form requires more hardware, but simplifies the software. The input/output device has to have some hardware to signal when it needs service or has some data or needs some data. The need is usually modeled by a 1-bit *ready state* which, when set, means that the device is ready for service, while, when clear, means that the device is not ready. In a gadfly loop, the program continually reads the ready state of the device, and loops until it finds this bit equal to 1 before going on. This is called a *gadfly loop,* in honor of the great philosopher Socrates, who was called the gadfly of Athens because he pestered the local politicians like a pesky little fly. He would ask them the same question over and over again until they gave the answer that he wanted. Often, they would believe that the answer was theirs, and Socrates would get his way. But then again, Socrates bothered someone a bit too much, as the politicians forced him to drink poisonous hemlock. This technique survives as the "Socratic method of teaching" and as the gadfly synchronization mechanism. In this mechanism, the program bothers the device with the same question (usually "Are you ready?") until it gets the desired answer ("I am ready!") before it goes on. The gadfly loop is easily implemented with the ACIA since the receiver ready and transmitter ready bits, when set, indicate that the device is ready to receive or transmit, respectively (see Figure 8-8). For example, the following program segment outputs the social security number using the gadfly synchronization mechanism with the ACIA.

```
         LDD     #$315        Initilization sequence for ACIA port
         STA     ACIASC
         STB     ACIASC
         .
         .
         .
         LDX     #SSN         Point X to SSN                        (2)
         LDB     #11
LOOP     LDA     ACIASC
         BITA    #2           Is transmitter ready bit set?
         BEQ     LOOP         If not, check again
         LDA     ,X+          Get next character.
         STA     XIS
         DECB
         BNE     LOOP
```

Since the status register is at location ACIASC and the transmitter ready bit is bit #1 in the status register, the gadfly loop

```
LOOP    LDA     ACIASC
        BITA    #2
        BEQ     LOOP
```

causes the program to cycle in this loop until the transmitter ready bit becomes 1. At this point, the ACIA is ready to receive another byte to send to the terminal.

The gadfly method is used extensively with the ACIA because the extra hardware needed with the gadfly technique over the real-time technique is already built into the ACIA and is therefore "free." The subroutine OUTCH, which outputs the byte in accumulator A through the ACIA using gadfly synchronization, is shown below.

```
OUTCH    PSHS    B          Save B
OUTCH1   LDB     ACIASC     Status/control register into B
         BITB    #2         Is the transmitter ready?
         BEQ     OUTCH1     Loop until ready
         STA     ACIAD      Put byte into transmitter data register
         PULS    B,PC
```

Note that the test for the ready state is done before the output of the character to prevent accidentally outputting data before the device is ready. The transmitter ready bit is cleared by the ACIA after the

```
STA      ACIAD
```

instruction. This subroutine needs to have the ACIA initialized before it is used, just like the program segment (2), to output the social security number. This is usually done by executing the initialization sequence once after the computer is turned on as discussed in the preceding section. The subroutine OUTCH is the output routine that is most commonly used in MC6809 programs and in almost all software except for the more powerful operating systems such as OS9.

We can similarly write the subroutine INCH for accepting an ASCII character from the terminal which is connected to the MPU through the ACIA.

```
INCH     LDA     ACIASC     Copy status/control register into A
         ASRA               Receiver ready bit into C
         BCC     INCH       Loop until new character is received
*
         LDA     ACIAD      Character from RDR into A
         RTS
```

In the preceding sequence, the ACIA will clear the receiver ready bit after the instruction

```
LDA        ACIAD
```

As one can see, the routines INCH and OUTCH that we have used in earlier chapters are quite simple.

The two techniques above are often referred to as *programmed input/output* because the program directly controls the input and output. (However, all such activity is ultimately controlled by the program in the other synchronization mechanisms, too, so we do not like this popular term.) They both waste computer power because the computer is unable to do anything else while looping in a delay loop or a gadfly loop. The other mechanisms will permit the computer to do something useful while waiting for a device to complete its work. The techniques of this type that we examine use interrupts. We will compare a simple interrupt model with the gadfly technique using a queueing example. The other synchronization techniques, direct memory access and context switching, will then be outlined, although the details of their operation will be omitted in this introductory treatment.

The interrupt mechanisms use more hardware to signal the computer as to the state of an input/output device. The computer can start a device, then do some other useful program, like invert a matrix, while the device is busy doing the operation. When the device is done, hardware sends a signal to the computer to stop the useful program, and execute a kind of subroutine, called an *interrupt handler,* to service the device. This may consist of restarting the device or stopping the device as appropriate. The interrupt handler is like any other subroutine in that any program segment can be used to service the device. (This will be contrasted to the direct memory access mechanism discussed later.) The interrupt handler ends with the instruction RTI that resumes execution of the useful program.

The program being interrupted must not be affected by the execution of the interrupt handler. The program must get the same results whether the interrupt occurs at all, or whenever it occurs during the execution of the useful program. This is done by the interrupt handler, by saving the *machine state* of the program and restoring it. The machine state is the contents of the accumulators and other registers, as well as any other variables that are used by the program and that might be altered by the interrupt handler. These data are saved at the beginning of the handler, often by pushing them on the stack, and restoring them at the end of the handler, often by pulling them back off the stack into the registers that they came from.

An interrupt handler may be written for one device, and that device may be the only one capable of causing an interrupt in the computer. But generally, more than one device will be capable of generating interrupts, and each such device will have a different handler. Determining which device caused an interrupt and then executing the appropriate handler is either done by a program segment or a hardware component.

The program segment that determines which device caused an interrupt is called a *polling* routine. The polling routine is similar to a gadfly loop, except that it checks each device to see if it has caused the interrupt, and it checks each device just once. It asks a device "Did you request an interrupt?" by examining its status register. If the answer is "yes," the polling routine jumps to the handler for that device. Otherwise, the polling routine asks another device, "Did you request an interrupt?", until it finds a device that did request an interrupt. Some call the gadfly loop and interrupt polling techniques by the same name, polling, but the two approaches do test different bits in the device's status register, are susceptible to different problems, and have different overall performance characteristics.

The polling of devices can take too long for devices that need to get service fast from their handler. On some machines, hardware can generate the address of the handler (or an indirect address which is the address of a double word that is the address of the handler) directly from the hardware signal from the device that requested the interrupt. The computer is vectored to the correct handler by this hardware rather like an airplane is vectored to fly in a certain direction by air traffic controllers. This eliminates the time needed to poll each device because the correct handler is started in just a few clock cycles after the device signals that it needs an interrupt.

The usual interrupt on the MC6809 is the IRQ (interrupt request) interrupt. When the I bit in the condition code register is set, signals on the IRQ pin of the MC6809 are ignored. However, if the I bit is clear, a device can cause an IRQ interrupt by putting the IRQ line low. When this happens, the instruction that is currently being executed is completed, the MPU then puts the E bit in the condition code register equal to 1 (we will explain why shortly), pushes all of its registers onto the S stack (except S itself), puts I equal to 1 preventing further IRQ interrupts, and loads the program counter with the address in locations $FFF8 and $FFF9. The address in these last two locations is the *IRQ vector*, the address of the start of the interrupt handler. The interrupt handler performs the necessary service to remove the low signal on the IRQ pin after which the instruction RTI is executed, restoring all of the MPU registers to their values just before the interrupt occurred (except for the E bit). Because the I bit is cleared when the condition code register is restored by the RTI, the interrupted program can continue and further IRQ interrupts can occur.

The FIRQ (fast interrupt request) interrupt behaves in a similar way to the IRQ interrupt except that the F bit is used instead of I, and when the FIRQ pin on the MC6809 is put low by a device, the E bit is put to 0 and only CC and

PC are pushed onto the stack. The F bit is then set, preventing further FIRQ interrupts, and the FIRQ vector is obtained from locations $FFF6 and $FFF7, the FIRQ vector. While an RTI still terminates the FIRQ handler, the MPU looks at the E bit of the CC saved on the stack and, if equal to 1, pulls twelve bytes off the stack to restore all of the registers, while if equal to 0, pulls off only three bytes to restore CC and PC. The E bit, for *entire,* thus allows the RTI instruction to restore the registers with both IRQ and FIRQ interrupts.

The NMI (nonmaskable interrupt) interrupt cannot be prevented from occurring and behaves exactly like the IRQ interrupt except that an interrupt occurs when a high-to-low transition takes place on the NMI pin and the interrupt handler begins at the address contained in locations $FFFC and $FFFD. The fact that the NMI interrupt is caused by a high-to-low transition rather than just a low signal keeps the NMI interrupt from repeatedly interrupting itself. For example, a device can have a line connected to the NMI pin which it keeps high until it wants an NMI interrupt. When it makes the high-to-low transition, the NMI request starts and the device keeps the line low to prevent further NMI interrupts. Further NMI interrupts become possible whenever the handler or the device allow the the NMI signal from the device to go high.

Notice that an IRQ interrupt cannot occur during the IRQ interrupt handler because the I bit is set before the start of the handler. In a similar way, a FIRQ interrupt cannot occur during a FIRQ interrupt handler because the F bit has been set before the start of the handler. However, a FIRQ interrupt can occur during an IRQ interrupt, and vice versa. An NMI interrupt can occur during either an IRQ or a FIRQ interrupt handler. Thus three levels of interrupts can occur at once in the MC6809. At each level, polling would be necessary if more than one device could cause an interrupt at that level. We will not deal further with these possibilities, however, and instead concentrate on how the ACIA works with one device with IRQ interrupts.

The ACIA has an interrupt line (see Figure 8-7) which can be connected to any of the MC6809 interrupt pins. We will assume in what follows that it is connected to the IRQ pin. If the receiver interrupt is enabled in the initialization sequence, then every time the receiver data register gets a byte that has not been read by the MPU, the ACIA puts a low signal on its interrupt line and sets the interrupt request and receiver ready bits in the control/status register (see Figure 8-8). When a byte is read from the receiver data register, both the receiver ready bit and the interrupt request bits are cleared. If the transmitter interrupt is enabled during the initialization sequence, every time that the transmitter data register can accept a new byte, the ACIA puts a low signal on the interrupt line and sets the interrupt request and transmitter ready bits in the control/status register. They are both cleared when a byte is written into the transmitter data register. If both the receiver and transmitter sections can cause interrupts, both a read and write at location ACIAD may be necessary to clear the interrupt request bit. The interrupt request bit is used in the polling part of the interrupt handler to determine if one of the devices connected to the ACIA has caused an interrupt. Because we will have only one device to consider in the examples that follow, we will not need the interrupt request bit. If both the receiver and the transmitter can cause interrupts, the interrupt handler will have to determine which section caused the interrupt by looking at the other two status bits, that is, the transmitter ready and receiver ready bits.

Let's look again at the problem of outputting a string of ASCII characters, but now we will assume that the string is terminated with the ASCII NUL character ($00). If we use the subroutine OUTCH discussed above and assume that the index register X points to the start of the string, the subroutine PRINT shown below will print the string, including the NUL character. (The NUL character does nothing when "printed" on most terminals.)

```
PRINT      LDA        ,X+
           LBSR       OUTCH
           BNE        PRINT
           RTS
```

Notice that the Z bit set by the LDA instruction is set exactly the same by the subroutine OUTCH. As noted earlier, subroutine PRINT wastes time in the gadfly loop of the subroutine OUTCH, preventing the MPU from doing useful work while the ASCII string is outputted. Consider, for example, an MPU handling the various control functions of an automobile. The MPU may have to print the message "engine oil level is low" on the dashboard display. Although this may take only half a second when ASCII characters are transmitted to the dashboard at 30 characters per second, it would probably be unacceptable for the MPU to leave the rest of its control functions for that period of time. One possibility is to have the transmitter section of the ACIA interrupt the program every time that it can accept a new character from the MPU. The subroutine MSGOUT in Figure 8-9 prints the first character of the string, while subsequent characters are printed with interrupts from the ACIA with the interrupt handler MSGINT. Notice particularly the sequence in MSGOUT that enables the transmitter interrupts of the ACIA. A gadfly loop is still necessary, however, to prevent a second message from being printed while the first one is still being outputted. Two global variables MPOINT and BUSY are used to point to the next character to be printed and to indicate that a message is currently being printed. At the beginning of the program, one will have the directives

```
ACIASC     EQU        $0000     Address of status/control registers
ACIAD      EQU        $0001     Address of data registers
*
```

```
SAVE        EQU     *
            ORG     $FFF8       IRQ vector address
            FDR     MSGINT      Address of interrupt handler
            ORG     SAVE
```

while the initialization segment will have

```
LDD     #$0315      Initialization sequence
STA     ACIASC      Transmitter interrupts disabled
STB     ACIASC
CLR     BUSY
```

In the main program, one might have the instructions

```
    .
    .
    .
LDX     #MSG1
LBSR    MSGOUT
    .
    .
    .
LDX     #MSG2
LBSR    MSGOUT
    .
    .
    .
```

Notice that if the first message MSG1 is not finished printing by the time that MSG2 is to be printed, the interrupt handler MSGINT will continually interrupt the gadfly loop of MSGOUT until the first message is printed.

Rather than wait in the gadfly loop with one message while another is being printed, one might instead put the messages to be printed in a queue, enabling the transmitter interrupt when a character is put into an empty queue and, thereafter, allowing the transmitter to interrupt the program to get the next character in the queue. If the queue is emptied by the transmitter, the interrupt handler would disable the transmitter interrupt before returning to the main program. When the queue is full, the program would still wait in a gadfly loop until there is room to put in the next character.

Although the preceding description is simple enough, a rather subtle situation that we have not met before can occur. Both the main program and the interrupt handler will be accessing the queue holding the characters to be printed and we will have to prevent the interrupt handler from accessing the queue while the main program is using it. Otherwise, the main program might be interrupted when there is only one character in the queue and when it is about to put another

```
*                    SUBROUTINE      MSGOUT
*
* MSGOUT prints the string of characters pointed to by X and
* terminated by an ASCII null character. MSGOUT prints the first
* character in the string, enables the transmitter interrupt of
* the ACIA, and then lets the ACIA interrupt the program when it
* can accept another character to be printed. The interrupt
* routine is MSGINT.
*
MPOINT   RMB   2              Pointer to next character
BUSY     RMB   1              Indicator of message being printed
*
MSGOUT   TST   BUSY           Is a message being printed?
         BNE   MSGOUT         Wait until current message is finished
         DEC   BUSY           Put $FF in BUSY
         LDA   ,X+            First character into A
         STX   MPOINT         Save X for MSGINT
         STA   ACIAD          Output first character
*
         LDD   #$0335         Master reset sequence
         STA   ACIASC         Transmitter interrupt enabled;
         STB   ACIASC         Other parameters exactly as before
         RTS
*
*                  Interrupt Handler MSGINT
*
MSGINT   LDX   MPOINT         Get address of next character
         LDA   ,X+            Next character into A
         BEQ   RESET
         STX   MPOINT         Save address of next character
         STA   ACIAD          Put out current character
         RTI
*
RESET    LDD   #$0315         Master reset sequence
         STA   ACIASC         Disable transmitter interrupts
         STB   ACIASC         Other parameters stay the same
         CLR   BUSY
         RTI
```

FIGURE 8-9.   MSGOUT and Its Interrupt Handler MSGINT

character in the queue. The interrupt routine would print the one character in the queue and then disable transmitter interrupts before returning to the main program. The main program, believing there is still one character in the queue, will put one more character in the queue but will not enable transmitter interrupts. From this point on, no more characters will be printed and the queue will fill up, stopping the program forever in the gadfly loop while it waits for a transmitter interrupt. This is a simple case of a more general situation, called a *lockout,* which is taken up when one studies operating systems.

Assuming that the queue is implemented with pushes onto the bottom of the queue and pulls from the top, the program allocates memory for the queue with the assembler directives

```
TOPPNT     RMB      2          Top pointer
BOTPNT     RMB      2          Bottom pointer
NUMQUE     RMB      1          Number in queue
QUEUE      RMB      200        Buffer for the queue
```

and initializes the queue with

```
CLR        NUMQUE        Initialize number in queue to 0
LDX        #QUEUE
STX        TOPPNT
LEAX       -1,X
STX        BOTPNT
```

assuming that the first push will be into location QUEUE. We will assume that the top and bottom pointers point to the top and bottom of the queue exactly, not one byte above or below, so that a push from accumulator A onto the bottom of the queue is achieved with the following macro.

```
PUSH    MACR
        PSHS      X               Save X
        LDX       BOTPNT          Get bottom pointer
        CMPX      #QUEUE+199      Bottom pointer at bottom of queue buffer?
        BNE       \.0             No reset necessary
        LDX       #QUEUE-1        Reset bottom pointer
\.0     LEAX      1,X
        STA       ,X              Push character onto the bottom
        STX       BOTPNT          Save bottom pointer
        PULS      X               Restore X
        ENDM
```

Similarly, a pull into accumulator A from the top of the queue is obtained with the following macro.

```
PULL    MACR
        PSHS      X               Save X
```

```
        LDX     TOPPNT          Get top pointer
        CMPX    #QUEUE+200      Top pointer below queue?
        BNE     \,0             No reset necessary
        LDX     #QUEUE          Reset top pointer
\,0     LDA     ,X+             Pull character from top
        STX     TOPPNT          Save top pointer
        PULS    X               Restore X
        ENDM
```

The subroutine MSGOUT is shown in Figure 8-10 together with the interrupt handler OUTINT. Note how the interrupt mask I is set in MSGOUT to prevent the lockout condition discussed above. When one starts with an empty queue in MSGOUT, the interrupt line from the ACIA will go low after the reset sequence. After the interrupt bit I is cleared, an interrupt will occur before the branch instruction

```
    BRA        MSGOUT
```

is executed, printing the first character before the BRA instruction is executed. As the first character is being transmitted to the terminal from the ACIA, the second character in the message will be put in the queue and the preceding process will be repeated with OUTINT putting the second character in the transmitter data register, emptying the queue again. At this point, MSGOUT will start filling up the queue with the remaining characters in the message, with perhaps another interrupt or two, before returning to the main program. In effect, two characters must be given to the ACIA before the queue can start filling up. (See the problems at the end of the chapter for an alternative way of implementing MSGOUT.) The initialization sequence for MSGOUT and OUT-INT is straightforward and is left as a problem. This completes our discussion of interrupts.

The last two synchronization techniques that we discuss are used for input/output devices that are faster than the computer. These are *direct memory access*, and its generalization *context switching*.

Direct memory access is very simple. The input/output device "steals a memory cycle" from the MPU so that it can transfer a word to or from memory without help from the MPU, and without disturbing the MPU and its contents. Here is a scenario that simply explains how direct memory access works. The MPU is executing a program. The device has just output a word, and needs to get another word from memory so that it can output it later. In this mode, the device signals the MPU to halt, the MPU signals the device that it has halted, and the MPU essentially disconnects itself from the address and data buses. The device has control of these buses, so that it can read a word from memory. After it has read the word, the MPU regains control of the buses and continues as if nothing happened in the stolen cycle. This method requires considerably

```
*                    SUBROUTINE MSGOUT
*
* MSGOUT prints the string of ASCII characters pointed to by X
* and terminated by an ASCII NUL character. MSGOUT places the
* characters in QUEUE, enabling transmitter interrupts whenever
* QUEUE is empty and busy-waiting if QUEUE is full. Registers D
* and X are changed by MSGOUT
*
MSGOUT    LDA     ,X+         Next character into A
          BNE     M0          Put nonnull character into QUEUE
          RTS                 Return if character is NUL
*
M0        PSHS    A           Save A
M1        LDB     NUMQUE
          CMPB    #200        Is queue full?
          BEQ     M1          Queue full; wait in gadfly loop
          ORCC    #$10        Mask interrupts while accessing queue
*
          TST     NUMQUE      Is queue empty?
          BNE     M2          Store character in queue
          LDD     #$0335      Master reset
          STA     ACIASC      Enable transmitter interrupt,
          STB     ACIASC      Leave other parameters unchanged
*
M2        PULS    A           Restore
          PUSH                Put character in queue
          INC     NUMQUE      Increment number in queue
          ANDCC   #$EF        Clear I; allow interrupts
          BRA     MSGOUT
*
*              Interrupt Handler OUTINT
*
OUTINT    LDA     NUMQUE      Get number in QUEUE
          CMPA    #1          Will QUEUE be empty after this output?
          BNE     LOAD        No, go to output sequence
          LDD     #$0315      QUEUE will be empty,
          STA     ACIASC      Disable transmitter interrupt with
          STB     ACIASC      Other parameters the same as before
*
LOAD      DEC     NUMQUE
          PULL
          STA     ACIAD
          RTI
```

FIGURE 8-10.   MSGOUT and Its Interrupt Handler OUTINT Using a Queue

more hardware since the device must have the means to generate the address as well as the data when it steals a cycle from the MPU. The device also has to change this address, and stop working after an appropriate number of words have been transferred. However, it has the capability of moving words very fast, ideally one word per memory cycle, into or out of memory. It is used for very fast input/output devices that require a high rate of data movement, such as Winchester disks and optical communications channels.

A less well known synchronization mechanism that is a generalization of direct memory access is context switching. We regard the main component of intelligence in a computer to be the program and data that have been entered by a human into memory. The MPU is really just an interpreter of the bits stored there. This interpreter has a *context,* which is its instruction set and the data in its registers (or more generally its machine state). The idea of this form of synchronization is that the interpreter, and its context, can be switched around to handle an "interrupt" if that suits the needs of the application. Here, two or more MPUs, which may or may not be the same type of MPU, are connected to the same address and data buses. An MPU is said to be *off* when it does not move data around inside it, and does not attempt to put signals onto the address and data buses. One MPU, the *background* MPU, is running some useful program. The other, a *handler* MPU, is off. When a device needs service, the background MPU is turned off, as if direct memory access were being used, and the handler MPU is turned on and runs the memory through the address and data buses to handle the device's needs. When the handler is done, it turns itself off and the background MPU is turned on to resume its activity as if nothing happened.

Context switching can use the same type of MPU for background as for the handler. This approach is very similar to interrupt handling, except that the machine state of the background MPU does not have to be saved in memory. It is saved in the background MPU because that MPU is frozen while the handler MPU services the device, and the handler MPU can have its registers, such as index registers, set up permanently so that they do not have to be loaded at the beginning of the interrupt and saved at the end of the interrupt handler routine.

Context switching can use different MPUs for the background and handler MPUs. Direct memory access is a special case of this type of context switching in which the device itself behaves as a microprocessor with a very limited instruction set that is optimized for moving data to or from the device. However, the handler MPU can have a full instruction set chosen for some special feature needed to service the device or chosen for reduced cost. It could also be a special-purpose integrated circuit chip used, for example, for floating-point operations. Such a chip is called a *floating-point coprocessor.*

Both approaches switch the context of the microcomputer, where the context is the contents of the registers—the machine state—and the instruction set that determines what words fetched from memory will mean to the MPU.

We conclude this section with a look at a more general state description of input/output devices. You may have already taken a course in logic design, where the notion of a sequential machine is studied. This notion is ideal for modeling the behavior of almost all input/output devices. Generally, we say that a given device has a *state* that can be either *idle, busy, or done*. When a device is in the idle state, no program is using it, and it is free to be used. To use the device, a program puts the device in the busy state (see Figure 8-11). When a device is in the busy state, it has been told to do something but has not yet done it. When the device is finished, it enters the done state on its own, without being told to do so by the computer. After the device is in the done state, the computer can prevent further action by putting the device in the idle state, or it can request another action by putting it in the busy state again.

Consider the example of a terminal that is to print a social security number where it can print at most one character each tenth of a second. The terminal is initially in the idle state. When the first character is sent to it with

```
STA        ACIAD
```

the terminal enters the busy state. It stays there for a tenth of a second as the character is being typed. Then it enters the done state. The program feeds it another character, putting it in the busy state, and then it goes to the done state. This cycle is repeated nine more times and, after the eleventh time, it goes to the idle state because the program does not command it to print another character.

In this real-time program, the notion of the idle, busy, and done states exist, but the program essentially keeps track of the state by implicitly associating parts of the program with each state, and using delays in the program to make the proper state transitions. However, the program has no way of checking that its accounting of the state is actually the correct state of the device. To check

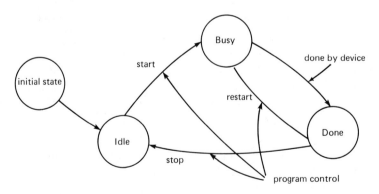

FIGURE 8-11. Generalized State Diagram for Input/Output Device

the state of the device, the device must have extra hardware to keep track of its own state, and the program must be able to read this state in a gadfly loop, as discussed earlier.

In this section we have detailed the two slowest synchronization mechanisms, real-time, and gadfly. We have also studied interrupts with one device and have sketched the other two synchronization mechanisms, direct memory access and context switching. You should be capable of writing and using an input or output routine that uses real-time or gadfly synchronization, on a simple device such as an ACIA, and you should have some understanding of the other synchronization mechanisms used for faster devices. However, we do caution you that, although the discussion showed how simple the notions of synchronization are, considerably more study is needed before you will be able to control more powerful input/output chips, and to use the faster synchronization techniques.

SUMMARY AND FURTHER READING

This chapter has introduced you to input/output programming, a somewhat obscure area because many texts, magazine articles, and courses define input/output to be beyond their scope, while they concentrate on some other topic. But it is not obscure. This chapter showed that the basic notion of input/output in a microcomputer is really a minor extension of reading and writing to memory. The input/output integrated circuit was discussed, and an example, the ACIA, was studied. We looked at enough of the chip to understand the way that the INCH and OUTCH subroutines work. The method of outputting several words one after another to the same device was discussed. This method, using buffers, was seen to be very straightforward. Then synchronization mechanisms were discussed, and the gadfly technique was detailed. The INCH and OUTCH subroutines were then shown, and their operation explained. You can now see how simple input/output programming can be. We also discussed other synchronization techniques, an area where new ideas are now being introduced and exciting possibilities for further microcomputer enhancements are becoming available.

If input/output programming interests you, we recommend the following books. Of course, we recommend the accompanying textbook, *Microcomputer Interfacing: Principles and Practices* (G. Jack Lipovski, D. C. Heath and Company, Lexington, Mass., 1980). It emphasizes the software used to control devices, using the MC6809 and chips in the 6800 family for concrete examples, experiments, and problems. The book *Microcomputer Architecture and Programming* (J. F. Wakerly, John Wiley & Sons, Inc., New York, 1981) has a more extensive, but still introductory, treatment of these topics. His appendix on the ACIA is quite readable. The book *Microcomputer Interfacing* (Bruce Artwell, Prentice-Hall Inc., Englewood Cliffs, N.J., 1979) emphasizes management-level issues, such as how fast a printer is needed for a given microcomputer. The book *Microcomputer Interfacing* (Harold Stone, Addison-Wesley Publishing Co., Inc., Reading, Mass., 1982) emphasizes the analog circuitry in these devices, especially in cassette and disk devices and in CRT controllers, and has a fine section on dynamic memory systems. Finally, two books by P Garrett, *Analog I/O Design* and *Analog Systems for Microprocessors and Minicomputers* (both published by Reston Publishing Co., Inc., Reston, Va., 1981 and 1978, respectively), give excellent discussions of operational amplifiers and filters used in input/output devices, and also discuss the characteristics of transducers and measurement hardware.

PROBLEMS

1. The most significant bit of an input port, as shown in Figure 8-5, is connected to a pushbutton switch. The signal from the switch is high if the button is not pressed, and low if it is pressed. However, when it is pressed, or released, it "bounces," that is, it changes value rapidly from high to low to high to low ... for about 10 milliseconds. Write a program segment that will loop until the button is down for at least 10 milliseconds without the signal changing value. (This is called a debouncer.)

2. Write a program to flash the LEDs in Figure 8-3. Only one LED should be lit at a time, and each LED should be lit for 1 second. Initially, the least significant LED should be lit. Then the LED for the next more significant bit should be lit, and so on. After the most significant LED is lit the least significant LED should be lit. This cycle should be repeated indefinitely.

3. Write a program segment that inputs a social security number into a buffer at location SSN using real-time synchronization. The ACIA is at location ACIASC (control/status) and ACIAD (data in/data out). The delay should be provided by a delay loop of 1/10 second as characters will be typed in at this rate. Discuss the timing assumptions necessary to make your program segment work.

4. Write a subroutine and interrupt handler that will take characters from a terminal connected through an ACIA at locations ACIASC and ACIAD. When the program wants an input character, it will get it from a queue. If the queue is empty, it should wait in a gadfly loop similar to the subroutine INCH. Characters typed at the terminal, unless asked for by the program with an empty queue, should be placed in the queue by the interrupt handler. If the queue is full, the interrupt handler should print "QUEUE FULL" at the terminal.

5. Explain why interrupts are useful when unexpected requests are made from a device, but are actually slower than gadfly routines when expected requests are made from a device.

6. Give the initialization segment for the MSGOUT subroutine with interrupt handler OUTINT (see Figure 8-10).

7. Give five concrete examples of devices that will require each of the following synchronization mechanisms, so that they should only use that mechanism and no other, and give reasons for your choice: real-time, gadfly, interrupt, direct memory access,

context switching using the same processor type. For example, a controller that selects channels on a television set should use real-time synchronization to pulse the motor that selects channels, because the computer is doing nothing else, and this is the least costly approach, requiring minimal hardware.

8. Write a program segment that delays N hours where the value of N is in accumulator A.

9. Show the graphs corresponding to Figure 8-4 when direct page addressing is used. Will the address decoder for $0000 work for any addressing mode with an effective address $0000? Explain.

10. Rewrite MSGOUT assuming that all of the characters in the message are put in the queue before the transmitter interrupts are enabled. Is there any difference in the performance of the two versions of MSGOUT?

An enlargement of the MC6805 chip. The large dark area on the chip is the **ROM** memory provided on the chip.

CHAPTER 9

Other Microcomputers

The microcomputer is a powerful tool, as we have learned in the preceding chapters. But the microcomputer is more than just one type of computer. There is a wide variety of microcomputers with different capacities and features that make them suitable for different applications. This chapter gives you some idea of this variety and the applications that particular microcomputers are useful for. To keep our discussion within the scope of this book, we examine those microcomputers that are related to the MC6809. This is particularly convenient for us since the MC6809 is ''in the middle'' of the Motorola family of microcomputers, so that being thoroughly familiar with the MC6809 makes it fairly easy to learn the other microcomputers in this family. This discussion of Motorola microcomputers will also help you approach microcomputers designed by other companies.

This chapter has two themes. The first consists of a discussion of Motorola microcomputers that are simpler than the MC6809 which include the MC6801, the MC6800, and the MC6805. The second theme is an overview of the MC68000, a machine more powerful than the MC6809. After this chapter is read, you should be able to write simple programs for the MC6800, MC6801, and MC6805 and their variants. You should be able to answer such questions as; Where should a 16-bit microcomputer be used, or where is an 8-bit microcomputer quite adequate? You should be able to approach a microcomputer designed along quite different lines than the Motorola family, with some idea of what to look for. You should appreciate the capacities of different microcomputers, and you should be able to pick a microcomputer that is suitable for a given application.

Although the MC6800 came first historically, we will treat the 8-bit microcomputers in order of their similarity to the MC6809. We begin with a discussion of the MC6801 followed by the MC6800 and the MC6805. The final sections cover the MC68000 and its variants, and present some observations about which microcomputer is most suitable for a given application.

9–1

THE MC6801

The MC6801, an older brother to the MC6809, was designed for a specific application, automotive control, and then made available for other applications. This chip can be used as a self-contained microcomputer because it has RAM and ROM inside the chip along with the MPU. A reduced version of the MC6801, the MC6803, has no ROM. A variant of the MC6801, the MC68701, has an EPROM memory which you can program yourself, in place of the ROM.

We can explain some of the excitement of this chip to those of you with hardware background: The key features of this microcomputer include 128 bytes of RAM and 2K bytes of ROM (in the MC6801) or EPROM (in the MC68701), a counter, ACIA, and three parallel ports for I/O interfacing. With these components all on one chip, all you need to add is a crystal for a clock oscillator, some capacitors for the reset and power supply filtering, and a 5-volt power supply, and you have a full-capability computer! This one chip can be used alone as described above, but it can also be used with external memory or I/O chips. The capabilities of this microcomputer are remarkable. We could spend a great deal of time discussing it. Also, there are similar chips sold by other manufacturers, and we would love to compare them with the MC6801 for you. However, we will concentrate here on the instruction set of the MC6801.

The register set for the MC6801 is similar to that of the MC6809, but is missing the direct page register, the Y and U index registers, and some condition code bits associated with interrupts (see Figure 9-1). You will be concerned mostly with the reduced number of index registers. This microcomputer also lacks some of the instructions and many of the addressing modes of the MC6809. We will discuss this below, and show some programs that illustrate how to get around these limitations. The instruction set and addressing modes are listed in Figure 9-2. Before we examine the differences, we should emphasize the

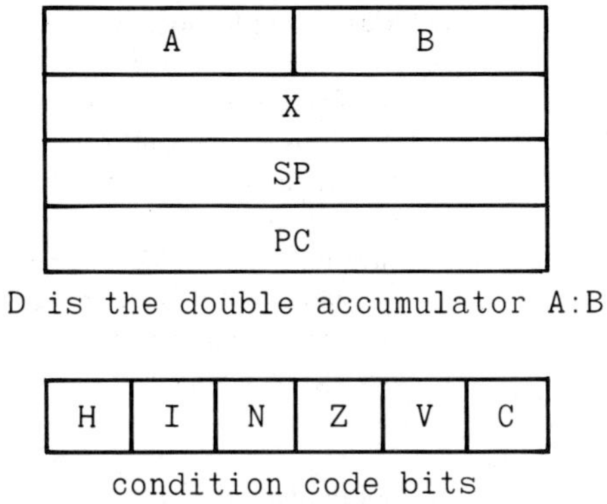

```
        A        |        B
             X
             SP
             PC
```

D is the double accumulator A:B

```
   H  | I | N | Z | V | C
```

condition code bits

FIGURE 9-1.   Register Set of the MC6801

similarities. The instruction sets are so similar that you can use many of the programs in earlier chapters with the MC6801. Some require moderate changes and, in the discussion below, we show how you can adapt instructions and addressing modes of an MC6809 program to make the program into an MC6801 program. The instructions of the MC6801 are classified as we did in Chapter 3. Some of the instructions behave identically to MC6809 instructions, except that they have different mnemonics in the standard assembler for the MC6801. If this is the case, we show the equivalent MC6809 instruction in parentheses. If the instruction behaves as a special case of the more general MC6809 instruction, so that the MC6809 instruction can do more than the MC6801 instruction, we put an asterisk after the MC6809 instruction.

The example that follows shows how similar an MC6801 segment is to an MC6809 segment. The example is the overused subroutine DOTPRD of Chapter 5 with the parameters passed in an in-line argument list.

```
*               SUBROUTINE DOTPRD
*
*               PARAMETERS
*
PARV    SET     0               Copy of the vector V
PARW    SET     2               Copy of the vector W
PARDP   SET     4               Dot product of V and W
PSIZE   SET     6
*               LOCAL VARIABLES
*
*               0
TERM    SET     2
NBYTES  SET
*
DOTPRS  PULX                    Address of the parameter list into X
        PSHX                    Put it back
```

```
            DES                              Make room for local variables
            DES
            LDAA      PARV,X                 Get first component of V
            LDAB      PARW,X                 Get firms component of W
            MUL                              First term of dot product into D
            TSX                              X points to stack
            STD       TERM,X                 Save the result in local storage
            LDX       NBYTES,X               Get address of parameter list
            LDAA      PARV+1,X               Get second component of V
            LDAB      PARW+1,X               Get second component of W
            MUL
            TSX
            ADDD      TERM,X                 Dot product into D
            LDX       NBYTES,X               Get back to parameter list
            STD       PARDP,X                Put dot product in output parameter
            INS                              Delete local variable
            INS
            INS                              Delete return address
            INS
            JMP       PSIZE,X                Return
```

Figure 9-2 shows that the instruction sets are very similar. Missing instructions include LBRA (etc.) EXG, LEAX (etc.), SEX, and an instruction SYNC that is used to synchronize with I/O devices. From the preceding example, we see that there are significant differences in the index registers and the addressing modes. The MC6801 has only the one index register X and the stack pointer SP, missing the other two index registers U and Y of the MC6809. This forces one to make the one index register X appear to be many index registers. (Remember, do not move the stack pointer around to use it like an index register!) This is done by saving copies of the other index registers in memory. Moreover, they have to be saved in global memory, preferably in some RAM words on page zero (RAM is available at locations $80 to $FF) because the addressing modes used to save them on the stack, such as

```
    STX       5,S
```

are missing. The program below highlights this difficulty. It also shows that the postincrement addressing mode is missing and that the index register has to be explicitly moved using the instruction INX instead of LEAX 1,X. This program moves ten bytes from a block beginning at the address SRC to a block beginning at the address DST.

```
            LDX       #SRC       Source address into X
            STX       SRCP       Save in pointer SRCP
            LDX       #DST       Destination address into X
            STX       DSTP       Save in pointer DSTP
            LDAA      #10        Set counter
        *
```

```
L1    LDX     SRCP      Get source pointer
      LDAB    0,X       Next byte into B
      INX               Move the pointer
      STX     SRCP      Save it
      LDX     DSTP      Get the destination pointer
      STAB    0,X       Place byte at destination
      INX
      STX     DSTP      Save this pointer
      DECA              Count down
      BNE     L1        Loop until all bytes are moved
```

Notice that a number of steps are needed to do a simple thing. We spend a lot of time saving and restoring the values of the ''index registers'' in memory. With three index registers in the MC6809, there is less need to save and restore the ''index registers'' than in the MC6801.

A related problem in the MC6801 is the lack of addressing modes. The MC6801 has immediate, direct page (where the direct page is forced to be page zero), 16-bit direct, inherent, and 8-bit relative for short branches only. The index addressing mode is available only with an 8-bit nonnegative offset. The relative address mode is available only in the BRA type of instructions, and such instructions behave exactly like their counterparts in the MC6809. For LDAA and similar instructions, the indirect, postincrement, predecrement, and program counter relative addressing modes are missing, and the index mode is only available in the form where an unsigned 8-bit offset in the instruction is added to the 16-bit index register X. Also, instructions that read, modify, and write the same word in memory, such as

```
INC     COUNT
```

may use only 16-bit direct or 8-bit unsigned offset indexed addressing. The reader should see that a MC6809 instruction such as

```
LDA     ,X+
```

has to be done in two instructions,

```
LDAA    0,X
INX
```

Similarly, an MC6809 instruction such as

```
LDA     [$1000]
```

is replaced by

```
LDX     $1000
LDAA    0,X
```

However, that kind of translation is fairly easy. You should be wary that all address arithmetic in the MC6801 is unsigned, so that if X contains $1000, then

```
LDA        OFF,X
```

can load accumulator A from locations $1000 to $10FF. The 16-bit index addressing mode of the MC6809, such as

```
LDA        $1000,X
```

has to be modified too, because the MC6801 has only an 8-bit addressing mode. You often have to calculate the address explicitly as the effective address is calculated within the MC6809 instruction, and put this effective address in the X register to use the instruction

```
LDA        0,X
```

While the calculation can be done in accumulator D, the MC6801 does not have instructions such as TFR X,D or TFR D,X to move the result to X. The best way to move data between D and X is to push and pull from the stack. For example, if the MC6809 were to use

```
LDA        $1000,X
```

at a time when X contains $2000, then, to get the same result in the MC6801, we would use the following:

```
PSHX                      Equivalent to PSHS X
PULA                      Equivalent to PULS A
PULB                      Equivalent to PULS B
ADDD       #$1000         Add the 16 bit offset
PSHB                      Equivalent to PSHS B
PSHA                      Equivalent to PSHS A
PULX                      Equivalent to PULS X
LDA        0,X            Get the data
```

The MC6809 has the LBRA and other 16-bit branch instructions which simplify the writing of position independent code. These instructions are missing in the MC6801. Writing position independent code is tedious. However, except for this capability, the MC6801 can be programmed to get the effect of the long branch instructions. For example, the MC6809 instruction

```
LBCC       L1
```

MOVE INSTRUCTIONS

LDAA (LDA)	LDAB (LDB)
STAA (STA)	STAB (STB)
PSHA (PSHS A*)	PSHB (PSHS B*)
PULA (PULS A*)	PULB (PULS B*)
LDD	
STD	
LDX	
STX	
LDS	
STS	
PSHX (PSHS X*)	
PULX (PULS X*)	
TAB (TFR A,B)	TBA (TFR B,A)
TSX (TFR S,X)	TXS (TFR X,S)
TAP (TFR A,CC)	TPA (TFR CC,A)
TSTA	TSTB TST
CLRA	CLRB CLR

ARITHMETIC INSTRUCTIONS

ADDA	ADDB	
ADCA	ADCB	
SUBA	SUBB	
SBCA	SBCB	
ADDD		
SUBD		
CMPA	CMPB	
CPX	(CMPX)	
ABA	(PSHS B ADDA ,S+)	
SBA	(PSHS B SUBA ,S+)	
CBA	(PSHS B CMPA ,S+)	
NEGA	NEGB	NEG
INCA	INCB	INC
DECA	DECB	DEC

INX (LEAX 1,X*)
DEX (LEAX −1,X*)
INS (LEAS 1,S*)
DES (LEAS −1,S*)
ABX
MUL
DAA

EDIT INSTRUCTIONS

ASLA	ASLB	ASL
ASRA	ASRB	ASR
LSRA	LSRB	LSR
ROLA	ROLB	ROR
RORA	RORB	
ASLD (ASLB ROLA)		
ASRD (ASRA ROLB)		
LSRD (LSRA (RORB)		

LOGIC INSTRUCTIONS

ANDA	ANDB	
ORA	ORB	
EORA	EORB	
BITA	BITB	
COMA	COMB	COM
CLV (ANDCC #$FD*)	SEV (ORCC #2*)	
CLI (ANDCC #$EF*)	SEI (ORCC #$10*)	
CLC (ANDCC #$FE*)	SEC (ORCC #1*)	

CONTROL INSTRUCTIONS

BCC	BCS	BEQ	BGE	BGT	BHI
BHS	BLE	BLO	BLS	BLT	BMI
BNE	BPL	BRA	BRN	BSR	BVC
BVS	JMP	JSR	RTI	RTS	SWI
NOP	WAI (CWAI #$FF*)				

ADDRESSING MODES

For LDAA: LDAA #$FF   LDAA <$FF   LDAA >$FFFF   LDAA $FF,X
For INC: INC >$FFFF   INC $FF,X

* Note: see text

FIGURE 9-2. Instruction Set and Addressing Modes of the MC6801

can be replaced by the MC6801 sequence

```
       BCS       L2
       JMP       L1
L2     (next instruction)
```

We spent a good part of Chapter 5 discussing the storage of local variables on the stack. Although this is possible on the MC6801, it is not quite as attractive because instructions such as LEAS and addressing modes such as 5,S are missing, and because the MC6801 is intended for smaller programs around 2K words long, where it is not so important to segment the program to prevent errors from propagating. Programs of this length may not need to be divided into smaller program segments with local variables since global variables should be manageable. But if you do need to use local variables on the stack, you have to transfer the stack pointer into the index register and then use index addressing. For example, the MC6809 instruction

```
   LDA       3,S
```

is carried out by

```
   TSX
   LDA       3,X
```

in the MC6801. The reader might note that, since X is used to address into the stack, it is difficult to save X on the stack. To allocate local storage and deallocate it later, put the instructions DES or INS in the program as many times as you need words of local storage. You can use a loop with a DES instruction inside it to allocate many words, or you can transfer S to D, add a constant, and transfer D to S.

With these modifications, you can take a program written for the MC6809 and rewrite it for the MC6801. Try a few programs. Scan through the earlier chapters and pick programs you have already written. Rewrite them for the MC6801. It is not too hard. However, we caution you that each computer has its strong points, and writing a good program by adapting a program from another computer for a new computer does not take full advantage of the strong points of the latter. In the MC6801, for instance, INX is one byte and takes three cycles; its equivalent in the MC6809, LEAX 1,X, is two bytes and takes five cycles. However, the MC6809 LEAX instruction can alter X in many ways in a single instruction whereas the INX instruction does just one operation. The MC6801 should use programs where the X register is incremented by one in preference to those programs where X is changed by a larger amount. You have to be more careful in the MC6801 to organize your data to avoid moving the pointer in X by more than one or two locations. For instance, you may select to store arrays by rows or by columns to avoid moving the pointer more than one word at a time.

Your MC6801 programs can be tested using the debugger LILBUG, which can be implemented in the on-board ROM of the MC6801. In fact, the minimum system can be implemented with this version of the MC6801, two other integrated circuits and a small number of other components. We strongly recommend that you try your programs on such a system to get a feeling for the MC6801.

THE MC6800

The MC6800 and similar microprocessors, the MC6802 and MC6808, are Motorola's first attempts at producing microcomputers. They are the oldest, and therefore the cheapest, microprocessors in the Motorola family. You may have to program them because they are built into a large number of existing systems. Some of the features of the MC6800 instruction set can be understood from its history. We will discuss some of the relevant history of this microcomputer. It is quite similar to the MC6801, which we just studied. We will show how you might program these microcomputers by comparing them to the MC6801.

Historically, the MC6800 was Motorola's answer to the surprising success of the Intel 8008. At the time of its development, the number of transistors that could be put on a chip was barely enough to implement an adder and a modest controller. At this time, the designers, mostly with backgrounds in transistor and small integrated circuit chip design, saw the microprocessor as a general-purpose chip that would serve to replace logic circuits in digital systems. At the time of the development of the MC6800, comparatively little thought was given to the cost of software. The designers of the MC6800, it is rumored, decided to take an evening course on minicomputers. Fortunately, the instructor was discussing the Digital Equipment PDP-11 minicomputer, thought by many to be the best minicomputer ever designed. It is fortunate that the designers of the MC6800 learned from it, rather than from some inferior minicomputer. They therefore tried to get as many of the features of the PDP-11 into the small chip that they were designing. They included the arithmetic and logical instructions of the PDP-11. However, the addressing modes took up too much room on the chip, and after all, for logic circuit applications they were thought to be unnecessary. As further improvements in integrated circuit technology permitted more transistors to be put on a chip, a clock and memory were included, using the same instruction set, to implement the MC6802. The MC6808 is an MC6802 without the memory. Given more room on the chip and a growing awareness of software costs, other designs with more instructions and addressing modes were implemented, such as the MC6801, the MC6809, and later the MC68000. Not surprisingly, these designs tended to look more like the PDP-11 as more features were added.

The register set for the MC6800 is the same as that for the MC6801 (see Figure 9-1). The instruction set and addressing modes for the MC6800 appear in Figure 9-3. We use the same conventions that we had for the description of the MC6801. Also, the previous discussion of missing addressing modes and instructions in the MC6801 applies to the MC6800. You can review the preceding section to see how to use the limited addressing modes and how to replace the missing instructions of the MC6800. The MC6801, designed next after the MC6800, corrected some of the most serious faults of the MC6800. We can understand the MC6800 by analyzing what was added to the MC6800 to get the MC6801. The instructions dealing with the combined 16-bit accumulator D (LDD, STD, ADDD, SUBD, CMPD, ASLD, LSLD) and some awkward gaps in the MC6800 instruction set (PSHX, PULX, ABX, MUL) were added, and the CPX and stack pointer errors were corrected in the MC6801.

The instructions dealing with accumulator D in the MC6801 and MC6809 can be replaced in the MC6800 in a simple way. For example,

```
ADDD        #$1234
```

is replaced by

```
ADDB        #$34
ADCA        #$12
```

The main advantage of the 16-bit instructions is efficiency, since 16-bit arithmetic is quite common. Without them, you can still do everything with the 8-bit instructions.

The MC6800 has a minor flaw regarding the stack pointer S. The S register points to the first free word above the stack. Pushing a word writes the word into the location pointed to by S and then decrements S. Pulling a word increments S and then reads the word pointed to by S. However, when TSX transfers the value in S to X, the value is incremented, and when TXS transfers the value in X to S, the value is decremented. Thus X will point to the top of the stack even though S does not, and index addressing using X will access words in the stack in the same way as the MC6809 except that only 8-bit positive offsets are available. We will see this in the next example.

The PSHX and PULX instructions are fairly awkward to implement in the MC6800 in a reentrant subroutine. Moreover, as we observed in the last section on the programming of the MC6801, PSHX and PULX are convenient ways to obtain the MC6809 instructions TFR X,D and TFR D,X so that arithmetic can be done on addresses used in X. Discarding the need for reentrance, you can use STX and LDX to save and restore X using a global variable. But if you want to have a reentrant subroutine to pull X from the stack, the only way we

MOVE INSTRUCTIONS

LDAA	(LDA)	LDAB	(LDB)
STAA	(STA)	STAB	(STB)
PSHA	(PSHS A*)	PSHB	(PSHS B*)
PULA	(PULS A*)	PULB	(PULS B*)
LDX			
STX			
LDS			
STS			

TAB (TFR A,B) TBA (TFR B,A)
TSX (TFR S,X) TXS (TFR X,S)
TAP (TFR A,CC) TPA (TFR CC,A)
TSTA   TSTB   TST
CLRA   CLRB   CLR

EDIT INSTRUCTIONS

ASLA	ASLB	ASL
ASRA	ASRB	ASR
LSRA	LSRB	LSR
ROLA	ROLB	ROL
RORA	RORB	ROR

ARITHMETIC INSTRUCTIONS

ADDA	ADDB
ADCA	ADCB
SUBA	SUBB
SBCA	SBCB
CMPA	CMPB
CPX	(CMPX)
SBA	(PSHS B SUBA ,S+)
CBA	(PSHS B CMPA ,S+)

NEGA   NEGB   NEG
INCA   INCB   INC
DECA   DECB   DEC
INX (LEAX 1,X*)
DEX (LEAX −1,X*)
INS (LEAS 1,S*)
DES (LEAS −1,S*)
DAA

LOGIC INSTRUCTIONS

ANDA	ANDB
ORA	ORB
EORA	EORB
BITA	BITB
COMA	COMB COM

CLC (ANDCC #$FE*) SEC (ORCC #1*)
CLV (ANDCC #$FD*) SEV (ORCC #2*)
CLI (ANDCC #$EF*) SEI (ORCC #$10*)

CONTROL INSTRUCTIONS

BCC	BCS	BEQ	BGE	BGT	BHI
BHS	BLE	BLO	BLS	BLT	BMI
BNE	BPL	BRA		BSR	BVC
BVS	JMP	JSR	RTI	RTS	SWI
NOP	WAI (CWAI #$FF*)				

ADDRESSING MODES

For LDAA: LDAA #$FF   LDAA <$FF   LDAA >$FFFF LDAA $FF,X
For INC: INC >$FFFF   INC $FF,X

* Note: see text

FIGURE 9-3. Instruction Set and Addressing Modes of the MC6800

know to do this is to execute an SWI instruction, and in the SWI handler move the data around to transfer the saved copy of X to a position on the stack where it will be left after the handler is finished. The SWI handler shown in Figure 9-4 illustrates this. The BEFORE picture shows the stack just after the SWI instruction is executed, and to its right, the AFTER picture shows the stack just

```
PULX     TSX                 Make X point to the top of the stack
         LDAA     5,X        Top byte of program counter
         LDAB     7,X           is exchanged with top byte
         STAA     7,X           of the word being pulled
         STAA     5,X
         LDAA     6,X        The second byte of the
         LDAB     8,X           program counter is exchanged
         STAA     8,X           with the second byte of the
         STAB     6,X           second byte of the word being pulled
         LDAA     2,X           and the saved value of B is moved
         STAA     4,X           to its position to be pulled by RTI
         PULA                Finally, the CC register is moved,
         PULB                The saved value of A is gotten,
         INS                    and two words are deleted
         INS                    from the stack
         PSHB                Restore the saved value of A
         PSHA                The CC is put back
         RTI                    and all registers are restored
```

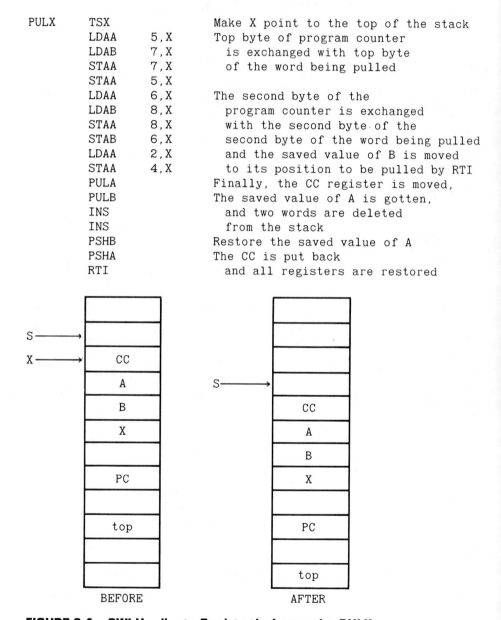

FIGURE 9-4. SWI Handler to Emulate the Instruction PULX

before the RTI instruction is executed. The initial positions of the X and S registers, and offsets from X used in the program, are shown to the left of the BEFORE picture, and the position of the S register just before the SWI instruction is shown to the left of the AFTER picture. You can see that the RTI instruction will replace the saved values of the registers, and effectively PULL the top two words from the stack into the X register. The SWI handler to push X onto the stack is similar to that shown in the figure.

The program of Figure 9-4 shows that any missing instruction can be implemented as a subroutine, but the subroutine can be expected to be much slower and to take up more memory than its MC6809 counterpart. Similar subroutines or SWI handlers can be written to replace the missing MUL and ABX instructions.

A serious problem with the MC6800 is the incorrect operation of the CPX instruction. The purpose of such an instruction is to compare X with an operand, setting the condition code bits according to the results of the compare. However, this instruction is incorrectly implemented in that it fails to propagate the middle carry between the addition of the low eight bits and the addition of the high eight bits. Thus the sign bit N is the sign of the result of subtracting the high byte of the operand from the high byte of register X and is independent of the low bytes of each. Additionally, instructions such as BHI or BLO do not work properly as unsigned compare branches. The only conditional branches that may be used are BEQ and BNE. These work correctly because the carry does not propagate from the low to high byte when the numbers are equal. If you want to perform a comparison, testing for greater or less than, you have to move the index register data to the accumulators to use SUBB and SBCA there.

Further information on programming the MC6800, MC6802, and MC6808 can be found in many paperbacks and texts, including the fine text *Introduction to Microcomputing* (Sydney B. Newell, Harper & Row Publishers, New York, 1982). However, after reading this chapter you should be able to use just the data sheet for the MC6800 to write programs for it. Finally, we recommend that you try out a few programs on an MC6800 if at all possible. The Heathkit model EE3401 experimenter's microcomputer system is one of many MC6800-based commercial products. You can get much more experience by playing with such a system than you can by simply reading about the MC6800 or even by doing the problems at the end of this chapter.

With these "patches," you can use the data sheet for the MC6800 to program it without much difficulty, although you will have a certain amount of frustration after being accustomed to the MC6809.

THE MC6805

The MC6805, like the MC6801, is a very powerful chip; it is a full computer on a single chip. All you have to add to it are a couple of capacitors and a power supply. Its cost will be several dollars per chip. What can you do with a $2 computer? Control your air conditioner, record the weather, control the speed of your car, or tune your television set. The MC6805 is ideal for these applications. We think it will be so important that every electrical engineer should know what it can do. It will show up in many system designs.

There are many versions of the MC6805, with different I/O devices built into the chip. All have a 2K-byte ROM, about 100 words of RAM, a counter/timer, and at least nineteen bits of parallel I/O available on pins of the chip. One version has an analog-to-digital converter, another has a phase-locked loop for controlling a television tuner, another has 3.2K bytes of ROM, and another has 32 bits of parallel I/O. Some MC6805 versions are CMOS (MC146805), which requires so little power that it can be powered by three lemons functioning as a battery, and some have EPROM in place of the ROM (MC68705) so that you can put the program into the MC6805 memory yourself.

We are focusing on the programming of this microcomputer in this section even though we are intrigued by the hardware, and spellbound by the possibilities of applying it. The MC6805 was designed specifically for simple control applications. These applications require very simple instructions and only a small number of registers. Thus the MC6805 has a rich set of addressing modes and bit manipulation instructions even though it has few registers. The register set for the MC6805 is shown in Figure 9-5, and its instruction set and addressing modes are shown in Figure 9-6. New or considerably revised instructions are shown with an asterisk. Note the short index register, and the lack of an

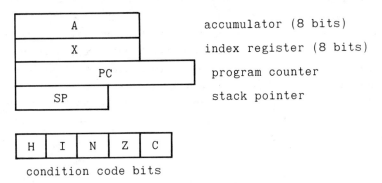

FIGURE 9-5. The Register Set of the MC6805. The size of PC varies between ten and twelve bits, and the size of the SP varies between five and six bits, depending on the version.

MOVE INSTRUCTIONS

LDA
STA

LDX
STX
RSP (LDS #$7F)
TAX (TFR D,X) TXA (TFR X,D)
TSTA   TSTX   TST
CLRA   CLRX   CLR

EDIT INSTRUCTIONS

ASLA   ASLX   ASL
ASRA   ASRX   ASR
LSRA   LSRX   LSR
ROLA   ROLX   ROL
RORA   RORX   ROR

ARITHMETIC INSTRUCTIONS

ADD (ADDA)
ADC (ADCA)
SUB (SUBA)
SBC (SBCA)
CMP (CMPA)
CPX (CMPX)
NEGA   NEGX   NEG
INCA   INCX   INC
DECA   DECX   DEC

LOGIC INSTRUCTIONS

AND
ORA
EOR
BIT
COMA   COMX   COM
BSET *
BCLR *
CLC (ANDCC #$FE) SEC (ORCC #1)
CLI (ANDCC #$EF) SEI (ORCC #$10)

CONTROL INSTRUCTIONS

BCC   BCS   BEQ   BHCC *   BHCS *   BHI
BHS   BIH *   BIL *   BLO   BLS   BMC *
BMI   BMS *   BNE   BPL   BRA   BRCLR *
BRSET *   BRN   BSR   JMP   JSR   RTI
RTS   SWI   NOP   STOP *   WAIT (CWAI #$FF) *

ADDRESSING MODES

For LDA: LDA #$FF LDA <$FF LDA >$FFFF LDA ,X LDA <$FF,X LDA >$FFFF,X

For INC: INC <$FF INC ,X   INC <$FF,X

* Note: see text

FIGURE 9-6. Instruction Set and Addressing Modes of the MC6805

accumulator B. The 8-bit X register behaves somewhat like X in the MC6809 in addressing operations such as LDA ,X (except that it can access only the first page of memory this way), and somewhat like accumulator B, in instructions such as ROLX or CLRX. The V condition code bit is absent, and the stack cannot be accessed because the only instruction (besides instructions such as

BSR and RTS) that changes it is RSP (reset stack pointer). DAA (decimal adjust accumulator) is removed but there are conditional branch instructions (BHCC and BHCS) that test the half carry. What really gives power to this little chip are the bit set instructions BSET, bit clear instructions BCLR, and conditional bit test instructions (BRSET, BRCLR).

The addressing modes in the MC6805 are more limited than those of the MC6809, but quite a bit more powerful than those of the MC6800. They include the inherent, immediate, 16-bit direct, and 8-bit offset index addressing modes of the MC6800, but also a zero-bit offset (pointer) addressing mode and a 16-bit offset index addressing mode. The instructions that read, modify, and then write a result back in the same location, such as INC, cannot use the 16-bit direct or the 16-bit indexed modes, but the instructions that use the accumulator as one operand (such as LDA) can use all the modes. However, only one index register X is available, and the X register is only eight bits long. The 16-bit offset mode is very useful for handling vectors that are placed anywhere in memory. The strategy most commonly used in the MC6805 is to put the address of a vector as the offset, and use the X register as an index into the vector. The following example shows how a few words (256) can be moved from one area (SRC) to another (DST) using this mode of addressing. Comparing this program to the program for moving words in the MC6801 shown earlier, you can see the advantages of the 16-bit offset type of index addressing—you may not need two index registers because the second may be a constant offset from the first.

```
          LDX     #10          Move 10 words
LOOP      LDA     SRC-1,X      Get a word
          STA     DST-1,X      Put it out
          DEX                  Count down
          BNE     LOOP         Until done
```

The following example illustrates the use of the X register as a substitute for accumulator B, and also shows that the MC6809 MUL instruction can be replaced by a subroutine without much effort.

```
*            SUBROUTINE MUL
*
*
* MUL multiplies the unsigned contents of A by the un-
* signed contents of X, putting the product into A:X.
*
          ORG     $10          Beginning of RAM
COUNT     RMB     1            Loop counter
TEMP      RMB     1            Storage for multiplier
*
          ORG     $80          Beginning of ROM or EPROM
```

```
MUL       STA      TEMP         Save A as multiplier
          LDA      #8           Set up counter
          STA      COUNT
          CLRA                  High byte of partial product
LOOP      LSLA                  Double byte shift left
          ROLX                     in A:X (like A:B in the MC6809)
          BCC      NOSHFT       If zero is shifted out
          ADD      TEMP            then add multiplier
NOSHFT    DEC      COUNT        Count loop
          BNE      LOOP
          RTS                   Exit subroutine
```

Other missing instructions can be implemented as subroutines. The implementation of the DAA instruction is particularly interesting. (See MC6805 HMOS/M146805 CMOS Family User's Manual, Motorola Inc., Prentice-Hall, Englewood Cliffs, N. J., 1983, p. 46.) Other subroutines are shown there for multiplication, division, and interfacing to keyboards and ACIA serial lines.

One of the most useful classes of instructions for small microcomputers is the class of bit set and bit test instructions. The instruction

```
BSET      3,$10
```

will set bit 3 in word $10, and

```
BCLR      3,$10
```

will clear the same bit. The instruction

```
BRSET     3,$10,L
```

will branch to location L if bit 3 of word $10 is set, and

```
BRCLR     3,$10,L
```

will branch to L if that bit is clear. Any bit (0 to 7) of any word on page zero ($0000 to $00FF) can be set, cleared, or tested this way. The input/output registers in the MC6805 are in locations $0000 to $00FF, so they can be modified and tested by these instructions. We note that the bit-handling instructions of the MC6809 (BIT, OR, AND) are still present in the MC6805, but the addition of the BSET, BCLR, and BTEST instructions permits further techniques in handling bits.

The following subroutine shows the use of the BSET instruction, but it shows the need for programming techniques that are not needed, and should never be used, on the other microcomputers that we have studied. The problem is to manage a vector of 75 bits, setting them, testing them, and so on. (This application showed up when we tried to run a bingo board from the MC6805.

The bit vector stored the bingo numbers that were called, and the subroutine is used to "call another number.") The vector is stored from location $10 to $19, such that bit 0 of the bit vector is bit 0 of word $10, bit 1 of the vector is bit 1 of word $10, ..., and bit 74 of the vector is bit 2 of word $19. The subroutine is called with "n" in accumulator A, and it sets bit "n" of the vector.

```
*                    SUBROUTINE SET
*
* SET sets bit n of the bit vector VECTOR by
* constructing an instruction in RAM and then
* executing it. The value of n is passed in
* accumulator A where the low three bits are the bit
* number, and the other bits (+ $10) are the address
* of the word containing the bit to be set.
*
            ORG     $10          Beginning of RAM
VECTOR      RMB     10           Storage for 75 bits
WORK1       RMB     1            The subroutine BSET n,l   RTS is
WORK2       RMB     1               constructed here
WORK3       RMB     1
*
            ORG     $80          Beginning of ROM or EPROM
SET         TAX                  Copy
            AND     #7           Get low 3 bits
            ASLA                 The op code for BSET n,l is $10 + 2 * n
            ADD     #$10
            STA     WORK1        Put it in RAM
*
            TXA                  Put word number into the second byte of
            LSRA                    the composed instruction
            LSRA
            LSRA
            ADD     #VECTOR
            STA     WORK2
*
            LDA     #$81         Op code for RTS
            STA     WORK3        Compose the whole subroutine
            JMP     WORK1        Go to the composed subroutine and exit
                                    from there
```

Although the preceding program exhibits impure code in its most outrageous form, it is effective in a small microcomputer. A similar self-creating instruction is effective in moving larger amounts of data than can be handled in the first subroutine shown in this section. When the facts do not fit the theory, an engineer has to go with the facts and ignore the theory. Other amusing subroutines for the MC6805 include one to transfer S to X (the stack area is searched for the return address of the subroutine, and that address, plus one, is the value in S before the subroutine was entered) and subroutines for pushing or pulling values from the stack. Programming such elementary computers is marvelous fun.

With this coverage, and the information in the data sheet for the MC6805, you should be able to write short programs for that microcomputer. For further reading, we highly recommend the Motorola manual mentioned earlier. It contains many complete programs that show how this mighty little chip can be used. Chapter 5 of this manual describes a 4-chip microcomputer with a debug monitor CBUG05 that enables you to get experience trying out MC6805 programs. Of course, if at all possible, you should use such a system to get hands-on experience programming the MC6805.

The MC68000

The preceding sections covered microcomputers that are less powerful than the MC6809. We now look at the MC68000 and similar 16-bit microcomputers (the MC68008, MC68010, and MC68020) to convey an understanding of the strengths and weaknesses of these microcomputers in particular, and of similar 16-bit microcomputers in general. However, we will at best be able to prepare you to write a few programs, similar to those written for the MC6809, for these microcomputers.

The register set for the MC68000 features seventeen 32-bit registers, a 32-bit program counter, and a 16-bit status register (see Figure 9-7). The eight data registers are functionally equivalent to the accumulators in the MC6809, and the nine address registers are equivalent to the index registers.

The low byte of the status register is similar to the MC6809 condition code register, having the familiar N, Z, V, and C condition code bits, and a new condition code bit X, which is very similar to the carry bit C. Bits X and C differ in that C is changed by many instructions and is tested by conditional branch instructions, while X is changed only by a few arithmetic instructions and is used as the carry input to multiple-precision arithmetic operations. Having two carry bits, X and C, avoids some dilemmas in the design of the computer that are inherent in simpler computers such as the MC6809. This allows X to be set specifically for multiple-precision arithmetic, and lets C be set for more instructions (such as MOVE) to facilitate testing using instructions (such as BLS).

The high byte of the status register contains a bit, S, that distinguishes the mode as user or system. When it is set, the program uses the system stack pointer whenever it uses address register 7, and when it is clear, the program uses the user stack pointer whenever it uses address register 7. Further, several instructions may only be executed when the program is in the system mode (S = 1), and hardware can be built so that some memory or I/O devices may be

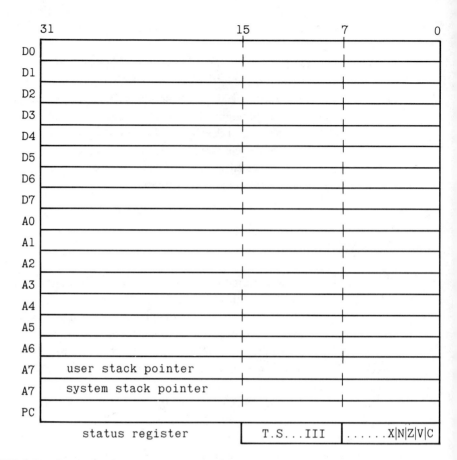

FIGURE 9-7. Register Set for the MC68000

accessed only when the program is in the system mode. This permits the writing of secure operating systems that can have multiple users in a time-sharing system, so that the users cannot accidentally or maliciously damage each other.

The MC68000 memory is organized as shown in Figure 9-8. The 16-bit-wide memory is actually addressed as an 8-bit memory, so that a 16-bit word (the unit of memory read or written as a whole) is logically two consecutive locations. Instructions can read or write half the word (the mnemonic ends in .B for byte), a word (these end in .W for word), or two consecutive words (these end in .L for long). If the suffix .B, .W, or .L is omitted, it is generally assumed to be a word (.W) instruction, unless such an option is not available. Word and long accesses must be aligned with memory so their addresses are even numbers, and byte accesses using even addresses will read or write the high byte, and those with odd addresses will access the low byte of a word. This is consistent with the MC6809 convention that puts the most significant byte at the lower-

Location 0	Location 1	Word 0 Long word 0
Location 2	Location 3	Word 2
Location 4	Location 5	Word 4 Long word 4
Location 6	Location 7	Word 6
. . .	. . .	
Location $FFFFFFFE	Location $FFFFFFFF	

FIGURE 9-8. Memory Organization for the MC68000

numbered address. Finally, bits are numbered from right (0) to left (7) in a byte exactly as the MC6809.

The instruction set and the addressing modes are shown in Figure 9-9. You may observe the general MOVE instruction, which has variations for moving one byte (MOVE.B), a word (MOVE.W), or two words (MOVE.L). The source is always the first (left) operand, and the destination is the second (right) operand. Any addressing mode may be used with the source or destination. This general instruction is equivalent to the MC6809 LDA, LDD, LDX, etc., and STA, STD, STX, etc., as well as the TFR A,B and TFR D,X instructions. It also includes a capability to move directly from memory to memory without storing the moved word in a register. In fact, there are over 12,000 different combinations of addressing modes that give different move instructions. There are similar byte, word, and long modes for arithmetic, logical, and edit instructions.

The addressing modes listed in Figure 9-9 can be used with almost all instructions. We will note those that are essentially the same as MC6809 modes first, and then we will examine those that are significantly different.

Data and address register modes are similar to those used in the MC6809 TFR instructions. Moving a byte, or word, into a 32-bit data register will result in replacing only the low byte, or word, in the register, leaving the other bits of the register untouched. Moving a word to an address register results in filling the high sixteen bits with the sign bit of the word that was moved, and moving a byte to or from an address register is not permitted. Immediate addressing can provide 16- or 32-bit operands. (Long) direct addressing uses a 32-bit address and can therefore address any word in memory. Pointer, postincrement and predecrement are the same as in the MC6809, except that a postincrement read of a word increments the pointer by 2, and a postincrement read of a long word increments the pointer by 4. Predecrement works similarly, and write

MOVE.*	MOVEM.**	MOVEQ.L	ABCD	SBCD	NBCD		
MOVEA.**	MOVEP.**		ADD.*	ADDA.**	ADDX.*	ADDI.*	AD
EXG	LEA	PEA	SUB.*	SUBA.**	SUBX.*	SUBI.*	SU
LINK	UNLINK		CMP.*	CMPA.**	CMPI.*	CMPM.*	CH
CLR.*	TST.*		NEG.*	NEGX.*			
			MULU	MULS	DIVU	DIVS	

EDIT INSTRUCTIONS

LOGIC INSTRUCTIONS

ASL.*				
ASR.*	AND.*	ANDI.*		
LSR.*	OR.*	ORI.*		
ROL.*	EOR.*	EORI.*		
ROR.*	NOT.*			
ROXL.*	BCLR	BSET	BCHG	BTST
ROXR.*	TAS	S***		
EXT.** SWAP				

CONTROL INSTRUCTIONS

BRA.S	B***.S	BSR.S	BRA.L	B***.L	BSR.L	DB***	JMP	JSR
NOP	RESET	RTE	RTR	RTS	STOP	TRAP	TRAPV	

Notes: Asterisks (*) are used here in lieu of alternative
letters:
   , B, W, or L (e.g., MOVE. may be MOVE.B, MOVE.W, or MOVE.L).
  , W or L (e.g., MOVEM. may be MOVE.W or MOVE.L).
 ***, CC, CS, EQ, F, GE, GT, HI, LE, LS, LT, MI, NE, PL, T, VC, or

FIGURE 9-9. Instruction Set and Addressing Modes for the MC68000

works similarly. Based on your experience with the MC6809, you should have no trouble learning these modes.

The remaining modes consistently use sign extension to expand 8- or 16-bit instruction offsets to 32 bits before using them in address calculations. (Short) direct addressing is somewhat like direct page addressing, requiring a short 16-bit instruction offset, but using sign extension, it can access locations 0 to $7FFF and $FFFF8000 to $FFFFFFFF. Similarly, index addressing uses sign extension, so if A0 contains $10000000, index addressing using A0 can access locations $0FFF8000 to $10007FFFF, as in the MC6809. Relative addressing works similarly.

Two new modes are available in the MC68000. The effective address can be the sum of three values. A general register is any address or data register. The sum of a general register, an address register, and a signed 16-bit offset is used as the effective address in base index addressing, and the sum of a general

Addressing Mode Name	Symbol	Example Instruction		Action
Data register	Dn	MOVE.L	D1,D0	(D1) -> D0
Address register	An	MOVE.L	A0,D0	(A0) -> D0
Immediate	#nnnnnnnn	MOVE.L	#$FFFFFFFF,D0	$FFFFFFFF -> D0
Direct (long)	nnnnnnnn	MOVE.B	$FFFFFFFF,D0	M($FFFFFFFF) -> D0
Direct (short)	nnnn	MOVE.B	$7FFF,D0	M($00007FFF) -> D0
Pointer	(An)	MOVE.B	(A0),D0	M(A0) -> D0
Postincrement	(An)+	MOVE.B	(A0)+,D0	M(A0) -> D0 A0+1 -> A0
Predecrement	-(An)	MOVE.B	-(A0),D0	A0-1 -> A0 M(A0) -> D0
Index	nnnn(An)	MOVE.B	$7FFF(A0),D0	M(A0+$7FFF) -> D0
Base index	nn(An,Xn)	MOVE.B	$7F(A0,A1),D0	M(A0+A1+$7F) -> D0
Relative	L1(PC)	MOVE.B	L1(PC),D0	M(PC+rrrr) -> D0
Relative indexed	L1(PC,Xn)	MOVE.B	L1(PC,A0),D0	M(PC+A0+rr) -> D0

Notes: Dn is any data register; An is any address register;
Xn is any An or Dn; nnnnnnnn is any 32–bit number;
nnnn is any 16–bit number; nn is any 8–bit number;
n is a number 0 to 7; rrrr is any 16–bit offset for
which PC+rrrr = L1; and rr is any 8–bit offset for
which PC+rr = L1.

FIGURE 9-9 (cont.)

register, the program counter, and a signed 8-bit offset is the effective address used in relative index addressing. These modes add quite a bit of flexibility to access tables, vectors, and arrays, which may be stored in the vicinity of an address register or the program counter address.

Several special move instructions are provided. A MOVE instruction can move data to or from the status register (although the user can only access the low byte using MOVE.B) and the user stack pointer can be set while in the system state using a special MOVE. An EXG instruction permits exchanging the bits in the data or address registers. The instruction MOVEM, for move multiple, is a generalized PSHS or PULS instruction. Registers to be pushed or pulled are specified by separators "/," meaning AND, and "-," meaning TO. The instruction

```
MOVEM       D0/D1/A0,-(A7)
```

will push D0, D1, and A0 onto the user's stack (or system stack if in the system mode), and

```
MOVEM        (A7)+,D0-D4
```

will pull D0, D1, D2, D3, and D4 from the same stack. However, any address register may be used in lieu of A7, so that the user may create many stacks or queues and use this instruction with them. MOVEA is a variation of MOVE that moves to an address register and that does not affect the condition codes, MOVEQ is a short version of MOVE immediate using an 8-bit signed immediate operand, and MOVEP is a MOVE that can be used to move data to an 8-bit I/O device that might be designed for the MC6809.

Other instructions from the move class include the LEA instruction, which works just like LEAX in the MC6809, PEA that pushes this effective address on the stack, and the familiar TST and CLR instructions. The LINK and UNLINK instructions are designed to simplify allocation and deallocation of local variables using the stack marker, as discussed in Chapter 5. The instruction

```
LINK        A0,#-10
```

will push A0 onto the stack, put the resulting stack address into A0, and add (negative 10) to the stack pointer to allocate ten bytes. The instruction

```
UNLINK      A0
```

deallocates by reversing this procedure, copying A0 into the stack pointer, and then pulling A0 from the stack.

Arithmetic instructions are again similar to MC6809 arithmetic instructions. As with MOVE instructions, ADD, SUB, and CMP have byte, word, and long forms, and ADDA and SUBA are similar to MOVEA. A memory-to-memory compare CMPM uses preincrement addressing to permit efficient comparison of strings. There are no INC or DEC instructions. Rather ADDQ can add 1 to 8, and SUBQ can subtract 1 to 8, from any register. These instructions are generalized INC and DEC instructions. Multiple-precision arithmetic uses ADDX, SUBX, and NEGX in the same way that ADC is used in the MC6809, except that the Z bit is not set, only cleared if the result is nonzero and only predecrement addressing is used. The handling of Z facilitates multiple-precision tests for a zero number. Decimal arithmetic uses ABCD, SBCD, and NBCD, and is designed to work like multiple-precision binary arithmetic such as ADDX. However, only bytes can be operated on in these instructions. A special compare instruction CHK is used to check addresses. For example,

```
CHK         D0,#1000
```

will allow the program to continue if D0 is between 0 and 1000; otherwise, it will jump to an error routine much as the SWI instruction does in the MC6809. Finally, this machine has multiply and divide instructions for signed and unsigned 16-bit operands that produce 32-bit results.

Logic instructions are again very familiar. We have AND, OR, and EOR as in the MC6809. As with ADD, the instructions AND and OR can operate on a data register and memory word, putting the result in the memory word. We have BCLR, BSET, and BTST as in the MC6805, and also a BCHG instruction that inverts a bit. Moreover, the chosen bit can be specified either by an immediate operand or by the value in a data register. The S*** group of instructions copies a condition code bit, or a combination of them that can be used in a branch instruction, into a byte in memory. (See Figure 9-8 and its footnotes.) For example,

```
SEQ        $100
```

copies the Z bit into all the bits of byte $100. The test and set instruction (TAS) is useful for some forms of multiprocessing. It sets the condition code bits as in the TST instruction based on the initial value of a byte and then it sets the most significant bit in the byte.

Edit instructions include the standard shifts, with some modifications. All shifts that shift the contents of a data register can be executed many times in one instruction. The instruction

```
ASL.B      #3,D0
```

will shift the low byte of D0 three times, as in the MC6809 sequence

```
ASLA
ASLA
ASLA
```

The number of shifts can be specified as an immediate operand or can be the number in a data register. However, when shifting memory words, an instruction can shift only one bit. Also, ROL and ROR are circular shifts of the 8-, 16-, or 32-bit numbers that do not shift through the X bit; ROXL and ROXR are 9-, 17-, or 33-bit shifts that shift through the X bit as the ROL and ROR instructions shift through the C bit in the MC6809. EXT is a sign extend instruction like the MC6809 instruction SEX, and SWAP exchanges the low and high words in the same data register.

Control instructions include the familiar conditional branch (B***.S), branch (BRA.S), branch to subroutine (BSR.S), long branch (BRA.L), conditional long branch (B***.L), long branch to subroutine (BSR.L), jump (JMP), and jump to subroutine (JSR) instructions, as well as the NOP, RTS, and RTE (equivalent to the MC6809 RTI). The instruction RTR is like RTS, which also restores the condition codes. Special instructions STOP and RESET permit halting the processor to wait for an interrupt and resetting the I/O devices.

The DB*** group of instructions permits decrementing a counter and simultaneously checking a condition code to exit a loop when the desired value

of the condition code is met. The condition code specified by *** in DB*** is
first tested, and if true, the next instruction below DB*** is begun. If the
condition is false, the counter is decremented, and if -1, the next instruction is
executed; otherwise, the branch is taken. The sequence

```
L1      CLR,B     (A0)+
        DBF       D0,L1
```

will execute the pair of instructions $n + 1$ times, where n is the number in D0.
This powerful instruction allows one to construct fast program segments to
move or search a block of memory. Moreover, in the MC68010 and MC68020,
such short loops are detected and, when they occur, the two instructions are
kept inside the MPU so that the op codes need not be fetched after the first
time, so that these loops run very fast.

We now consider a few simple programs that illustrate the MC68000 instruction
set. The first is the familiar program that moves a block of 10 words from SRC
to DST. This program shows the way to specify the byte, word, or long form
of most instructions, and it shows the powerful DB*** instruction.

```
        MOVEQ     #9,D0
        MOVE,W    #SRC,A0
        MOVE,W    #DST,A1
L1      MOVE,B    (A0)+,(A1)+
        DBF       D0,L1
```

Let us now look at the overused inner product subroutine, passing the
parameters in the in-line argument list by value. Although this method of passing
parameters is not the best for the MC68000 because it has plenty of registers
to pass parameters by registers, it illustrates the use of data and address registers.
The subroutine evaluates the expression

$$DP = V(0)*W(0) + V(1)*W(1)$$

where, as in the earlier examples, V(0), V(1), W(0), and W(1) are 1-byte
unsigned numbers and DP is a 2-byte unsigned number.

```
*
*                   SUBROUTINE DOTPRD
*
*        PARAMETERS
*
PARV    SET       0
PARW    SET       2
PARDP   SET       4
PSIZE   SET       6
*
```

```
DOTPRD   CLR.L    D0              Clear D0 and D1 bits
         CLR.L    D1
         MOVE.L   (A7)+,A0        Similar to LDX ,S++
         MOVE.B   (A0),D0         Like LDA ,X
         MOVE.B   2(A0),D1        Like LDB 2,X
         MULU     D0,D1           Like MUL
         CLR.L    D0              Clear D0 and D2 bits
         CLR.L    D2
         MOVE.B   1(A0),D0        Note that the result is saved in D1 and the
         MOVE.B   3(A0),D2            same method is used to load to get the
         MULU     D0,D2              other operands
         ADD.W    D1,D2           We now combine the products and put the
         MOVE.W   D2,4(A0)        result in the argument list
         JMP      PSIZE(A0)       Finally we return to the caller
```

Our third example is the fairly familiar subroutine that converts an ASCII character into a hexadecimal nibble. The ASCII character is passed into the subroutine ATOH in the least significant byte of D0, and the resulting nibble is left in its place. Errors are reported by a long branch to an error handler at address ERROR, and uppercase or lowercase letters A to F can be used. Note the comparison order: CMP subtracts the source (first argument) from the destination (second argument) and sets the condition codes according to whether the result is higher, lower, or equal to zero. The branch following it senses the resulting condition codes. Note that the branches have the form B***.L, which forces the long form of the branch having a 16-bit offset, or B***.S, which forces the short form. If B*** is used without a .S or .L, the assembler will try to use the short form if possible, but a two-pass assembler will not use it for forward references. We often need to force the short form using .S, but we do not have to force the long form using .L with the standard assembler.

```
ATOH     CMP.B    #$30,D0         If below ASCII 0
         BLT.L    ERROR               then report/correct error
         CMP.B    #$39,D0         If above ASCII 9
         BGT.S    L2                  then analyze below L2
L1       AND.B    #$F,D0          Else return low nibble
         RTS                          and exit
L2       AND.B    #$5F,D0         Convert lowercase to uppercase
         CMP.B    #$41,D0         If below ASCII A
         BLT.L    ERROR               then error
         CMP.B    #$46,D0         If above ASCII F
         BGT.L    ERROR               then error
         SUBQ     #7,D0           Else reduce by 7
         BRA      L1                  and exit
```

With these short examples, some of the flavor of the MC68000 can be seen. The machine offers a very large address space, over sixteen megabytes, and seventeen data and address registers. This largeness is typical of minicomputers and larger computers, and makes it easier to write large programs. However, many of the techniques are the same as those you have already learned, passing parameters and handling local variables, writing clear programs, and testing them. You are prepared to learn to program the MC68000 with comparatively little effort. However, the greater size and complexity of this microcomputer requires a longer time to master all of its peculiarities, to enable you to write really good programs.

The complexity of the MC68000 can be seen from a few examples that we give here. The DB*** group of instructions, such as DBF D0,L1, decrements until the result is -1, so if you want to execute a loop 10 times, you must put 9 in the counting register D0. (There is a reason for this. The counting is specially designed for programs written in C, where vectors have a zero origin, so you want to do the loop the last time with 0, to access the 0th element, and terminate when the loop counter is -1.) However, almost every assembly language program that uses DB*** has an instruction that decrements the counter before the loop is entered. This is annoying. Moreover, the usual way that zero origin indexing is handled is to subtract 1 from the offset rather than the loop count, for example, use

```
MOVE.B          LABEL-1(A0,D0),D1
```

where the counter D0 runs from n to 1, rather than using

```
MOVE.B          LABEL(A0,D0),D1
```

where D0 runs from n − 1 to 0.) It would be tempting to clear all the registers by first clearing D0, then executing

```
MOVEM.L         D0,D1-D7/A0-A6
```

However, that particular version of MOVEM is illegal. As Wakerly pointed out in a book that we recommend below, TST and CLR do not work on address registers. As the MC6800 had a few problems, being the first 8-bit microcomputer designed by Motorola, so the MC68000 has a few problems, being its first 16-bit computer. However, we agree with a substantial number of experts who hold this computer to be one of the best 16-bit microcomputers.

There are a few variations on the MC68000 which are the MC68008, MC68010, and the MC68020. The MC68008 is an MC68000 with an 8-bit data bus which allows 8-bit systems to be connected to a machine with the instruction set of the MC68000. Programs for the MC68000 will work on the MC68008, but will take longer to execute. The MC68010 is an MC68000 that has been modified to use a special integrated circuit called a memory management unit (MMU). The MC68010 and the MMU can address memory using the concept of virtual memory. In this technique, the MC68010 may send an address to memory, to read location $100, but the MMU may translate that address to

$1000100. This permits a smaller amount of real memory to appear like a large memory in which only the part of the program that is now in use is actually in real memory. That is, the addresses 0 to $1FFF, $5000 to $6FFF, and $A000 to $BFFFF sent by the MC68010 may be translated into addresses sent to memory, for which real memory actually exists, while other addresses sent by the MC68010 are translated to addresses to memory that do not exist as real memory words. If the program generates an address that is not translated to a real memory word, an interrupt occurs and a page of memory is brought in (from a disk) that contains the required address, and the program is resumed. The programmer can write programs as if all memory 0 to $FFFFFF exists, even though only a small amount of memory actually exists in hardware. This is analogous to your using a magnifying glass to get a virtual image of the real object, which essentially makes the object appear bigger or smaller than it really is. Special instructions have been added to the instruction set and modifications have been put in the hardware to permit the MC68010 to react properly when it addresses a memory word that is not in real memory. However, the programming of the MC68010 is essentially identical to that of the MC68000 as described above. Also, the MC68020 is an MC68000 that has been expanded to have a 32-bit address bus and a 32-bit data bus, and requires a 32-bit wide memory. It also incorporates the virtual memory capability of the MC68010 and is essentially programmed the same way as the MC68000.

The book *Microcomputer Architecture and Programming* (J. Wakerly, John Wiley & Sons, Inc., New York, 1981) has a very good chapter on the MC68000, as well as many other microcomputers. This book has a lot of insight, and we recommend it for the advanced reader. Motorola's MC68000 16-bit Microprocessor User's Manual accurately defines the instruction set. Finally, if at all possible, you should try out your programs on the MC68000. The Motorola MEX68KECB/D2 Educational Computer Board is a fairly inexpensive way to become acquainted with the MC68000.

9-5

SELECTING A MICROPROCESSOR FOR AN APPLICATION

Suppose you are designing a product that will have a microprocessor in it. Which one should you use? You have to look at many different alternatives, such as the ones we looked at in this chapter and similar microcomputers made by other companies. You should not select one with which you are very familiar, such as the MC6809, or one that you are overwhelmed with, such as the MC68020, unless you have good reason to select it. You have to analyze the needs of the application to pick the most suitable microcomputer.

The larger the microprocessor, the easier it is to write large programs. The MC68000 has capabilities to handle high-level languages, such as Pascal or C, and has an instruction set that allows assembly language programs to be written that can handle fairly complex operations in short fashion (such as the LINK instruction). It is easy to say that the larger the microprocessor, the better, and to select the largest one you can get. But consider some other aspects.

The smaller microcomputers such as the MC6805 are very inexpensive. You can build a fully functioning microcomputer using just the MC6805 and a couple of resistors and capacitors. The MC68000 requires about 70 extra integrated circuits (based on the number of chips on the MEX68KECB/D2 board) to make a working computer. The cost of the integrated circuits, the printed circuit board, and the testing needed to get the board working make the MC68000 system nearly two orders of magnitude more expensive than the MC6805 system. This can make a big difference to the cost of your product, especially if you intend to make thousands of copies of the product.

The trend toward networking should be observed. If you divide your problem in half, each half may fit on a smaller microcomputer. We read a news article that claimed the Boeing 767 jet had over a 1000 microcomputers scattered throughout the wing tip, landing gear and cockpit to control the plane. The distributed computer system saved wire and thus weight. Offices are using personal computers so that each person has a microcomputer dedicated to his or her work, rather than time-sharing a large computer. Small jobs, or small parts of a larger job, should be put on small computers.

The main criterion for selecting a microprocessor (within a family such as the Motorola family described here) is the size of the program stored in it. The microcomputer should be able to store the programs and data, with a little to spare to allow for correcting errors or adding features. That is, as the program and data approach the maximum size of the microprocessor, the cost of programming rises very sharply because squeezing a few extra instructions in will require moving subroutines around and cause errors to propagate as assumptions are forgotten and violated. The MC6805 is the best choice when the program size is about 1K bytes. The MC6801 is better when the size is above that, but less than about 4K bytes. The MC6809 is excellent when the size is less than the 64K-byte capacity of that microprocessor. The MC68000 is the best choice when the program size exceeds 64K bytes.

Other criteria include the requirements for I/O and speed. The MC6805 and MC6801 have some peripherals in the MPU chip. If the application needs more than the chip has, the advantage of that chip relative to memory size may be overshadowed by the extra cost of peripherals needed for the application. Speed can be a factor. Especially in communication systems and control of electronic systems, the fastest microprocessor may be needed. However, speed is often overrated. In most systems having I/O, the microprocessor will spend much, if not most, of its time waiting for I/O. The faster microprocessor will spend more time waiting. If you can select faster I/O (such as a Winchester disk in place of a floppy disk) the overall performance of the system will be much better than if you spend a great deal more money on the microprocessor.

A final, and often overwhelming criterion, is available software. Your company may have been using the MC6800 for years and may therefore have millions of lines of code for it. This may force you to select the MC6800 even though another may be indicated due to memory size, I/O, or speed requirements. Often, the availability of operating systems and high-level languages selects the microprocessor. The Z80 microprocessor from Zilog and the 8080-8085 microprocessors from Intel run the popular operating system CP/M, which will support a very wide range of languages and other programs for business data processing.

This section has pointed to the need to consider different microprocessors. You should be able to select a microprocessor for an application and defend your selection. You should extend your understanding and appreciation of microprocessors made by other manufacturers.

9–6

SUMMARY

This chapter has examined other microcomputers related to the MC6809. There are smaller microcomputers, such as the MC6805 and the MC6801, that are ideal for controlling appliances and small systems, and there are larger microcomputers, such as the MC68000, that are excellent for larger programs. Moreover, having learned to program the MC6809, you are well prepared to learn the languages for the MC6805 and the MC68000. It is rather like learning a second foreign language after you have learned the first. Although you may err by mixing up the languages, you should find the second easier to learn because you have been through the experience with the first language. After learning these languages for the Motorola family, you should be prepared to learn the languages for other microcomputers, and become a multilingual programmer.

This text has taken you through the world of microcomputer programming. You have learned how the microcomputer actually works, at the level of abstraction that lets you use it wisely. You have learned the instruction set and addressing modes of a good microcomputer and have used them to learn good techniques for handling subroutine parameters, local variables, data structures, arithmetic operations, and input/output. You are prepared to program small microcomputers such as the MC6805, which will be used in nooks and crannies all over, and you have learned a little about programming the MC68000, which will introduce you to programming larger computers. But that should be no problem. A computer is still a computer, whether small or large, and programming it is essentially the same.

PROBLEMS

1. Write an MC6801 subroutine DOTPRD that passes parameters on the stack as that subroutine was written in Chapter 5. It should be reentrant, position independent and as short as possible.

2. Write a shortest MC6801 subroutine SRCH that finds a string of ASCII characters in a text. The label STRNG is the address of the first letter of the string, STLEN is the length of the string, TXT is the address of the first letter of the text, TXLEN is the length of the text, and the subroutine will exit with C = 1 and the address of the first occurrence of the first letter of the string in the text in X, if it is found, or C = 0 if it is not found. The calling sequence for the subroutine is

```
BSR        SRCH
FDB        STRNG
FDB        STLEN
FDB        TXT
FDB        TXTLEN
```

3. Write a shortest reentrant MC6800 SWI interrupt handler ABX that will add B to X, exactly as the MC6809 instruction ABX works.

4. Write a shortest reentrant MC6800 SWI interrupt handler MUL that will multiply A by B, putting the result in A:B, exactly as the MC6809 MUL works. Ignore CC bits.

5. Write a shortest reentrant MC6800 SWI interrupt handler PSHX that will push X on the stack as the MC6801 instruction PSHX works. This instruction must be reentrant.

6. Write a shortest MC6805 subroutine MOVE that can move any number of words from any location to any other location in memory. The calling sequence will put the beginning address of the source in page zero global variable SRC, the beginning address of the destination in DST, and the length in LEN. Use impure coding if necessary.

7. Write a shortest MC6805 program segment that will jump to subroutines L0 to L7 depending on the value of X. If (X) = 0, jump to subroutine L0; if (X) = 1, jump to subroutine L1; and so on. Assume that there is a table JTBL as shown below:

```
JTBL        FDB        L0,L1,L2,L3,L4,L5,L6,L7
```

Use self-modifying code if necessary.

8. Write a shortest MC6805 subroutine DOTPRD similar to that subroutine in Chapter 5 which passes parameters through global variables. However, use global variables TEMP1, TEMP2, and so on in place of local variables in the subroutine.

9. Write a shortest MC6805 subroutine to divide the unsigned number in X by the unsigned number in A, leaving the quotient in X and the remainder in A. Use only TEMP1 and TEMP2 to store variables needed by the subroutine.

10. Write a shortest MC6805 subroutine to clear bit n of the 75-bit vector similar to the subroutine SET at the end of Section 9-3. The instruction BCLR N,M clears bit N of byte M, and has op code $11 + 2 * N followed by offset M. Use self-modifying code.

11. Write an MC6805 subroutine to transmit the bits of the 75-bit vector set by the SET subroutine described in Section 9-3, bit 0 first, serially through the least significant bit of output port O1 at location 0. Each time a bit is sent out, the second least significant bit of that output port is pulsed high and then low. The least significant bit happens to be connected to a serial data input, and the second least significant bit is connected to a clock of a shift register that controls display lights. This subroutine sends the bit pattern

into the shift register to display the lights on a BINGO board, corresponding to the numbers that are set to one in the bit vector, which are the bits that had been set by the SET subroutine.

12. Write a shortest MC68000 subroutine CLRREG to clear all the registers except A7. Assume that there is a block of 60 bytes of zeros, after LOC0, which is not in part of your program (i.e., use 32-bit direct addressing and do not count these bytes when calculating the length of your subroutine) Be careful since this one must be checked out and the obvious solutions do not work.

13. Write a fastest MC68000 subroutine MULT that multiplies two 32-bit unsigned binary numbers in D0 and D1, to produce a 64-bit product in D0:D1.

14. Write a position independent, reentrant, fastest MC68000 subroutine DOTPRD that passes parameters on the stack, in the same manner as that subroutine in Chapter 5.

15. Write a position independent, reentrant, fastest MC68000 subroutine CAH that converts a string of ASCII characters representing a hexadecimal number, whose first character is pointed to by A0 and whose length is in D0, to an unsigned binary number in D0.

16. Select the most suitable microprocessor or microcomputer among the MC6805, MC6801, MC6809, or MC68000 for the following applications.

(a) A graphics terminal needing 250K bytes of programs and 100K bytes of data

(b) A controller for a boat motor, requiring 1.5K bytes of program storage and needing the MUL instruction to evaluate polynomials quickly

(c) A text editor for a "smart terminal" needing 8K for programs and 40K for data storage

(d) A keyless entry system (combination lock for a door) requiring 500 bytes of program memory and 2 parallel I/O ports.

Number Representations and Binary Arithmetic

This appendix contains material needed for the rest of the book and is usually found in an introductory course on logic design. The two topics are the representation of integers with different bases and binary arithmetic with unsigned and two's-complement numbers.

A1–1

NUMBER REPRESENTATIONS

If b and m are positive integers and if N is a nonnegative integer less than b_m, then N can be expressed uniquely with a finite series

$$N = c_{m-1}*b^{m-1} + c_{m-2}*b^{m-2} + \cdots + c_0*b^0 \qquad (1)$$

where $0 \leq c_i < b$ for $0 \leq i \leq m - 1$. The integer b is called the *base* or *radix* and the sequence $c_{m-1}\cdots c_0$ is called a *base-b representation* of N. If b = 2, the digits $c_{m-1},\cdots,c_0$ are called *bits* and the sequence $c_{m-1}\cdots c_0$ is called an *m-bit representation* of N.

Binary, octal (base-8) and hexadecimal (base-16) representations, as well as the ordinary decimal representation, are the ones used when discussing computers with hexadecimal being particularly useful with 8-bit microprocessors. When the hexadecimal representation is used, the numbers 10 through 15 are replaced by the letters A through F, respectively, so that hexadecimal sequences such as 112 will be unambiguous without the use of commas (e.g., without commas, 112 could be interpreted as 1,1,2 or 11,2 or 1,12, which are the decimal numbers 274, 178, or 28, respectively). Unless stated otherwise, all numbers will be given in decimal and, when confusion is possible, a binary sequence will be preceded by a "%" and a hexadecimal sequence by a "$." For example, 110 denotes the integer one hundred and ten, %110 denotes the integer six, and $110 denotes the integer two hundred seventy-two.

To go from a base-b representation of N to its decimal representation, one has only to use (1). To go from decimal to base-b, notice that

$$N = c_0 + c_1*b^1 + \cdots + c_{m-1}*b^{m-1}$$
$$= c_0 + b*(c_1 + b*(c_2 + \cdots) \cdots)$$

so that dividing N by b yields a remainder c_0. Dividing the quotient by b again yields a remainder equal to c_1 and so on. Although this is a fairly convenient method with a calculator, we shall see later that there is a more computationally efficient way to do it with an 8-bit microprocessor.

To go from binary to hexadecimal, or octal, one only needs to generalize from the following example.

$$\%1101 \quad 0011 \quad 1011 = \$D3B$$

Thus, to go from binary to hexadecimal, one first partitions the binary representation into groups of four 0's and 1's from right to left, adding leading 0's to get an exact multiple of four 0's and 1's, and then represents each group of four 0's and 1's by its hexadecimal equivalent. To go from hexadecimal to binary is just the reverse of this process.

A1-2

BINARY ARITHMETIC

One can add the binary representations of unsigned numbers exactly like the addition of decimal representations except that a carry is generated when 2 is obtained as a sum of particular bits. For example,

1010	1100	1110
+0111	+0111	+0111
10001	10011	10101

Notice that when two 4-bit representations are added and a carry is produced from adding the last or most significant bits, five bits are needed to represent the sum.

Similarly, borrows are generated when 1 is subtracted from 0 for a particular bit. For example,

$$
\begin{array}{ccc}
1111 & 1011 & 1000 \\
-0101 & -0100 & -1001 \\
\hline
1010 & 0111 & (1)1111
\end{array}
$$

In the last of the examples above, we had to borrow out of the most significant bit, effectively loaning the first number 2^4 to complete the subtraction. We have put a "(1)" before the 4-bit result to indicate this borrow. Of course, when a borrow occurs out of the most significant bit, the number being subtracted is larger than the number that we are subtracting it from.

When handling numbers in microprocessors, one usually has instructions that add and subtract m-bit numbers, yielding an m-bit result and a carry bit. Labeled C, the carry bit is put equal to the carry out of the most significant bit after an add instruction, while for subtraction, it is put equal to the borrow out of the most significant bit. The bit C thus indicates *unsigned overflow*; that is, it equals 1 when the addition of two positive m-bit numbers produces a result that cannot be expressed with m-bits, while with subtraction, it equals 1 when a positive number is subtracted from a smaller positive number so that the negative result cannot be expressed with equation (1).

We can picture the m-bit result of addition and subtraction of these nonnegative numbers (also called *unsigned* numbers) using Figure A1-1, where m is taken to be four bits. For example, to find the representation of $M + N$, one moves N positions clockwise from the representation of M while, for $M - N$, one moves N positions counterclockwise. Mathematically speaking, we are doing our addition and subtraction *modulo-16* when we truncate the result to four bits. In particular, we get all the usual answers as long as unsigned overflow does not occur, but with overflow, $9 + 8$ is 1, $8 - 9$ is 15, and so on.

We also want some way of representing negative numbers. If we restrict ourselves to m binary digits $c_{m-1} \cdots c_0$, then we can clearly represent 2^m different integers. For example, with (1) we can represent all of the nonnegative integers in the range 0 to $2^m - 1$. Of course, only nonnegative integers are represented with (1), so that another representation is needed to assign negative integers to some of the m-bit sequences. With the usual decimal notation, a plus and minus sign is used to distinguish between positive and negative numbers. Restricting ourselves to binary representations, the natural counterpart of this decimal convention is to use the first bit as a sign bit. For example, put c_{m-1} equal to 1 if N is negative and put c_{m-1} equal to 0 if N is positive or zero. The remaining binary digits $c_{m-2} \cdots, c_0$ are then used to represent the magnitude of N with (1).

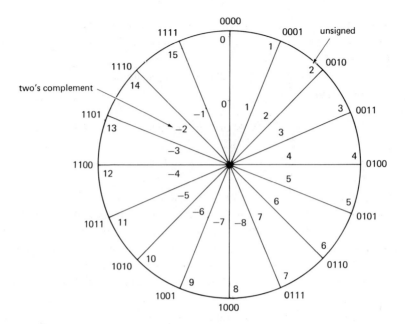

FIGURE A1-1.   4-Bit Binary Representations

This particular representation, called the *signed-magnitude* representation, has two problems. First, carrying out addition and subtraction is clumsy, particularly from a logic design point of view. Second, the number zero has two representations, 10...0 and 00...0, which, at best, has a perplexing feeling to it. The following representation, the *two's-complement* representation, essentially solves both of these problems.

Looking again at Figure A1-1, notice that when we subtract the representation of N from M, we get the same thing as adding the representation of M to that of $2^4 - N$ since moving N positions counterclockwise is the same thing as moving clockwise $2^4 - N$ positions. Thus, as far as modulo-16 addition is concerned, $M - 1 = M + (-1)$ is the same as $M + 15$, $M - 2 = M + (-2)$ is the same as $M + 14$, and so on. Letting -1 be represented with the sequence for 15, -2 with the sequence for 14, and so on, we get the two's-complement representation shown in Figure A1-1 for m equal to four.

We choose to represent the negative integers -1 through -8 in Figure A1-1 because, with this choice, the leading bit is a sign bit, as with the signed-magnitude representation (e.g., 1 for minus, 0 for plus). Additionally, the number zero, which is now considered positive, is represented by the single sequence 0000. However, the nicest feature is that the two's-complement representation of $M + N$ is obtained by simply adding the two's-complement representations of M and N and truncating to four bits. This works, of course, as long as there is no *signed* overflow, that is, adding two m-bit two's-complement numbers whose sum cannot be represented with an m-bit two's-complement number. For addition, notice that signed overflow occurs when, and only when, the sign of the two representations added are the same but different from the sign of the result. A similar observation can be made for the two's-complement representation of $M - N$.

We can now summarize the facts for m-bit two's-complement representations. With m fixed and $-2^{m-1} \leq N < 2^{m-1}$, the m-bit two's complement representation of N is given by:

1. The m-bit representation of N for $0 \leq N < 2^{m-1}$.
2. The m-bit representation of $2^m + N$ for $-2^{m-1} \leq N < 0$.

The first bit of the representation is a sign bit and, after a little thought, you should be able to see that if $c_{m-1} \cdots c_0$ is the m-bit two's-complement representation of N, then

$$N = -c_{m-1}*2^{m-1} + c_{m-2}*2^{m-2} + \cdots + c_0*2^0 \qquad (2)$$

The difference between equations (2) and (1), of course, is that the first term in (2) is negative. Finally, the two's-complement representation of $M + N$ is obtained by adding the two's-complement representations of M and N and truncating to m bits. The answer is correct except when signed overflow occurs or, equivalently, when the signs of the two representations are the same but different from that of the result.

If N is positive, its m-bit two's-complement representation y is just its ordinary m-bit representation. It is not difficult to see that the m-bit two's-complement representation of $-N$ can be obtained by subtracting each bit of y from 1 and then adding 1 to the result. This procedure, sometimes called "taking the two's-complement" of y, works even if N is zero or negative, with two exceptions. If N is zero, the result needs to be truncated to m bits. If $N = -2^{m-1}$, one will just get back the two's-complement representation of -2^{m-1}. To see why this works for $-2^{m-1} < N < 2^{m-1}$, suppose that $y = c_{m-1} \cdots c_0$ and let $d_j = 1 - c_j$, $0 \leq j \leq m-1$. Then it is easy to see from (2) that $d_{m-1} \cdots d_0$ is the m-bit two's-complement representation of $-N-1$. That the procedure works now follows from the fact above for the addition of two's-complement representations.

One situation frequently encountered when two's-complement representations are used with microprocessors is that of finding the hexadecimal equivalent of the 8-bit two's-complement representation of a negative number. For example, for a -46 you could find the 8-bit representation of 46, use the technique just mentioned, and then find its hexadecimal equivalent. You could also use the two's-complement definition, finding the 8-bit representation of $2^8 - 46$, and then converting this to hexadecimal. It would, however, usually be quicker just to convert $2^8 - 46 = 210$ to hexadecimal. Finally, one could also use a "16's-complement" approach, that is, convert the number to hexadecimal, subtract each hexadecimal digit from 15, and then add 1 to get the result. For example, $46 = \$2E$ and the 16's-complement of $\$2E$ is $\$D1 + 1 = \$D2$, the desired result. You should try to understand how this works. (See the problems at the end of this appendix.)

A1–3

REMARKS

The material discussed here can be found in any introductory text on logic design. We recommend the book *Fundamentals of Logic Design, 2nd ed.* (C. H. Roth, West Publishing Co., St. Paul, Minn., 1979).

PROBLEMS

1. Find the hexadecimal equivalents of the 8-bit two's-complement representations of -44 and -121.

2. Explain why the 16's-complement technique works when used for calculations such as Problem 1.

3. Suppose that you were going to add a 16-bit two's-complement representation with an 8-bit one. How would you change the 8-bit representation so that the 16-bit result would be correct? This process is sometimes called *sign extension*.

4. Give a simple condition for signed overflow when two's-complement representations are subtracted.

5. One textbook reason for preferring the two's-complement representation of integers over the signed-magnitude representation is that the logic design of a device that adds and subtracts numbers is simpler. For example, suppose that M and N have m-bit two's-complement representations x and y. To subtract M from N, one can take the two's-complement of x and then add it to y, presumably simpler from the logic design viewpoint than dealing with signed-magnitudes. Does this always work? Try it with m = 8, N equal to -1, and M equal to -128. What is the condition for overflow? Does this work when N and M are interpreted as unsigned numbers? Interpret.

6. Suppose that we add two m-bit representations x and y, where x is the unsigned representation of M and y is the two's-complement representation of N. Will the answer, truncated to m bits, be correct in any sense? Explain.

Instruction Set
Summary

Operation Code Bytes[a]

Instruction	Forms	Immediate Op	~	#	Direct Page Op	~	#	Index Op	~	#	Direct Op	~	#	Inherent Op	~	#	Description	H	N	Z	V	C
ABX														3A	3	1	$B+X \to X$ (B) unsigned	.	.	.	.	.
ADC	ADCA	89	2	2	99	4	2	A9	4+	2+	B9	5	3				$A+M+C \to A$	↕	↕	↕	↕	↕
	ADCB	C9	2	2	D9	4	2	E9	4+	2+	F9	5	3				$B+M+C \to B$	↕	↕	↕	↕	↕
ADD	ADDA	8B	2	2	9B	4	2	AB	4+	2+	BB	5	3				$A+M \to A$	↕	↕	↕	↕	↕
	ADDB	CB	2	2	DB	4	2	EB	4+	2+	FB	5	3				$B+M \to B$	↕	↕	↕	↕	↕
	ADDD	C3	4	3	D3	6	2	E3	6+	2+	F3	7	3				$D+M:M+1 \to D$	.	↕	↕	↕	↕
AND	ANDA	84	2	2	94	4	2	A4	4+	2+	B4	5	3				$A \wedge M \to A$	.	↕	↕	0	.
	ANDB	C4	2	2	D4	4	2	E4	4+	2+	F4	5	3				$B \wedge M \to B$	.	↕	↕	0	.
	ANDCC	1C	3	2													$CC \wedge IMM \to CC$					6
ASL	ASLA													48	2	1		.	↕	↕	↕	↕
	ASLB													58	2	1		.	↕	↕	↕	↕
	ASL				08	6	2	68	6+	2+	78	7	3					.	↕	↕	↕	↕
ASR	ASRA													47	2	1		7	↕	↕	.	↕
	ASRB													57	2	1		7	↕	↕	.	↕
	ASR				07	6	2	67	6+	2+	77	7	3					7	↕	↕	.	↕
BIT	BITA	85	2	2	95	4	2	A5	4+	2+	B5	5	3				Bit Test A $(M \wedge A)$	.	↕	↕	0	.
	BITB	C5	2	2	D5	4	2	E5	4+	2+	F5	5	3				Bit Test B $(M \wedge B)$	.	↕	↕	0	.
CLR	CLRA													4F	2	1		.	0	1	0	0
	CLRB													5F	2	1		.	0	1	0	0
	CLR				0F	6	2	6F	6+	2+	7F	7	3				$0 \to M$	.	0	1	0	0

Condition code bit positions: H (5), N (3), Z (2), V (1), C (0)

Instruction	Forms	Immediate Op	~	#	Direct Op	~	#	Indexed Op	~	#	Extended Op	~	#	Inherent Op	~	#	Description	H	N	Z	V	C
CMP	CMPA	81	2	2	91	4	2	A1	4+	2+	B1	5	3				Compare M from A	[7]	↕	↕	↕	↕
	CMPB	C1	2	2	D1	4	2	E1	4+	2+	F1	5	3				Compare M from B	[7]	↕	↕	↕	↕
	CMPD	10 83	5	4	10 93	7	3	10 A3	7+	3+	10 B3	8	4				Compare M:M+1 from D	•	↕	↕	↕	↕
	CMPS	11 8C	5	4	11 9C	7	3	11 AC	7+	3+	11 BC	8	4				Compare M:M+1 from S	•	↕	↕	↕	↕
	CMPU	11 83	5	4	11 93	7	3	11 A3	7+	3+	11 B3	8	4				Compare M:M+1 from U	•	↕	↕	↕	↕
	CMPX	8C	4	3	9C	6	2	AC	6+	2+	BC	7	3				Compare M:M+1 from X	•	↕	↕	↕	↕
	CMPY	10 8C	5	4	10 9C	7	3	10 AC	7+	3+	10 BC	8	4				Compare M:M+1 from Y	•	↕	↕	↕	↕
COM	COMA													43	2	1	$\overline{A} \to A$	•	↕	↕	0	1
	COMB													53	2	1	$\overline{B} \to B$	•	↕	↕	0	1
	COM				03	6	2	63	6+	2+	73	7	3				$\overline{M} \to M$	•	↕	↕	0	1
CWAI		3C	≥20	2													CC ∧ IMM → CC Wait for interrupt	[6]	[6]	[6]	[6]	[6]
DAA														19	2	1	Decimal Adjust A	•	↕	↕	0	↕
DEC	DECA													4A	2	1	$A - 1 \to A$	•	↕	↕	↕	•
	DECB													5A	2	1	$B - 1 \to B$	•	↕	↕	↕	•
	DEC				0A	6	2	6A	6+	2+	7A	7	3				$M - 1 \to M$	•	↕	↕	↕	•
EOR	EORA	88	2	2	98	4	2	A8	4+	2+	B8	5	3				$A \veebar M \to A$	•	↕	↕	0	•
	EORB	C8	2	2	D8	4	2	E8	4+	2+	F8	5	3				$B \veebar M \to B$	•	↕	↕	0	•
EXG	R1,R2	1E	8	2													R1 → R2[2]	•	•	•	•	•
INC	INCA													4C	2	1	$A + 1 \to A$	•	↕	↕	↕	•
	INCB													5C	2	1	$B + 1 \to B$	•	↕	↕	↕	•
	INC				0C	6	2	6C	6+	2+	7C	7	3				$M + 1 \to M$	•	↕	↕	↕	•
JMP					0E	3	2	6E	3+	2+	7E	4	3				EA[3] → PC	•	•	•	•	•

Operation Code Bytes[a] (continued)

Instruction	Forms	Immediate Op	~	#	Direct Page Op	~	#	Index Op	~	#	Direct Op	~	#	Inherent Op	~	#	Description	H	N	Z	V	C
JSR					9D	7	2	AD	7+	2+	BD	8	3				Jump to Subroutine	·	·	·	·	·
LD	LDA	86	2	2	96	4	2	A6	4+	2+	B6	5	3				$M \rightarrow A$	·	↕	↕	0	·
	LDB	C6	2	2	D6	4	2	E6	4+	2+	F6	5	3				$M \rightarrow B$	·	↕	↕	0	·
	LDD	CC	3	3	DC	5	2	EC	5+	2+	FC	6	3				$M:M+1 \rightarrow D$	·	↕	↕	0	·
	LDS	10 CE	4	4	10 DE	6	3	10 EE	6+	3+	10 FE	7	4				$M:M+1 \rightarrow S$	·	↕	↕	0	·
	LDU	CE	3	3	DE	5	2	EE	5+	2+	FE	6	3				$M:M+1 \rightarrow U$	·	↕	↕	0	·
	LDX	8E	3	3	9E	5	2	AE	5+	2+	BE	6	3				$M:M+1 \rightarrow X$	·	↕	↕	0	·
	LDY	10 8E	4	4	10 9E	6	3	10 AE	6+	3+	10 BE	7	4				$M:M+1 \rightarrow Y$	·	↕	↕	0	·
LEA	LEAS							32	4+	2+							$EA^3 \rightarrow S$	·	·	·	·	·
	LEAU							33	4+	2+							$EA^3 \rightarrow U$	·	·	·	·	·
	LEAX							30	4+	2+							$EA^3 \rightarrow X$	·	·	↕	·	·
	LEAY							31	4+	2+							$EA^3 \rightarrow Y$	·	·	↕	·	·
LSL	LSLA													48	2	1	$\left. \begin{matrix} A \\ B \\ M \end{matrix} \right\}$ $\underset{c}{\square} \leftarrow \underset{b_7}{\square}\boxed{} \underset{b_0}{\square} \leftarrow 0$	·	↕	↕	↕	↕
	LSLB													58	2	1		·	↕	↕	↕	↕
	LSL				08	6	2	68	6+	2+	78	7	3					·	↕	↕	↕	↕
LSR	LSRA													44	2	1	$\left. \begin{matrix} A \\ B \\ M \end{matrix} \right\}$ $0 \rightarrow \underset{b_7}{\square}\boxed{} \underset{b_0}{\square} \rightarrow \underset{c}{\square}$	·	0	↕	·	↕
	LSRB													54	2	1		·	0	↕	·	↕
	LSR				04	6	2	64	6+	2+	74	7	3					·	0	↕	·	↕
MUL														3D	11	1	$A \times B \rightarrow D$ (unsigned)	·	·	↕	·	↕8

6809 Instruction Set (continued)

Instruction	Forms	Immediate (Op ~ #)	Direct (Op ~ #)	Indexed (Op ~ #)	Extended (Op ~ #)	Inherent (Op ~ #)	Description	H	N	Z	V	C
NEG	NEGA					40 2 1	$0 - A \rightarrow A$	7	↕	↕	↕	↕
	NEGB					50 2 1	$0 - B \rightarrow B$	7	↕	↕	↕	↕
	NEG		00 6 2	60 6+ 2+	70 7 3		$0 - M \rightarrow M$	7	↕	↕	↕	↕
NOP						12 2 1	$PC + 1 \rightarrow PC$	•	•	•	•	•
OR	ORA	8A 2 2	9A 4 2	AA 4+ 2+	BA 5 3		$A \vee M \rightarrow A$	•	↕	↕	0	•
	ORB	CA 2 2	DA 4 2	EA 4+ 2+	FA 5 3		$B \vee M \rightarrow B$	•	↕	↕	0	•
	ORCC	1A 3 2					$CC \vee IMM \rightarrow CC$	6	6	6	6	6
PSH	PSHS	34 5+ 2					Push registers on S Stack	•	•	•	•	•
	PSHU	36 5+ 2					Push registers on U Stack	•	•	•	•	•
PUL	PULS	35 5+ 2					Pull registers from S Stack	•	•	•	•	•
	PULU	37 5+ 2					Pull registers from U Stack	•	•	•	•	•
ROL	ROLA					49 2 1	A) rotate left, $c \leftarrow b_7 \ldots b_0$	•	↕	↕	↕	↕
	ROLB					59 2 1	B)	•	↕	↕	↕	↕
	ROL		09 6 2	69 6+ 2+	79 7 3		M)	•	↕	↕	↕	↕
ROR	RORA					46 2 1	A) rotate right, $c \rightarrow b_7 \ldots b_0$	•	↕	↕	•	↕
	RORB					56 2 1	B)	•	↕	↕	•	↕
	ROR		06 6 2	66 6+ 2+	76 7 3		M)	•	↕	↕	•	↕
RTI						3B 6/15 1	Return from Interrupt	6	6	6	6	6
RTS						39 5 1	Return from Subroutine	•	•	•	•	•
SBC	SBCA	82 2 2	92 4 2	A2 4+ 2+	B2 5 3		$A - M - C \rightarrow A$	7	↕	↕	↕	↕
	SBCB	C2 2 2	D2 4 2	E2 4+ 2+	F2 5 3		$B - M - C \rightarrow B$	7	↕	↕	↕	↕
SEX						1D 2 1	Sign Extend B into A	•	↕	↕	0	•

Operation Code Bytes[a] (continued)

Instruction	Forms	Immediate Op	Immediate ~	Immediate #	Direct Page Op	Direct Page ~	Direct Page #	Index Op	Index ~	Index #	Direct Op	Direct ~	Direct #	Inherent Op	Inherent ~	Inherent #	Description	H (5)	N (3)	Z (2)	V (1)	C (0)
ST	STA				97	4	2	A7	4+	2+	B7	5	3				A→M	•	↔	↔	0	•
	STB				D7	4	2	E7	4+	2+	F7	5	3				B→M	•	↔	↔	0	•
	STD				DD	5	2	ED	5+	2+	FD	6	3				D→M:M+1	•	↔	↔	0	•
	STS				10 DF	6	3	10 EF	6+	3+	10 FF	7	4				S→M:M+1	•	↔	↔	0	•
	STU				DF	5	2	EF	5+	2+	FF	6	3				U→M:M+1	•	↔	↔	0	•
	STX				9F	5	2	AF	6+	2+	BF	6	3				X→M:M+1	•	↔	↔	0	•
	STY				10 9F	6	3	10 AF	6+	3+	10 BF	7	4				Y→M:M+1	•	↔	↔	0	•
SUB	SUBA	80	2	2	90	4	2	A0	4+	2+	B0	5	3				A − M→A	7	↔	↔	↔	↔
	SUBB	C0	2	2	D0	4	2	E0	4+	2+	F0	5	3				B − M→B	7	↔	↔	↔	↔
	SUBD	83	4	3	93	6	2	A3	6+	2+	B3	7	3				D − M:M+1→D	•	↔	↔	↔	↔
SWI	SWI													3F	19	1	Software Interrupt 1	•	•	•	•	•
	SWI1													10 3F	20	2	Software Interrupt 2	•	•	•	•	•
	SWI2													11 3F	20	1	Software Interrupt 3	•	•	•	•	•
SYNC														13	≥4	1	Synchronize to Interrupt	•	•	•	•	•
TFR	R1,R2													1F	6	2	R1→R2[2]	•	•	•	•	•
TST	TSTA													4D	2	1	Test A	•	↔	↔	0	•
	TSTB													5D	2	1	Test B	•	↔	↔	0	•
	TST				0D	6	2	6D	6+	2+	7D	7	3				Test M	•	↔	↔	0	•

Post Bytes for Index Addressing Options[a]

Type	Forms		Direct Assembler Form	Post Byte	+~	+#	Indirect Assembler Form	Post Byte	+~	+#
Pointer addressing			.R	1RR00100	0	0	[,R]	1RR10100	3	0
Index addressing	5-bit offset		n,R	0RRRnnnnn	1	0	Defaults to 8 bit			
	8-bit offset		<n,R	1RR01000	1	1	[<n,R]	1RR11000	4	1
	16-bit offset		>n,R	1RR01001	4	2	[>n,R]	1RR11001	7	2
Accumulator indexed	A-register offset		A,R	1RR00110	1	0	[A,R]	1RR10110	4	0
	B-register offset		B,R	1RR00101	1	0	[B,R]	1RR10101	4	0
	D-register offset		D,R	1RR01011	4	0	[D,R]	1RR11011	7	0
Postincrement/predecrement R	Increment by 1		,R+	1RR00000	2	0	Not allowed			
	Increment by 2		,R++	1RR00001	3	0	[,R++]	1RR10001	6	0
	Decrement by 1		,−R	1RR00010	2	0	Not allowed			
	Decrement by 2		,−−R	1RR00011	3	0	[,−−R]	1RR10011	6	0
Program counter relative	8-bit offset		<n,PCR	1XX01100	1	1	[<n,PCR]	1XX11100	4	1
	16-bit offset		>n,PCR	1XX01101	5	2	[>n,PCR]	1XX11101	8	2
Indirect	16-bit address		—	—	—	—	[n]	10011111	5	2

R = X, Y, U, or S   RR:00 = X   10 = U

X = don't care   01 = Y   11 = S

[a] See the footnotes in the operation code bytes table.

Instruction	Forms	Addressing Mode Relative			Description	5 H	3 N	2 Z	1 V	0 C
		OP	~5	#						
BCC	BCC / LBCC	24 / 10 24	3 / 5(6)	2 / 4	Branch if C = 0	• •	• •	• •	• •	• •
BCS	BCS / LBCS	25 / 10 25	3 / 5(6)	2 / 4	Branch if C = 1	• •	• •	• •	• •	• •
BEQ	BEQ / LBEQ	27 / 10 27	3 / 5(6)	2 / 4	Branch if Z = 1	• •	• •	• •	• •	• •
BGE	BGE / LBGE	2C / 10 2C	3 / 5(6)	2 / 4	Branch if N⊕V = 0	• •	• •	• •	• •	• •
BGT	BGT / LBGT	2E / 10 2E	3 / 5(6)	2 / 4	Branch if Z∨[N⊕V] = 0	• •	• •	• •	• •	• •
BHI	BHI / LBHI	22 / 10 22	3 / 5(6)	2 / 4	Branch if C∨Z = 0	• •	• •	• •	• •	• •
BHS	BHS / LBHS	24 / 10 24	3 / 5(6)	2 / 4	Branch if C = 0	• •	• •	• •	• •	• •

Instruction	Forms	Addressing Mode Relative			Description	5 H	3 N	2 Z	1 V	0 C
		OP	~5	#						
BLS	BLS / LBLS	23 / 10 23	3 / 5(6)	2 / 4	Branch if C∨Z = 1	• •	• •	• •	• •	• •
BLT	BLT / LBLT	2D / 10 2D	3 / 5(6)	2 / 4	Branch if N⊕V = 1	• •	• •	• •	• •	• •
BMI	BMI / LBMI	2B / 10 2B	3 / 5(6)	2 / 4	Branch if N = 1	• •	• •	• •	• •	• •
BNE	BNE / LBNE	26 / 10 26	3 / 5(6)	2 / 4	Branch if Z = 0	• •	• •	• •	• •	• •
BPL	BPL / LBPL	2A / 10 2A	3 / 5(6)	2 / 4	Branch if N = 0	• •	• •	• •	• •	• •
BRA	BRA / LBRA	20 / 16	3 / 5	2 / 3	Branch Always	• •	• •	• •	• •	• •
BSR	BRN / LBRN	21 / 10 21	3 / 5	2 / 4	Branch Never	• •	• •	• •	• •	• •

Branch Instructions[a] (continued)

Instruction	Forms	OP	~[5]	#	Description	H (5)	N (3)	Z (2)	V (1)	C (0)
BLE	BLE	2F	3	2	Branch if Z∨[N∀V] = 1	•	•	•	•	•
	LBLE	10 2F	5(6)	4						
BLO	BLO	25	3	2	Branch if C=1	•	•	•	•	•
	LBLO	10 25	5(6)	4						

Instruction	Forms	OP	~[5]	#	Description	H (5)	N (3)	Z (2)	V (1)	C (0)
BVC	BSR	8D	7	2	Branch to Subroutine	•	•	•	•	•
	LBSR	17	9	3						
	BVC	28	3	2	Branch if V = 0	•	•	•	•	•
	LBVC	10 28	5(6)	4						
BVS	BVS	29	3	2	Branch if V = 1	•	•	•	•	•
	LBVS	10 29	5(6)	4						

Simple Branches

	OP	~	#
BRA	10	3	2
LBRA	16	5	3
BRN	21	3	2
LBRN	1021	5	4
BSR	8D	7	2
LBSR	17	9	3

Simple Conditional Branches[1-4]

Test	True	OP	False	OP
N = 1	BMI	2B	BPL	2A
Z = 1	BEQ	27	BNE	26
V = 1	BVS	29	BVC	28
C = 1	BCS	25	BCC	24

Signed Conditional Branches[1-4]

Test	True	OP	False	OP
r > m	BGT	2E	BLE	2F
r ≥ m	BGE	2C	BLT	2D
r = m	BEQ	27	BNE	26
r ≤ m	BLE	2F	BGT	2E
r < m	BLT	2D	BGE	2C

Unsigned Conditional Branches[1-4]

Test	True	OP	False	OP
r > m	BHI	22	BLS	23
r ≥ m	BHS	24	BLO	25
r = m	BEQ	27	BNE	26
r ≤ m	BLS	23	BHI	22
r < m	BLO	25	BHS	24

[a] In additional to the following notes, see the footnotes in the operation code bytes table.

Notes:
1. All conditional branches have both short and long variations.
2. All short branches are two bytes and require three cycles.
3. All conditional long branches are formed by prefixing the short branch op code with $10 and using a 16-bit relative offset.
4. All conditional long branches require four bytes and six cycles if the branch is taken or five cycles if the branch is not taken.
5. 5(6) means: five cycles if branch not taken, six cycles if taken.

Push/Pull Post Byte

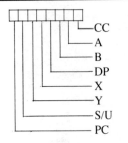

CC
A
B
DP
X
Y
S/U
PC

The bits are set if the corresponding registers are being pushed or pulled in the instruction.

6809 Stacking Order

Pull Order
↓
CC
A
B
X Hi   increasing
X Lo   memory
Y Hi   ↓
Y Lo
U/S Hi
U/S Lo
PC Hi
PC Lo
↑
Push Order

Transfer/Exchange Post Byte

Source   Destination

Register Field

0000 = D(A:B)	1000 = A
0001 = X	1001 = B
0010 = Y	1010 = CC
0011 = U	1011 = DP
0100 = S	
0101 = PC	

6809 Vectors

FFFE	Restart
FFFC	MMI
FFFA	SWI
FFF8	IRQ
FFF6	FIRQ
FFF4	SWI2
FFF2	SWI3
FFF0	Reserved

ASCII Character Set

Hex	Most Significant Character							
	0	**1**	**2**	**3**	**4**	**5**	**6**	**7**
0	NUL	DLE	SP	0	@	P		p
1	SOH	DC1	!	1	A	Q	a	q
2	STX	DC2	"	2	B	R	b	r
3	ETX	DC3	#	3	C	S	c	s
4	EQT	DC4	$	4	D	T	d	t
5	ENQ	NAK	%	5	E	U	e	u
6	ACK	SYN	&	6	F	V	f	v
7	BEL	ETB	'	7	G	W	g	w
8	BS	CAN	(	8	H	X	h	x
9	HT	EM	)	9	I	Y	i	y
A	LF	SUB	*	:	J	Z	j	z
B	VT	ESC	+	;	K	[	k	{
C	FF	FS	,	<	L	/	l	|
D	CR	GS	−	=	M	]	m	}
E	SO	RS	·	>	N	∧	n	~
F	SI	US	/	?	O	__	o	DEL

Least Significant Character

Floating-Point Subroutines

The main subroutines below, FPADD and FPMUL, are for single-precision floating-point addition and floating-point multiplication. The format of the floating-point numbers is

31		23	22		0
s		e		f	

where the number represented equals

$$(-1)^s * 2^{e-127} * 1,f \qquad \text{for } 0 < e < 256$$
$$0 \qquad \qquad \qquad \text{for } e = 0$$

In particular, no denormalized floating-point numbers are used and all numbers with an e of 0 are assumed to be zero. When an underflow occurs, the result is flushed to zero and an underflow flag is returned set. When an overflow occurs, the maximum result consistent with the sign of the answer is returned and an overflow flag is returned set. Rounding in these subroutines is to the nearest represented number as prescribed by the IEEE standard, except that results are flushed to zero if an underflow occurs.

```
*
* LDXB MACRO: LDXB loads X from \0 with index
* addressing and B from \1 with immediate addressing.
* Registers B, CC, and X are changed.
*
LDXB      MACR
          LEAX      \0
          LDB       #\1
          ENDM
*
*
* LDXYB MACRO: LDXYB loads X and Y from \0 and \1
* using index addressing and loads B from \2 using
* immediate addressing. Registers X, Y, CC, and B are
* changed
*
LDXYB     MACR
          LEAX      \0
          LEAY      \1
          LDB       #\2
          ENDM
*
*
* LDXYU MACRO: LDXYU loads X, Y, U from \0, \1, and \2
* using index addressing. Registers X, Y, CC, and U
* are changed.
*
LDXYU     MACR
          LEAX      \0
          LEAY      \1
          LEAU      \2
          ENDM
*
*
* TCOMP MACRO: TCOMP replaces the #\1 byte signed-
* magnitude number at \0 with its two's-complement
* equivalent. It also replaces the two's-complement
* number at \0 with its signed-magnitude equivalent
* except that the most negative two's-complement
* number is changed to a minus zero. No registers are
* changed except CC. TCOMP should not be used with
* local variables since the stack pointer is changed
* within TCOMP.

TCOMP     MACR
          PSHS      A,B,X
```

```
              LEAX    \0
              LDB     #\1
              TST     ,X          Is the number positive?
              BPL     \,0         The number is positive; no change
              LSL     ,X          The number is negative; subtract from 0
              LSR     ,X          Replace sign bit with 0 and clear carry
              ABX                 Position X for least significant byte
*
\,1           LDA     #0          Subtract number from zero
              SBCA    ,-X
              STA     ,X
              DECB
              BNE     \,1
\,0           PULS    A,B,X       Balance stack
              ENDM
*


*
* FPADD adds the two binary floating-point numbers at
* X and Y, putting the sum at the address passed in U.
* All numbers are normalized in the IEEE format. An
* underflow is flushed to zero with 1 returned in A,
* while 0 is returned otherwise. The largest signed
* number compatible with the result is returned when
* overflow occurs while 1 is returned in B. Zero is
* returned in B otherwise. Registers A, B, and CC are
* changed.
*
*           LOCAL VARIABLES
*
SIGNX   SET     0           Sign of number at X; $80 for minus
MANX    SET     SIGNX+1     Significand magnitude of number at X
RBITSX  SET     MANX+3      Round bits for number at X
SIGNY   SET     RBITSX+1    Sign of number at Y; $80 for minus
MANY    SET     SIGNY+1     Significand magnitude of number at Y
RBITSY  SET     MANY+3      Rounds bits for number at Y
SGNSUM  SET     RBITSY+1    Sign of sum; $80 for minus
MANSUM  SET     SGNSUM+1    Significand magnitude of sum
EXPX    SET     MANSUM+3    Exponent of number at X
EXPY    SET     EXPX+1      Exponent of number at Y
EXPSUM  SET     EXPY+1      Exponent of sum
OFLOW   SET     EXPSUM+1    Overflow indicator
UFLOW   SET     OFLOW+1     Underflow indicator
NBYTES  SET     UFLOW+1
*
FPADD   PSHS    X,Y,U       Registers at NBYTES+0, +2, and +4
        LEAS    -NBYTES,S   Allocate space for local variables
        CLR     OFLOW,S     Initialize overflow indicator
        CLR     UFLOW,S     Initialize underflow indicator
        CLR     RBITSX,S    Initialize the round bits
```

```
            CLR    RBITSY,S
*
* We now bring in the two numbers to local variables,
* make the hidden bit explicit, put the exponents in
* local variables and extend the significands to four
* bytes. For example, SIGNY,S and MANY,S contains the
* 4-byte signed-magnitude number at Y, and EXPY,S
* contains its exponent.
*
            LDXYB  ([NBYTES,S]),(SIGNX,S),4
            LBSR   MOVE
            LEAX   EXPX,S
            LBSR   EXAJST
            LDXYB  ([NBYTES+2,S]),(SIGNY,S),4
            LBSR   MOVE
            LEAX   EXPY,S
            LBSR   EXAJST
*
* We now test to see if one of the numbers is zero,
* returning the other number as the answer if zero is
* encountered.
*
            TST    EXPX,S
            BNE    FPA1
            LDXYB  ([NBYTES+2,S]),([NBYTES+4,S]),4
            LBSR   MOVE
            LBRA   FPA14          Return
FPA1        TST    EXPY,S
            BNE    FPA2           Neither exponent is zero
            LDXYB  ([NBYTES,S]),([NBYTES+4,S]),4
            LBSR   MOVE
            LBRA   FPA14          Return
*
* We now unnormalize the number with smallest exponent
* until the two exponents are equal.
*
FPA2        LDA    EXPX,S
            CMPA   EXPY,S
            BNE    FPA3
            STA    EXPSUM,S
            BRA    FPA6           Two exponents equal, add significands
FPA3        BLO    FPA4
            STA    EXPSUM,S
            LDA    EXPY,S         Smallest exponent in A
            LEAX   MANY,S         Point X to significand to be unnormalized
            BRA    FPA5
*
FPA4        LDB    EXPY,S
            STB    EXPSUM,S
            LEAX   MANX,S         Point X to significand to be unnormalized
```

```
*
* We now begin the unnormalizing step with the
* smallest exponent in A, and X pointing to the
* significand (with round bits) to be unnormalized.
*
FPA5    LDB     #4
FPA5A   LBSR    SHIFTR              Shift four bytes right
        BCC     FPA5B               Adjust round byte
        LDA     3,X                 Get round byte
        ORA     #1                  Set sticky bit to 1
        STA     3,X
FPA5B   INCA                        Increment smallest exponent
        CMPA    EXPSUM,S            Is unnormalization completed?
        BNE     FPA5A
*
* We now add the significands with the round bits. No
* overflow is possible since the significands have
* been extended to four bytes.
*
FPA6    LDXYU   (SIGNX,S),(SIGNY,S),(SGNSUM,S)
        TCOMP   ( ,X),5
        TCOMP   ( ,Y),5
        LDB     #5
        LDXYU   (B,X),(B,Y),(B,U)
        CLRA
*
FPA7    LDA     ,-X
        ADCA    ,-Y
        STA     ,-U
        DECB
        BNE     FPA7
        TCOMP   ( ,U),5
*
* Check now to see if the sum has overflowed from
* three bytes.
*
        LDA     SGNSUM,S
        BITA    #1                  Overflow from three bytes iff Z=0
        BEQ     FPA8
*
        LDXB    (SGNSUM,S),5
        LBSR    SHIFTR
        BCC     FPA7A               Adjust round byte
        LDA     4,X                 Get round byte
        ORA     #1                  Set sticky bit equal to 1
        STA     4,X
FPA7A   LSL     SGNSUM,S            Restore sign bit
        INC     EXPSUM,S
        BNE     FPA10               Round result
        BRA     FPA12A              Overflow; put result to maximum
```

```
*
* We now test for an exact zero.
*
FPA8    TST    MANSUM,S
        BNE    FPA8A
        TST    MANSUM+1,S
        BNE    FPA8A
        TST    MANSUM+2,S
        BEQ    FPA9A
*
* We now execute the renormalization\rounding
* sequence.
*
FPA8A   LDA    MANSUM+3,S    Round bits into A
        ANDA   #$FE          Clear sticky bit
FPA9    TST    MANSUM,S      Round or renormalize?
        BMI    FPA10         Go to round sequence
*
        LSLA                 Renormalize
        ROL    MANSUM+2,S
        ROL    MANSUM+1,S
        ROL    MANSUM,S
*
        DEC    EXPSUM,S
        BNE    FPA9
        INC    UFLOW,S
*
FPA9A   LDXB   (MANSUM,S),3  Underflow; flush result to 0
        LBSR   CLEAR
        CLR    EXPSUM,S
        BRA    FPA13
*
FPA10   LDA    MANSUM+3,S    Begin round sequence
        BPL    FPA13
        BITA   #$7F          Check round and sticky bits
        BNE    FPA12         Round upward
        ROR    MANSUM+2,S    Check least significant bit
        BCC    FPA11         Don't round upward
        ROL    MANSUM+2,S    Restore least significant bit
        BRA    FPA13
FPA11   ROL    MANSUM+2,S    Restore least significant bit
FPA12   INC    MANSUM+2,S
        BNE    FPA13
        INC    MANSUM+1,S
        BNE    FPA13
        INC    MANSUM,S
        BNE    FPA13
*
        ORCC   #1
        ROR    MANSUM,S
```

```
          ROR    MANSUM+1,S
          ROR    MANSUM+2,S
          INC    EXPSUM,S
          BNE    FPA13
*
FPA12A    INC    OFLOW,S
          LDXB   (MANSUM,S),3
          LBSR   MAXSET
          STA    EXPSUM
*
* Below, the roles of SGNSUM and EXPSUM are exchanged.
*
FPA13     ROL    SGNSUM,S       Sign bit into carry
          ROL    OFLOW,S        Save sign bit
          LDA    EXPSUM,S
          STA    SGNSUM,S
          CLRA
          LSR    OFLOW,S        Sign bit into carry bit
          RORA
          STA    EXPSUM,S       Sign into EXPSUM
          LDXYU  (SGNSUM,S),(EXPSUM,S),([NBYTES+4,S])
          LBSR   RESTOR
*
FPA14     LDA    UFLOW,S
          LDB    OFLOW,S
          LEAS   NBYTES,S
          PULS   X,Y,U,PC
*
*
*         SUBROUTINE FPMUL
*
* FPMUL multiplies the two floating-point numbers
* pointed to by X and Y, returning the answer at the
* address passed in U. All numbers are in the IEEE
* format with the inputs assumed normalized. The
* answer is returned normalized. Rounding is to the
* closest represented number with ties decided by
* rounding to the closest number whose last
* significand bit is 0. Underflow is handled by
* flushing the result to zero and returning 1 in A.
* Zero is returned in A otherwise. Overflow is handled
* by putting the result equal to the maximum magnitude
* and returning 1 in B. Zero is returned in B
* otherwise. Registers A and B are changed by FPMUL.
*
* Subroutine FPMUL uses subroutines MULT, SHIFTL,
* MOVE, CLEAR, MAXSET, RESTOR, and FPAJST. It also
* uses the macros LDXYB and LDXYU.
*
*         LOCAL VARIABLES
```

```
*
SIGNP   SET   0                Sign of the product; $80 if minus
EXPX    SET   SIGNP+1          Exponent of number at X
MANX    SET   EXPX+1           Significand magnitude of number at X
EXPY    SET   MANX+3           Exponent of number at Y
MANY    SET   EXPY+1           Significand magnitude of number at Y
EXPP    SET   MANY+3           Exponent of product
MANP    SET   EXPP+1           Significand magnitude of product
OFLOW   SET   MANP+6           Overflow indicator; 1 for overflow
UFLOW   SET   OFLOW+1          Underflow indicator; 1 for underflow
DEXP    SET   UFLOW+1          Temporary double byte exponent
NBYTES  SET   DEXP+2           Number of bytes for local variables
*
FPMUL   PSHS  X,Y,U            Save X, Y, and U
        LEAS  -NBYTES,S        Allocate space for local variables
*
* We first find the sign of the product, using $80 for
* minus.
*
        LDA   ,X               High byte of first number
        ANDA  #$80             (A) = $80 if first number is minus
        LDB   ,Y               High byte of second number
        ANDB  #$80             (B) = $80 if second number is minus
        PSHS  B
        EORA  ,S+              $80 if product is minus
        STA   SIGNP,S
*
* We now put the magnitudes of the input numbers into
* local stack variables, making the hidden bit
* explicit. The exponent is shifted left one bit to
* make room for the hidden bit in FPAJST.
*
        LDXYB ([NBYTES,S]),(EXPX,S),4
        LBSR  MOVE
        LBSR  FPAJST
        LDXYB ([NBYTES+2,S]),(EXPY,S),4
        LBSR  MOVE
        LBSR  FPAJST
*
        CLR   OFLOW,S          Initialize overflow indicator
        CLR   UFLOW,S          Initialize underflow indicator
*
* We now multiply the 3-byte significand magnitudes,
* putting the 6-byte product in MANP,S. The binary
* point is to the right of the most significant two
* bits.
        LDXYU (MANX,S),(MANY,S),(MANP,S)
        LDA   #3
        LDB   #3
        LBSR  MULT
```

```
*
* We next add the exponents, keeping the sum as a 2-
* byte number in accumulator D. If either exponent is
* zero, the result is put equal to zero. Because the
* exponent is biased by 127 in the IEEE format, the
* number in D is high by 127.
*
          LDB     EXPX,S
          BEQ     FPM5            Number is zero; put result to zero
          TST     EXPY,S
          BEQ     FPM5            Number is zero; put result to zero
          CLRA                    Sign extend EXPX,S to two bytes
          ADDB    EXPY,S          Add exponents
          ADCA    #0              Propagate carry
          ADDD    #1              Move binary point of significand left
          STD     DEXP,S          Save exponent
*
* We next check the significand, normalizing it if
* necessary.
*
          TST     MANP,S          Is number normalized?
          BMI     FPM1            Significand is normalized
          LDXB    (MANP,S),6
          LBSR    SHIFTL          Normalize significand
          LDD     DEXP,S          Get exponent
          SUBD    #1              Decrement exponent
*
FPM1      CMPD    #127
          BLS     FPM4            Underflow
          CMPD    #382
          BHI     FPM3            Overflow
*
* At this point, the significand is normalized and the
* actual exponent is within the range -126 to 128, so
* that we can now remove the extra bias of 127 and
* place the exponent in EXPP,S.
*
          SUBD    #127            Bias the exponent to IEEE format
          STB     EXPP,S
*
* We next round the significand.
*
          LDA     MANP+3,S
          CMPA    #$80
          BHI     FPM2            Round upward
          BLO     FPM6            Truncate
          LDA     MANP+4,S
          BNE     FPM2            Round upward
          LDA     MANP+5,S
          BNE     FPM2            Round upward
```

```
*
          LDA     MANP+2,S          Check LS bit for 0 since tie exists
          BITA    #1
          BEQ     FPM6              Truncate
*
FPM2      INC     MANP+2,S          Increment 3-byte significand
          BNE     FPM6
          INC     MANP+1,S          Propagate carry
          BNE     FPM6
          INC     MANP,S
          BNE     FPM6
          ORCC    #1                Set carry
          ROR     MANP,S            Renormalize significand
          ROR     MANP+1,S
          ROR     MANP+2,S
          INC     EXPP,S
          BNE     FPM6
*
FPM3      INC     OFLOW,S           Set overflow indicator
          LDXB    (EXPP,S),4
          LBSR    MAXSET
          BRA     FPM6
*
FPM4      INC     UFLOW,S           Set underflow indicator
*
FPM5      LDXB    (EXPP,S),4
          LBSR    CLEAR
*
* We now move the result to the location pointed to
* initially by U, removing the explicit hidden bit and
* putting in the sign bit.
*
FPM6      LDXYU   (EXPP,S),(SIGNP,S),([NBYTES+4,S])
          LBSR    RESTOR
*
          LDA     UFLOW,S
          LDB     OFLOW,S
          LEAS    NBYTES,S          Remove local variables
          PULS    X,Y,U,PC          Restore registers and return
*
*
*         SUBROUTINE MULT
*
* MULT multiplies the M-byte unsigned number whose
* address is passed in X with the N-byte unsigned
* number whose address is passed in Y. The value of M
* and N are passed in A and B, respectively, while the
* result placed at the address passed in U by the
* calling routine. Registers X, Y, U, A, B, and CC are
* changed.
```

```
*
M        SET     0
N        SET     M+1
MCOUNT   SET     N+1
NCOUNT   SET     MCOUNT+1
XBYTE    SET     NCOUNT+1
SAVEU    SET     XBYTE+1
NBYTES   SET     SAVEU+2
*
MULT     LEAS    -NBYTES,S      Holes for local variables
         STA     M,S
         STB     N,S
*
         ADDA    N,S            M + N into A
         DECA
M1       CLR     A,U            Initialize result
         DECA
         BPL     M1
*
         LDA     M,S
         STA     MCOUNT,S
         LEAX    A,X            Position X for lowest order byte
         LEAU    A,U            Initialize U
*
M2       LDB     N,S
         STB     NCOUNT,S
         LEAY    B,Y            Position Y for lowest order byte
         LEAU    B,U            Position U for current LS output byte
         LDA     ,-X
         STA     XBYTE,S
*
M3       LDA     XBYTE,S
         LDB     ,-Y            Next Y byte
         MUL
         ADDD    ,--U
         STD     ,U+
*
         BCC     M5
         STU     SAVEU,S
         LEAU    -1,U
M4       INC     ,-U            Propagate carry
         BEQ     M4
         LDU     SAVEU,S
*
M5       DEC     NCOUNT,S
         BNE     M3
*
         LEAU    -1,U           Position U for next X byte
         DEC     MCOUNT,S
         BNE     M2
```

```
*
        LEAS    NBYTES,S        Balance stack
        RTS
*
*
*       SUBROUTINE MOVE
*
* MOVE moves the M-byte number at X to Y. The value of
* M is in B. No registers are changed by MOVE except
* CC.
*
MOVE    PSHS    A,B,X,Y
MOV1    LDA     ,X+
        STA     ,Y+
        DECB
        BNE     MOV1
        PULS    A,B,X,Y,PC
*
*
*       SUBROUTINE SHIFTR
*
* SHIFTR shifts the M-byte number at X one bit to the
* right, bringing zero in on the left and putting the
* least significant bit into the carry bit. The value
* of M is in B. No registers are changed by SHIFTR
* except CC.
*
SHIFTR  PSHS    B,X
        ANDCC   #$FE
SHR1    ROR     ,X+
        DECB
        BNE     SHR1
        PULS    B,X,PC
*
*
*       SUBROUTINE SHIFTL
*
* SHIFTL shifts the M-byte number at X one bit to the
* left, bringing in zero on the right and putting the
* least significant bit into the carry bit. The value
* of M is in B. No registers are changed by SHIFTL
* except CC.
*
SHIFTL  PSHS    B,X
        ANDCC   #$FE
        ABX
SHL1    ROL     ,-X
        DECB
        BNE     SHL1
        PULS    B,X,PC
```

```
*
*
*        SUBROUTINE FPAJST
*
* FPAJST takes the IEEE binary floating-point number
* at Y, removes the sign bit by shifting the exponent
* into the high byte, and then puts in the hidden bit
* in the position left vacant by shifting the
* exponent. No registers are changed by FPAJST except
* CC.
FPAJST LSL    1,Y
       ROL    ,Y               Shift exponent into high byte
       TST    ,Y               Is exponent zero?
       BEQ    FP1
       ORCC   #1               Put hidden bit to 1
       BRA    FP2
FP1    ANDCC  #$FE             Put hidden bit to 0
FP2    ROR    1,Y              Rotate in hidden bit
       RTS
*
*
*        SUBROUTINE CLEAR
*
* CLEAR clears the M-byte number at X. The value of M
* is passed in B and no registers are change by CLEAR
* except CC.
*
CLEAR  PSHS   B,X
CLR1   CLR    ,X+
       DECB
       BNE    CLR1
       PULS   B,X,PC
*
*
*        SUBROUTINE MAXSET
*
* MAXSET puts $FF into the M-byte number at X. The
* value of M is passed in B. Only registers A and CC
* are changed by MAXSET, which returns $FF in A.
*
MAXSET PSHS   A,B,X
       LDA    #$FF
MX1    STA    ,X+
       DECB
       BNE    MX1
       PULS   A,B,X,PC
*
*
*        SUBROUTINE RESTOR
*
* RESTOR combines the 4-byte magnitude of a binary
```

```
* floating-point number, including the hidden bit, at
* X with its sign at Y, placing the result at U. No
* registers are changed by RESTOR except CC.
*
RESTOR PSHS  A,B
       LDB
            #4
       EXG   Y,U
       LBSR  MOVE           Move 4-byte magnitude to U
       EXG   Y,U
*
       LSL   3,U            Remove hidden bit
       ROL   2,U
       ROL   1,U
       EXG   X,U
       LBSR  SHIFTR         B still contains 4
       EXG   X,U
       LDA   ,U
       ORA   ,Y             Get sign
       STA   ,U
       PULS  A,B,PC
*
*
*        Subroutine EXAJST
*
* EXAJST takes the IEEE binary floating-point number
* at Y, puts the exponent at X, and sign extends the
* significand to four bytes at Y. No registers are
* changed except CC.
*
EXAJST PSHS  B
       ROL   ,Y             Sign bit into carry bit
       ROL   ,-S            Save sign bit
       LSR   ,Y             Reposition exponent
       LBSR  FPAJST
       LDB   ,Y             Get exponent
       STB   ,X             Place exponent
       CLRB
       LSR   ,S+            Place sign bit into carry
       RORB
       STB   ,Y             Sign extend significand to four bytes
       PULS  B,PC
*
```

Using the TRS-80 Color Computer

An inexpensive computer system that can be used to run virtually all of the programs and subroutines in this text consists of the following items.

1. The TRS-80 Color Computer (at least 16K).
2. Audio cassette recorder.
3. EDTASM+ ROM (and manual).
4. A black-and-white, or color, television set.

Assuming that you have a television set, this package can be purchased for about $300, depending on the supplier. An inexpensive dot matrix printer is also useful to get hard copies of assembler listings, but this is not absolutely necessary.

The editor, assembler, and debugger (EDTASM+) manual and the standard manuals supplied with the TRS-80 Color Computer are quite straightforward, so operation of the color computer should present little difficulty for the reader. In this appendix we explain the differences in this assembler and the one described in the text, which is the standard Motorola macro assembler.

There are four simple differences between the EDTASM+ assembler and the Motorola assembler. First, the EDTASM+ assembler does not have macro or conditional assembly capabilities, so that, in particular, calling sequences for subroutines will have to be written out. Other macros can be replaced by subroutines. Second, the NAM directive is not used in the EDTASM+ assembler, so that it should be omitted in all your programs run on the color computer. Third, repeated FDB and FCB directives such as

```
TABLE        FDB           100,200,300,400
```

which are used in the text must be written

```
TABLE        FDB           100
             FDB           200
             FDB           300
             FDB           400
```

for the EDTASM+ assembler. Fourth, the directive OPT is not used in the EDTASM+ assembler. Some options can be specified as part of the command line that starts the assembler. For example, a symbol table is always part of the assembler listing unless "/NS" is attached to the assembler command line.

The last difference between the two assemblers is in the use of the ORG directive, the use of which requires a little care with the color computer. If one chooses the assembler command that puts the object code onto tape to be loaded and executed later, the ORG directive can be used exactly as described in the text. (One must be careful, however, to make sure that the program is being put into the available RAM of the color computer. See Figure A4-1 and the EDTASM+ manual for further details.) When one is writing programs and debugging them as part of the process of learning assembly language, the simplest thing to do is to avoid the outputting to and inputting from tape and let the assembler put the object code in available RAM. When this is done, the EDTASM+ debugger ZBUG can be used with the labels of the program to set breakpoints, access variables, and so on. This makes the whole debugging process much easier. When the assembler puts the machine code for your program into memory, it puts it just below the source code and the symbol table for your program (see Figure A4-1). At first you may feel lost without being able to specify the location of your program, but you should soon appreciate the advantages of being able to use the symbolic debugger ZBUG and, perhaps, the philosophy of position independent code.

Letting the assembler choose the origin of your program will force the assembler to use direct addressing instead of direct page addressing for data or variables using the FCB, FDB, and RMB directives. This is because these variables or data will be placed in memory below the symbol table, that is, in RAM locations with addresses greater than $0800. One can still put variables

```
$0000  ┌──────────────┐   area for global variables
       │              │
$0069  ├──────────────┤   do not use this part of RAM;
       │        .     │   it is used for the video
       │        .     │   display and variables used
       │        .     │   for BASIC
$0600  │        .     │
       ├──────────────┤   area used for stack and other
       │        .     │   EDTASM+ variables; use the
       │        .     │   stack for local variables
$0800  │        .     │
       ├──────────────┤
       │        .     │   area for source code (ASCII)
       │        .     │
       │ .      .     │
       │        .     │   area for symbols table
       │        .     │
       ├──────────────┤
       │        .     │   machine code placed here
$3FFF  │        .     │   end of 16K RAM
       ├──────────────┤
       │//////////////│
       │//////////////│
       │//////////////│
       │//////////////│
       │//////////////│   unused
       │//////////////│
       │//////////////│
       │//////////////│
       │//////////////│
$8000  ├──────────────┤
       │              │   extended BASIC ROM (if present)
$A000  ├──────────────┤
       │              │   BASIC ROM
$C000  ├──────────────┤
       │              │   EDTASM+ ROM
$E000  ├──────────────┤
       │//////////////│   unused
$FF00  ├──────────────┤
       │              │   input/output
       └──────────────┘
```

FIGURE A4-1. Memory Map for a System with 16K of RAM.

on page 0 to use direct page addressing by using the following technique with the RMB directive.

```
REF     RMB     0           Put REF to the current location counter value
        RMB     -*          Put location counter to zero
VAR1    RMB     N1          Put variable VAR1 on page zero
          .
          .
          .
VARM    RMB     NM          Put variable VARM on page zero
        RMB     REF-*       Restore location counter to original value
```

This method of putting variables on page zero is encouraged for global variables. (It does not work with EDTASM+, however, for the FCB and FDB directives.) There are 105 bytes available for global variables on page zero. Also, most of the examples of text could be "hand assembled" on page zero and, using ZBUG, loaded into memory.

The stack pointer is loaded with $0777 at the beginning of the EDTASM+ debugger ZBUG. Looking at Figure A4-1, this gives more than a page of memory for the stack, which should be adequate for storing local variables for all of the programs in the text. You can, of course, always reload the stack pointer S at the beginning of your program to incorporate a larger stack buffer. The usual choice would be $4000 or 16K systems and $8000 for 32K systems.

The subroutines INCH and OUTCH used in Chapters 6, 7, and 8 can be written with the color computer ROM routines POLCAT and CHROUT, respectively. For example, using

```
CHROUT  EQU     $A002
OUTCH   TSTA                    Set CC bits for LDA instruction
        PSHS    CC
        JSR     [CHROUT]
        PULS    CC,PC
```

yields the OUTCH subroutine used in the text with the condition code bits set exactly like a STA instruction. Similarly, INCH can be written in terms of POLCAT as shown below.

```
POLCAT  EQU     $A000
INCH    JSR     [POLCAT]
        BEQ     INCH
        TSTA                    Set bits in CC for load instruction
        RTS
```

The bits in CC have been set exactly as a LDA instruction by INCH. With both INCH and OUTCH, however, C may be changed. Notice that indirect addressing is used for the subroutines CHROUT and POLCAT above. By examining the two bytes at locations $A002 and $A003 with ZBUG one could find the actual ROM location of CHROUT.

Finally, we mention that the TRS-80 Color Computer does not have an ACIA for input/output so that the subroutines of Chapter 8 involving interrupts cannot be run. While the color computer does have a PIA (parallel interface adapter), analogous subroutines are difficult to run because one can not get direct access to the PIA without without hardware modifications. If one does make the necessary hardware modifications, or uses interrupts in some other way, there are RAM locations for your interrupt handler. For example, the IRQ vector is in ROM and contains the address $010C which is in RAM. The RAM locations of other interrupt vectors can easily be found using ZBUG.

Index

Calling and returning mechanism, 136, 170
Calling routine, 151
Calling sequence, 152
Carry, 15
Carry bit, 15, 349
Checksum, 120
Clarity, 18
Clock cycle, 5, 283
Clock rate, 5
Clock signal, 5, 283
Column major array, 214
Comment field, 95
Compiler, 66, 121
Condition code bits, 15
Condition code register, 15
Conditional assembler, 123
Conditional branch instruction, 40, 71
Context switching, 305, 307
Control instructions, 56, 71
Control lines, 283
Control register, 291
Controller, 3
Coroutine, 171, 178
Coroutine local variable, 180
CPU, 4
Cross-assembler, 117

Data bus, 5
Data operator, 3
Data structure, 23, 210
Deallocate, 142
Debug, 9
Debugger, 176
Delay loop, 295
Denormalized floating-point number, 260
Deque, 220
Direct addressing, 13, 25
Direct memory access, 305
Direct page addressing, 26, 28
Direct page register, 28
Down-line loader, 118
Driver, 187
Dynamic efficiency, 18

Edit instructions, 56, 69
Editor, 118
Effective address, 8, 24
Emulate, 177
Entry point, 138
Entry symbol, 121
Execute phase, 7
Exit point, 138
Exponential part, 259
Expression, 94

Extended addressing, 28
Extended indirect addressing, 30
Extended local access, 147
External symbol, 120

Fetch, 7
Fetch phase, 7
Fetch/execute cycle, 7
Field, 93
First-in first-out buffer, 224
Fixed-point representation, 258
Floating-point number, 260
Floating-point representation, 259
Flushing to zero, 264
Fork, 181
Formal parameter, 125
Forward reference, 104

Gadfly loop, 296
Gadfly synchronization, 296
Global variable, 139, 153
Guard bit, 265

Half-carry bit, 15
Hand assembly, 89
Hardware interrupt, 171, 177
Hardware stack, 60
Hidden bit, 260
High-level language, 121
High signal, 5
Higher-order, 4
Host, 117

Immediate addressing, 10, 26
Implied addressing, 25
In-line argument list, 159
INCH, 297
Index, 212
Index addressing, 32, 35
Index register, 31
Indexable data structure, 212
Indirect addressing, 29
Inherent addressing, 25
Initialize, 142
Input argument, 138
Input device, 284
Input parameter, 136, 138
Input port, 284
Input routine, 281
Input/output, 3
Input/output instructions, 56, 76
Instruction, 6